THE BUSINESS OF THE F WORLD CUP

The FIFA World Cup is arguably the biggest sporting event on earth. This book is the first to focus on the business and management of the World Cup, taking the reader from the initial stages of bidding and hosting decisions, through planning and organisation, to the eventual legacies of the competition.

The book introduces the global context in which the World Cup takes place, surveying the history and evolution of the tournament and the geopolitical background against which bidding and hosting decisions take place. It examines all the key issues and debates which surround the tournament, from governance and corruption to security and the media, and looks closely at the technical processes that create the event, from planning and finance to marketing and fan engagement. Analysis of the Women's World Cup is also embedded in every chapter, and the book also considers the significance of World Cup tournaments at age-group level.

No sport business or management course is complete without some discussion of the FIFA World Cup, so this book is essential reading for any student, researcher or sport business professional looking to fully understand global sport business today.

Simon Chadwick is a Global Professor of Sport at Emlyon Business School, France. Chadwick's specific interests are in the geopolitical economy of football, which embraces matters of globalisation, digitalisation, environmentalism and lifestyle change. He has worked with some of world football's key stakeholders including UEFA, several clubs and national associations, and sponsors such as Mastercard and Coca-Cola.

Paul Widdop is a Senior Lecturer in Sport Business at Leeds Beckett University, UK. His research explores social and economic networks on the consumption and production of sport. He has published widely in areas of sport and popular culture including articles in the *Journal of Consumer Culture, Cultural Sociology, Cultural Trends, Political Behavior, Electoral Studies* and *Leisure Sciences.*

Christos Anagnostopoulos is a Deputy Dean of the School of Business and Management at the British University of Central Lancashire in Cyprus, and Associate Professor in sport management at the Faculty of Business Administration and Social Sciences at Molde University College, Norway. He is an editorial board member for nine international scientific journals related to sport management. He served on the EASM board of directors and is the Secretary General of the charitable foundation of the Cyprus Basketball Federation. He also consults with Cyprus Sport Organisation on issues related to the governance of sport federations.

Daniel Parnell is an Associate Professor at the University of Liverpool, UK. His research interests lie in business management, policy and social and economic networks in sport. Dan serves as co-Editor-in-Chief of the journal *Managing Sport and Leisure.* He is a co-editor of the Routledge book series *Critical Research in Football* and co-edited the *Routledge Handbook of Football Business and Management.* He is Head of Football Research at Dundee United Football Club and CEO of the Association of Sporting Directors.

THE BUSINESS OF THE FIFA WORLD CUP

Edited by Simon Chadwick, Paul Widdop, Christos Anagnostopoulos and Daniel Parnell

LONDON AND NEW YORK

Cover image: Kirill Neiezhmakov / Shutterstock

First published 2022
by Routledge
4 Park Square, Milton Park, Abingdon, Oxon OX14 4RN

and by Routledge
605 Third Avenue, New York, NY 10158

Routledge is an imprint of the Taylor & Francis Group, an informa business

British Library Cataloguing-in-Publication Data
A catalogue record for this book is available from the British Library

Library of Congress Cataloging-in-Publication Data
Names: Chadwick, Simon, 1964- editor. | Widdop, Paul, editor. | Anagnostopoulos, Christos, 1978- editor. | Parnell, Daniel, editor.
Title: The business of the FIFA World Cup / edited by Simon Chadwick, Paul Widdop, Christos Anagnostopoulos and Daniel Parnell.
Other titles: Federation Internationale de Football Association World Cup
Description: New York : Routledge, 2022. | Includes bibliographical references and index.
Identifiers: LCCN 2021053355 | ISBN 9780367640200 (Hardback) | ISBN 9780367640170 (Paperback) | ISBN 9781003121794 (eBook)
Subjects: LCSH: Hosting of sporting events--Economic aspects. | World Cup (Soccer)--Economic aspects. | Soccer--Economic aspects.
Classification: LCC GV721 .B87 2022 | DDC 796.334/668--dc23/eng/20220126
LC record available at https://lccn.loc.gov/2021053355

ISBN: 978-0-367-64020-0 (hbk)
ISBN: 978-0-367-64017-0 (pbk)
ISBN: 978-1-003-12179-4 (ebk)

DOI: 10.4324/9781003121794

Typeset in Bembo
by MPS Limited, Dehradun

CONTENTS

CONTRIBUTORS

Gerard A. Akindes earned a Masters in Sports Administration and a PhD in Sports Media Studies at Ohio University, where he taught Sport Management in the College of Business. He also taught sports management as an adjunct and visiting professor for Universities in Qatar, England, and the United States. His research focuses on international sport management, the political economy of sports, sports broadcasting and athletes' migration.

Mahfoud Amara is Associate Professor in Sport Social Sciences & Management at College of Education, Qatar University. Amara has a specific interest in sport business, culture, and politics in Arab and Muslim contexts. His other research interest is sport, multiculturalism and intercultural dialogue, including the provision of sport for ethnic minorities, and debate on sport and social inclusion.

Michael Anagnostou is an international football industry expert with a strong interest in sports marketing research. He holds a PhD in Sports Science, University of Thrace, Greece; an MSc in Sports and Recreation Management, University of Sheffield, UK, and a Bachelors' Degree in Sports Science and Physical Education, University of Thrace.

Austin Anahory is an Environmental Science master's student at the University of South Florida, USA. He is a mentee of the Sport Ecology Group, working on numerous research projects to bridge sport and environmental studies. He has a bachelor's degree in Business Management and has played soccer his entire life.

Alexander J. Bond is a Senior Lecturer in Sport Management at Leeds Beckett University's Carnegie School of Sport, UK. He leads the Management and Governance Theme for the Research Centre of Social Justice in Sport and Society at Leeds Beckett University.

Youcef Bouandel a graduate of the Universities of Algiers, Algeria and Glasgow, Scotland, is Full Professor of International Affairs at Qatar University. He taught at the University of Lincoln England and was visiting professor in Sweden, Bulgaria and the United States of America. His work has appeared in DOMES-Digest of Middle East Studies, Mediterranean Politics, The Journal of Modern African Studies, The Journal of North African Studies, Third World Quarterly and Cambridge Review of International Affairs and has contributed several chapters on Algeria's politics.

Estelle E. Brun is an Associate Research Fellow at the Institute for Strategic and International Affairs (IRIS). Her research mainly focuses on French identity, race and nationalism. She has notably used sports as a window through which to study such issues, as well as broader dynamics surrounding systemic inequalities and identity politics.

André Bühler is a Professor for Marketing and Sports Management at Nuertingen-Geislingen University in Germany and the Academic Director of two part-time MBA-programmes in the field of Sports Management. He also serves as the Director of the German Institute for Sports Marketing.

Bram Constandt is a Postdoctoral Research Fellow in Sport Management at Ghent University, Belgium, as well as an Affiliated Scholar at the Global Institute of Responsible Sport Organizations (GIRSO) at the University of Minnesota, USA. His main research interests include integrity issues and integrity management in sport. He was awarded the 2020 ESMQ New Researcher Award of the European Association for Sport Management for his research on gambling in sport. Through his position as Board Member of the Center for Ethics in Sport (ICES), he tries to translate the insights of his academic work into the policies and practices of sport organisations.

Rony Epelbaum Edwabne is a Sustainable Development master's student at the University of St. Andrews, in Scotland. He holds a bachelor's degree in Sports Administration from the University of Miami and has worked in hospitality and operations for major international sporting events such as the PGA Tour and Olympic Games. He embraces the power of sport as a catalyst for positive change.

Alex Gillett is a Senior Lecturer in Marketing at the York Management School, University of York, UK. His research interests are relatively broad, but much of his work has focused on organisational networks, relationships and interaction. As well as studying contemporary contexts, Dr Gillett has a keen interest in management/business history, and is a founding member of the Management and Business History Special Interest Group of the British Academy of Management.

Michael M. Goldman is an Associate Professor with the Sport Management Program at the University of San Francisco, USA, while also working with the Gordon Institute of Business Science in South Africa. He works with students, managers and clients to enhance their abilities to acquire, grow and retain profitable customers and fans.

Carole Gomez is a Senior Research Fellow at Institute for Strategic and International Affairs (IRIS) on international sports. She holds a Master's Degree in International and European Law from Queen's University of Belfast, and a Master's degree in International Public Law, International Relations, at the University of Panthéon Assas and International Security and Defense of Pierre University Mendès France in Grenoble. She also worked in the Ministry of Sports between 2011 and 2013. Her research work focuses on sports diplomacy, integrity and governance reform in sport.

Lingling Liu is an international sports marketing communication expert with expertise in sports business and media interaction. She has worked as a FIFA Media Officer and a Senior Sales Manager of FIFA Commercial. She holds a Liverpool University MBA and a PhD in sports marketing from Coventry University, UK.

Jan Andre Lee Ludvigsen is a Lecturer in the School of Justice Studies at Liverpool John Moores University, UK. His research interests lie in the sociology and criminology of sports and he has published widely on the topics of sports mega-events, 'security', and 'risk'.

Rauf Mammadov is a Doctorate in Business Administration student at the IE Business School. His research focuses on the influence of mega sporting events on the entrepreneurial ecosystems in host countries. Rauf's professional experience covers the areas of public policies, finance, mega sporting events, development banking and management consulting.

Argyro Elisavet Manoli is an Associate Professor in Sport Marketing and Communications in Loughborough University, UK, following a career in the professional sport industry. Her research focuses on sport branding, crisis communications, and marketing and media management, having won funding, and been published and presented extensively.

Sebastian Merten is a practitioner and researcher in the areas of sport marketing, digital transformation and strategic management. He is lecturer in sport management at LUNEX International University of Health, Exercise and Sports, Luxembourg and PhD candidate at WHU-Otto Beisheim School of Management, Germany. Prior to joining LUNEX University he worked in various management positions in the sports sector and currently advises different sports organisations on management issues.

Jessica R. Murfree is a member of The Sport Ecology Group, and a Visiting Assistant Professor in the Division of Sport Management at Texas A&M University, USA, where she researches the social and legal implications of the effects of climate change on sport. She also serves as a research contributor for Divers for Climate.

Georgios Nalbantis is a Research Associate at the Department of Sport Economics, Sport Management and Media Research at the University of Tübingen, Germany.

Madeleine Orr is a researcher in the Faculty of Management at The University of British Columbia at Okanagan, Canada. She is also the Founder of The Sport Ecology Group, a non-profit consortium of academics working to accelerate climate action in the sport sector through research and industry-academy knowledge exchange.

Tim Pawlowski is Full Professor of Sport Economics and Head of the Research Group on Sport Economics, Sport Management and Media Research at the University of Tübingen, Germany.

Renan Petersen-Wagner is a Senior Lecturer in Sport Business and Marketing and Researcher at the Research Centre for Social Justice in Sport and Society at Leeds Beckett University, UK. His current research explores the intersection of media, technologies, digital transformations, and sport. His research has appeared in *Current Sociology, International Review for the Sociology of Sport*, and *Journal of Sport & Social Issues*. He tweets as @renanpwagner and blogs at https://petersen-wagner.biz.

Daniel Plumley is a Senior Lecturer in Sport Finance in the Sheffield Business School at Sheffield Hallam University, UK. His PhD focuses on holistic performance measurement in professional team sports and how financial and sporting indicators impact on club performance. His research interests include the financial health of professional team sports and leagues, performance measurement in professional team sports, the economics and finance of professional team sports and competitive balance in team sports and he has published numerous peer reviewed research articles in these areas. He is an active researcher within the football industry, consulting for organisations such as the English Football League and delivering funding research projects for ESRC examining the financial impact of COVID-19 on football clubs and their communities.

Travis Richardson is a PhD student at the Department of Sport Economics, Sport Management and Media Research at the University of Tübingen, Germany.

J. Simon Rofe is a Reader in Diplomatic and International Studies in the Centre for International Studies and Diplomacy, at SOAS University of London, and Programme Director for the MA Global Diplomacy, following a role in the London Organising Committee of the Olympic Games (LOCOG) in 2012.

Eric C. Schwarz has been an academic and practitioner in sport business management for 20+ years in Australia, China, and the United States. His research focuses on sport marketing, sport facility, and event management. He is the lead author of three textbooks; has published numerous articles, book chapters, and encyclopaedia entries; and made over 70 presentations worldwide.

Kamilla Swart is an Associate Professor in the Masters of Science in the Sport and Entertainment program, Division of Engineering Management and Decision Sciences, College of Science and Engineering, Hamad Bin Khalifa University, Qatar Foundation. Her work focuses on sport, tourism and events in the developing context, and global South in particular.

Kevin D. Tennent is a Senior Lecturer in Management. He is a management historian whose research focuses on the development of strategy, purpose and governance within the broad corporate economy, and with specific reference to the transport and sport industries. He is founding chair of the British Academy of Management's Management and Business History SIG, the Secretary of the Management History Research Group, and sits on the editorial board of the Journal of Management History.

Rob Wilson is a Head of Department for Finance, Accounting and Business Systems in the Sheffield Business School at Sheffield Hallam University, UK. He has been involved in academic and applied work in football finance and governance since 2010 and has published extensively on topics including, financial health, governance, economic decision-making and resilience with his PhD focusing on the factors affecting financial performance in professional team sport. He presents his work all over the world, serves on several editorial boards for leading journals and has a rich network in board rooms of professional clubs.

Mathieu Winand is a Professor of Sport Management and Head of Department of International Sport Management at LUNEX International University of Health, Exercise and Sports, Luxembourg. Prior to joining LUNEX University in 2017, he was lecturing at the University of Stirling, UK. Mathieu is an expert in sport governance, performance management and innovation in sport.

Géraldine Zeimers is a Lecturer of Sport Management at the Faculty of Motor Sciences and Researcher at the Louvain Research Institute in Management and Organizations at Université Catholique de Louvain, Belgium. Her main research interests are in the area of sport governance and social change in national and regional sport organisations in Belgium, Australia and in India. She is the Review Editor of Frontiers in Sports and Active Living for Sports Management, Marketing and Business and reviews for several sport management, non-profit and management journals.

ACKNOWLEDGEMENTS

Simon thanks family, friends, colleagues and others who have helped influenced his career and writing. He nevertheless reserves particular thanks for his contribution to this book for his mother. Although she no longer remembers, our time together has profoundly shaped my life.

Christos thanks the "dream team No 2" of contributors that brought this volume to life. Big thanks also goes to the "line-up" of co-editors, with whom – after the influential Routledge Handbook of Football Business and Management – Christos enjoys working. Special thanks to University of Central Lancashire Cyprus and Molde University College that both afforded him the time and resources to co-edit this volume. Demetra (his wife) remained patient and supportive although she knew that this second football-focused book would intensify the "football discussions" into the house! Charis is old enough now to watch (or even attend) his first ever football World Cup; but it is Filippos, Charis' younger brother, who deserves the attention this time. Christos spent less time with him over holidays in August 2021, and thus this book is dedicated to him.

Paul thanks everyone who contributed to the book and the support staff at Routledge. Paul also thanks Dan, Christos and Simon, the co-authors of the book, they have such knowledge of the world of sport. He is glad to have shared the platform with them. Further afield, he thanks his mentor Professor Dave Cutts. Last but not least, his family Jayne, Heidi, Paddy, Elsie and Betsy.

Daniel thanks his colleagues at the University of Liverpool Management School for their ongoing support and friendship, especially Professor Bridgewater, Professor Ian McHale and Dr David Cockayne. He is also indebted to the professionalism and collaboration of the stellar line-up of contributors, and his co-editors who have helped make this new book happen. He thanks his family, Olive, Stephen, Linda, Sarah, George, Niamh, Betty and Rupert. He dedicates the books to the football students and scholars globally who endeavour to help build a better game for future generations.

1

INTRODUCTION

Simon Chadwick, Paul Widdop, Christos Anagnostopoulos, and Daniel Parnell

The FIFA World Cup is one of the world's biggest mega-events and, on this basis alone, is worthy of analysis. However, nearly 100 years since the tournament's first edition took place, in 1930 in Uruguay, understanding how and why World Cup tournaments are planned, organised, staged and evaluated has never been more imperative. What started as a football competition between nations has now grown into something that is of immense economic, political and sporting significance.

Radio and television coverage may initially have captured the attention of football fans and non-fans alike, but the digital era has propelled the competition to a position of global prominence. Social media, Over-the-Top broadcasting and mobile technology are now pervasive influences on the World Cup and the way that people engage with it. At the same time, industrial and commercial influences mean that the World Cup is now an opportunity to build business, create products and sell brands. Furthermore, globalisation has led to nations such as Qatar and China becoming important constituents of world football's eco-system. At the same time, socio-cultural change over the past century means that women's football is now gaining parity with men's football, fans are increasingly seeking tournament experiences rather than just 90-minute matches, whilst concerns about preserving the natural environment are challenging everyone. All the while, despite widespread protestations that football and politics do not mix, staging World Cup tournaments has always been an inherently political process. In tandem, countries are increasingly staging tournaments for political reasons, whether it be to project soft power or to build a nation's brand.

At the time of writing, the global pandemic was still a problem and therefore a significant challenge for in staging FIFA World Cups – whether qualifying games, or the various tournaments themselves. Looking ahead, unless there is an instantaneous or miraculous eradication of the virus, then COVID-19 will loom on

DOI: 10.4324/9781003121794-1

the event's landscape for some time to come. The 2022 World Cup in Qatar will be the first held in the Middle East; in 2023 (Australia and New Zealand) and 2026 (Canada, Mexico and the United States) competitions will be held with an increased number of competing teams; and then in 2030, speculation is rife that China will seek to secure hosting rights. It therefore seems likely that the World Cup will retain its place as one of the world's most important sport events; indeed, it seems likely to grow in stature albeit in a way that brings further challenges and complexity. At the same time, the world is in a state of flux and perhaps encountering one of the most dynamic periods in human history. Bidding for and staging a football World Cup must therefore be viewed against this backdrop.

Thus, this book has been compiled with the specific purpose being to provide an analysis of how to plan, organise and deliver successful World Cup tournaments. The book is firmly rooted in the fields of leadership and management, drawing from other disciplines including politics and technology. It will provide readers with an understanding of fields ranging from fan engagement to managing environmental impacts. The chapters take you from the start of the bidding process, right through to establishing and managing the legacies of World Cup events. It is also important to note that the book focuses on both male and female tournaments, and should be read in the context of both. The book is not specifically or exclusively about what happens on the field of play, or does its analyses extend to, for example, matters such as the management of injuries or national team performance. Furthermore, the book does not seek to judge but rather to inform, adopting a balanced and analytical approach that is not intended either to support or condemn one host or another, or FIFA itself. Indeed, the essence of the chapter collection presented herewith is one based on promoting understanding and identifying lessons for improved leadership and management.

In broad terms, the book's structure is based on the notions of where the World Cup has come from, where it is now, and where it is heading. The book starts by examining the World Cup's business history (Chapter 2), something which the editors believe has never been undertaken before. This is remiss of the writers in the field, as the tournament's commercial background reveals a great deal about both its current and past incarnations. Thereafter, the book moves onto examine bidding, covering what is involved in this process, why countries bid and how FIFA members vote for a particular nation to host the competition (Chapter 3). Often, such decisions are based on the internal politics of the continental associations, and of the global geopolitical situation in which bids are made. Equally, it is important to note that countries often bid for tournament hosting rights for political reasons, which are often linked to matters pertaining to international relations, diplomacy and soft power (all of which are covered in Chapters 4 and 5).

A crucial, though often ignored, part of World Cup tournaments is how they are designed as competitions (Chapter 6). In Uruguay in 1930, 13 nations competed (7 from South America, 4 from Europe and 2 from North America). By the time we get to 2026, there will be 48 teams competing in the men's edition, with 30 teams being present in Australia and New Zealand during 2023. How to design a qualifying competition as well as the tournament itself are key issues. In making such decisions, as well as those linked to hosting decisions, good governance is vital. This is an area in which FIFA and World Cup have sometimes struggled; indeed, despite recent changes to processes and procedures, some observers remain cynical about and critical of issues of governance, ethics and corruption. In Chapter 7, we consider the issues, challenges and developments in these areas. Perhaps, the biggest issue of all that is facing the various World Cups is environmental change. The carbon footprint of tournaments, the rubbish that fans generate, the pollution caused by air travel and their consequences (such as erratic and extreme weather patterns) are a major concern and must be addressed (an examination of which appears in Chapter 8).

FIFA is not a business, and it is reliant on irregular revenue streams (which are dictated by when tournaments take place). The organisation therefore has to address how it ensures financial sustainability whilst at the same time generating revenues that are of benefit to world football. Similarly, host nations must ensure that they have the financing in place to successfully deliver tournaments and are not left with debts and white elephant facilities (see Chapter 9). Financial decisions are part of planning and organisational processes that extend to a multitude of issues that require good management and leadership. How many venues there will be, whether some of these venues will need to be newly constructed, where training facilities are available, how many hotels are needed, whether civic infrastructure is adequate and so forth, are all important considerations for FIFA and its World Cup host nations (Chapter 10). In addressing such matters, sourcing and managing resources is crucial when planning and organising the World Cup (Chapter 11). Issues of how many volunteers will be needed, how water supplies can be secured, and where space for fan zones can be allocated, are all part of a complex decision-making landscape.

The latter example, pertaining to fans, is an especially salient one. Fans are the lifeblood of any World Cup – co-producers of the excitement, tension and drama; a source of ticket, merchandise and other revenues; and one of the reasons why sponsors and broadcasters pay so much money to be associated with the tournament. The book considers fans in Chapter 12, then in Chapter 13 explores issues related to risk and security, which are clearly of direct relevance to those who attend matches. Risk and security are also important in terms of protecting not only the infrastructure and amenities being used by the World Cup, but also the revenue streams and operating models that underpin the tournament's staging. Thereafter, the book moves onto examine marketing, sponsorship and merchandising (Chapter 14), broadcasting and the media (Chapter 15), and digital and social media (Chapter 16). Each of these is important as a means through which to engage fans, though they are also important in terms of working with sponsors, commercial partners, media outlets, and digital corporations. Whilst FIFA looks towards generating revenues and providing football fans with a compelling tournament experience, companies associated with the event will want to achieve a return on the investments they make into the competition. The notion of event returns on investment are something that host nations pay attention to and are typically labelled as being a tournament legacy. Chapter 17 examines the notions of legacy and legacy management, whilst highlighting the role that tourism plays both during and subsequent to a country hosting the World Cup.

Given the scale of World Cup events and their associated qualifying campaigns, a text of this nature can never be completely exhaustive. If one considers the impact of local cultures and business practices upon competing teams and the tournament at various levels, the complexity of planning and staging the tournament becomes apparent. For instance, one continental association's winter is another's summer; and playing qualifying matches in Africa or Asia is a very different proposition to staging them in Europe. The editors of this book nevertheless hope that it provides a strong introduction to the business of the FIFA World Cup, by offering structured insights, informed analysis and relevant examples. As such, we hope that readers will find the text engaging and inspiring. For students, it is important that you go beyond the headlines to understand the mechanics of running a tournament. For academics and researchers, the book is intended to prompt further, much needed analysis. As for practitioners, our intention has been to deliver new perspectives on the issues and challenges you face. We invite you to read and enjoy this ground-breaking text.

2

A BRIEF HISTORY OF THE FIFA WORLD CUP AS A BUSINESS

Kevin D. Tennent and Alex Gillett

Introduction

This chapter provides an overview of the historic development of the FIFA World Cup as a business entity while recognising the broader cultural, political, economic and social context to the event. This broader context has meant that the event has become internationally prestigious and therefore it has taken on a level of scholarly significance, perhaps outweighing its economic contribution (Gillett and Tennent, forthcoming). The development of the World Cup tournament has been one of remarkable institutional continuity supported by a system of increasingly powerful monopolies. These monopolies have worked with forces of global political and economic change to shape the evolution of the FIFA World Cup. From the very first iterations of the tournament through to its most recent staging, this chapter highlights key events, patterns and trends in the business and management of the World Cup. Important elements that we consider are the early history of the tournament, which is often overlooked in terms of relative importance, through to the more recent themes of the introduction of sponsorship, broadcasting and other media developments, the proliferation of other tournaments using the FIFA World Cup identity, and various corruption scandals. Space here precludes us from offering a tournament by tournament narrative, but we aim to deal with some of the more important aspects while continuing to pay attention to historical context.

The World Cup in Historical Perspective

Increasing scholarly attempts have been made to understand the evolution of the FIFA World Cup and similar sporting mega-events of scale such as the summer and winter Olympic Games, yet, because of its episodic quadrennial nature a satisfying discussion of its essential character as a business remains elusive. Fett (2020)

DOI: 10.4324/9781003121794-2

draws our attention to the need for an overall approach to the historic narration of FIFA World Cups, comparing the "dimensions" of visitor attractiveness, broadcasting rights, organisation, stadiums, transformation and inheritance (or legacy), while expressing concern at the episodic nature of many previous studies (Baade and Matheson, 2004; Gillett and Tennent, 2017; Kassens-Noor et al., 2015; Maharaj, 2011; Müller and Gaffney, 2018; Schausteck de Almeida et al., 2015; Tennent and Gillett, 2018; Wong and Chadwick, 2017). Fett perpetuates the teleological angle of this literature by pointing to the increasing trend of gigantism as each World Cup appears to get bigger and better as innovation is added over time. We argue, however, that while the dollar value of and opportunities for commercial exploitation of the World Cup has undoubtedly increased, this approach understates the relative importance of early World Cups to understanding later expansion. This creates a "jumpers for goalposts" myth, suggesting that early World Cups were on too small a scale to be commercially relevant, yet when viewed in historical context, the FIFA World Cup has been from its inception a globally impactful event characterised by high political and social intervention and interest. Meanwhile, the governing body, FIFA, has always relied on the men's tournament and the development of other versions, such as the women's tournament after 1991, for revenue generation. By closing off study, we lose the opportunity to understand how external factors have made the World Cup such an enduring business form.

Understanding the overall impact of past World Cups from a qualitative perspective is therefore challenging and requires an understanding of historical context – what appeared big in the1930s or the 1960s may not appear to be big in retrospect, but the competition still derives meaning and legitimacy from the memory and reputation of those earlier editions. In a resource-based view perspective (Barney, 1991), this legacy forms an intangible resource for FIFA which can be likened to the "social memory assets" described by Foster et al. (2011). Each tournament took place in a different historical and spatial context, embedded in very diverse cultural and national settings, with very different endogenous conditions prevailing – from the shadow of European fascism which characterised the 1934 (Italy) and 1938 (France) editions, to the earthquakes which complicated preparations for the 1962 (Chile) and 1986 (Mexico) editions. Technological development also matters, with radio in its infancy at the time of the inaugural tournament, held in Uruguay during 1930 (but this did not preclude impact through newsprint) and the use of floodlights in soccer some distance in the future. If understood through Ansoff, these locally nested developments enabled FIFA to follow a business strategy (though not always deliberate) of market penetration and development around the men's tournament, asserting greater rights around that, before adding product development later, by adding versions for women, other age groups and beach soccer.

This historical and spatial context particularly matters for the FIFA World Cup because it exists in franchise form. The tournament is subject to local interpretation and variation allowing local organisers, including national Football

Associations/Federations (FAs) as well as those outside of football such as national and local governments, to apply their own approaches. The international diffusion of the tournament therefore also presents research challenges as the participation of multiple stakeholder organisations was often required to deliver World Cup tournaments, scattering documentary traces between repositories. Meanwhile, a "silence of the archives" (Decker, 2013) problem also exists – some modest but lasting changes made for World Cups out of larger tranches of funding, such as the concreting of existing stadium car parks at USA 1994 were actioned on the fly leaving few traces but an oral tradition that the facility had been improved for the event. Other archival sources again may be locked in languages unfamiliar to the researcher. Similarly, there has been a great diversity in the reporting of each World Cup, with those taking place in the Internet era inevitably leaving more traces when compared to earlier editions, perhaps as a consequence of the expansion of sport management academia in itself.

We also hope that as the COVID-19 pandemic places the status of sport and the mega event at something of a crossroads as we approach Qatar 2022 and USA, Mexico and Canada 2026 that we can highlight the relevance of historical consciousness for decision-making. Tennent et al. (2020) highlight the need for decision-makers to develop historical consciousness by using archival sources and the insights gained from them to learn reflexively, becoming more aware of their own contribution to historical processes.

Unlike the 2020 Tokyo Olympics or the "Euro 2020" European Football Championship, the next edition of The FIFA World Cup, to be held in Qatar during 2022 may escape COVID-19 disruption. Historically, however, we see the FIFA World Cup institution has proved its durability specifically after 1938 due to the outbreak of World War II, returning successfully in 1950, and would likely do so again – it is not always necessary to go bigger and better to ensure a successful tournament, as the symbolism and significance of the competition can be important in itself (Gillett and Tennent, 2017).

Early History of the World Cup

FIFA was founded in 1904 by seven European FAs, as the global organiser and governing body of football, although the first FIFA World Cup tournament was not held until 1930. However, it was not the first attempt to create a football world championship – international football had started among the four British "Home Nations" in the 1870s. These matches along with club football fixtures proved commercially popular on a "gate money" basis (Vamplew, 2004) and it is not surprising that attempts to promote a World Cup followed. The British Lipton grocery and tea company sponsored a "World Cup" between invited club sides known as the Sir Thomas Lipton Trophy in 1909 and 1911 (Tennent and Gillett, 2016). A much more direct precursor to the FIFA World Cup was the Olympic football tournaments, the first of which officially recognised by FIFA, took place parallel to the London Summer Olympic Games of 1908. At this time, the institutional structure of international sport was in its infancy and the English FA collaborated with the Olympic organisers to put together the first tournament, while the 1912 Stockholm Summer Games featured the innovation of hosting fixtures around Sweden, rather than only in Stockholm itself. The Olympic tournaments continued after the World War I, being held in 1920, 1924 and 1928, by which time FIFA was becoming more assertive of its rights.

A further important precursor, given the Eurocentric nature of the early FIFA, was the Copa America. This was a tournament between South American teams, first played in 1916, which was also the inaugural year of the CONMEBOL (*Confederación Sudamericana de Fútbol*) the regional body for South American football associations, which began to vote together to increase their power in the FIFA organisation (Vonnard and Quin, 2017).[1]

The International Olympic Committee (IOC), however, continued to favour strict amateurism. This stood at odds with the development of football as a professional sport around the world, threatening football's status at the Olympic Games, while Jules Rimet (FIFA President 1921–1954), favoured a softer line on broken time payments. Acceptance of professional football was an essential precondition for the FIFA World Cup as a showcase involving the best players, with an active transfer market already forming between Europe and South America (Vonnard and Quin, 2017). At this point, the organisation had two main sources of revenue – the contributions of member associations and a small license fee paid on each international match played (Homburg, 2008). The 1927 FIFA Congress tasked the Executive Committee with organising an independent tournament, the hosting rights for which were awarded at FIFA's 1929 Congress to Uruguay, winners of the 1924 and 1928 Olympic titles. However, Uruguay was not a popular choice among European countries, and only four participated, with the rest of the 13 entrants coming from North and South America.

The Uruguayan tournament, though it seems modest by contemporary standards, demonstrates that even from the beginning the FIFA World Cup was a large-scale event, requiring intervention "off-the-pitch" in the host country, whilst proving extremely profitable for FIFA. D'Amado (2020) shows that the hosting rights were awarded on the basis that the Uruguayans pay the travel expenses of the visiting teams. This necessitated the Uruguayan FA (AUF) to lobby parliament for state support, as well as the municipality of Montevideo building a new stadium, the Estadio Centenari. The tournament was promoted as complementary to Uruguay's centenary celebrations and the government made available a 300,000 pesos grant allowing the AUF to promise to pay travel and

1 Membership of FIFA had by this point begun to expand beyond Europe, beginning with South Africa's application in 1909, then Argentina in 1912, Canada and Chile in 1913, and the United States in 1914.

subsistence for each visiting FA to send a delegation of 20, as well as loaning the municipality 200,000 pesos interest free (p. 852).[2] This support was secured prior to the presentation of the bid at the 1929 Congress in Barcelona and used to successfully campaign against alternative bids by Hungary, Spain and Italy. This diversion of public funds to an elite sporting event that would be charging entry fees did attract opposition in parliament, and a compromise was reached that ticket prices in a third of the Estadio Centenario be capped to make them affordable to the working class (p. 852). This did not restrict FIFA from making a near 200% return on investment from the tournament – their costs amounted to 11,251.48 Dutch guilders (FIFA was at this time based in Amsterdam) and their revenue 30,410.41 Dutch guilders, being composed of a small entry fee for each team plus 5% of gate receipts (Homburg, 2008, p. 38). Even in fledgling form Uruguay 1930 set expectations – the tournament would be a "mega" event requiring public sector involvement beyond sport. The host country would use it as an opportunity to exhibit its prowess at organising sporting events, and the logistics of travel in 1930 necessitated the whole tournament to take place over a three week period with a neutral host country as a meeting place.

Gate receipts remained the tournament's sole source of revenue until the 1950s, yet the public were eager to watch the matches to the extent that FIFA-derived monopoly rents from them. It was the realisation of these monopoly rents, enough to sustain the organisation for four years, which put FIFA onto a sustainable financial footing independent of its members. This allowed it to develop a professionalised managerial hierarchy and bureaucracy, while President Jules Rimet, who had preserved FIFA as a unit and except for the CONMEBOL had resisted the idea splitting the FIFA "family" into regional confederations,[3] saw his role as to political standing in the organisation much enhanced (Tomlinson, 2000, 2020). In 1932, the organisation, previously run on a part-time "honorary" basis, first employed a paid General Secretary to manage its day-to-day affairs. It also moved to Zurich to take advantage of Swiss tax law allowing the establishment of FIFA as a non-profit corporation which reinvested its income in football development (Conn, 2017; Homburg, 2008).

The business model of FIFA was therefore established as one which relied on a four year cycle of income from the World Cup tournament, sustaining the Zurich administration, and where possible, providing football development activities. From the start, the tournament was a form of foreign direct investment licensing in which the hosting is contracted out, removing from FIFA the financial risk of directly investing in the host country (Tennent and Gillett, 2016). This was cemented by the introduction of "World Cup Regulations" for each competition

2 Conversion values are difficult to find for years before the 1950s, so no currency conversions are given for World Cups before WW2. All conversion values are approximations based on figures from fxtop.com.

3 Shortly after Jules Rimet's retirement, in 1954 regionalisation did begin, the European confederation UEFA was formed in June of that year.

which set out the duties of FIFA and the host FA as well as the division of revenues and profits between them (Homburg, 2008). Each tournament from 1930 until 1982 ran with some variant of a model in which the "surplus of receipts" after the tournament was divided between FIFA (10–15%), and after 1950 the Host FA (25–30%) and the participating FAs (usually 55–70%, thus providing national teams with an incentive to participate even when travel was far, and later, attempt to qualify). FIFA also claimed a 5–10% share of the gross gate receipts. These revenues were later augmented by broadcasting rights, payments for advertising and sponsorships, and the profits of merchandising and marketing rights. FIFA could enjoy supranormal profits even before technology and rising disposable incomes around the world made these things possible. We give a sense of the upward trajectory of FIFA's supranormal profits in Table 2.2.

Following the success of Uruguay, the Italian government under Mussolini enthusiastically signed up to host in 1934. This continued the fusion of sport and state already established in Italy since the regime had taken over the national FA in 1926. Sport was thought to encourage the "Fascist Man" ideal, a man physically and mentally suited to giving his life for his country. The World Cup gave the opportunity to build three stadiums celebrating the ideal - the "Partenopeo" in Naples, the "Giovanni Berta" in Florence and the "Mussolini" in Turin (Sbetti and Serapiglia, 2020). Italy won the tournament, much to the propaganda benefits of the fascist state, both in Italy and in terms of global prestige, and FIFA derived "total receipts" of CHF 53,226 (Homburg, 2008, p. 42). Thus, again political involvement had happily enabled local football to bear the risk for FIFA, and indeed while definitive "tournament costs" are hard to find, this happened in a country where GDP per capita ($4,466) was less than that of Uruguay in 1930 ($5,590). Broadly, as shown in Table 2.1, it was rare for the tournament to be hosted by a regime that was not Democratic and centrist in orientation, and despite the Cold War, Communist countries were avoided entirely for the men's tournament (though the women's has been hosted twice in China).

The 1938 edition of the tournament in France was less politically controversial in its hosting. From the perspective of footballing governance, the 1938 FIFA World Cup was an "anchoring of tradition and eurocentrisism" (Dietschy, 2014, p. 85) although there were concerns that France did not have the stadium infrastructure to host (ibid). In deliberate contrast to the fascist governments of Germany and Italy, the Popular Front government was generally not favourable towards spectator sports, instead proclaiming to focus on accessibility and playing field provision. It was not until the beginning of 1938 that the French government pledged 1 million francs towards upgrading a stadium to the specifications required to host the Final. The French FA and the Racing Club de France (RCF) thus needed to provide a further 1,300,000 francs each to upgrade RCFs stadium, originally built cheaply for the Olympic Games of 1924, though other fixtures were hosted by existing stadiums around the country. Regardless of these challenges, the 1938 edition still allowed FIFA to derive an income of CHF 59,963 (Homburg, 2008). The World War II then denied FIFA of the opportunity of the

TABLE 2.1 CAGE (Ghemawat, 2007) Factors of World Cup Hosting Nations

	Country	*Culture*	*Administrative*	*Geographic*	*Economic*	
		Language	*Form of Government*	*Country Size (sq km)**	*Population ('000s)***	*GDP per capita 2011 US$***
1930	Uruguay	Spanish	Democratic, centre-left	176,215	1,713	5,950
1934	Italy	Italian	Fascist, far-right	301,340	42,093	4,466
1938	France	French	Democratic, centre-left	551,500	41,960	7,119
1950	Brazil	Portuguese	Democratic, centre-left	8,515,770	53,443	2,236
1954	Switzerland	German, French, Italian, Romansch	Democratic, centre-right	41,227	4,929	13,171
1958	Sweden	Swedish	Democratic, centre-left	450,295	7,409	12,884
1962	Chile	Spanish	Democratic, centre-right	756,102	7,961	7,071
1966	England	English	Democratic, centre-left	129,113	54,643	15,757
1970	Mexico	Spanish	Authoritarian, left	1,964,375	52,775	6,873
1974	West Germany	German	Democratic, centre-left	248,577	78,966	19,228
1978	Argentina	Spanish	Military, right	2,780,400	27,440	12,444
1982	Spain	Spanish	Democratic, centre-left	505,370	37,983	14,045
1986	Mexico	Spanish	Authoritarian, left	1,964,375	78,442	9,283

(*Continued*)

TABLE 2.1 (Continued)

	Country	*Culture Language*	*Administrative Form of Government*	*Geographic Country Size (sq km)⋆*	*Economic Population ('000s)⋆⋆*	*GDP per capita 2011 US$⋆⋆*
1990	Italy	Italian	Democratic, centre-right	301,340	56,743	26,003
1994	USA	English	Democratic, centre-right	9,833,517	263,662	38,807
1998	France	French	Democratic, centre-right	551,500	60,103	31,323
2002	Japan	Japanese	Democratic, centre-right	377,915	127,503	33,195
2002	South Korea	Korean	Democratic, centre-left	99,720	47,645	25,251
2006	Germany	German	Democratic, centrist	357,022	82,322	38,014
2010	South Africa	isiZulu, isiXhosa, Afrikaans, Sepedi, English, Sesotho, Xitsonga, siSwati, Tshivenda, isiNdebele	Democratic, populist	1,219,090	51,087	11,319
2014	Brazil	Portuguese	Democratic, centre-left	8,515,770	205,045	15,258
2018	Russia	Russian	Authoritarian, right	17,098,242	146,476	24,669

Notes

⋆ CIA (2020). West Germany from (CIA, 1986), p. 91.

⋆⋆ Bolt, Jutta and Jan Luiten van Zanden (2020). 1966 England population and GDP is for whole UK.

1942 and 1946 tournaments, with a deleterious effect on finances. FIFA was reliant on the license fees from matches between the South American associations to stay afloat (Dietschy, 2013).

The first postwar World Cup took place in Brazil in 1950, amidst the background of the country's attempt at democratisation. Despite Brazil of 1950 still being relatively the poorest country that has held the tournament with a GDP per capita of just $2,236 (see Table 2.1), there was a conspicuous return to FIFA's reliance on the largesse of public authorities. Indeed, Brazil saw the highest expenditure on stadia until Italy 1990 ($291.88 million 2018 US dollars), according to Fett (2020). The tournament was awarded in 1947 on the condition that new stadiums be built in Rio de Janeiro (then the capital) and Belo Horizonte. The Rio stadium, the Estádio Municipal, or Maracanã was a monumental bowl, accommodating 179,000 people, and which featured a vast popular section called the *geral*, intended to give access to people from all social classes (Gaffney, 2010). The event was again used to symbolise populist rule, and over 1 million cumulative spectators watched matches (Fett, 2020) giving FIFA a total net benefit of CHF 1,322,281, or over $30m at 2021 prices (Homburg, 2008). This was a remarkable financial success for FIFA and allowed for the comfortable restoration of the four-year cycle. The 1954 tournament in Switzerland was relatively low-key by comparison with just $6.48m being spent on stadiums at 2018 prices (Fett, 2020) in a country about six times as wealthy as Brazil had been in 1950, having a GDP per capita of $13,171 (Table 2.1).

The 1950s and 1960s were a period of rapid technological change and commercial innovation globally, and new opportunities began to emerge for the exploitation of World Cup revenue streams, though FIFA were sometimes slow to assert control. The Switzerland and Swedish World Cups were the first to be broadcast live on television to a European audience through deals between FIFA and the European Broadcasting Union (EBU), meaning that even in 1954 far more people would see the matches on television than in person. FIFA was slow to monetise this, not yet seeing the potential to flip the business model towards TV rights. In the 1958 tournament, gate receipts were £716,000 ($19.4m at 2021 prices), but radio and television rights were sold for only £103,448 ($2.8m). Rous and Winterbottom (1961) imagined that rights for England 1966 might reach only £250,000 ($6m at 2021 prices) versus possible gate receipts of about £1m ($24.2m). Ultimately, FIFA and the EBU agreed a contract which covered both the 1962 edition in Chile, and the 1966 event in England, the EBU paying $75,000 ($688,479 at 2021 prices) suggested by the EBU for Chile, and the £300,000 ($7.7m at 2021 prices) demanded by FIFA for 1966 (Chisari, 2007). Over 400 million people tuned in to the 1966 final, a number thought to be more than the 1969 moon landings, but the TV rights were dwarfed by gate receipts of £1,548,280 ($37.5m at 2021 prices) (Tennent and Gillett, 2016) suggesting that these rights may have been undersold. The Chilean rights consisted of highlights packages only, because transatlantic broadcasting was not yet possible, but the EBU was dominated by public broadcasters run on Reithian lines and this may have restricted the amount broadcasters were prepared to contribute.

Subsidiary commerce also emerged around the early World Cups. FIFA were slow to realise the sales potential of pitch-side advertising, which was already common in club football around the world, and certainly did not move to claim the rights to it until the 1970 edition, when an array of global brands bought pitch-side advertising space (Homburg, 2008). Indeed, partly due to article 10 of FIFA's own agreement with the EBU which stated that FIFA could not authorise third parties to profit from the broadcasts, in 1966, the BBC were allowed to insist that there was no pitch-side advertising at all (Chisari, 2007; Tennent and Gillett, 2016). The event of 1966 did see innovation in the commercial sphere however, with the English FA introducing a World Cup mascot for the first time; Willie, a cartoon lion whose image could be licensed and used on anything from beer to bathmats (Tennent and Gillett, 2016, 2018). World Cup Willie appears to have only been promoted in the United Kingdom and financial returns were modest, but FIFA asserted their rights over the global commercial exploitation of the tournament in the 1970 World Cup regulations which were agreed in 1967 (Homburg, 2008). This also included rights over the souvenir programme, which the English FA had produced in 1966. There is some evidence that earlier World Cups also involved merchandising on a small scale – certainly souvenir badges were produced for the 1954, 1958 and 1962 editions (Rous and Winterbottom, 1961). Alongside these products and publications made by organisers, there were unofficial publications – many newspapers and magazines ran special supplements for World Cups, and sponsored tourist guides were produced, in multiple languages, while businesses tried to use the World Cup to advertise their products (Tennent and Gillett, 2016, 2018) a phenomenon which continues to date with increasing sophistication as sport mega-event ambush marketing (Chadwick and Burton, 2011). The United Kingdom and local governments also used the tournament in attempts to boost regions through tourism and to showcase the National Plan of infrastructure developments, industry, and technology, although most overseas visitors preferred to stay in London (Gillett and Tennent, 2017, 2019; Tennent and Gillett, 2016, 2018; Warwick, 2017).

The World Cup was bigger than a normal football competition – it was already attracting entrepreneurial opportunity, but FIFA's early conservatism may not only have been a hangover from the earlier amateur ethos, but also a legacy of the "gate money" business model of Victorian and Edwardian British football which dominated in the UK into the 1980s (Vamplew, 2004; Walvin, 1986). The legacy of this formative period, ending with the Presidency of Sir Stanley Rous, was that FIFA would come to realise the greater potential for commercial exploitation of the tournament that would be further asserted later.

Development of the World Cup as a Mega-event

The size and scale of the FIFA World Cup as a tournament and commercial venture increased rapidly after changes in the leadership of FIFA. In 1974, Brazilian Joao Havelange was elected to become the seventh president of FIFA.

Havelange was a former Olympic athlete and had enjoyed some business success in his professional life, demonstrating an individualistic and marketing-orientated, entrepreneurial outlook (Tomlinson, 2000). He had fostered support across the African continent after promising to target FIFA's development spending there as well as recognising decolonisation by allowing increased participation in the World Cup tournament. Havelange worked with the British sports marketing pioneer Patrick Nally and Horst Dassler, of Adidas, to attract Coca-Cola's sponsorship for the 1978 tournament (Conn, 2017; Tomlinson, 2000; Sugden and Tomlinson, 1998).

Through the 1970s and 1980s, the men's World Cup expanded dramatically as measured by the number of teams participating, the aggregate stadium attendances, and the financial value of the television rights (Fett, 2020). The development of corporate sponsorship programmes by FIFA at the 1982 World Cup and the IOC at the 1984 Los Angeles Olympics initiated category exclusivity and commercial rights bundling in sponsorship with global brands, which have been key drivers in sponsorship's subsequent growth (Chadwick and Burton, 2011). Geographically though, the tournament had still only ever been hosted in Europe and Latin America. Mexico had become the first nation to host two editions in 1986, when they replaced FIFA's original choice, Colombia (Kioussis, 2020). As shown in Table 2.1, Mexico's GDP per capita in 1986 was lower than that of South Africa in 2010 (a world cup lauded for its development focus), though Mexico had seen considerable economic growth since 1970.

In 1988, the United States was awarded the hosting rights for the 1994 edition, thus fulfilling a long-held ambition of US football (soccer) administrators since the 1970s, and signifying FIFAs ambitions to develop football in "new" global markets (Tennent and Gillett, 2018). USA '94 as well as the previous edition (Italia '90, the second nation to host a second tournament) were by far the most profitable World Cups to date and continued the trend for growing attendances and television rights. As well as being the world's largest economy, the USA was also the richest nation to host in GDP per capita terms. Merchandising opportunities have also expanded with technology, and other media were opened, including the sales of soundtrack albums and official video games after 1990 (Porro and Conti, 2014). As Table 2.2 shows, when correcting for inflation FIFA's share of the profits, however defined, sharply increased after the 1986 edition, and especially so for the 1998 and 2002 editions, largely because of these broader merchandising and sponsorship opportunities.

A notable moment in the business history of World Cups occurred when in 1990, shortly before the start of the negotiation process with FIFA, the World Cup 94 organising committee (World Cup 94 Inc.) trademarked multiple permutations of the name "USA '94" in the English and Spanish languages, strengthening licensing rights and a legal foundation to protect marketing revenue. This allowed for the creation of a new category for World Cup sponsorship, "Local Marketing Partner"; six tiers of sponsorship were offered, ranging from national level "Official Sponsors" to "Equipment Suppliers" and "Official Licensees," in tandem with

TABLE 2.2 Men's World Cup FIFA Share of Profits

	Country	*Receipts (CHF, '000s)**	*defined in sources as**	*2021 CHF equivalent ('000s)***	*2021 USD equivalent ('000s)***
1930	Uruguay	38	Total Receipts		
1934	Italy	53	Total Receipts		
1938	France	59	Net Receipts		
1950	Brazil	1,322	Net Benefit	5,668	3,073
1954	Switzerland	928	Net Benefit	3,979	2,158
1958	Sweden	1,810	Profit	7,800	3,866
1962	Chile	2,117	Active Balance	9,152	4,287
1966	England	4,374	Active Balance	18,935	8,171
1970	Mexico	6,154	Active Balance	26,558	9,533
1974	West Germany	8,693	Active Balance	22,025	17,584
1978	Argentina	6,139	Income	9,965	14,860
1982	Spain	9,517	Receipts	18,991	13,000
1986	Mexico	21,711	Receipt	31,811	32,220
1990	Italy	34,431	Receipts/ WC share FIFA	43,924	53,578
1994	USA	57,101	Receipts/ WC share FIFA	65,044	77,364
1998	France	273,260	Total Receipts	302,347	321,852
2002	Japan	1,442,350	Gross Profit	1,528,035	1,531,458

Notes

* Figures based on (Homburg, 2008) p. 42.

** Calculated on 9 April 2021 using fxtop.com using Jan 1 of the year following the World Cup finals, adjusted for CPI inflation. CHF adjusted for CPI only after Mexico 1986.

FIFA's established Global Marketing Partners. USA '94 was also notable for its prominent use of tiered ticketing packages, which it released in phases, to heighten demand (Hopkins, 2010; Tennent and Gillett, 2018; Gillett and Tennent, 2020).

The value of broadcasting rights increased with every edition up to and including the most recent edition at the time of writing, Russia 2018 (Fett, 2020). The global development of football through the tournament was a continuing trend, with the first Asian World Cup Finals event hosted by Japan and South Korea jointly in 2002 (the first ever co-hosted edition), and the first African tournament hosted by South Africa in 2010. Between 1998 and 2016, there were also second times for France, Germany, and Brazil. For 2026, FIFA has awarded hosting rights again to a joint-host, the "United 2026" bid signifies a first for Canada, second for the United States and an unprecedented third time for Mexico. Except for 2010 and 2014, the tournament was also hosted in higher income countries that one might argue could afford the largesse required to host (Table 2.1).

This spread and increasing commercialisation of the World Cup product has corresponded with controversy around the behaviours and allegations of corruption amongst FIFA and some of its members. Most notably were allegations of bribery for the awarding of television rights involving Havelange and his son-in-law, the FIFA executive committee member Ricardo Teixeira (Conn, 2012). Indeed, rumours of corruption had haunted Havelange and Teixeira for some time, resulting in Havelange banning former Brazilian superstar player Pele from the 1994 World Cup draw (WorldGame, 2016). Havelange retired from FIFA presidency in 1998, succeeded by his Secretary General Sepp Blatter. Blatter was in post until 2015 but he, too, was dogged by allegations of corruption. Like Havelange, he had lobbied African and CONMEBOL members promising, and often delivering, development funds under the "Goal" initiative, to provide FIFA-funded headquarters and playing facilities in "developing" nations whose football associations were otherwise without funds to afford them independently (Conn, 2017). According to former head of the English Football Association, Greg Dyke, some of the FIFA culture of "gifts" was seen as normal by the cultural values of some FIFA members, but not by the values of others, particularly those of the western hemisphere (Dyke et al., 2018). Patience ran out as the finances of FIFA were under investigation by the United States Federal Bureau of Investigation and the Internal Revenue Service Criminal Investigation Division for various problems including bribery to influence the World Cup selection process (The United States Department of Justice, 2015).

Whilst the progression of football and the World Cup into new geographic frontiers was in some ways a success story, the alternative narrative identified a legacy of white elephant stadiums in developing countries where that money could have been used towards healthcare, social and infrastructure challenges (Majendie, 2015). This diversion of resources away from more productive or social welfare uses has related to the allegations of corruption around the game, and a sense that the tournament was being used to enhance the image of host countries in the short run without genuinely benefiting the sport. Perhaps, most controversially of all the hosting rights for the 2022 edition were awarded to the small Persian Gulf state of Qatar. The Qatari motives appear to be to raise the national profile and its "soft power" of acceptance and cultural influence for a future beyond reliance on its oil and gas exports. However, the benefit for football was unclear: the heat of Qatar's desert climate and lack of any suitable stadiums necessitated arguably the most significant investment in new facilities and infrastructure of any FIFA World Cup in a territory with no prior track record of hosting anything of equivalent scale. More tragically, the stadium building programme has been dogged by reports of poor and dangerous working conditions, including allegations of the deaths of thousands of construction workers (Guardian, 2021).

Product Development: The Women's FIFA World Cup

Women's football is today pursued as a growth market by FIFA, for example, the European regional group UEFA operated its Women's Football Development Programme (WFDP) between 2010 and 2016 (UEFA, 2019). In England, the FA initiated its "Gameplan for Growth" strategy in 2017, aiming to more than double attendance at international fixtures, women's superleague attendances, and broadcast viewing figures. Reporting in 2020, the FA announced that these targets had all been exceeded (The FA, 2020a, 2020b).

As with the men's game, the story of the women's World Cup has its roots before FIFA's involvement. Women's football teams have existed since at least 1895, when the British Ladies' Football Club was founded. Sizeable crowds were attracted to see "ladies teams" playing throughout Britain's industrial heartlands of northern England, particularly during World War I, when spectators had limited access to men's football. The first international fixtures are thought to have been held in 1920 between an English works' team (Dick, Kerr Ladies FC) and a side from France, and then between England and Scotland. However, the English FA reacted by banning women's football from FA-affiliated pitches, and women's football clubs lost much of their commercial and participatory momentum (Tennent and Gillett, 2016).

Regardless of this institutional discouragement, 50 years later the first World Cup (the "Coppa del Mondo") was hosted in Italy, organised by FIEFF (Federazione Internazionale Europea Football Femminile). Its success resulted in a second edition a year later in Mexico (The "Campeonato de Fútbol Femenil"). Both tournaments were sponsored by Martini & Rossi, the Italian multinational alcoholic beverage company, and the Mexican tournament is also notable for adopting the sort of mascot and merchandising campaign pioneered by the English FA, and later by FIFA, for men's World Cups (National Football Museum, n.d.a, n.d.b).

It was not until 20 years later, in 1991, that the first FIFA sanctioned event took place in China, with the support of the global confectionery company Mars. FIFA had also held an unofficial "International Women's Football Tournament" in China in 1988 as a pilot, though the announcement of the dates and lineup in *FIFA News* seemed to take secondary importance behind the construction of a new stadium in Pyongyang (FIFA, 1988a, 1988b). Despite a low-profile start, with just 12 countries participating in the first official World Cup, the event has operated quadrennially since, gradually expanding participation. Though a cumulative gate of over 500,000 spectators was attracted together with global TV coverage, FIFA does not seem to have been confident enough to call this first tournament a World Cup, calling it the rather lengthy "1st FIFA World

Championship for Women's Football for the M&Ms Cup" instead (FIFA, 1991a, p. 91–92). This reflected FIFA's relative slowness in realising the potential for women's football to complement the men's game, prioritising indoor men's football instead – indeed the first men's "five a side" (later futsal) FIFA World Cup was held in 1989 (FIFA, 1989).

In 1996, a Women's Olympic Football Tournament was added to the schedule of the summer Olympics, where it has remained ever since as a regular fixture alongside the men's edition. At this point, it is useful to return briefly to the history of Olympic football, which began as a men's-only event. Although part of the Olympic Games, and thus the organisation of the IOC, the association football component as with other events is "outsourced" to the sport's governing body, in this case FIFA. To differentiate from its own World Cup, FIFA has imposed restrictions ever since the IOC had itself opened to professional players in 1988, prior to which Olympic football had been an amateur competition, albeit open to allegations of "shamateurism" as particular nations, particularly from the Eastern Bloc, dominated the medal board. With the allowance of professional players in 1988, FIFA initially insisted on no prior World Cup experience, replaced by an age cap of 23 years in 1992, augmented with an allowance of three "overage" players since 1996. For the reorganised 2020 edition, this age cap is lifted to 24 years.

Returning to women's football, the technical report of the 1996 Olympic Football Tournament refers to the introduction of women's Olympic football as an "innovation" that was "a natural progression of FIFA's continuing support for women's football and the successful organisation of two Women's World Cups in the past five years" (FIFA, 1996, p. 8).

Some FAs – notably the US, China, Germany, and the Nordic countries – did more to encourage the development of women's football, and the women's tournament has continued to grow, reaching maturity quickly. This was reflected in the choice of Women's World Cup tournament hosts in the early years, which tended to be countries with a strong national team – Sweden in 1995, the US twice (1999 and 2003), China again in 2007 and Germany in 2011. The US double-hosting, in particular, reflected the popularity of football (soccer) in the US after the 1994 men's World Cup edition, as well the women's side having won the 1991 and 1999 Women's World Cups, as well as Olympic gold in 1996 and silver in 2000. China had been expected to host the 2003 edition but the US Soccer Federation stepped in due to the SARS epidemic, making use of MLS facilities such as the Home Depot Centre near Los Angeles (FIFA, 2003). By 2015, the tournament attracted 1.35 million spectators and was viewed in 188 territories (FIFA, 2015), though as Table 2.3 shows the record of the tournament in terms of match attendance has been inconsistent, with the tournaments held in the US and China in 1999 and 2007 respectively generally being more popular than elsewhere. Data on financial returns is vague, but in their 2019 Annual Report, FIFA show that their expenses for the tournament ran to $156.9m (FIFA, 2018) suggesting that incomes raised, while aggregated with other FIFA tournaments, would probably exceed this figure.

TABLE 2.3 Spectators at Women's World Cup Games

	Country	*Average number of spectators*
1991	China	19,615
1995	Sweden	4,315
1999	USA	37,319
2003	USA	21,239
2007	China	37,218
2011	Germany	26,430
2015	Canada	26,029
2019	France	21,756

Source: (Lange, 2020).

The Women's World Cup has helped FIFA to diversify from its historic reliance on the men's tournament, though the potential for this did not seem to be fully realised until the late 2010s, with the formal launch of a global strategy for women's football (FIFA, 2018). This document directly recognised the opportunity for FIFA to create new revenue streams from women's football, reflecting a realisation that women's football could open new markets while also serving existing markets. There was also a desire to implement this strategy by involving women more closely in the governance of the game itself, with a commitment for women to be on the executive committees of all member FAs by 2026, and to take up at least a third of FIFA's own committee seats by 2022.

Other Versions: U-17, U-20 and Beach Football

Since association football spread through the schools and universities of England, the organisation of the game had a physical education dimension, and FIFA had looked to expand a World Championship for male youth football as early as 1948, when a competition for players aged 17–19 was held. This was taken over by UEFA in 1957, and remained a European tournament. In a pattern that would become familiar in launching new tournaments, FIFA leveraged their partnership with Coca-Cola to hold the first under 20s World Cup in Tunisia in 1977, a commercial partner being necessary to underwrite the travel and organisation costs of a tournament unlikely to bring in the gate money or TV rights of the men's World Cup. To give more up-and-coming players a chance to participate, this competition was held bi-annually instead of quadrennially. Age group tournaments were later expanded and proliferated, with an U-16 (U-17 after 1991) version first held in China in 1985, sponsored by Kodak, complete with a cuddly Panda mascot (FIFA, 1985).

The strategic importance to FIFA of these tournaments is that they could be used as market development for football in nations such as China, Australia or New Zealand where football was an emerging sport, and perhaps also as a test bed for a future World Cup, as in Japan in 1993. In other cases, such as Trinidad and

Tobago (2001), the tournaments could be used to give smaller nations the opportunity to host and to extend FIFA patronage.[4] Alternatively, as in Scotland (1989) the tournament, with its lower crowds, could be held in existing top division football stadiums without incurring the need for extensive public works. As with senior women's football, age group tournaments were somewhat slower to be proliferated, but an U-19 version was started in 2002, and an U-17 in 2008 (e.g. Allan, 2018). These early women's tournaments were run on a relatively small scale. For example, the 2002 edition was held over three cities (Vancouver, Victoria, and Edmonton) in Western Canada involving 12 teams, but 47,000 spectators were attracted to the final; this allowed for the metaphoric water to be tested prior to the Women's World Cup taking place in Canada in 2015 (FIFA, 2002).

FIFA has also expanded the World Cup umbrella to include two new formats of football: futsal, and beach football. In the technical report for the first FIFA Indoor (Five-a-Side) World Cup in 1989, Sepp Blatter emphasised that the development of the new format was intended to expand the overall sport, particularly through participation, rather than compete with the outdoor version. He also stressed that only four indoor halls or arenas were required to host a World Cup. This meant that the entry requirements for hosting were much lower, and bespoke state involvement was not required as futsal could even be supported by existing state leisure centre provision. Further tournaments followed in Hong Kong in 1992 and Spain in 1996, again under the sponsorship of Mars. Similar to the age group tournaments, futsal was used to expand football and FIFA patronage by giving smaller countries, including Guatemala (2000) and Chinese Taipei (2004), the chance to host. FIFA formally renamed their competition from the FIFA Indoor (Five-a-Side) World Championship to the Futsal (Indoor) World Championship in 1996, although Futsal also retains its own independent governing body, the Asociación Mundial de Fútsal (AMF), which organises its own World Cups.

Beach soccer originated in Brazil in the late 1950s and started to take place in organised form from the 1990s onwards. It was originally organised by the Beach Soccer Worldwide Federation, which organised a series of tournaments before joining formally with FIFA in 2005. That year the first official FIFA Beach Soccer World Cup was held in Brazil, involving twelve teams. France, player-managed by Eric Cantona, won the first edition, held in Rio de Janerio (Beachsoccer.com, 2020). This event settled into a biennial schedule, initially held in countries known for their beaches including Tahiti, Portugal and the Bahamas, but in 2019, demonstrating the increasing seriousness of the competition and the building of bespoke facilities for it, it was held in landlocked Paraguay, and the 2021 competition took place in Moscow (Ruskiy Mir Foundation, 2019). However, the infrastructure requirements which appear to involve providing sand, nets and

4 Jack Warner, notoriously also a FIFA Vice President chaired the organising committee.

temporary stands are perhaps the lowest of any FIFA tournament, and this has given territories with populations as small as the Bahamas (385,000) and Tahiti (189,517) the opportunity to host a FIFA event. Neither the Futsal nor the Beach World Cups have yet spawned women's or age group competitions.

Conclusion: The Nature of the World Cup as a Business

Emerging in 1930, the FIFA World Cup is easily the most high-profile and globally marketable single-sport mega-event. For its first two decades, hosting alternated between South America and Europe, typically in established football markets which had previously hosted the Olympics and also had a good track record in the amateur Olympic football event. The tournament is also usually won by teams representing countries from the same continent as the hosts, sometimes it has been the hosts themselves, which only seems to heighten the excitement and spectacle for "World Cup fever." While more recent tournaments have become bigger in terms of infrastructure building and revenue, earlier tournaments still made a considerable impact both on their host nations and on football fans globally.

Since the first edition (Uruguay 1930) FIFA operated its World Cup on a franchise basis whereby host FAs took responsibility for providing stadium infrastructure and other expenses at their own risk, and often with substantial public subsidy. The proceeds of the tournament included a contribution to FIFA, which in its earliest years were required to sustain the organisation for the four-year cycle until the next tournament. The tournament became associated with increasing advertising/sponsorship revenues and television rights correspondingly, with progress in broadcast technology which made highlights packages possible, and then live transmission, globally. FIFA also became more assertive of its branding and merchandising rights after England 1966, when the host FA demonstrated the possibilities with the first global sporting mega-event mascot, World Cup Willie, which was licensed across many product categories.

A pivotal moment occurred in 1974, when Joao Havelange replaced Stanley Rous as FIFA President. This increased the involvement and "voice" of FAs outside of Europe and Latin America, because of the one-member/one-vote policy, further solidifying Havelange's position. It also diluted the power of the European members, which constituted the geographic and historic "home" of the organisation. Havelange and his Technical Director, later General Secretary (and eventually successor) Sepp Blatter accelerated the involvement of sponsors, perhaps most significantly Coca-Cola and Adidas, to fund the global reach of FIFA by funding football development programmes particularly across Africa and island nations. This grew the market for football as well as the potential for interest and involvement in its flagship event, the World Cup, and thus the sponsorship and the television rights that could be increasingly leveraged for the quadrennial event.

FIFA has used its World Cup to open-up markets in countries (and continents) identified as high-potential growth for football consumption, participation, and thus broadcasting and sponsorship: The USA (North America) in 1994, Korea-Japan (Asia) in 2002, and South Africa (Africa) in 2010. USA'94 is a particularly interesting case for this chapter as the most profitable tournament, taking place in the most politically and economically powerful country of the 20th century. The US Soccer Federation circumnavigated FIFA's copyrights, allowing them more latitude for branding and licensing, as well as its manipulation of supply/demand in ticketing tiering and release, and the introduction of a local partners tier of sponsorship.

The World Cup (and FIFA's) global and financial growth have also been associated with controversy: criticism over the use of public finance to fund lavish stadiums, and criticisms over the conduct of individuals within (and at the top) of the organisation which have sometimes overshadowed the game itself, at least when measured in news media headlines. This is partly a consequence of the concentration of political and economic power brought about by FIFA's monopoly status which is reinforced by the IOC position that each affiliated sport may have only one governing body. Despite the attempted emergence of non-FIFA affiliated "pirate" associations over the decades, and most recently a proposed unaffiliated "European Superleague," FIFA has sustained its existence as the world's governing body for football, not least because of the popularity of its World Cup flagship footballing product. While these controversies are more recent, it is important to recognise the institutional entrepreneurship of earlier administrators such as Jules Rimet and Sir Stanley Rous in using the World Cup tournament to consolidate FIFA's power.

Since the late 1970s, FIFA has extended its range of tournaments to include age categories, indoor and beach editions, as well as a deliberate strategy to grow women's football with its own World Cup, Olympic football event, and age-categories. These other tournaments are used by FIFA as test-beds for "new" or potential World Cup locations, as well as developing football markets generally. These tournaments continue to be big business and it will be interesting to see where FIFA goes next, assuming it maintains its global monopoly. Perhaps the "virtual" environment is the next great frontier, with an FIFA e-sports cup having existed since 2004, this is a potentially lucrative market space for FIFA to grow; its "FIFA" computer games have been a market leading digital product for many years already. FIFA budgets $12 million USD for the 2021 tournament, compared to just $7 million for its Beach Soccer World Cup in the same year, and equal to its budget for the Refereeing Assistance Programme (RAP) (FIFA Finance Division, 2020).

References

Allan, M. (2018) Assessing the Perceptions of Local Residents on the Positive and Negative Impacts of FIFA U-17 Women's World Cup in Jordan 2016, *Journal of Environmental Management and Tourism*, 9(26), 255–266.

Baade, R.A. & Matheson, V.A. (2004) The Quest for the Cup: Assessing the Economic Impact of the World Cup, *Regional Studies*, 38(4), 343–354.

Barney, J. (1991) Firm Resources and Sustained Competitive Advantage, *Journal of Management*, 17(1), 99–120.

Beachsoccer.com (2020) *Eric Cantona: Winning the World Cup was one of the Best Moments in my Life*. Available at: https://www.beachsoccer.com/news/winning-the-world-cup-was-one-of-the-best-moments-in-my-life [Accessed 27 April 2021].

Bolt, J. & van Zanden, J.L. (2020) *Maddison Style Estimates of the Evolution of the World Economy. A New 2020 Update*. Available at: https://www.rug.nl/ggdc/historicaldevelopment/maddison/releases/maddison-project-database-2020?lang=en [Accessed 30 April 2021].

CIA (1986) *The World Factbook*. Washington, DC: US Government Printing Office.

CIA (2021) *The World Factbook*. Available at: https://www.cia.gov/the-world-factbook/ [Accessed 30 April 2021].

Chadwick, S. & Burton, N. (2011) The Evolving Sophistication of Ambush Marketing: A Typology of Strategies, *Thunderbird International Business Review*, 53(6), 709–719.

Chisari, F. (2007) *The Age of Innocence: A History of the Relationship Between Football Authorities and the BBC Television service*, 1937–1982 (Doctoral dissertation, De Montfort University).

Conn, D. (2012) *Sepp Blatter Faces Calls to Step Down at FIFA over 'Bribery Cover-up.'* Available at: https://www.theguardian.com/football/2012/jul/12/sepp-blatter-joao-havelange-fifa [Accessed 15 April 2021].

Conn, D. (2017) *The Fall of the House of FIFA*. New York: Random House.

D'Amado. L.J. (2020) Montevideo 1930: Reassessing the Selection of the First World Cup host, *Soccer & Society*, 21(8), 848–860.

Decker, S. (2013) The Silence of the Archives: Business History, Post-colonialism and Archival Ethnography, *Management & Organizational History*, 8(2), 155–173.

Dietschy, P. (2013) Making Football Global? FIFA, Europe, and the Non-European Football World, 1912–74. *Journal of Global History*, 8(2), 279–298.

Dietschy, P. (2014) The 1938 World Cup. Sporting Neutrality and Geopolitics, or All-Conquering Fascism?. In Rinke, S. and Schiller, K. (eds.) *The FIFA World Cup 1930-2010: Politics, Commerce, Spectacle and Identities* (pp. 85–102). Wallstein: Verlag.

Dyke, G., Gillett A.G. & Tennent, K.D. (2018) The Business of World Cup Football in *Presentation at York Festival of Ideas University of York*, June 12th, 2018.

Fett, M.(2020) The Game Has Changed – A Systematic Approach to Classify FIFA World Cups, *International Journal of Sport Policy and Politics*, 12(3), 455–470. 10.1080/19406940.2020.1784978

FIFA (1985) *I FIFA U-16 World Tournament for the Kodak Cup, China '85 Technical Report*. Zurich, Switzerland: FIFA.

FIFA (1988a) 150,000 Seating Accommodation in the Pyongyang Stadium. *FIFA News*, p. 4

FIFA (1988b). International Women's Tournament in China, *FIFA News*, p. 4.

FIFA (1989) *First FIFA World Championship for 5-a-Side Football Technical Report*. Holland: KNVB.

FIFA (1991) *1st FIFA World Championship for Women's Football for the M&M's Cup China '91 technical report*. Zurich, Switzerland: FIFA.

FIFA (1996) *Atlanta '96 Olympic Soccer Technical Report*. Zurich, Switzerland: FIFA.

FIFA (2002) *U-19 Women's World Championship Canada 2002: Report and Statistics*. Zurich, Switzerland: FIFA.

FIFA (2003) *FIFA Women's World Cup USA 2003 Technical Report and Statistics*. Zurich, Switzerland: FIFA.

FIFA (2015) *FIFA Women's World Cup 2015 Technical Report and Statistics*. Zurich, Switzerland: FIFA.

FIFA (2018) *Women's Football Strategy*. Zurich, Switzerland: FIFA.

FIFA Finance Division (2020) *FIFA 2021 Budget*. Zurich, Switzerland: FIFA.

Foster, W.M., Suddaby, R., Minkus, A. & Wiebe, E. (2011) History as Social Memory Assets: The example of Tim Hortons, *Management & Organizational History*, 6(1), 101–120.

Fx.com (2021) *Historical Converter*. Available at: https://fxtop.com/en/historical-currency-converter.php [Accessed 9 April 2021].

Gaffney, C. (2010) Mega-events and Socio-spatial Dynamics in Rio de Janeiro, 1919-2016, *Journal of Latin American Geography*, 7–29.

Gillett, A.G. & Tennent, K.D. (2017) Dynamic Sublimes, Changing Plans, and the Legacy of a Megaproject: The Case of the 1966 Soccer World Cup, *Project Management Journal*, 48(6), 93–116.

Gillett, A.G. & Tennent, K.D. (2019) 'Filip'or Flop? Managing Public Relations and the Latin American Reaction to the 1966 FIFA World Cup, *Soccer & Society*, 20(7-8), 923–935.

Gillett, A.G. & Tennent, K.D. (2020) (online first). Hybrid Goals: Institutional Complexity and 'Legacy' in a Global Sporting Mega-event, *Public Management Review*. 10.1080/14719037.2020.1833609

Gillett, A.G. & Tennent, K.D. (forthcoming) *Managing British Olympic Games Projects: Institutions through Time*. Bingley, UK: Emerald

Ghemawat, P. (2007) *Redefining Global Strategy: Crossing Borders in a World Where Differences Still Matter*. Boston, MA: Harvard Business School Press.

Guardian (2021) *Revealed: 6,500 Migrant Workers Have Died in Qatar Since World Cup awarded*. Available at: https://www.theguardian.com/global-development/2021/feb/23/revealed-migrant-worker-deaths-qatar-fifa-world-cup-2022 [Accessed 24 April 2021].

Homburg, H. (2008) Financing World Football. A Business History of the Fédération Internationale de Football Association (FIFA). *Zeitschrift für unternehmensgeschichte/Journal of Business History*, 53(1), 33–69.

Hopkins, G. (2010) *Star-Spangled Soccer*. London, UK: Palgrave Macmillan.

Kassens-Noor, E., Wilson, M., Müller, S., Maharaj, B. & Huntoon, L. (2015) Towards a Mega-event Legacy Framework, *Leisure Studies*, 34(6), 665–671.

Kioussis, G.N. (2020) A Bid Denied: The U.S. Application to Host the 1986 World Cup, *Soccer & Society*, 21(8), 946–959. 10.1080/14660970.2020.1793628

Lange, D. (2020) *Women's Soccer World Cup Average Per Game Attendance 1991–2019*. Statista.com. Available at: https://www.statista.com/statistics/272800/average-number-of-spectatators-at-the-fifa-womens-world-cup/ [Accessed 30 April 2021].

Maharaj, B. (2011) 2010 FIFA World Cup^{TM}: (South)'Africa's Time Has Come'? *South African Geographical Journal*, 93(1), 49–62.

Majendie, M. (2015) *The World's Most Expensive Car Park, Empty Seats at the Maracana and More: FIFA's Unwanted World Cup legacy in Brazil*. Available at: https://www.standard.co.uk/sport/football/the-world-s-most-expensive-car-park-empty-seats-at-the-maracana-and-more-fifa-s-unwanted-world-cup-legacy-in-brazil-10342016.html [Accessed 20 April 2021].

Müller, M. & Gaffney, C. (2018) Comparing the Urban Impacts of the FIFA World Cup and Olympic Games from 2010 to 2016, *Journal of Sport and Social Issues*, 42(4), 247–269.

National Football Museum (n.d.a) *1970 Coppa del Mondo poster*. Available at: https://artsandculture.google.com/asset/1970-coppa-del-mondo-poster/eQE-wgTkBrgSdA?hl=en [Accessed 20 April 2021].

National Football Museum (n.d.b) *1971 Women's World Cup Pennant*. Available at: https://artsandculture.google.com/asset/1971-women-s-world-cup-pennant/UwHCCFVQTHM25w?hl=en [Accessed 20 April 2021].

Porro, N. & Conti, F. (2014) Italia Novanta. "Magic Nights", Globalization and a Country at the Crossroads. In Rinke, F. and Schiller, K. (eds.), *The FIFA World Cup 1930–2010*. Wallstein: Verlag.

Rous, S.F. & Winterbottom, W. (1961) *World Cup 1966: Organization*. FIFA Document Centre, File KA.

Ruskiy Mir Foundation (2019 *Russia Will Host First Beach Soccer World Championship In 2021*. Available at: https://russkiymir.ru/en/news/264039/ [Accessed 27 April 2021].

Sbetti, N. & Serapiglia, D. (2020) Was Football Fascist? The 1934 World Cup in the Postwar Memory, *Soccer & Society*, 21(8), 889–903.

Schausteck de Almeida, B., Bolsmann, C., Marchi Junior, W. & de Souza, J. (2015) Rationales, rhetoric and realities: FIFA's World Cup in South Africa 2010 and Brazil 2014, *International Review for the Sociology of Sport*, 50(3), 265–282.

Sugden, J. & Tomlinson, A. (1998) *FIFA and the Contest for World Football: Who Rules the People's Game?* Oxford: Polity Press.

Tennent, K.D. & Gillett, A.G. (2016) *Foundations of Managing Sporting Events: Organising the 1966 FIFA World Cup*. London: Routledge.

Tennent, K.D. & Gillett, A.G. (2018) Opportunities for all the Team: Entrepreneurship and the 1966 and 1994 Soccer World Cups, *The International Journal of the History of Sport*, 35(7-8), 767–788.

Tennent, K.D., Gillett, A.G. & Foster, W.M. (2020) Developing Historical Consciousness in Management Learners, *Management Learning*, 51(1), 73–88.

The FA (2020a) *Every Target Hit as Gameplan for Growth Delivers for Women's and Girls' Football*. Available at: https://www.thefa.com/news/2020/jun/25/gameplan-for-growth-season-four-report-250620 [Accessed 24 April 2021].

The FA (2020b) *The Gameplan for Growth Final Review and Report*. London, UK: The Football Association.

The United States Department of Justice (2015) *Nine FIFA Officials and Five Corporate Executives Indicted for Racketeering Conspiracy and Corruption*. Available at: https://www.justice.gov/opa/pr/nine-fifa-officials-and-five-corporate-executives-indicted-racketeering-conspiracy-and [Accessed 15 April 2021].

Tomlinson, A. (2000) FIFA and the Men Who Made It, *Soccer & Society*, 1(1), 55–71.

Tomlinson, A. (2020) *Sir Stanley Rous and the Growth of World Football: An Englishman Abroad*. Cambridge Scholars Publishing.

UEFA (2019) *Women's football | Inside UEFA*. Available at: https://www.uefa.com/insideuefa/football-development/womens-football/ [Accessed 26 April 2021].

Vamplew, W. (2004) *Pay Up and Play the Game: Professional Sport in Britain, 1875–1914*. Cambridge University Press.

Vonnard, P. & Quin, G. (2017) Did South America Foster European football?: Transnational Influences on the Continentalization of FIFA and the Creation of UEFA, 1926–1959, *Sport in Society*, 20(10), 1424–1439.

Walvin, J. (1986) *Football and the Decline of Britain*. Basingstoke: Macmillan.

Warwick, T. (2017) Northernness, Sheffield and the 1966 World Cup: The "Steel City" on Display, *International Journal of Regional and Local History*, 12(2), 92–106.

Wong, D. & Chadwick, S. (2017) Risk and (in) Security of FIFA Football World Cups–Outlook for Russia 2018. *Sport in Society*, 20(5-6), 583–598.

World Game (2016) *Havelange Was the King of Corruption, Blatter Merely the Prince*. Available at: https://theworldgame.sbs.com.au/havelange-was-the-king-of-corruption-blatter-merely-the-prince [Accessed 28 March 2021].

3

BIDDING AND HOSTING DECISIONS

Kamilla Swart and Rauf Mammadov

Introduction

Sport mega-events such as the FIFA World Cup and Olympic Games are complex matters which generally arise from distinctive economic objectives but have far-reaching political and social ramifications. These events are considered by policy makers as catalysts of economic activities in host cities, regions and nations. Moreover, they are utilised to reposition nations, enhance their image and gain soft power. Host cities and countries tend to have huge expectations regarding the legacies of sport mega-events. A legacy is considered positive when a territory leverages the sporting tournament by generating results that are positive in one or more areas such as political, human capital, cultural, urban and social, based on a strategic approach (Ruta and Manzoni, 2015). However, not all legacies are positive and coupled with the increasing contestation and controversies associated with the selection of host cities and countries as was the case with Russia 2018 and Qatar 2022, bidding contests have attracted much media scrutiny and public attention.

FIFA, which was founded in 1904, is the highest football governing body whose primary role is to oversee the international competitions among its 211 national member associations (Stanwick and Stanwick, 2020). According to Parent (2017), FIFA has excellent relationships with its stakeholders. FIFA organises and promotes football's leading international tournaments that attract millions of fans globally. The main sporting tournament is the (men's) World Cup, which began in 1930, and the Women's World Cup that began much later, in 1991. FIFA generates a lot of revenue from its tournaments. Human Rights Watch (2020) indicates that in the 2015–2018 cycles, FIFA had a net profit of $1.2 billion and cash reserves of more than $2.7 billion. FIFA uses the World Cup and other tournaments to produce quality content to broadcasters globally and subsequently

DOI: 10.4324/9781003121794-3

deliver the best football viewing experience to fans watching on television (FIFA, n.d.a). Media convergence has been increasing, and the content's proliferation has been significant for the right holders, advisors, sponsors and other entities standing out from the crowd.

The bidding process is essential for FIFA to achieve its objectives and permits the assessment of the logistics, planning and operations needed to deliver a great sporting tournament experience (Borkowski, 2009). The FIFA World Cup has a bidding process specific for the men, women and U20 tournaments with the men's World Cup being the most widely known. The purpose of this chapter is to discuss the bidding process and hosting decisions made by FIFA when organising its sport mega-events. The remaining sections of this chapter have been structured to include the review of the bidding processes for the World Cups, bidding process reforms, differences between successful and unsuccessful bids as well as the outlook for the future of bidding and hosting.

Bidding Processes for the World Cups

Event bidding contests or "bidding wars" are viewed as mechanisms "whereby entrepreneurial cities engage in inter-urban competition to ensure they are visible to residents, visitors and investors" (McGillivray and Turner, 2017, p. 2). Due to the changing geopolitical landscape regarding the bidding and hosting of the FIFA World Cup, and the men's edition in particular, more cities and nations have joined the bidding race in recent years. Sport mega-events are generally driven by political and corporate elites; moreover, the political economy has developed to such a degree globally that these "events have gained a self-perpetuating dynamic of their own, characterized by distinct coagulations of interests and predominance of certain corporate actors" (Cornelissen and Swart, 2006, p. 108), as explored further next.

FIFA World Cup (Men's)

The FIFA (men's) World Cup is a quadrennial tournament deemed the most popular sporting tournament globally. The first men's World Cup, held in 1930, was won by Uruguay (Lisi, 2011). Table 3.1 presents the bidding nations together with the successful host nations for the FIFA (men's) World Cup. (van der Merwe, 2009) emphasises that just as in today's intense bidding process, Uruguay lobbied hard to beat the four European opponents who subsequently withdrew from the tournament. The first men's World Cup only had 13 teams competing, and only increased marginally to 16 teams in 1934. From 1934 to 1966, Europe strengthened its hold on the World Cup and hosted it six times, with the exception of South America in 1950 (Brazil) and 1962 (Chile) (van der Merwe, 2009). Consequently, South American teams boycotted the event in protest especially after they had been given the impression that FIFA would rotate host status between the two continents. To prevent further controversy, FIFA implemented a

TABLE 3.1 FIFA (men's) World Cup host nations, bidding countries and participating teams

Year	*Bidding countries*	*Host*	*Participating teams*	*Winner*
1930	Italy, Sweden, Netherlands, Spain, Hungary and Uruguay	Uruguay	13	Uruguay
1934	Italy and Sweden	Italy	16	Italy
1938	France, Argentina and Germany	France	15	Italy
1950	Brazil, Argentina and Germany	Brazil	13	Uruguay
1954	Switzerland	Switzerland	16	West Germany
1958	Sweden	Sweden	16	Brazil
1962	Chile, Argentina and West Germany	Chile	16	Brazil
1966	England, West Germany and Spain	England	16	England
1970	Argentina, Australia, Colombia, Japan, Mexico and Peru	Mexico	16	Brazil
1974	West Germany, Spain, Italy and Netherlands	West Germany	16	West Germany
1978	Argentina, Colombia and Mexico	Argentina	16	Argentina
1982	Spain, West Germany and Italy	Spain	24	Italy
1986	Canada, Mexico and USA	Mexico	24	Argentina
1990	Italy, Soviet Union, Austria, England, France, Greece, Iran, West Germany and Yugoslavia	Italy	24	West Germany
1994	USA, Morocco, Brazil and Chile	USA	24	Brazil
1998	France, Morocco, Switzerland, England and Germany	France	32	France
2002	South Korea, Japan and Mexico	Japan/South Korea	32	Brazil
2006	Germany, South Africa, England and Morocco	Germany	32	Italy
2010	South Africa, Morocco, Egypt, Tunisia/Libya and Nigeria	South Africa	32	Spain
2014	Brazil, Argentina and Colombia	Brazil	32	Germany

(*Continued*)

TABLE 3.1 (Continued)

Year	*Bidding countries*	*Host*	*Participating teams*	*Winner*
2018	Russia, Portugal/Spain, Belgium/ Netherlands and England	Russia	32	France
2022	Qatar, Australia, Korea Republic, Japan and USA	Qatar	32	?
2026	Canada/Mexico/USA and Morocco	Canada/ Mexico/ USA	48	?

rotational policy between Europe and the Americas in the late 1950s which continued until 1998 (van der Merwe, 2009).

The tournament continued to grow and by 1982 there were 24 participating countries; and expanded further to 32 countries in 1998 (Glanville, 2014). This expansion could be attributed to several reasons. First, the increasing commercialisation and globalisation of world football resulted in further penetration of new markets in Africa, Asia and the Americas, and served the self-interest of FIFA and its sponsors (van der Merwe, 2009). Second, the creation of newly independent states in the developing world increased the membership of FIFA and contributed to greater diversification of world football and more competitive bidding processes (van der Merwe, 2009). While the period from the 1970s to 1990s was still dominated by Europe and the Americas, North America started to play a more prominent role with Mexico hosting the event twice (1970 and 1986) and the USA in 1994.

Despite the significant costs associated with hosting the FIFA (men's) World Cup, FIFA has generally been able to recruit bidding applicants (Solberg, 2017), as per Table 3.1.

By 2002, Asia entered the fray and while Korea and Japan bid separately, before the vote they agreed with FIFA to co-host jointly. Interestingly, at the time FIFA said that co-hosting would unlikely to happen again due to the many logistical and organisational challenges. Furthermore, while its statutes in 2004 stated that it did not permit co-hosting, yet Asian market penetration was a strategic move by FIFA.

Africa, although lagging behind in the bidding contests, had Morocco bid for several editions (1994, 1998) and South Africa bid for the 2006 World Cup. South Africa lost controversially by one vote to Germany when Charles Dempsey from New Zealand abstained from voting. Germany was also accused of bribery and corruption that secured the Asian votes and included payments to FIFA (Spiegel, 2015). A continental rotational system was subsequently introduced by FIFA for the 2010 World Cup in an attempt to level the playing fields (albeit revoked again in 2007 with Brazil being the only contender for the 2014 edition).

The 2010 World Cup presented an opportunity to grow the game beyond the traditional power bases of Europe and South America to further globalise the sport on the periphery of world football (van der Merwe, 2009). South Africa was successful in its bid to host the first World Cup in Africa, eighty years after its inception. South Africa's 2006 and 2010 bids were positioned to enhance the international image of the country, grow tourism, and instil national pride and unity in the "new" post-apartheid country. Moreover, it was viewed as "Africa's turn"; as an opportunity to redress the negative stereotypes of Afro-pessimism.

For the 2014 World Cup, Brazil became the only contender after Colombia withdrew and the Argentinian bid not materialising. In contrast, the 2018 and 2022 World Cups included six (Russia, Portugal/Spain, Belgium/Netherlands and England) and five (Qatar, Australia, Korea Republic, Japan and USA) bidding countries, respectively. It is interesting to note that this included two joint bids. The 2018 World Cup bids were made predominantly by the European nations whereas the bids for 2022 World Cup were made by nations from all regions apart from South America. The expectation that the 2022 World Cup would be the largest football tournament made the bidding process fierce. The awarding of Russia 2018 and Qatar 2022 World Cups simultaneously were mired in controversy.

Qatar will be the first Arab country to host the men's World Cup tournament in 2022. Dorsey (2018) states that the decision has sparked several controversies since Qatar has been accused of bribing FIFA to host the tournament. The other controversy is that Qatar has a poor human rights record that contravenes FIFA's human rights principles. The state-sponsored Kafala system has caused many human rights organisations to criticise FIFA's decision. The sponsorship system has been equated to modern-day slavery as migrant workers must have a sponsor who are able to exert significant control (Peltz-Steele, 2016). Ter Haar (2018) suggested that hosting the 2022 World Cup will likely change Qatar's approach to labour laws considering that it has already indicated intentions to abolish the Kafala system to reduce human rights criticisms. Several initiatives were launched such as the development of a Worker's Charter in 2013 and Workers' Welfare Standards in 2014, and more recently the adoption of Laws No. 17 and 18 of 2020 on the 30 August 2020. The former law provides for the introduction of a "non-discriminatory minimum wage"; the first for a country in the region, whereas the latter ends the requirement for migrant workers to obtain their employer's permission to change jobs (Swart et al., 2020).

Blake and Calvert (2015) contend that Qatar paid to host the 2022 World Cup. Some journalists have evidence showing that Qatar paid USD 880 million to FIFA to host the men's World Cup, which contravenes the principle of openness and corruption avoidance (California Western International Law, 2012). Some of the FIFA officials, such as mysterious Mr. Seedy, received money in their personal accounts from Qatari officials in exchange for marketing the nation to host the World Cup (Blake and Calvert, 2015). Although controversial, Qatar's winning bid was very inspiring considering the nation has never hosted a sport mega-events of this magnitude. The 2022 World Cup will upgrade Qatar's status since it may consider to bid for other sport mega-events due to the upgraded infrastructure and new stadia. Qatar has recently been awarded the 2030 Asian Games and has aspirations to host Olympic Games, having unsuccessfully bid for both the 2016 and 2020 Games.

In 2018, FIFA announced that the first joint bid by three countries (Canada, Mexico and the United States) for the 2026 World Cup was successful. FIFA agreed to honour the request of the South American Football Confederation, CONMEBOL, among other institutions, to expand the qualifications to 48 teams to allow for more countries to take part in the tournament (Millward and Parnell, 2014). This joint bid received 67% of the votes in comparison to Morocco's 33% (FIFA, 2018). It was Morocco's fifth failed bid. While Morocco focused its bid on the country's passion for football, access, accessibility in relation to European time zones, and the compact geolocation of potential match venues (similar to Qatar), its lack of infrastructure in terms of stadiums, transport, accommodation were considered high risk (Morgan, 2019). In contrast, the joint North American bid was infrastructurally more sound and offered FIFA an estimated windfall of USD 14 billion, USD 2 billion more than the Moroccan bid (Morgan, 2019). With Morocco entering the bid race again for 2030 World Cup, it is argued that the country is likely to stand a better chance if it considers joining the bid of Portugal and Spain (Kelly, 2021).

FIFA World Cup (Women's)

The women's World Cup was initially known as the FIFA Women's World Cup. Similar to the men's World Cup, FIFA governs the Women's World Cup that takes place every four years (Tomlinson, 2014). However, since it is held on a smaller scale, it is considered a tier 2 sport mega-event (Dickson et al., 2015). The first Women's World Cup involved 12 teams but expanded to 16 teams in 1999 and 24 teams in 2015 (Fonio and Pisapia, 2014). In the past, football was dominated by male players such as Lionel Messi and Christiano Ronaldo. However, the situation is changing and there are female football players who are gaining popularity, such as Marta Vieira da Silva from Brazil and Megan Rapinoe from the United States. The increased coverage of women in sporting tournaments has increased the prominence of female sports stars in the media (Göral, 2019). It has also improved the marketing of female-focused sporting tournaments which will likely generate more funding for female sports. Daprano (2013) argues that in 2019, more than one billion people watched the women's football matches. FIFA (2018) indicates that 82.18 million in-home viewers watched the 2019 World Cup final, which was 56% more compared to the 2015 World Cup's final. The hosting nations and cities of the Women's World Cup have been positively affected. Woodward (2018) claims that in 2019, more than 720,000 tickets had been sold 50 days prior to the tournament's kickoff in France. The Women's World Cup led to an induced, direct and indirect contribution of USD 389 million to the GDP of

TABLE 3.2 FIFA Women's World Cup host nations, bidding countries and participating teams

Year	*Bidding countries*	*Host*	*Participating teams*	*Winner*
1991	China and USA	China	12	USA
1995	Bulgaria and Sweden	Sweden	12	Norway
1999	Sweden, Australia, Canada and England	USA	16	USA
2003	USA, Canada, Australia and China	USA	16	Germany
2007	China, USA, Germany and Japan	China	16	Germany
2011	Australia, Canada, France, Germany, Peru and Switzerland	Germany	16	Japan
2015	Canada and Zimbabwe	Canada	24	USA
2019	England, France, South Korea, New Zealand and South Africa	France	24	USA
2023	Japan, Colombia, Australia and New Zealand	Australia/ New Zealand	32	?

France while the net capital gain FIFA obtained was USD 122 million (Woodward, 2018). Given the success of the 2019 edition, it is no surprise that FIFA has increased the number of participating teams to 24 (see Table 3.2). Furthermore, it is evident that the Women's World Cup is not as contested as its male counterparts and has resulted in bids from smaller and emerging nations (e.g., Peru in 2011 and Zimbabwe in 2015). Besides China hosting the first and fifth editions, the hosts have been from Europe and North America. Seemingly, the geopolitical distribution was addressed somewhat with the joint bid by Australia and New Zealand.

The Women's World Cup has provided a platform to showcase talented women players but there is a long way to make men's and women's football equal (Kenschaft et al., 2015). Kenschaft et al. (2015) state that masculinised sports, such as football and basketball, receive more funding at the institutional and national levels. The low funding women football teams make it impossible for them to meet most of their obligations as characterized by stagnant growth (Kenschaft et al., 2015). The Women's World Cup has been increasing the coverage of female sports to increase demand for the tournament (Darby, 2013). With the record-breaking viewership of the 2019 Women's World Cup, FIFA has promoted better marketing of the women's sporting tournaments, which has played an important role in increasing coverage. According to Kampmark (2018), the media is able to influence people subconsciously and advertisements they watch are able to affect their emotions, feelings and thoughts. The Women's World Cup awards of the best performing sportswomen has also led to their prominence. Female athletes have been given a chance to voice their opinions as well. For example, Megan Rapinoe has used social media and her success from the Women's World Cup to openly speak about gender discrimination, racism and LGBTQ rights.

FIFA World Cup (U20)

The U20 World Cup is a biennial football through which football players under 20 years of age get a chance to showcase their talent. The first U20 World Cup tournament took place in Tunisia in 1977 after which the tournament is held every two years (Rockerbie, 2016). The sporting tournament name was changed to FIFA World Cup (U20) in 2005 from FIFA World Youth Championship (Molinaro, 2009). Twenty-two U20 tournaments, which have been held in different host nations (see Table 3.3), were won by 11 nations (Moore, 2018). It is apparent that this event is a lot more equally distributed in comparison to the host nations of both the Men's and Women's World Cups.

The U20 World Cup, which was scheduled for 2021 (Moon, 2017), was cancelled due to the COVID-19 pandemic (Reuters Staff, 2020). Five bids were submitted to host the tournament on 23 May 2019, which included a joint bid by Bahrain, Saudi Arabia and the UAE, and another by Myanmar with Thailand as well as individual bids from Brazil, Indonesia and Peru. Myanmar and Thailand withdrew their joint bid in favour of Indonesia, followed by the joint Arab bid and then Brazil. On 4 September 2019, Indonesia was announced by the FIFA Council in Shanghai, China as the winner (Glass, 2020). The tournament would be the first to take place in Southeast Asia since 1997 but was cancelled due to the COVID-19 pandemic. Indonesia was subsequently awarded the rights to host the 2023 edition.

Raithel (2014) indicates that the U20 World Cup tournaments have received a lot of negative publicity as they have been associated with injuries of the youths. Parent (2017) and Bunc, Ravnik and Velnar (2017) indicate that head trauma cases among young footballers have been on the rise. Despite such injury risks, some of the youths have continued to shine with the support of the U20 World Cup (Rockerbie, 2016).

Bidding Processes Reform

This section reviews how FIFA has reformed the bidding processes in the wake of the recent scandals. Moreover, the most recent bidding processes for the 2026 FIFA World Cup, the 2023 FIFA Women's World Cup and the 2021 U20 FIFA World Cup are presented.

FIFA World Cup (Men's)

The bid assessment involves evaluating the bidding nation's compliance with FIFA policies, risks, and technical capabilities. Unlike the previous bidding processes for

TABLE 3.3 U20 World Cup host nations, bidding countries and participating teams

Year	*Bidding countries*	*Host*	*Participating teams*	*Winner*
1977	Soviet Union, Brazil and Spain	Tunisia	16	Soviet Union
1979	Yugoslavia, Brazil and Chile	Japan	16	Argentina
1981	Saudi Arabia, USA and Japan	Australia	16	West Germany
1983	Nigeria, South Korea, Portugal and Brazil	Mexico	16	Brazil
1985	Australia, Yugoslavia and Nigeria	Soviet Union	16	Brazil
1987	Nigeria, Qatar, England and USA	Chile	16	Yugoslavia
1989	Uruguay, Argentina, Australia and West Germany	Saudi Arabia	16	Portugal
1991	Nigeria, Spain, Japan and Brazil	Portugal	16	Portugal
1993	Ghana, Argentina, Spain and Australia	Australia	16	Brazil
1995	Brazil, United Arab Emirates (UAE), USA and Finland	Qatar	16	Argentina
1997	Netherlands, Argentina and Morocco	Malaysia	24	Argentina
1999	Egypt, Ghana, Brazil and USA	Nigeria	24	Spain
2001	Colombia, Argentina, Nigeria and UAE	Argentina	24	Argentina
2003	Turkey, UAE and Uzbekistan	UAE	24	Brazil
2005	New Zealand, Peru and Tunisia	Netherlands	24	Argentina
2009	Azerbaijan, Bahrain, England, France, Ireland, Mexico, Poland and Saudi Arabia	Egypt	24	Ghana
2011	Poland, India and Colombia	Colombia	24	Brazil
2013	Indonesia, Peru, Myanmar and Saudi Arabia	Turkey	24	France
2015	New Zealand, Peru, Tunisia and Wales	New Zealand	24	Serbia
2017	Azerbaijan, Bahrain, England, France, Republic of Ireland, Mexico, Poland, Saudi Arabia, South Africa, South Korea, Tunisia and Ukraine	South Korea	24	England
2019	India and Poland	Poland	24	Ukraine
2021	Brazil, Indonesia, Peru, Bahrain/Saudi Arabia/UAE and Myanmar/Thailand	Indonesia	24	Cancelled
2023	Indonesia and Peru	Indonesia	24	?

the FIFA World Cup, failure to comply with the minimum hosting requirements under the technical evaluation leads to the exclusion of the bid. The bids that meet the minimum requirements under the technical evaluation are submitted to the FIFA Congress, which opens the voting process. The bidding process of the Men's World Cup has been enhanced to maintain the integrity of FIFA (Sugden and Tomlinson, 2017). FIFA rules indicate that the bidding nations must collaborate with FIFA to apply the ethical principles. Gifts are considered inappropriate since they may be viewed as a form of corruption (FIFA, 2020). Throughout the bidding process, any form of unethical collaboration between the member associations is prohibited.

The bidding process has evolved since all promotional activities, such as meetings with the members and decision-making bodies, have to be reported comprehensively (FIFA, n.d.b). The bidding member associations must appoint independent compliance and ethics officers to support compliance with the bid rules. Clause 3.4 of the bidding registration has changed as FIFA must appoint independent auditors (Sugden and Tomlinson, 2017). The auditors monitor the rate at which FIFA complies with the rules of the bidding process. Currently, auditors from BDO company are providing the FIFA Congress and FIFA Council with written reports that contain the findings and observations of the bidding process. A final written report of the findings is presented to FIFA a month before any nation is selected to host the tournament after which FIFA makes the final report available through its website.

The revised bidding process of the men's World Cup is based on four essential principles. The first is *objectivity* as evaluation of bids must be unbiased and straightforward. California Western International Law (2012) indicates that experts in the committees and administration form the task force. Appraisal of bids is guided by a precise objective that leads to the production of the evaluated reports. The second principle is *participation* as the process of decision-making determines the hosts of the tournament (Daprano, 2013). Sugden and Tomlinson (2017) argue that the decision-making process must be open and vast, and for the first time in 50 years, FIFA Congress, which has 211-member associations, has the final vote on the host. *Transparency* is the third principle as each step of the bidding process should be publicised. The content of the bids and hosting requirements are available to everyone. FIFA (n.d.c) states that the individual votes are disclosed during the final decision-making process and shortlisting of the bids. The final principle is related to the commitment to *sustainability* and *human rights*. Wenner (2012) argues that the FIFA is committed to working with other entities to ensure that the tournaments are successful. This collaboration is based on incorporation of sustainability and management principles based on the International Standards of Organisations (ISO) 20121. The regulation states that human rights and labour standards must be respected and be compliant with the UN's guiding principles for business and human rights. These standards apply to the bidding member associations and other entities involved in the tournaments such as airports, hotels, stadiums and even training sites (Table 3.4).

TABLE 3.4 Bidding sequence of FIFA Men's World Cup 2026 (FIFA, n.d.d)

Date	*Bidding Sequence*
14 October 2016	FIFA Council approves general principles governing the process for the selection of the host(s) of the 2026 FIFA World Cup
10 January 2017	FIFA Council unanimously decides on the expansion of the FIFA World Cup to a 48-team competition as of 2026
9 May 2017	FIFA Council approves bidding process, bidding requirements, hosting structure and slot allocation
11 May 2017	FIFA Congress following stages of the bidding process, including a first candidature phase to be voted in June 2018
11 August 2017	Deadline for member associations (from CAF, CONCACAF, CONMEBOL and the OFC only) to express their interest in hosting the tournament
13 September 2017	FIFA dispatches bidding registration documents to the member associations that have expressed interest
15 October 2017	Deadline for the submission of the completed bidding registration documents
16 October 2017	FIFA dispatches bidding agreement, hosting agreement and further bidding and hosting documents to candidate member associations
30 November 2017	Deadline for the submission of the completed bidding agreement to FIFA
16 March 2018	Submission of bids to FIFA
June 2018	Shortlisting of bids by the FIFA Council to be voted on by the FIFA Congress
13 June 2018	68th FIFA Congress to decide whether to select one of the candidates

Source: Adapted from FIFA (n.d.d).

FIFA World Cup (Women's)

FIFA has improved the bidding process of the Women's World Cup as indicated by the one that will be held in 2023 (see Table 3.5). The bidding process has evolved to adhere to the FIFA Code of Ethics that each stakeholder must follow FIFA (n.d.e). FIFA (2020) claims that Women's World Cup bidding process is based on several principles. The first principle is *objectivity* as the evaluation of bids must be quantified to determine their commercial and infrastructure aspects. Bids are excluded if they do not meet the minimum requirements provided by FIFA. The second principle is *vision* as Women's World Cup is considered as a catalyst for popularising women's football. Woodward (2018) argues that the Women's World Cup has become a common football competition. This has led FIFA to consider three abilities that each bidder should demonstrate in optimising commercial and sporting elements of the tournament. *Transparency*, which entails publishing the Bid Books produced by the bidding member associations and FIFA's Evaluation Report, is the third principle. FIFA Council makes decisions

TABLE 3.5 Bidding sequence of FIFA Women's World Cup 2023

Date	*Bidding Sequence*
19 February 2019	FIFA launches bidding process
15 March 2019	Deadline for member associations to express interest in hosting tournament
16 April 2019	Deadline for submission of completed bidding registration
18 April 2019	FIFA dispatches all bidding and hosting documents to bidding member associations
June 2019	Bid information workshop
4 October 2019	Submission of bids to FIFA
November/ December 2019	Inspection visits
Early 2020	Publication of Bid Evaluation Report
Q1 2020	Appointment of host(s) of FIFA Women's World Cup 2023 by FIFA Council

Source: Adapted from FIFA (n.d.f).

according to the suggestions of the member associations appointed to host the World Cup. The FIFA Council opens the results of each ballot and other related votes. The final principle is a commitment to *sustainability* and respect for *human rights* that member associations must implement, as per the Men's edition.

FIFA and its decision-making bodies play an important role in applying ethical principles and prohibiting inappropriate gifts that are viewed as a form of bribery and promoting ethical collaborations. The Rules of Conduct include transparency in the selection and designation of possible hosts. Risk assessment is part of the Women's World Cup bidding process. (Impey, 2019) claims that risks based on the security of the people, legal, human rights, and even those related to compliance are used to provide ratings. Technical evaluation involves assessing specific commercial and infrastructure criteria by using an evaluation system that FIFA has developed. Darby (2013) states that description of the host facilities is also part of the bidding process, which involves summarising relevant information provided and highlighting essential issues. The decision-making process is also part of the bidding process in which qualified bids are submitted to the FIFA Council to take a final decision.

FIFA's Women Football Strategy is based on five pillars. The first is developing and growing Women's World Cup by increasing the number of female football players to 60 million by 2026 (FIFA, n.d.g). It aims to encourage member associations to develop their comprehensive women's football strategies by 2022. The second pillar is exposure of women footballers to develop the women's tournament with new improved competitions globally (FIFA, n.d.g). The third pillar is communicating and commercialising women football. Glass (2020) argues that the 2027 bidding process will change since the commercial side of the women's tournament will have a concrete shape, and the female role models will interact with their audience through FIFA and other communication platforms. The fourth pillar is governing and leading women's football supported by the increased participation of women in the decision-making process (FIFA, n.d.g). FIFA (n.d.h) states that each of the institution's committee must comprise 30% women by 2022 and have at least one woman in the executive committee by 2026. Patel and Rajgor (2016) claim that the last principle is educating and empowering sportswomen.

FIFA World Cup (U20)

FIFA determined that there was a low legal risk when governments support U20 World Cup. The bidding process takes place over a much shorter period as illustrated in Table 3.6. The member associations selected to host the U20 World Cup must be fully supported by the local government authorities at the municipal and state levels. FIFA has requested the local governments to amend visa requirements to ensure that young players can visit the host countries without discrimination due to their age. Kolmakov (2018) states that the government should also amend labour laws to make it easier for the young players and officials involved in the competition to acquire work permits.

FIFA aims to ensure that the safety and security of young players and officials involved U20 World Cup are upheld during the tournament. Darby (2013) underscores that the nations must take anti-discrimination pledges to ensure that players are not discriminated against due to their ages, gender and nationalities. The government exempts taxes to FIFA and other involved parties during specific periods when activities related to the tournament are held, as with the other tournaments. The government, which is hosting the U20 tournament, must also facilitate protection of commercial rights (Duvall and Guschwan, 2013).

Moore (2018) adds that the U20 World Cup must meet the statutory objectives such as developing youth football globally. The U20 tournament has continued to

TABLE 3.6 Bidding sequence of FIFA U20 2021 World Cup (FIFA, 2020)

Date	*Detail*
23 April 2019	FIFA launches bidding process
21 May 2019	Deadline for member associations to express intertest in hosting the tournament
24 May 2019	FIFA dispatches all bidding and hosting documents to interested member associations
21 June 2019	Deadline for member associations to reconfirm their interest in bidding by submitting the signed terms and conditions
30 August 2019	Deadline for submission of bids to FIFA
Q4 2019	Appointment of host(s) of FIFA U20 World Cup 2021 by FIFA Council

Source: Adapted from FIFA (2020).

develop and the number of teams is expected to increase in the coming years since it is still young compared to the men's and women's World Cups. While the U20 World Cup has not gained significant popularity, it has continued to attract large number of spectators.

What Distinguishes a Successful Bid from not Successful Ones?

A successful bid is the one in which a country is selected to host the next World Cup tournament. Countries that express interest to host the tournament are expected to meet all FIFA requirements before application. FIFA usually prefers nations that have met all the requirements and rates infrastructure, risk, human rights and stadia development aspects to determine the best among applicants (FIFA, n.d.i).

Technical expertise needs to be demonstrated in wide-ranging areas in the form of a bid book which is generally prepared by a bid committee together with consultants (McGillivray and Turner, 2017). They are also generally supported by a celebrity figure or an ambassador. For example, Zinedine Zidane served as the key spokesperson for Qatar's 2022 bid. Bid committees are also supported by subject matter experts who assist in the production of the bid documentation and operationalisation of the bid, as well as prominent business and political elite who provide legitimacy, power and urgency to the bid (McGillivray and Turner, 2017).

The most widely criticised aspect of the bidding process is the physical infrastructural requirements resulting in unused or under-utilised "white elephants" as was the case with several stadia in Brazil. Similar concerns are being raised regarding Qatar 2022, which seems to underscore that the "requirements of the awarding body can be seen to take precedence and overrule the development needs of the host" (McGillivray and Turner, 2017, p. 30).

Intangible skills and soft infrastructure are also considered to be important. A successful track record in bidding and hosting mega-events usually increases chances to win as it demonstrates the necessary experience and capability that has been developed by the bidding nation. Maennig and Vierhaus (2016) state that FIFA and the International Olympic Committee (IOC) usually prioritise countries that have hosted other sport mega-events because they already have sporting facilities such as stadia and infrastructure. However, the period after hosting the last tournament determines whether a country is suitable. Maennig and Vierhaus (2016) contend that the FIFA and IOC consider nations that have had at least one sport mega-event in the past ten years. Spain was considered for the Olympics ten years after hosting the World Cup in 1982 while Brazil and the United States were considered as possible Olympics hosts just two years after hosting the World Cup in 2014 and 1994, respectively. These factors have discriminated many nations from hosting the World Cup.

Furthermore, bid campaigns have been increasingly professionalised with bid narratives playing a greater role in distinguishing successful bidders amidst growing competition. These bid narratives tend to support technically competent bids or redirect attention away from the technical criteria by appealing to more subjective and emotional aspects of the bid. Thus, the best technical bid is not always the winning bid as successful candidates need to be able to respond to their competitors within the context of the current edition as well as in relation to the recent history of the mega-event (McGillivray and Turner, 2017). In the case of Germany's 2006 World Cup, the narrative was linked to a long-term destination development strategy from an established candidate (Grix, 2012), whereas in the South African case the narrative centred on it being "Africa's turn," as highlighted previously. Similarly, the narrative for Qatar's successful 2022 bid was that the World Cup has never been hosted in the Middle East and also linked to its long-term strategic 2030 vision. McGillivray and Turner (2017) claim that prospective bidders can gain competitive advantage by assessing how their bid fits within the broader political environment of FIFA as well as contemporary global issues related to sustainability and legacy.

Besides political and public support, well-designed and executed bid campaigns are also central to a successful bid. South Africa's bid for 2010 World Cup is used as an illustrative case of event lobbying. The selection of South Africa as the host of 2010 World Cup started with campaigns led by the former president Nelson Mandela and Danny Jordan after FIFA announced in the year 2000 that the next World Cup would be held in Africa (Baller et al., 2013; FIFA, 2010). The nation already had a better infrastructure and stadia compared to the other bidders which made it the favourite among the five candidates (Baller et al., 2013).

It is evident that subjective criteria played a significant role in influencing FIFA's decision-making as a successful bid is determined by the vote of the appointed FIFA officials conducted by a secret ballot. Voting is also determined by bloc votes from continents or voter trading from countries in relation to future support. Seemingly, this contributed to the positive outcome for the bids of Russia 2018 and Qatar 2022. As a result of several investigations, previous World Cups (2006, 2010 and 2014) have also come under scrutiny and led to the downfall of several senior FIFA officials including its President, Sepp Blatter, in 2015. Furthermore, bidding processes have been reformed as discussed previously.

Bidding cities and nations can leverage from the process even when their bids are unsuccessful. According to Bason and Grix (2018), unsuccessful bids can help in community building by fasttracking the development of projects that have been planned. Moreover, bids usually bring different stakeholders together in which case they may work together towards proposed development plans. Furthermore, they indicate that the networks created among stakeholders at such times is instrumental in future development even when a bid is unsuccessful. In their research, Bason and Grix (2020) have studied the failed Olympic bids of Toronto and Cape Town to show that acceleration effect, taking stock, and national support are among the major opportunities offered by the bidding process even if bids are unsuccessful. In the case of South Africa, the unsuccessful bid for the 2006 FIFA World Cup laid the foundation to build on for the 2010 FIFA World Cup.

The Future of Bidding and Hosting

The popularity of the World Cup and associated bidding and hosting, has led to unprecedented levels of interest by countries, especially by emerging nations who use these events to consolidate a new national identity, for soft power gains and global (re)positioning. This has been coupled with increased public scrutiny due to the high levels of bribery, corruption and lack of transparency that have emerged. Calls for reform have led to some changes to the bidding processes, however, it is still unclear as to whether these efforts will lead to greater transparency and accountability. Furthermore, (McGillivray and Turner, 2017) question the idea of "global bid gurus" who offer their expertise to prospective hosts, following a successful bid elsewhere, with little consideration to the unique challenges of each country's context and institutional memory for a strategic approach to future bidding. Challenges related to "white elephants" have also resulted in greater flexibility, the return to joint bids to reduce the financial burden on single host nations and adoption of more sustainable bidding processes. Joint bids have the potential to create more equitable distribution of host countries, including smaller, emerging nations.

Additionally, sustainability, legacy and human rights will become even more significant aspects of future bidding and hosting. Protests and opposition will also become more central elements as seen with Qatar 2022 World Cup where even teams, most notably in Europe, are voicing their concerns. However, Qatar's case also demonstrates that a World Cup can catalyse change. It remains to be seen whether bidding and hosting one of the biggest sporting events can lead to meaningful and sustainable changes.

References

Baller, S., Miescher, G., & Rassool, C. (eds.). (2013) *Global Perspectives on Football in Africa: Visualising the Game*. London: Routledge.

Bason, T. & Grix, J. (2018) Planning to Fail? Leveraging the Olympic bid, *Marketing Intelligence & Planning*, 36(1), 138–151.

Bason, T. & Grix, J. (2020) Every Loser Wins: Leveraging "Unsuccessful" Olympic Bids for Positive Benefits, *European Sport Management Quarterly*, 1–21.

Blake, H. & Calvert, J. (2015) *The Ugly Game: The Corruption of FIFA and the Qatari Plot to Buy the World Cup*. New York: Scribner.

Borkowski, R.P. (2009) The Football Coach and Football Safety, *Safety in American Football. ASTM International*, 167–167–5. 10.1520/STP11784S.

Bunc, G., Ravnik, J. & Velnar, T. (2017) May Heading in Soccer Result in Traumatic Brain Injury? A Review of Literature, *Medical Archives (Sarajevo, Bosnia and Herzegovina)*, 71(5), 356–359. 10.5455/medarh.2017.71.356-359.

California Western International Law (2012) FIFA World Cup 2022: Why the United States Cannot Successfully Challenge FIFA Awarding the Cup to Qatar and How the Qatar Controversy Shows FIFA Needs Large-scale Changes, *California Western International Law Journal*, 42(2), 541–553.

Cornelissen, S. & Swart, K. (2006) The 2010 Football World Cup as a Political Construct: The Challenge of Making Good on an African Promise, *The Sociological Review*, 54(2_suppl), 108–123. 10.1111/j.1467-954X.2006.00656.x.

Daprano, C. (2013) Women's Association Football (FIFA), Attire in. In: Stange, M.Z., Oyster, C.K. and Sloan, J.E. (eds.) 2013. *The Multimedia Encyclopedia of Women in Today's World Encyclopedia of Women in Today's World* (pp. 2160–2163), 2nd edn. Thousand Oaks, CA: Sage. 10.4135/9781452270388.n471.

Darby, P. (2013) *Africa, Football and FIFA: Politics, Colonialism and Resistance* (1st ed.). London: Routledge. 10.4324/9781315039527.

Dickson, T.J., Darcy, S., Edwards, D.A., & Terwiel, F.A. (2015) Sport Mega-event Volunteers' Motivations and Post-event Behaviour: The Sydney World Master Games, 2009. *Event Management*, 19(2), 227–245.

Dorsey, J.M. (2018) Trouble in Sport Paradise: Can Qatar Overcome the Diplomatic Crisis? *Revista Crítica de Ciências Sociais*, 116, 179–196.

Duvall, S. & Guschwan, M.C. (2013) Commodifying Global Activism and Racial Unity During the 2010 FIFA World Cup, *Communication, Culture & Critique*, 6(2), 298–317.

FIFA (2018) *Canada, Mexico and USA selected as hosts of the 2026 FIFA World Cup™*. Available at: https://www.fifa.com/worldcup/fifaworldcup2026/news/canada-mexico-and-usa-selected-as-hosts-of-the-2026-fifa-world-cuptm.

FIFA (2020) *FIFA women's World Cup 2023™ bid evaluation report published – three bids submitted to FIFA council*. Available at: https://www.fifa.com/who-we-are/news/fifa-women-s-world-cup-2023tm-bid-evaluation-report-published-three-bids-submitt [Accessed 4 February 2021].

FIFA (2010) *Mandela's Role in Football Success*. Available at: https://www.fifa.com/worldcup/news/mandela-role-football-success-1168775 [Accessed 7 February 2021].

FIFA (n.d.a) *Broadcaster Service*. Available at: https://www.fifa.com/what-we-do/tv/broadcaster-servicing/ [Accessed 4 February 2021].

FIFA (n.d.b) *Guide to the Bidding Process for FIFA Women's World Cup 2026*. Available at: https://img.fifa.com/image/upload/hgopypqftviladnm7q90.pdf [Accessed 7 February 2021].

FIFA (n.d.c) *FIFA Regulations*. Available at: https://img.fifa.com/image/upload/stwvxqphxp3o96jxwqor.pdf [Accessed 7 February 2021].

FIFA (n.d.d) *Guide to the Bidding Process for the 2026 FIFA World Cup™*. Available at: https://img.fifa.com/image/upload/hgopypqftviladnm7q90.pdf [Accessed 7 February 2021].

FIFA (n.d.e) *FIFA Women's World Cup 2023: Bid Evaluation Report. FIFA World Cup and Beyond*. Available at: https://img.fifa.com/image/upload/hygmh1hhjpg30lbd6ppe.pdf [Accessed 7 Feburary 2021].

FIFA (n.d.f) *Guide to The Bidding Process for FIFA Women's World Cup 2023*. Available at: https://resources.fifa.com/image/upload/guide-to-the-bidding-process-for-the-fifa-women-s-world-cup-2023tm.pdf?cloudid=gfuxttuixv3s10jvidbn [Accessed 7 February 2021].

FIFA (n.d.g) *Women's Football Strategy*. Available at: https://resources.fifa.com/image/upload/women-s-football-strategy.pdf?cloudid=z7w21ghir8jb9tguvbcq [Accessed 7 February 2021].

FIFA (n.d.h) *Women's Football Administrator Handbook*. Available at: https://img.fifa.com/image/upload/nduju6vk2fyr7d8doyu3.pdf [Accessed 7 February 2021].

FIFA (n.d.i) *Bid Evaluation Report 2026 FIFA World Cup*. Available at: https://resources.fifa.com/image/upload/2026-fifa-world-cup-bid-evaluation-report.pdf?cloudid=yx76lnat3oingsmnlvzf [Accessed 2 February 2021].

Fonio, C. & Pisapia, G. (2014) Security, Surveillance, and Geographical Patterns at the 2010 FIFA World Cup in Johannesburg, *The Geographical Journal*, 181(3), 242–248.

Glanville, B. (2014) *The Story of the World Cup: 2014: The Essential Companion to Brazil 2014*. London: Faber & Faber.

Glass, A. (2020) Australia and New Zealand to host the 2023 FIFA Women's World Cup. *Forbes*. Available at: https://www.forbes.com/sites/alanaglass/2020/06/25/australia-and-new-zealand-to-host-the-2023-fifa-womens-world-cup/ [Accessed 2 February 2021].

Göral, K. (2019) The Importance of Set-Pieces in Soccer: Russia 2018·FIFA World Cup Analysis, *Journal of Human Sciences*, 16(3), 885–893.

Grix, J. (2012) 'Image' Leveraging and Sports Mega-events: Germany and the 2006 FIFA World Cup, *Journal of Sport & Tourism*, 17(4), 289–312, 10.1080/14775085.2012.760934.

Human Rights Watch (2020) *FIFA: 2026 World Cup Bids Test Reforms*. Available at: https://www.hrw.org/news/2018/06/12/fifa-2026-world-cup-bids-test-reforms [Accessed 4 February 2021].

Impey, S. (2019) FIFA receives four hosting bids for 2023 women's World Cup. *SportsPro Media*. Available at: https://www.sportspromedia.com/news/fifa-soccer-womens-world-cup-2023-hosting-rights-bids [Accessed 3 February 2021].

Kampmark, B. (2018) Conflicting Traditions: The FIFA World Cup, Australia, and Football Identities, *FIFA World Cup and Beyond*, 66–80. 10.4324/9781351181921-6.

Kelly, R. (2021). World Cup 2030: Which Countries Are Bidding to the Host the Tournament? *Goal*. Available at: https://www.goal.com/en-qa/news/world-cup-2030-which-countries-bidding-host-tournament/cjf37div77mq1axfim3rybsw1.

Kenschaft, L., Clark, R. & Ciambrone, D. (2015) *Gender Inequality in Our Changing World: A Comparative Approach*. New York: Routledge.

Kolmakov, S.Y. (2018) Legitimacy of Restriction on Freedom of Meetings in Russia During the World Cup FIFA 2018 and FIFA Confederations Cup 2017, *Prologue: Law Journal*, (2). 10.21639/2313-6715.2018.2.1.

Lisi, C.A. (2011) *A History of the World Cup, 1930-2010*. Lanham, MD: Scarecrow Press.

Maennig, W. & Vierhaus, C. (2016) Which Countries Bid for the Olympic Games? Economic, Political, and Social Factors and Chances of Winning. Economic, Political, and Social Factors and Chances of Winning (February 2016). *Hamburg Contemporary Economic Discussions*, 55

McGillivray, D. & Turner, D. (2017) *Event Bidding: Politics, Persuasion and Resistance*. Oxon: Routledge.

Millward, P. & Parnell, D. (2014) FIFA: The Men, the Myths, and the Money, *Leisure/Loisir*, 38(2), 199–202. 10.1080/14927713.2014.984922.

Molinaro, J.F. (2009) *1977-2009: The Evolution of the FIFA U-20 World Cup*. Available at: https://www.cbc.ca/sports/soccer/1977-2009-the-evolution-of-the-fifa-u-20-world-cup-1.844504 [Accessed 7 February 2021].

Moon, K. (2017) The Relationships Among Regional Benefits, Regional Image, Loyalty, and Behavioral Intention: A Study of FIFA U-20 World Cup, *Korean Journal of Sports Science*, 26(6), 673–689. 10.35159/kjss.2017.12.26.6.673.

Moore, K. (2018) A Second 'Maracanazo'? The 2014 FIFA World Cup in Historical Perspective, *FIFA World Cup and Beyond*, 9–25. 10.4324/9781351181921-2.

Morgan, E. (2019) *Why Does Morocco Keep Bidding and Failing to Host the World Cup? These Football Times*. Available at: https://thesefootballtimes.co/2019/04/02/why-does-morocco-keep-bidding-and-failing-to-host-the-world-cup/.

Patel, M. & Rajgor, M. (2016) A Review on Strategy of Bidding and Competitive Bidding Process, *International Journal of Advanced Engineering and Research Development*, 3(04): 206–212. 10.21090/ijaerd.030435.

Parent, M.M. (2017) The organizing committee's perspective. In Parent, M.M. and Chappelet, J. (eds.). *Routledge Handbook of Sports Event Management* (pp. 43–64). London: Routledge. 10.4324/9780203798386-3.

Peltz-Steele, R.J. (2016) The FIFA World Cup, human rights goals and the gulf between. In Human Rights Goals and the Gulf Between (September 27, 2016). *Presented at the Sport project: Probing the boundaries: 5th Global Meeting*, Oxford. UK: Mansfield College (pp. 13–15).

Raithel, T. (2014) The German Nation and the 2006 FIFA World Cup, *The FIFA World Cup 1930 – 2010*, 353–371. 10.5771/9783835326064-353.

Reuters Staff (2020) *Soccer-FIFA U-20, U-17 World Cups Moved to 2023 due to COVID-19.* Available at: https://www.reuters.com/article/uk-health-coronavirus-soccer-worldcup-idUKKBN28Y1N7.

Rockerbie, D.W. (2016) The Importance of Domestic Football Leagues to International Performance: Predicting FIFA Points, *Soccer & Society*, 20(1), 21–38. 10.1080/14660970.2016.1267627.

Ruta, D. & Manzoni, B. (2015) City Capacity Building – Preparing to Exploit the Legacy of a Large-scale Sports Event. In Holt, R. & Ruta, D. (eds.). *Routledge Handbook of Sport and Legacy* (pp. 231–244). 10.4324/9780203132562-18. London: Routledge.

Solberg, H.A. (2017) Why Cities Are Willing to Host Them, Despite the Lack of Economic Benefits. In Brittain, I., Bocarro, J., Byers, T. & Swart, K. (eds.), *Legacies and Mega Events: Facts or Fairytales* (pp. 43–59). New York: Routledge.

Spiegel (2015) *Germany Appears to Have Bought Right to Host 2006 Tournament.* Available at: https://www.spiegel.de/international/world/documents-indicate-slush-fund-used-in-german-world-cup-bid-a-1058212.html.

Stanwick, P. & Stanwick, S. (2020) *International Management: A Stakeholder Approach.* Cheltenham: Edward Elgar.

Sugden, J. & Tomlinson, A. (2017) Bidding wars: Winners and losers in the World Cup hosting game. In Sugden, J. & Tomlinson, A. (eds). *Football, corruption & lies. Revisiting 'Badfellas', the book FIFA tried to ban.* London: Routledge.

Swart, K., Jureidini, R. & Jones, S. (2020) *Migrant Workers Sport Tournaments – Al Khor. Case Studies of Sport in the MENA Region.* Doha: Josoor Institute.

Ter Haar, B. (2018) FIFA, Qatar, Kafala: Can the World Cup Create a Better World of Work? by Beryl ter Haar, Assistant Professor on European and International Labour Law, Leiden University, The Netherlands, *International Labor Rights Case Law*, 4(1), 128–132.

Tomlinson, A. (2014) FIFA: Beginnings, Tensions, Trajectories. In Rinke, S. & Schiller, K. (eds.). *The FIFA World Cup 1930 – 2010* (pp. 30–46). Göttingen: Wallstein Verlag.

van der Merwe, J. (2009) The road to Africa: South Africa's hosting of the 'African' World Cup. In Pillay, U., Tomlinson, R. & Bass, O. (eds.). *Development and Dreams: The Urban Legacy of the 2010 Football World Cup* (pp. 18–32). Pretoria: HSRC Press.

Wenner, J. (2012) Playing the Possession Game: Development through Hosting the FIFA World Cup. *University Honors in International Studies.*

Woodward, K. (2018). Women's time? Time and temporality in women's football. *FIFA World Cup and Beyond*, 143–154.

4

POLITICS AND GEOPOLITICS IN STAGING THE FIFA WORLD CUP: WHAT IS AT STAKE FOR THE HOSTING NATIONS?

Estelle E. Brun and Carole Gomez

Introduction

Sport has been a highly political subject since the advent of modern sports at the end of the 19th century, and its modern history cannot be dissociated from politics (Cha, 2016). Yet, social sciences have only begun to address issues related to sports in the past 30 years (Pigman and Rofe, 2014). Mega-sporting events (MSE) like men's football World Cups and the Olympic Games (with the notable exception of the Paralympic Games) have become a point of focus for both the academia and the media.

The political dimensions of the *Fédération Internationale de Football Association* (FIFA) World Cup have been studied within the field of social sciences, particularly that of history and sociology. Historical accounts of football underline the long-standing relationship between politics and sports (Bromberger, 1998; Pivato, 1994) in which the men's World Cup has become a place, in a globalised world, where national identities and political ideologies can be expressed (Armstrong and Giulianotti, 1999; Dietschy, Gastaut and Mourlane, 2006; Hare, 2003). These MSE are effectively used by represented countries to instill sentiments of national belonging (Ravenel, 2019) and pride (Cha, 2016), while increasing their influence at the international level (Grix, Brannagan and Houlihan, 2015) and reinforcing political legitimacy of their regimes, both on the national and international stage (Tomlinson and Young, 2006). Anholt (2002) also underlined the importance of nation branding, considering "that a proper national branding campaign can unite a nation in a common sense of purpose and national pride" (p. 234).

In terms of sports diplomacy, if participating in and performing at MSE such as football World Cups is a traditional axis developed by many states to symbolise the prowess and success of the nation (Cronin and Mayall, 2005), hosting one, appears to be a "privilege" reserved for some "happy few." Indeed, if FIFA has 211

DOI: 10.4324/9781003121794-4

affiliated federations, only 22 countries will have hosted a men's or women's World Cup between 1930 and 2026, in 33 editions. Hence, countries may consider that hosting a World Cup, and especially the men's one, can allow them to be part of a "select club," meaning that their country and national capital will be in the limelight, at the heart of political and media attention during the bidding process, the preparation of the event, and finally the competition.

Bidding campaigns have become even more fierce with new actors interested by this "sport power" (Verschuuren, 2013). Between 2002 and 2023, eight new countries have already hosted or will host all or part of the men's or women's competition. It is also interesting to underline the geographical distribution of these host countries: five of them are located within the Asian football confederation (Japan, South Korea, China, Qatar and Australia). According to FIFA, Asia seems to become (again) the centre of the world (of football).

Moreover, becoming the host of an MSE, rather than simply participating in it, increases even further the political dimensions of the event as domestic policies are actively involved in its structural organisation. Stadiums and other sites dedicated to the sports competition become "governable spaces" in which socio-spatial dynamics developed by the host country help in producing governable subjects (Gaffney, 2010). The complex relationship between spatial, cultural, political and commercial interests has driven many nations around the world to aspire to stage MSE (Guttmann, 2002; Hill, 1992) such as the World Cup.

The purpose of this chapter is to examine the political dimensions associated with bidding for and hosting the World Cup. Special attention will be paid to several case studies such as France, Russia, Qatar and China. Although mainly illustrated by men's World Cups, this chapter also highlights some relevant examples of women's editions.

The Domestic Politics of Hosting the World Cup

Hosting an MSE, and especially a football World Cup, is way more than a mere organisational challenge, considering the huge investment of time and money spent from the bidding state through the actual event. States which are willing to take on this challenge do so for domestic and foreign policy reasons. When focusing on internal politics, depending on the time period or the states concerned, several objectives can be targeted: developing a strong nation, legitimising a regime, asserting its leadership at the national and/or regional level, or restructuring the public space.

Developing a strong nation

Sport has long been used as a tool to strengthen national identities. As early as the 19th century, Germany developed educational programmes centred around gymnastics intended to instill values of liberalism and democracy among its youth (Pivato, 1994). In addition to sports programs, MSE have also participated in creating and enforcing identities (Vidacs, 2006). Eric Hobsbawm (1990) famously associated national sports teams with the representation of entire nations or "imagined communities" (p. 143), echoing Benedict Anderson's concept of nationalism (1983). As sports competitions allow for national teams to symbolise their nations, their sporting performances contribute to a national narrative enhancing collective consciousness.

MSE such as the World Cup also allow for expressions of "banal nationalism," a concept developed by Michael Billig, which theorise how everyday symbols and rituals "flag" nations. Indeed, sports events include various practices that convey national symbols: waving the national flag, singing the national anthem, wearing a national sport jersey, etc. Hosting a World Cup provides even further opportunities for the host country than for the mere participating nations, as national symbols and messages can be displayed way beyond short-lived moments of actual football games. Opening and closing ceremonies, visuals and other marketing-related communication tools around the event represent important political opportunities for the host country to formulate expressions of banal nationalism. For example, the opening ceremony of the 2018 men's World Cup in Russia featured Russian singer Aida Garifullina, who performed alongside international star singer Robbie Williams, as well as Russian President Vladimir Putin who gave a speech welcoming fans to an "open, hospitable and friendly" Russia. The presence of 21 national leaders at Moscow's Luzniki stadium, the largest number ever gathered during a World Cup, also testifies to the importance of the ceremony and the competition more broadly in terms of foreign policy.

These symbols, meant to represent a positive image of the nation to be displayed across the host country and on the international level, are concrete political motivations for the regime in place to bid for and host a World Cup. Indeed, whereas participating in an international sports competition is a way of staging national identity and therefore contributing to national pride (Meier and Mutz, 2018), hosting it represents new opportunities through which a political regime can instrumentalise the power of sports performance to further bolster national identity. The strengthened attachments to the nation can in turn strengthen the political legitimacy of the regime under which the World Cup is bid for or organised, both nationally and internationally.

Fostering a strong regime

Host countries are interested in promoting positive images of their nations as it can bolster the political legitimacy of nation's political elite (Elling, Van Hilvoorde and Van Den Dool, 2014; Meier and Mutz, 2018; Tomlinson and Young, 2006). Indeed, Putin's words during the 2018 World Cup's opening ceremony particularly resonate when inscribed in a tensed geopolitical context in which Russia had repeatedly been criticised by Western powers, notably for its illegal annexation of Ukraine's Crimea in 2014 or its support of Bashar al-Assad's regime in the Syrian civil war since 2011. The former Soviet power is also regularly criticised by international watchdog organisations regarding state corruption, the lack of freedom or anti-LGBT propaganda, for example. Therefore, there is a particularly powerful symbolism behind Putin's intervention in one of the most popular events in the world, as its country is staging it. It contributes to normalising both the country and its politics through the representation of a "friendly" and well-organised regime capable of successfully hosting a major sporting tournament.

Authoritarian political regimes such as Russia have an even stronger need for legitimacy (Scharpf, 1997) and are therefore more likely to use sport-centred identity policies (Meier and Mutz, 2018). The staging of the World Cup allows for the political elite to shape public attitudes and promote national pride, which can translate into new forms of tolerance to undemocratic regimes by the people. That was the case in Italy for example, in which the 1934 men's World Cup staged under the fascist regime of Benito Mussolini led to a positive depiction of the country amid a "perfect organisation" and modern broadcasting services according to the foreign press (Dietschy, 2010). Few decades later, Argentina hosted the 1978 men's World Cup, two years after the coup d'état which installed the military junta rule in 1976. After having considered to abandon the event, the General Jorge Rafael Videla decided to maintain the competition as he believed it would transform the international image of the regime. A major American advertising agency, Burston-Marsteller, was even asked to contribute 1.1 million US dollars to optimise "the risks and opportunities of such a prospect [which] are obvious" (Contamin and Le Noé, 2010, p.28). Moreover, thanks to the Albiceleste's final victory against the Netherlands, the regime was convinced that "it had achieved an important symbolic and real goals through football: the image of a victorious nation projected to the entire world" (Novaro and Palermo, 2003)

The staging of the World Cup can also be used as a way to restore the political legitimacy of recently democratic and/or post-colonial countries, whose political elites need to assert or rehabilitate their new ideologies both nationally and internationally (Tomlinson and Young, 2006). The case of Post-Apartheid South Africa and its use of sports policy to restore its international reputation and position itself as an African power is particularly relevant. After decades of international boycotts against South African national sports teams, used by the International Olympic Committee (IOC) or FIFA as a way to pressure the apartheid regime to end its racist policies, the nation developed sport-centred policies as a way through which to introduce its newly democratic regime to the world stage. The new regime, under the leadership of South African President Nelson Mandela, famously organised and won the 1995 men's Rugby World Cup, three years after the end of the apartheid era in 1992. In 2010, thanks to sports policies centred around the building of infrastructures, it became the first African country to host a men's FIFA World Cup. Here, political ambitions at the regional level should also be noted, with the staging of the 2010 men's World Cup which highlighted the regional politics of the post-apartheid regime with its winning bid describing "a true African bid" and developed around a Pan-Africanist imagery (Bolsmann, 2011).

Although it has not hosted any World Cups, the case of post-colonial Morocco remains interesting. Indeed, the country has bid to host the World Cup five times (1994, 1998, 2006, 2010 and 2026), unsuccessfully thus far. The last two bids are particularly relevant to study because they can be analysed through a continental prism. As said earlier, in the case of the 2010 bid, this campaign was considered to be the "turn of Africa" (Cornelissen, 2004), between South Africa and Morocco. The challenge for the then-president Jacob Zuma, the South African Football Association and FIFA as a whole was to "portray the tournament as an 'African showpiece', a force for continental unity, solidarity and peace" (Brannagan and Giulianotti, 2014, p. 705; Cornelissen, 2004; Pillay and Bass, 2008). By winning the bid, Zuma effectively positioned itself as a leader in Africa, after notably competing against Morocco which had also proposed a bid. Both countries, through their bids to host men's World Cups, respond to a political agenda aiming at growing their influence on the regional level while consolidating their political legitimacy.

For the 2026 bid, Morocco has had to compete against an alliance made of Canada, the United States and Mexico. After an interesting campaign, highlighting the African identity, Morocco received only 65 votes from national federations, that is, 33% of those who voted. Beyond the defeat, the votes highlighted how other African countries did not uniformly vote for its neighbour, with 11 African federations which did not support the Moroccan bid (South Africa, Benin, Botswana, Cape Verde, Guinea, Lesotho, Liberia, Mozambique, Namibia, Sierra Leone and Zimbabwe), giving their votes instead to the North American candidature. To partially explain these votes, it is useful to recall that former United States president Donald Trump did not hesitate to put pressure, *via* Twitter, on the 52 African presidents, reminding them how this bid was important to him and that he would not hesitate to cut aid to countries that did not vote for the threefold candidacy. It should also be noted that seven federations from the Middle East did not vote for the Moroccan bid, following Saudi Arabia's choice to vote for the North American bid.

Restructuring the public space

Public policies centred around infrastructures, particularly concerned with stadiums in the case of the World Cup, help governments to reconstitute public spaces through the hosting of sports events (Tomlinson and Young, 2006). As the stadium creates a dynamic of space and power, the construction and legacy of the sports space constitutes another political dimension of the World Cup situated at the local level of politics which is peculiar to the hosting of MSEs. Indeed, whereas high-level performances during sports competitions can contribute to the reputation of a certain national ideology or improve national pride of the winning nation's population, staging an MSE allow for the political elite to develop and promote socio-spatial dynamics through the stadiums in which the competition takes place.

Scholarship on stadiums shows how they combine urban political economy and popular culture and influence "cultural identities, nationalist discourses, ritualised identity performance, and the production and consumption of spectacles in the public space" in Buenos Aires and Rio de Janeiro (Gaffney, 2010, p.9). In 1950, when Brazil hosted the men's World Cup for the first time, it branded itself as a progressive, innovative and productive nation, both to local and international audiences, through the construction of stadiums (Gaffney, 2010).

Therefore, the socio-spatial power dynamics held in stadiums, organised through state public policies on infrastructure, are intimately linked with other political ambitions linked to bidding for and eventually staging World Cup competitions. The stadium is a concrete physical item available to regimes which wish to demonstrate their productivity and technical skills and a concrete space in which demonstrations of banal nationalism take place, hence promoting state's ideologies and nationalisms.

Leaving long-term legacies

Although the term legacy in sports first appeared in the mid-1950s (Leopkey and Parent, 2012), this concept has been regularly invoked since the 1990s by organising committees and international sports bodies (Chappelet, 2013), particularly because of the increasingly pressing questions related to the costs and benefits of hosting an MSE.

The legacy of an MSE is considered as a multi-dimensional (Attali, 2019) and multi-scalar concept (Attali and Viersac, 2021). It is also characterised by several components (Scheu, Preuss and Könecke, 2019): urban development; environmental enhancement; policy and governance; skills, knowledge and networks; beliefs and behaviour like new or changed beliefs regarding the image of a city or country; behavioural changes, for instance in terms of service quality, use of public transportation, sport participation. The complexity of these components can lead to confusion in its understanding (Preuss, 2019; Thomson, Schlenker and Schulenkorf, 2013) and consequently, the task of organisers is made more difficult when they are expected to translate these principles into reality (Orr and Jarvis, 2018).

As an example, in addition to displaying modernity and productivity through the preparation and construction of stadiums before and during World Cups, those sports buildings add to the long-term legacies of the host countries. For example, the French collective memory of winning the 1998 World Cup is paired with the building of the Stade de France, still central to sports culture in contemporary France. Public discussions around the building of the stadium followed the French bid's selection for the hosting of the 1998 World Cup. It was built in 1995 with the French Council of State acting as an active chaperon both in technical and financial terms. In January 1998, former president Jacques Chirac attended the first game ever hosted in the stadium, hence showing yet again how involved the political elite is in the creation of such long-term socio-spatial dynamics.

The case of the World Cup legacies stemming from the Stade de France also highlights that the political dimensions associated with hosting the World Cup are not limited to non-democratic or post-colonial host nations but instead to all bidders and hosts, including well-established democratic regimes and ideologies such as France. Indeed, another legacy of the 1998 World Cup was instrumentalised by the French regime to promote its ideology nationally through the branding of its victorious national team as "Black-Blanc-Beur" [Black, White, Arab]. The nickname gave birth to the myth of a multi-cultural France whose integration system proper to the French ideology functions and of which Zinedine Zidane becomes an icon (Blanchard, 2010). In other words, the staging of the 1998 men's World Cup paired with the victory of the French national team allowed France's political elites to reassert their state ideology and national ideals far beyond the actual organisation of the event.

In the case of women's World Cups, legacy is obviously also an important element. In the case of the World Cup held in France in the summer of 2019, the stated aim of the French Football Federation (FFF) was to use this competition to develop women's football and the feminisation of football. After unsuccessfully bidding to organise the 2011 competition, the FFF won the right to organise it in 2019. After the success of the World Cups organised in Germany (2011) and then in Canada (2015), the main issue for the host country, as well as for FIFA, was to confirm the interesting dynamics of this event and above all its attractiveness for public, media, investments. The publication by FIFA of the first global strategy for the development of women's football in October 2018 also enabled France to test and implement various strategies, particularly in terms of media coverage. The long-term effects may occur several years after the event, so it will be essential to try to measure and analyse the impact of this MSE on the French territory, nuanced by the consequences of the COVID-19.

Those concepts of socio-spatial dynamics, banal nationalism, bolstering of the regime, as well as long-term legacies are also variables which are difficult to measure. How exactly did the 1998 staging of the men's World Cup or the 2019 staging of the women's World Cup in France impact the host country? The next section of this chapter explores some of the concrete ramifications of hosting the World Cup.

Case Study: China, the future of football?

While China's power in sports is recognised and unchallenged, particularly during the Olympic and Paralympic Games, the results of the men's and women's football teams have been far less impressive. This is set to change irrevocably as a result of the decisions currently being taken in Beijing. President Xi Jinping, apart from being a fervent supporter of Manchester City, wants to turn China into a "great sports nation," with the most-followed sports in the world as the cynosure around the "three World Cup dreams": participating in the World Cup, hosting the World Cup and eventually winning the men's World Cup.

To reach these dreams, the Chinese government has launched in April 2016 the "football development plan in the medium and long term (2016-2050)," which highlights the development of football in the short (2020), medium (2030) and long (2050) terms:

- By 2020, efforts have been made to get the Chinese population to play football, with the creation of training and education centres. Partnerships with clubs were also signed to bring skills within the Chinese training camps. Moreover, massive investments and recruitments were made within the Chinese Super League to make it more attractive. At this time, the government wanted to reach 50 million Chinese, boys and girls, young and old.
- By 2030, Chinese football wants to become a major force in Asia, giving pride to "Tsu Chu." Beijing expects its women's national team to be a world leader, and its men's team a regional leader. Linked to this strategy, the large wave of Chinese investors in European clubs (AC Milan, Inter Milan, Atletico Madrid, OGC Nice or SK Slavia Praha) is also significant. These clubs are indeed particularly renowned for the quality of their training centres, and thus allowing them to come, observe good practices to develop them within Chinese clubs. Beyond the sporting aspect, this is also a gateway to interesting economic markets for Beijing.

Furthermore, and as a symbol of its desire to establish itself on the international scene, China has regularly expressed its interest in hosting the men's World Cup in the next editions, in 2030, or more probably in 2034, considering the geographical rotation of the men's World Cup.

- By 2050, Xi Jinping wants to make China a football superpower, able to compete with the best teams in the world.

On the national level, the Chinese Super League has not performed as well as in previous years, experiencing a slow down in the recruitment of international players since 2016. Between 2017 and 2018, stricter regulations were implemented by the Chinese federation, to slow down the financial boom that affected football in the country. Such decisions were made to prevent certain clubs from spending millions of yuan (Chinese currency) to attract world-class players and then potentially finding themselves in financial difficulties, in addition to sending a message to clubs to encourage the training of young national players rather than relying solely on the talent of foreign recruits. Thus, several measures have been implemented, such as taxing the transfer of foreign players at 100% for clubs exceeding the 45-million-yuan threshold. The money collected was injected directly into a national development fund for young Chinese players, further supporting Xi Xinping's national development strategy.

Through this strategy, this case study shows the aforementioned stakes for the political elite to develop and invest in football, notably through the staging of

World Cup competitions, as a way to enhance national and international legitimacy and build long-term political legacies through sports.

Hosting a World Cup: Take the Risk or Lose the Chance?

The politics of hosting the World Cup are organised around the political elite's ambitions to strengthen national belonging among its population while bolstering its legitimacy, both to its own people and on the international stage. It does so notably through demonstrations of banal nationalism and their organisational skills, enabled by the appropriation of the local space, such as the renovating or building of stadiums, whose newly created socio-spatial dynamics increase the political elite's power and serve both its national and international ambitions. However, the concrete impact of hosting and participating in MSE onto the political elite's legitimacy or the national belonging of its nation is very hard to measure. Recently, an increasing range of literature has attempted to measure such impact using concrete economic variables.

Limited tangible effects

The existing literature on the economics of staging MSE mostly agrees that its effects are mostly limited. Bidding for the right to host an MSE in the first place, otherwise called a scarce resource, often results in substantial waste if it is done so via lobbying process (Mitchell and Stewart, 2015). On the relationship between tourism and the hosting of the World Cup, a case study looking at the 1995, 2002 and 2006 men's World Cups found very little positive impact on the tourism industry from these three events (ibid).

Considering the limited economic impact of hosting the World Cup, a political economy theory suggests that nations still continue hosting MSE as they are attracted by a "feel good effect" produced by such events, a "temporary, transient sense of relief from the troubles and tensions of the days" (Tomlinson and Young, 2006; Mitchell and Stewart, 2015). In the case of the 1978 World Cup staged by Argentina, this "large-scale event can provide temporary, transient sense of relief from the troubles and tensions of the day" (Tomlinson and Young, 2006, p. 12). Yet, economic studies have yet to find concrete evidence that MSE do make people happy and proud (De Nooij and van den Berg, 2017).

International spotlight: A poisoned gift for the host country?

Hosting such a World Cup could be perceived as a great gift for the selected country, as the global attention directs itself to one geographical location for an entire month, highlighted by dynamism, tourism, renovation of reception facilities, transports, etc. However, it becomes a double-edged sword when the country is subjected to showing both its strengths and weaknesses, while under the international spotlight. The 1978 World Cup in Argentina sparked an intense debate among many of the qualifying teams as whether to boycott the tournament, thereby isolating the military junta on the international stage. These same thoughts were also raised during the 2018 men's World Cup in Russia, especially after the annexation of Crimea and the Skripal affair, triggering major tensions between London and Moscow.

More recently, the upcoming men's World Cup in Qatar has also raised ethical questions. Since the awarding of the competition to Doha in December 2010, there have been a number of forums and press releases calling for the withdrawal or boycott of the event, highlighting suspicions of corruption in the context of the awarding of the competition, the ecological footprint of the event and the conditions of foreign workers in Qatar.

White elephants: The difficulties behind long-term legacies

Initially confidential, the question of legacy is now taking on an increasingly important role in the discourse of international sports federations, as well as in that of the bidding and organising committees. After focusing on revenues, the cost side – especially regarding investment in venues and infrastructures – is now studied. The majority of existing scholarship on public financing of stadiums finds that the financial payoff from such public investment is very limited and cannot justify the use of limited public funds. Often absent from debates about sports, the theme of "white elephants" has also gradually imposed itself on host countries (Alm et al., 2014), which have often been accused of building expensive and top-level infrastructures for only a few weeks of competitions, without having anticipated the longer-term legacy of staging MSE.

In the context of the global economic crisis, infrastructures of the 2004 Athens and 2008 Beijing Games, as well as the 2010 men's World Cup in South Africa, were particularly scrutinised and criticised. They went on during the 2014 World Cup in Brazil, where four stadiums with 42,000 to 65,000 seats were built specially for this tournament. It has been the Arena Amazônia, in Manaus, which has particularly been subjected to criticism.

The 2018 men's edition was also exceptional in size: nine of the 12 stadiums were built specifically for the occasion, and the Central Stadium in Yekaterinburg was rebuilt and expanded for the competition. This gigantism could explain the exceptional cost of this World Cup: $14 billion. More recently, concerns have been raised about some of the stadiums being built in Qatar for the next men's World Cup and their potential future use. In this case, various bids for other MSE, such as the 2027, or 2031 men's Rugby World Cup, are apparently being considered. The 2026 Men's World Cup, which will be played in the United States, Canada and Mexico, should avoid this trap as many infrastructures are already in place. Nevertheless, the risks could be present for all other infrastructures linked to the hosting of an MSE, particularly in the context of an increase in the number of participating teams from 32 to 48.

Although the phenomenon of white elephants has been identified and decried, the host countries of the men's World Cup and FIFA do not seem to be fully aware of the situation. The question remains for future editions, especially with the interest of China and even Saudi Arabia in hosting a future World Cup. However, it should be noted that this phenomenon does not seem to concern the organisation of women's World Cups. Indeed, the organisation committee tend to reuse infrastructures that have already been built, and thus allowing the event to be planned for the long term.

Civil society: The main opponent of the World Cup?

Given the constant increase of the number of participating national teams (13 in 1930, 24 in 1982, 32 in 2002, 48 from 2026 for the men's World Cup; 32 from 2023 for the women's World Cup), organisational costs have exponentially risen, with new stadiums and infrastructures specifically build for the competition. In a context of a global economic crisis in the early 21st century, such investments and expenses were very difficult to justify for the organising committees to the public. The massive protests in Brazil in June 2013, during the Confederations Cup, is a relevant example during which the population denounced both the increase in the price of bus tickets and the financial mismanagement linked to the organisation of the World Cup.

As a new actor in international relations, civil society is now particularly active during campaigns for the awarding of MSE to denounce the risks of these "white elephants" and a broader reticence of hosting highly expensive events with little tangible proof of economic gains. If this is particularly obvious with the hosting of the Olympic and Paralympic Games (Bourbillères and Koebel, 2020), the mistrust of FIFA and its competitions seems to be moving towards the same direction. Indeed, hosting an MSE "can provide a forum for refusal or contestation, if not outright resistance" (Tomlinson and Young, 2006, p. 12).

Last but not least, athletes could also become key players in the coming years. Silenced in the name of the principle of apolitical sports, the main actors on the field seem to have become increasingly relevant political actors in recent months. Through statements during press conferences, the featuring of social justice messages on their jerseys during the 2022 World Cup qualifying matches, or the repetition of the anti-racist gesture of taking a knee during the 2020 men's European football championship, suggest that a small revolution is currently underway in the world of football and in the world of sports more generally. These recent changes will need to be confirmed and analysed carefully from a political point of view, including their impact of the bidding and the staging of World Cups.

Conclusion

There are highly relevant political stakes involved for nations when they choose to bid for and host World Cup competitions. Indeed, considering the limited impact on the economy, as shown by studies on the limited tourism impact of the staging of MSE, and the risks associated with long-term legacies and civil society's opposition, national and foreign policies play a crucial role in the motivations behind the staging of the World Cups. Organising a men's World Cup brings international spotlight to the hosting nation, allowing it to show a positive image to the rest of the world as part of a foreign policy strategy. Nationally, it may bolster national belonging and the legitimacy of the ruling political party/regime. Beyond the significant opportunity for host nations to promote banal nationalism throughout the competition, they can also reorganise urban spaces through the building of new stadiums or the improvement of public transportations.

However, to effectively measure the political ramifications of organising this type of events, more research needs to be conducted on the quantification of those political variables to see how effective those political ambitions are implemented before, during, and after the event.

As a double-edged sword, new urban spaces can become white elephants in the long-term while, before and during the competition, the host nation may demonstrate socio-economic and political weaknesses to a world that might have been unaware of such dynamics prior to the event. This is the case with Qatar for example, which has been largely criticised for the treatment of its migrant workers, with a civil society increasingly involved in denouncing such social injustice and expressing rising reticence regarding the hosting of such MSE in the first place. When conducting future research on the concrete political and geopolitical impact of staging World Cups and MSE more generally, it will be important to consider the new role played by civil society and athletes.

References

Alm, J., Arne Solberg, H., Storm, R.K. & Jakobsen, T.G. (2014) Hosting Major Sports Events: the Challenge of Taming White Elephants, *Leisure Studies*, 35, 5.

Anderson, B. (1983) *Imagined Communities: Reflections on the Origin and Spreading of Nationalism*. London: Verso.

Anholt, S. (2002) Foreword,*Journal of Brand Management*, 9(4-5), 229–239.

Armstrong, G. & Giulianotti, R. (eds) (1999) *Football Cultures and Identities*. London: MacMillan Press Ltd.

Attali, M. (2019) Les défis de l'héritage des Jeux olympiques et paralympiques: De la croyance aux possibilités. *Revue internationale et stratégique, n°114, IRIS Editions*, 127–137.

Attali, M. & Viersac, M. (2021) Discuter l'héritage social et culturel des grands événements sportifs. Une revue de littérature internationale. *Staps*.

Blanchard, P. (2010) Black-Blanc-Beur, l'équipe nationale aux "couleurs de l'histoire", in Boli, C., Gastaut, Y., and Grognet, F. (eds), *Allez la France! Football et immigration*. Paris: Gallimard.

Bolsmann, C. (2011) Thoughts on the First African World Cup: Football, Representation and Exclusion, *Journal des anthropologues*, 124–125, 359–371.

Bourbillères, H. & Koebel, M. (2020) Les processus de contestation dans le cadre des candidatures des villes européennes aux Jeux olympiques et paralympiques 2024. *Movement & Sport Sciences – Science & Motricité*, 107 (1), 17–29.

Brannagan, P.M. & Giulianotti, R. (2014) Soft Power and Soft Disempowerment: Qatar, Global Sport and Football's 2022 World Cup finals, *Leisure Studies*, 34(6), 703–719.

Bromberger, C. (1998) *Football, la bagatelle la plus sérieuse du monde.* Paris: Bayard Éditions.

Cha, V. (2016) Role of Sport in International Relations: National Rebirth and Renewal, *Asian Economic Policy Review*, 11(1), 139–155.

Chappelet, J.-L. (2013) Mega Sporting Event Legacies: A Multifaceted Concept. *Papeles de Europa*, 25, 76–86.

Contamin, J. & Le Noé, O. (2010) La coupe est pleine Videla! Le Mundial 1978 entre politisation et dépolitisation, *Le Mouvement Social*, 230, 27–46.

Cornelissen, S. (2004). 'It's Africa's turn!' The narratives and legitimations surrounding the Moroccan and South African bids for the 2006 and 2010 FIFA finals, *Third World Quarterly*, 25:7, 1293–1309.

Cronin, M. & Mayall, D. (2005) Sport and Ethnicity: Some Introductory Remarks, in Cronin, M. and Mayall, D. (eds),*Sporting Nationalisms: Identity, Ethnicity, Immigration and Assimilation*, 1–13. London: Routledge.

De Nooij, M. & van den Berg, M. (2017) The Bidding Paradox: Why Politicans Favor Hosting Mega Sport Events Despite the Bleak Economic Prospects, *Journal of Sport and Social Issues*, 42(1), 68–92.

Dietschy, P. (2010) La Coupe du monde: un enjeu politique et économique pour les États?, *Géoéconomie*, 54(3), 31–38.

Dietschy, P., Gastaut, Y. & Mourlane, S. (2006) *Histoire politique des Coupes du monde de football.* Paris: Vuilbert.

Elling, A., Van Hilvoorde, I. & Van Den Dool, R. (2014) Creating or Awakening National Pride through Sporting Success: A Longitudinal Study on Macro Effects in the Netherlands, *International Review for the Sociology of Sport*, 49(2), 129–151.

Gaffney, C. (2008) *Temples of the Earthhound Gods: Stadiums in the Cultural Landscapes of Rio de Janeiro and Buenos Aires.* Austin, TX: University of Texas Press.

Gaffney, C. (2010) Mega-Events and Socio-Spatial Dynamics in Rio de Janeiro, 1919-2016, *Journal of Latin American Geography*, 9(1), 7–29.

Grix, J., Brannagan, P. & Houlihan, B. (2015) Interrogating States' Soft Power Strategies: A Case Study of Sports Mega-Events in Brazil and the UK, *Global Society*, 29(3), 463–479.

Guttmann, A. (2002) *The Olympics--A History of the Modern Games.* Chicago, IL: University of Illinois Press.

Hare, G. (2003) *Football in France: A Cultural History*. New York, NY: Berg.

Hill, C.R. (1992) *Olympic Politics.* Manchester: Manchester University Press.

Hobsbawm, E. (1990) *Nations and Nationalism since 1780.* Cambridge: Cambridge University Press.

Leopkey, B. & Parent, M. (2012) Olympic Games Legacy: From General Benefits to Sustainable Long-Term Legacy. *International Journal of The History of Sport*, 29, 924–943.

Meier, H.E. & Mutz, M. (2018) Political Regimes and Sport-Related National Pride: A Cross National Analysis, *International Journal of Sport Policy and Politics*, 10(3), 525–548.

Mitchell, H. & Stewart, M.F. (2015) What Should You Pay to Host a Party? An Economic Analysis of Hosting Sports Mega-Events. *Applied Economics*, 47(15), 1550–1561.

Novaro, M. & Palermo, V. (2003) *La Dictadura militar (1976-1983)*, Buenos Aires, éditorial Paidos.

Orr, M. & Jarvis, N. (2018) Blinded by Gold: Toronto Sports Community Ignores Negative Legacies of 2015 Pan Am Games, *Event Management*, 22, 367–378.
Pigman, G.A. & Rofe, J.R. (2014) Sport and Diplomacy: An Introduction, *Sport in Society: Cultures, Commerce, Media, Politics*, 17(9), 1095–1097.
Pillay, U. & Bass, O. (2008) Mega-Events as a Response to Poverty Reduction: The 2010 FIFA World Cup and Its Urban Development Implications, *Urban Forum*, 19, 329–346.
Pivato, S. (1994) *Les enjeux du sport*. Florence: Giunti Editore.
Preuss, H. (2019) Event Legacy Framework and Measurement, *International Journal of Sport Policy and Politics*, 11(1), 103–118.
Ravenel, L. (2019) Les sportifs sont-ils les premiers citoyens universels ou les derniers patriotes? Une étude sur l'identité des athlètes, *Revue internationale et stratégique*, 114, 151–161.
Scharpf, F.W. (1997) Economic Integration, Democracy and the Welfare State, *European Public Policy*, 4(1), 18–36.
Scheu, A., Preuss, H. & Könecke, T. (2019) The Legacy of the Olympic Games: A Review, *Journal of Global Sport Management*, 6(3), 212–233.
Thomson, A., Schlenker, K. & Schulenkorf, N. (2013) Conceptualizing Sport Event Legacy, *Event Management*, 17(2), 111–122.
Tomlinson, A. & Young, C. (eds) (2006) *National Identity and Global Sports: Culture, Politics, and Spectacle in the Olympics and the Football World Cup*. Albany, NY: State University of New York Press.
Verschuuren, P. (2013) Les multiples visages du « sport power ». *Revue internationale et stratégique, n°89, IRIS Editions*, 131–136.
Vidacs, B. (2006) Through the Prism of Sports: Why Should Africanists Study Sports? *Afrika Spectrum*, 41(3), 331–349.

5

DIPLOMACY, INTERNATIONAL RELATIONS, SOFT POWER AND THE FIFA WORLD CUP

J. Simon Rofe

Introduction

This chapter addresses football World Cups in three dimensions of global affairs: *diplomacy*, *international relations* and *soft power*. The multiple versions of, and topics associated with, the FIFA World Cup described in this *Handbook* provide for multiple opportunities, or "sites" in the words of Iver Neumann, for diplomatic activity to play out (Neumann, 2013). The international relations of World Cups will be addressed, as bidding for and hosting these events have a multitude of motivations, costs and potential outcomes including the accrual of soft power. Each element has a wealth of literature and numerous debates within them. For the purposes of this chapter, *diplomacy* will be considered as "a fundamental activity that has been undertaken throughout history and around the world with a single goal: to mediate the intercultural communication that underlies the connections between all people and all societies" (Rofe and Holmes, 2016, p. 2). *International relations* can be understood as the relationships between different polities or actors in the international sphere, while also being both a distinct discipline – or area of study within academia, and a short-hand or synonym for global affairs. *Soft power* is a term, coined in the early 1990s by scholar Joseph Nye to describe the power of attraction and trust in relations amongst different polities, rather than the "hard" power of coercion. While not an absolute dichotomy; they are relational, soft power and its relationship with sports, particularly sport mega events and therefore football World Cups, has been much debated in the past the 25 years (Anholt 2007; Brannagan and Giullianoti, 2015; Grix and Donna Lee, 2013). Together these three dimensions provide a lens to understand the different forces at work in our exploration of World Cups.

In addressing the bidding for and hosting World Cups it is necessary to comprehend two significant, context building factors that shape and influence our understanding of World Cups. The first of these is to recognise three essential

DOI: 10.4324/9781003121794-5

characteristics of diplomacy: representation, negotiation and communication. Importantly, these are not the preserve of those who inhabit "embassies," international organisations such as the United Nations, or are explicitly concerned with the Vienna Convention on Diplomatic Relations (Vienna Convention on Diplomatic Relations, 1961). Instead, diplomacy can be most usefully understood as an everyday occurrence; one that is as relevant to football World Cups as it is to intergovernmental discussions at the G-20. This is because diplomatic practice is played out whenever "representation," "negotiation" and "communication" are aligned (Rofe and Holmes, 2016). In the realm of football World Cups, this is clear when teams representing nations compete at a set time and place under rules and regulations that are the result of negotiation, and messages are communicated by players, fans, sponsors and others to a variety of audiences deliberately and as part of wider narratives that sporting events facilitate.

The second significant contextual factor in understanding the diplomacy of World Cups speaks directly to both the range of different polities or "actors" involved – be they individuals, teams, organisations within and without football and sport; and the audiences who engage with the sporting event. In other words, it is more than the 22 players on the pitch. The quantity and variety of these different actors who can exert an influence includes the following: individual athletes, coaches and spectators and also their collected representative bodies, such as player's unions and fan groups at professional levels; a range of sponsors from multi-national corporations to local firms; journalistic and media channels from transcontinental conglomerates to local outlets; the full gamut of social media, commentators and contributors – and service providers; support services for facilities management, transportation, health care; government at national, regional and local levels; and national and international governing bodies under the umbrella of FIFA. This is not an exhaustive list, and they do not all have an equal voice in football's decision-making. Importantly also, this is not just a breadth of actors associated with the elite game, as World Cups have connections directly and indirectly to the local and amateur game. So, there is breadth and depth, to the cast involved in bidding for and hosting a World Cup. Together the two dimensions, that is, the key characteristics of diplomacy and the range of actors, help our understanding of the complexity of World Cup bidding and hosting.

Importantly for the purpose of our chapter on bidding for and hosting World Cups, this diverse cast of actors and the networks that they are party to create a consistently evolving ecosystem that is at the heart of what has in the past decade been identified as "sports diplomacy" (Murray, 2018; Rofe, 2018). This approach recognises that *Sport Diplomacy* operates at the "intersection of the realms of sport and diplomacy" providing an "explanatory overlay to the network of evolving networks within the two worlds of sport and diplomacy" (Rofe, 2018, p. xi). Equally, it has been described as "new term that describes an old practice: the unique power of sport to bring people, nations and communities closer together via a shared love of physical pursuits. It is a young field of studies and growing area of practice for governments the world over." (Murray and Price, 2020, p. 7).

Murray and Price go on to say that sports diplomacy is the "strategic use of sport to build relationships and amplify profile, policy and attractiveness as a place to invest or study in, trade with, or visit" (Murray and Price, 2020, p. 7). In the case of World Cups at various levels, one can see how these occasions provide the opportunity to bring together the realms of sport and diplomacy, bring different actors together and offer the opportunity to advance interests of those actors. In other words, how World Cups provide nations, and particularly the hosts, with the opportunity to enhance their relations with others, through the practice of diplomacy and to project their soft power.

Before looking in more detail at World Cup bidding, it is important to also recognise the place of football World Cups in the context of global public occasions, and in particular as Sport Mega Events (SMEs). A discourse has emerged around SMEs with football's World Cups playing a significant role, but as Müller states "mega-events are much discussed, but seldom defined" (Müller, 2015, p. 1). Beyond a sense of scale that comes with mega, Müller notes the absence of anything further and so proposes a fourfold typography: tourist attraction – to the physical space of the SME; mediated reach – the ability of the SME to be consumed away from the physical space; cost – associated with infrastructure and operations; and transformation – urban renewal and regeneration. There may be some additional considerations that shape certain SMEs and each one will have a unique configuration set against any typography, but what is clear from Müller and the other literature is the sheer complexity of SMEs.

In seeking to address this complexity, what Müller has called the "mega-event syndrome," the Institute for Human Rights and Business compiled a Mega Sporting Event lifecycle. Amongst its salient features are that the competition – the most prominent public facing element of an SME is only one of eight dimensions and one that comes as the penultimate element. Equally as important is that the lifecycle begins and ends with legacy giving a clear sense of dynamism to the process. A particular discourse has emerged around the term "legacy" in SMEs since it was given prominence in the bid for London 2012 summer Olympics. This as bled into the bidding for and hosting of World Cups. The purported absence of legacy planning was a critique of the 2014 tournament in Brazil, while the 2022 hosts Qatar, have made legacy a key element of their preparations in establishing the "Supreme Committee for Delivery and Legacy" as the primary organisation body – the local organising committee in Olympic parlance – for the 2022 tournament. In settling upon this title, the organisation seeks to address both the short-term project management dimension of delivery, and the longer-term legacy of hosting in one body.

The lifecycle also prompts consideration of the key elements of what it takes to bid for a World Cup. The simplest answer here is money. In the days of Sepp Blatter's FIFA presidency, this money may have been used to influence decision-making in a nefarious fashion, but beyond such notions there are significant financial costs to bidding for and hosting a World Cup (see Chapter 9 in this *Handbook* for a more detailed account on these financial matters). The estimated costs of the Qatar 2022 tournament are over 100 billion dollars; over 10 times as much as the initially staggering figure of 11 billion dollars spent on Russia 2018. This latter figure was in some regards considered moderate for the Russian hosts, who had spent over 50 billion dollars on the Sochi Winter Olympics in 2014. Whatever the precise figure for an individual World Cup the costs are huge and decisions of this magnitude, and of this cost, cannot divorced from their geopolitical environment.

World Cup Bidding: Process and Action

The process for the bidding for FIFA World Cups is officially governed by the sport's international federation, *Fédération Internationale de Football Association (FIFA):* but it does not happen in isolation from the geopolitical context. FIFA, the body formed in 1904 amongst eight European states, now comprises 211 members (2021) and is responsible for the range of different tournaments since organising the first men's FIFA World Cup in 1930. These tournaments cover different age groups and formats across the men's and women's games and not all warrant SME classification. With men's competitions in Under 15s, U17s, U20s, Futsal and Beach Soccer, and at U23 level, the football competition at the Summer Olympic Games, and the World Cup; and women's competition in at U15s, U17s, U20s, the Summer Olympics and the Women's World Cup. In addition, FIFA supports the FIFAe World Cup an eSports football tournament staged annually (https://www.fifa.gg/).

Thus far, global attention falls mainly in the men's quadrennial tournament, the longest standing of FIFA's World Cups as a pre-eminent SME. The many histories of the individual tournaments are covered elsewhere in this *Handbook* (see Chapter 2), but the salience of recounting the different editions here is that each requires hosting and some form of bidding that precedes that. With each, therefore, is an opportunity for a differentiated form of international relations, diplomacy and soft power to play out. This chapter duly notes those different tournaments and acknowledges that it consciously mimics a hierarchy of importance in having as its main focus the Men's World Cup.

Bidding for a World Cup is a political undertaking. Nations and states, their national football federations, the continental federations, and ultimately global audiences have an influence on the process. Some of this range of actors have more influence than others as noted previously, but the process makes a national federation, or federations for joint bids, the key actor on the stage of the World Cup drama. A national federation is itself a political body, and a bid an act of public policy – that is a series of actions by a governance body to address a real-world concern of a public. There are three important implications for this chapter.

1. The relationship between national FAs and nations is intertwined in many regards, perhaps most notably, FAs are often in receipt of taxpayer's money. Though mechanisms will vary from nation to nation, in the majority of nations, and particularly those who are candidates to bid for the World Cup, FAs receive public money to fund their activities. For example in England, a potential host for the 2030 Men's World Cup, the FA receives money from Sport

England – a body that exists to support sport and physical activity – which in turn derives its money from a National Lottery and the national exchequer (https://www.sportengland.org/why-were-here accessed 12.7.21). What this means is that the taxpaying public are stakeholders in the process.

2. The second point here is in relation to political interference in football. FIFA statues (15.c) state for member associations and confederations that they need to be "independent and avoid any form of political interference" https://digitalhub.fifa.com/m/4b2bac74655c7c13/original/viz2gmyb5x0pd24qrhrx-pdf.pdf Yet simultaneously, FIFA require bidding associations to have the support of government. "As a condition for their appointment to host and stage the competition," FIFA's bid guide states, "member associations are required to secure the full support of the governmental authorities at federal, state and municipal level in their respective countries" (FIFA, 2017). There is a tension here in relation to World Cups between interference and support at the heart FIFA mandate that FA's need to be free from political influence, and to receive whole-hearted government support for a bid.
3. A third important point here is that national FAs are part of international organisations in their own right aside from the global system of nation states. FAs are members of regional federations such as the Confederation of African Football (CAF) or the Asian Football Confederation (AFC); have bilateral relations with each other and their organisational structures, practices and personnel are often interchangeable.

Together, these three elements demonstrate that the body responsible for submitting a bid to FIFA – a Football Association – is itself part of the public policy process within a sovereign state and as part of a broader geopolitical and diplomatic network of actors. This context shapes the ability of different FAs to even begin the process of bidding for FIFA's World Cups, and thus their nation's ability to engage in the associated diplomatic activity

FIFA now recognises the political context in which bids are developed and considered.

FIFA produced extensive support to the bidding process for the 2026 Men's tournament, which was awarded to the United 2026 bid from CONCACAF nations the United States, Mexico and Canada at the 2018 Congress in Moscow on the eve of the 2018 tournament. This support centred on 35-page document entitled "Guide to the Bidding process for the 2026 FIFA World Cup" and may come to be regarded as current best-practice in aligning the prerogatives of the global governing body and the capabilities of potential hosts (FIFA, 2017). FIFA identifies here five requirements for hosting the World Cup:

- Hosting Vision and Strategy – including legacy and political support
- Host Country Information – political, economic, media and marketing data
- Technical matters – stadiums, facilities, accommodation, transportation and security

- Other event-related matters – PR, Fan events, volunteers, health/medical systems
- Sustainable event management, human rights and environmental protection.

The requirement for support to the bidding process was stark in the aftermath of controversies that beset FIFA for a generation. These controversies have been addressed elsewhere by the likes of Sugden and Tomlinson (1998, 2017), and Conn (2018), and centre on financial corruption, the concentration of executive power, and the award of the 2018 and 2022 Men's World Cups to Russia and Qatar, respectively. The 2026 bid process was one that need to be reformed to restore credibility to the organisation. The 2017 bid document reflected the desire from then newly elected President Gianni Infantino to demonstrate his leadership in reform. In looking to the expansion of the tournament from 32 to 48 teams, the document pledges FIFA to an "impeccable process" for determining the host based on four "Key Principles of the Reformed Bidding Process." These begin with "Transparency," and go on to include "Participation, Commitment to HR and sustainability, [and] Objectivity." That transparency was the first principle was little surprise given the dénouement of the Blatter regime but spoke to a longer history within FIFA – and other sports governing bodies notably the International Olympic Committee – of secrecy. Infantino pledged FIFA to an open process where "[n]ot a single decision is guarded away from public scrutiny" (FIFA, 2017). With respect to the 2026 bidding process, and with the rotation of the event away from UEFA 2018, and AFC 2022, only two bids emerged; one from Morocco in CAF, and the eventual winner in the UNITED bid from CONCACAF. Therefore, it is perhaps too early to judge the success of the reforms in the 2026 process, and the 2030 process may be a better test ground with at least five confirmed bids as of 2021.

To emphasise the point, it is important to recognise that even contemplating bidding for a World Cup at any level is a diplomatic act. The opportunity for a nation and its Football Association to state their intent to enter the bidding process stands them apart from their peers who do not. In doing so, it gives them a platform to engage publics at home and abroad – the essence of public diplomacy. By signalling intent to bid, they are also engaging in a process that is an international competition: akin to that on the pitch in so far as it is governed by a series of rules and protocols, and in that there are potential multiple entrants but only one victor. As such, bidding, regardless of success, provides the opportunity for potential soft power benefits in terms of enhancing a nation's international reputation (Guala, 2021). This potential plays into what Simon Anholt identifies as nation branding. He states: "the reputation of a country has a direct and measurable impact on just about every aspect of its engagement with other countries, and plays a critical pole in its economic, social, political and cultural progress" (Anholt 2007, p. 99). Anholt goes on to note that hosting mega-events as a means "for countries, cities and regions to earn a better and stronger reputation," which in turn may lead to economic and political benefits (Anholt 2007, p. 25). This is in essence the appeal of soft power. Anholt's more recent work, through the Good Country Index, suggests the impact of hosting may be more transient than is sometimes thought: a temporary altering of perceptions with a post-event correction. Nonetheless, Anholt's work and the broader body of literature speaks to is the confluence of the literatures on sport mega-events and that on soft power and public diplomacy that this chapter explores.

Before moving to the diplomacy of hosting FIFA World Cups, a note on non-FIFA World Cups in the shape of the CONIFA and the Homeless World Cups. Both began with men's competitions in 2014 and 2003, respectively, and have expanded to include women, and both have gained a growing a distinct profile in the global sporting social conscious. The latter highlights a specific cause with global resonance, and the former a further indication of the range of actors engaged in the global sportscape. The CONIFA tournament has particular relevance for diplomacy and international relations. The competing "members" come from unrecognised and/or contested territories such as the County of Nice, Abkhazia or Karpatalja (the winners from 2014, 2016 and 2018, respectively). Their sovereignty is not acknowledged amongst the international relations system of nation states governed by those same states. CONIFA, operates in a liminal space at the margins of this system often mimicking both FIFA and state behaviour but not fully participating nor fully recognised (McConnell, Moreau and Dittmer, 2012). So, CONIFA has a President, a General Secretary and a regional representation along the same lines as FIFA, yet the organisation consciously avoids using the terms "nation" or "state" given potential implications for claims of sovereignty for the territories or in being subjugated by existing members of the system of states. While it may seem fanciful for the likes of Abkhazia to gain access to the full diplomatic system as outlined in the Vienna conventions, Ganohariti and Dijxhoorn argue that participation in CONFIA aids in "nation branding through hosting rights and media attention," in terms Anholt would appreciate, and "contributes to strengthening the 'national' identity of the participants" through mutual recognition (Ganohariti and Dijxhoorn, 2020, p. 329). Equally, sport, and particularly football has been a key part of the journey to statehood for other nations. The case of Kosovo is a notable one, with the province declaring independence in 2008 and seeking to use the "door" of sport as a means of gaining further recognition. Brentin and Tregoures plot how recognition by the IOC in 2014 was an integral step as "sport can play a very particular and increasingly significant role for young and contested states" diplomatic endeavours towards full international recognition (Brentin and Tregoures, 2016, p. 361). Recognition by FIFA followed in 2018, as Kosovo continues a journey towards participation both in a World Cup and full acknowledgement by the international community. This intertwining of recognition within sport and in diplomacy speaks to the opportunity here as the increasing number of participants in the men's World Cup and the proliferation of tournaments allows for greater scope for aspiring nations to participate as competitors and in the bidding/hosting process.

The Diplomacy of World Cup Hosting

The hosting of an SME such as the men's FIFA World Cup provides explicit opportunities for diplomatic activity and enhancing soft power. Hosting places a sharp focus on the host nation, its facilities, and its populace. Importantly also for this chapter, the host's reputation is under scrutiny as the message a host seeks to share can be more important than the sport itself. Former South African President Thabo Mbeki wrote to then FIFA president Sepp Blatter with a vision for the 2010 World Cup tournament that would see it enter the pages of history as "a moment when Africa stood tall and resolutely turned the tide on centuries of poverty and conflict" (Quoted in Alegi, 2010). With implications for enhancing South African, and African soft power, Mbeki stated "[w]e want, on behalf of our continent, to stage an event that will send ripples of confidence from the Cape to Cairo." Mbeki's vision chimed with Blatter who had pledged FIFA to take the men's World Cup to the African continent and the tournament in South Africa can be regarded as the pinnacle of his leadership. Yet, the impact of the tournament is highly contested. The costs of hosting significantly exceeded estimates with the budget for stadium refurbishment of 225 million US dollars swelling to over two billion dollars. Equally, the prospect of recouping these costs through additional revenues such extra tourist income is debated. Maennig's extensive research in this regard demonstrates "no evidence of a net increase in World Cup related overseas tourism beyond approximately 90,000 to 118,000 persons, equivalent to a short-term impact of the tournament of 0.1% of GDP". Allied to observable increases in prices for travel and accommodation, the benefits of hosting is further removed from local populations. Dowse noted that although "South Africa's political elite presented the 2010 FWC as an opportunity to support a range of policy priorities" and justified the hosting as having "domestic and largely economic policy," the "government systematically prioritised event interests over these social concerns" (Dowse, 2018, p. 81). Once more, in terms that emphasise the diplomatic and soft power dimensions of hosting a World Cup, Dowse goes on to suggest "that it was diplomatic potential of securing foreign policy interests and developing soft power resources through symbolic messaging and image rehabilitation opportunities that underpinned the political value associated with the hosting opportunity" (Dowse, 2018, p. 81). Cornelissen agreed that the South African hosting of the 2010 tournament was more about post-apartheid South African statehood than the impact of football in transforming the lives of the South African people (Cornelissen, 2008).

Assessments of the impact remain challenging, even ephemeral, and the South African case was made harder to assess due to the more tangible blow of the 2008 global financial crisis. Its impact on sport in the years that followed (Parnell et al., 2018) mean a similarly contested history of the impact of hosting the World Cup in Brazil in 2014 has emerged. A year before the 2014 tournament, during FIFA's "dry run" of the Confederations Cup, millions of Brazilians took to the streets to protest at government expenditure including the costs of the 2014 men's World

Cup and the 2016 Summer Olympic and Paralympic Games. Brazil's fall from grace at the same time as hosting the two most prestigious SMEs was as stark as it was surprising. "In terms of local and international opinion," Winter wrote from the vantage point of 2017, "a country that had been almost universally heralded as a success story – a vibrant democracy, a Latin American economy growing at China-like rates, the "B" in BRICS – would by 2016 be synonymous with dysfunction, instability and failure" (Winter, 2017). President Dilmar Rouseff's fall was particularly hard, as by the end of 2016 she was facing impeachment and removal from office. A significant factor in the demise of Rouseff was the distance between declarations by political leaders about the value of hosting the SME, and the reality for local populations. This rhetorical "gap," and the difficulties it exposes as a host, presents a countervailing narrative to the premise that hosting the World Cup brings broader benefits to the host. The case of the 2010 and 2014 World Cups stand as examples of the risks involved in seeking to deliver deliberate soft power messages through a football World Cup when an audience has an ability to shape the outcome before, during or after the event.

A particular element of both the 2010 and 2014 tournaments were the costs of the stadia being used. The South African edition used 10 stadiums of which 6 were newly built, and Brazil used 12 with 7 being new constructions. The financial and environment costs of these stadia is huge and the risk of creating "white elephants" – a recurrent concern for those invested in World Cups – a legacy that has become increasingly unpalatable.

Beyond the costs, and importantly for this chapter, the stadia that are used for any World Cup provide distinct sites for diplomacy (Neumann, 2013). In a stadium's executive boxes business deals can be negotiated; in the training facilities technical knowledge can be communicated amongst different teams; and on the concourses and in the stands, representation is to the fore amongst fans bedecked in the colours of "their" team. Iconic stadia are a key element of both bids, and the tournaments themselves, and come with considerable operational costs and logistical chains. While sustainability concerns have seen a greater emphasis on use of existing stadia (see Chapter 8 in this *Handbook*), they provide a visual and physical focus for the host. Art critic Robert Hughes purportedly said from the vantage point of the mid-20th century that train stations were the "cathedrals of the modern age"; many would now suggest that stadia hold that mantle. The complexity and cost of their construction and maintenance; their architectural majesty, and the emotional attachment that acts as a place of pilgrimage for many, make them churches to congregations who may never see them in person. The Maracanã, Wembley, the Azteca, the Stade de France are locations that resonate with millions of people. Whilst many will be football fans, these sites transcend football also as they are (meant to be) multi-purpose facilities recognised for hosting other mass gatherings and cultural events as pop concerts and religious festivals. That, arguably, the biggest diplomatic gathering of the 20th first century, the memorial service for Nelson Mandela (5 December 2013), was held in the same location – Soccer City Stadium – as the 2010 World Cup final is testament to how hosting the World Cup provides an opportunity for diplomatic activity long after the final whistle has been blown.

Conclusion: Bidding and Hosting in Diplomacy

World Cups are fora for discussion; some of it is about the merits of a particular player, a controversial decision, or a glorious goal; and sometimes that discussion extends to issues which may appear to have little overlap with the field of play. It is the congruence of "football" and "diplomacy" in those moments that has been the focus of this chapter exploring the bidding for and hosting of World Cups within FIFA's age group and gender structure, and beyond in the CONIFA and Homeless World Cups. These moments do not arrive by accident: they can be facilitated, coached and nurtured, but – like any deflection on the pitch – they can be diverted in unexpected directions and with unintended consequences.

The coming together of football and diplomacy is epitomised in World Cup. They provide numerous opportunities for cooperation and can also expose tensions. There is a notable overlap in mission but not a precise mapping of one to another. The relationship between the two realms is seen in the simple acknowledgement that the pre-eminent global organisation of nation states, the United Nations, has 192 members, while football's global governing body has 211. Yet to talk in terms of solely nation states or football associations overlooks the range of stakeholders who participate both in the global diplomacy and football. Nations and states, their national football federations, the continental federations

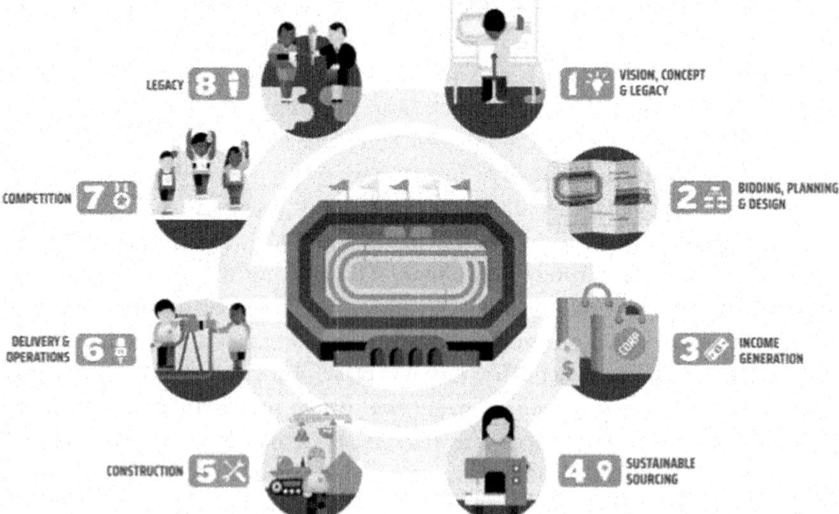

FIGURE 5.1 The mega-sporting event lifecycle: embedding human rights from vision to legacy (Institute for Human Rights and Business IHRB, Mega-Sporting Events Platform for Human Rights, 2018)

and ultimately the global organisation that is FIFA are all part of the diplomatic theatre, but they are joined by a plethora of others from athletes, coaches and support staff, to sponsors, the media and fans. In its simplest manifestation this practice of diplomacy – people to people diplomacy – takes place when a ball is kicked between two individuals. The cultural exchange, the dialogue and the opportunity that is provided by the roll of the ball is the basis for all of the grandeur of a World Cup tournament.

The bidding for and hosting of World Cups brings a level of scrutiny to the network of relationships that football facilities. The focus on the men's FIFA World Cup is not to ignore the importance of other tournaments, but to recognise that it sits as one of two sport mega events – possibly even a "giga" event – alongside the Summer Olympic and Paralympic games. In doing so, the chapter has explored how football World Cups provide the opportunity for a range of actors in the global diplomatic theatre – most notably nation states and their football associations – to build stronger international relations, proactively engage in diplomacy and project soft power (Figure 5.1).

References

Ahlfeldt, G. & Maennig, W. (2010) Stadium Architecture and Urban Development from the Perspective of Urban Economics, *International Journal of Urban and Regional Research*, *34*(3), 629–646.

Allmers, S. & Maennig, W. (2009) Economic impacts of the FIFA Soccer World Cups in France 1998, Germany 2006, and outlook for South Africa 2010, *Eastern Economic Journal, 35*, 500–519.

Alegi, P. (2010) *African Soccerscapes: How a Continent Changed the World's Game*. London: Hurst.

Brannagan, P. & Giullianoti, R. (2015) Soft Power and Soft Disempowerment: Qatar, Global Sport and Football's 2022 World Cup Finals, *Leisure Studies*, 34(6), 703–719.

Brentin, D. & Tregoures, L. (2016) Entering Through the Sport's Door? Kosovo's Sport Diplomatic Endeavours Towards International Recognition, *Diplomacy & Statecraft*, 27(2), 360–378, 10.1080/09592296.2016.1169799 [Accessed 25 August 2021].

Chadwick, S., Parnell, D., Widdop, P., & Anagnostopoulos, C. (2018) *Routledge Handbook of Football Business and Management*. London: Routledge.

Conn, D. (2018) *The Fall of the House of FIFA*. London: Yellow Jersey.

Cornelissen, S. (2008) Scripting the Nation: Sport, Mega-events, Foreign Policy and State Building in Post-Apartheid South Africa, *Sport in Society*, 11, 4.

Dowse, S. (2018) Mega sports events as political tools: a case study of South Africa's hosting of the 2010 FIFA Football World Cup, in Rofe, J.S. (eds), *Sport and Diplomacy: Games Within Games*. Manchester: Manchester University Press.

FIFA (2017) *Guide to the Bidding Process for the 2026 FIFA World Cup*. Available at: https://www.fifa.com/about-fifa/official-documents [Accessed 26 May 2021].

Ganohariti, R. & Dijxhoorn, E. (2020) Para- and Proto-Sports Diplomacy of Contested Territories: CONIFA as a Platform for Football Diplomacy, *The Hague Journal of Diplomacy*, 15, 3, 329–354, Brill 10.1163/1871191X-BJA10027 [Accessed 22 August 2021].

Gillet, A., & Tennent, K. (2021) Populism and political motives for hosting the FIFA World Cup: Comparing England 1966 and Russia 2018, in Clift, B. & Tomlinson, A. (eds), *Populism in Sport, Leisure, and Popular Culture*. London: Routledge.

Goldblatt, D. (2008) *The Ball Is Round: A Global History of Soccer*. New York: Riverhead.

Gold, J.R. & Gold, M.M. (eds) (2016) *Olympic Cities: City Agendas, Planning, and the World's Games, 1896–2020*. London: Routledge.

Grix, J. & Donna Lee, D. (2013) Soft Power, Sports Mega-Events and Emerging States: The Lure of the Politics of Attraction, *Global Society*, 27(4), 521–536, 10.1080/13600826.2013.827632

Grix, J., Brannagan P., & Lee, D., (2019) *Entering the Global Arena: Emerging States, Soft Power Strategies and Sport Mega-Events*. London: Palgrave.

Guala, A. (2021) To Bid or Not to Bid: the Legacy of the Failed Bids, *Academia Letters*, Article 3138. 10.20935/AL3138

Institute for Human Rights and Business IHRB, Mega-Sporting Events Platform for Human Rights, (2018) The Mega-Sporting Event Lifecycle: Embedding Human Rights from Vision to Legacy. Available at: https://www.ihrb.org/focus-areas/mega-sporting-events/mse-lifecycle-embedding-human-rights-from-vision-to-legacy [Accessed 26 May 2021].

McConnell, F., Moreau, T. & Dittmer, J. (2012) Mimicking State Diplomacy: The Legitimizing Strategies of Unofficial Diplomacies, *Geoforum*, 43, 804–814.

Müller, M. (2015) What Makes an Event a Mega-Event? Definitions and Sizes, *Leisure Studies*, 35(6), 627–642.

Murray, S. & Price, G. (2020) *Towards a Welsh Sports Diplomacy*. British Council Wales.

Murray, S. (2018) *Sports Diplomacy: Origins, Theory and Practice*. London: Routledge.

Neumann, I. (2013) *Diplomatic Sites: A Critical Enquiry*. London: Hurst Press.

Parnell, D., Millward, P., Widdop, P., King, N. & May, A. (2018) Sport Policy and Politics in an Era of Austerity, *International Journal of Sport Policy and Politics*, 10 (1), 1–5.

Postlethwaite, V. & Grix, J. (2016) Beyond the Acronyms: Sport Diplomacy and the Classification of the International Olympic Committee, *Diplomacy and Statecraft*, 27(2), 295–313. 10.1080/09592296.2016.1169796

Rofe, J.S. (ed.) (2018) *Sport and Diplomacy: Games Within Games*. Manchester: Manchester University Press.

Rofe, J.S. & Holmes, A.R. (2016) *Global Diplomacy: Theories, Types and Models*. London: Routledge.

Sugden, J. & Tomlinson, A. (2017) *Football, Corruption and Lies Revisiting 'Badfellas', the Book FIFA Tried to Ban*. London: Routledge.

Sugden, J. & Tomlinson, A. (1998) *FIFA and the Contest for World Football: Who Rules the People's Game?* Cambridge, UK: Polity.

Vienna Convention on Diplomatic Relations. (1961) United Nations, Treaty Series Vol. 500. Available at: https://treaties.un.org/pages/ViewDetails.aspx?src=TREATY&mtdsg_no=III-3&chapter=3&clang=_en [Accessed 26 May 2021].

Winter, B. (2017), Revisiting Brazil's 2013 Protests: What did they really mean?, *Americas Quarterly*. Available at: https://www.americasquarterly.org/article/revisiting-brazils-2013-protests-what-did-they-really-mean/ [Accessed 28 August 2021].

6

COMPETITION DESIGN OF THE FIFA WORLD CUP

Travis Richardson, Tim Pawlowski, and Georgios Nalbantis

Introduction

This chapter examines how the FIFA World Cup as well as the FIFA Women's World Cup competitions are structured and organised, along with how they have changed over the years. As such, the chapter provides an overview on competition format and seeding systems for the World Cup Final competition, as well as an emphasis on the Qualifying tournaments for each of the six FIFA confederations.

FIFA Men's World Cup Qualifiers

With a limited number of nations able to compete in the FIFA World Cup Finals (32 in 2022; 48 in 2026), yet 211 nations from 6 different confederations longing to participate, qualifying tournaments and play-offs are exceptionally necessary. Qualifying for the Finals is a lengthy, extensive process taking place during the four years between each Final. Each of FIFA's six confederations determine their own qualification system to produce their rightful number of nations for the Final. The six confederations are as follows: Africa (CAF), Asia (AFC), Europe (UEFA), North and Central America and Caribbean (CONCACAF), Oceania (OFC), and South America (CONMEBOL). Differing greatly in structure and World Cup representatives, this section gives insight into the substantial differences *between* and *within* confederations over time. In this regard, we review the last ten qualifying formats starting with FIFA World Cup 1986 for each confederation.[1]

---

1 Unless stated otherwise, information on structure, format, and tournament design presented in this chapter was retrieved from the website of each respective confederation and the RSSSF Archive (Rec.Sport.Soccer Statistics Foundation: www.rsssf.com).

DOI: 10.4324/9781003121794-6

Africa (CAF)

In Africa, both the number of participating nations in the Qualifiers (29 in 1986 and 54 in 2022)[2] and the number of representatives for the Finals (2 in 1986, 5 in 2022) have increased considerably during recent years. At the same time, however, financial and geopolitical conditions in the continent have led FIFA to suspend national associations either before or during the Qualifiers on several occasions (e.g., Zimbabwe in 2018 Qualifiers). Likewise, some associations decided to voluntarily withdraw (e.g., Central African Republic in 2010 Qualifiers).

With the exception of the 1994 and 2002 Qualifiers, where all participating nations took part in the first stage, CAF organises the first stage of the Qualifiers as knockout (KO) games between its lowest ranked associations. A number of best ranked associations, which number widely varies on tournament (i.e., three for the Qualifiers of 1986, 26 for the Qualifiers of 2022), qualifies automatically to the second stage of the competition. Overall, this design is expected to foster both competitive balance (CB) and homefield advantage (HA) at later stages (Pollard and Gómez, 2014) since home teams are more likely to win when both teams are of equal strength (considering travel fatigue, stadium familiarity or support effects, see Ponzo and Scoppa, 2018). In fact, empirical evidence shows that among all six confederations Africa has the highest HA in the Qualifiers. In CAF, group stage teams (from 2006 to 2014) averaged about 1.93 points at home (Pollard and Armatas, 2017).

With having ten different formats in the last ten Qualifiers, CAF has been the most susceptible to changes amongst the six confederations. In this regard, the number of teams, the number of stages, as well as the format of the final stage have constantly changed throughout the years. For instance, in the last ten Qualifiers, four times the World Cup participants were decided after a KO stage and six times after a group stage, while in the last four Qualifiers CAF switches back and forth between group stage and KO games in the final stage. During the last ten Qualifiers, the teams representing CAF in the Finals were decided one time after the fourth stage, four times after the second stage and five times after the third stage of the competition.

Asia (AFC)

Like in Africa, the number of participating nations from Asia in the Qualifiers (27 in 1986, 46 in 2022) and the representatives in the Finals (two in 1984, five guaranteed in 2022) have increased considerably during recent years. Also, the number of eligible nations does not always correspond to the actual number of teams that participate in the Qualifiers. For instance, in the 2014 Qualifiers Brunei were suspended by FIFA, while Bhutan and Guam voluntarily withdraw their

2 If not stated otherwise, all years refer to the corresponding years when the World Cup Finals took place.

participation. Since 2006, Australia participates in the AFC Qualifiers with the hope to increase its chance to participate in the Finals. Indeed, Australia's probability of participating in the 2018 FIFA World Cup increased by 75% after leaving OFC and joining AFC (Csato, 2021a).

Until 2002 all eligible nations had to participate in the first stage of the Qualifiers. However, since 2006, there is a KO stage between the lowest ranked nations, with the highest ranked nations automatically qualifying for the second stage.[3] While this design is similar to CAF Qualifiers, the number of nations taking part in AFC's first stage KO rounds is considerably lower (28 in CAF, just 12 in AFC in 2022). This might, at least to some extent, explain the comparably lower level of CB and HA in the consecutive stages of AFC Qualifiers. In fact, AFC has (together with UEFA) the lowest HA among all confederations with teams scoring, on average, about 1.58 points in group stage games at home between 2006 and 2014 (Pollard and Armatas, 2017).

The participants in the 2010 and 2014 Finals were decided after the fourth stage: playing KO rounds in the first two stages and in groups in the latter two. In the 2018 and 2022 Qualifiers, AFC eliminated the fourth stage, by implementing groups in the second and third stage of the Qualifiers. Since 2006, the final stage consists of two different groups with varying numbers of teams (four in 2006, six in 2022) with the two group winners and the two group runners-up qualifying for the Finals. In 2022, Qatar automatically qualifies as host nation tallying the guaranteed representatives for AFC in the Finals to five.

Next to these representatives, an additional AFC nation, coming from a head-to-head matchup against the two third-place group finishers, has the opportunity to enter the Finals via the "Inter-Confederation Play-off" by winning the two-legged ties against another nation coming from AFC, CONCACAF or CONMEBOL.

Europe (UEFA)

The Qualifiers in Europe have always represented the most participating nations (32 in 1986 and 55 in 2022) and the most representatives (13 since 1986) in all Finals. With 12 titles since 1930, UEFA has produced the greatest amount of FIFA World Cup winners over time.

In contrast to CAF and AFC Qualifiers, the basic competition design of UEFA Qualifiers has not changed much over time. Each tournament (besides 1990 and 1994) has two rounds. The first round is a group stage; the winner of these groups automatically qualifies for the Finals. Given the changes in the number of eligible nations. there have been several occasions where also group runners-up (1990, 1994), the four best (1986) or the two best (2006) runners-up qualified.

3 An exception occurred in 2010, where the five highest ranked teams received automatic qualification into the third stage, bypassing the competition in the first and second stages.

In contrast to AFC and CAF, all eligible nations compete in the first stage of the Qualifiers. Without sorting out weaker nations, UEFA has the lowest HA among all confederations in the group stage, signalling a wide performance gap between stronger and weaker nations (Armatas and Pollard, 2014; Pollard and Armatas, 2017). In stage two, the format is KO and the nations winning their KO draw join the stage one winners in the finals. The inclusion criteria for teams in stage two has changed several times; ranging from the best runners-up to the worst runners-up, to being randomly selected into the stage.

For the 2022 FIFA World Cup, UEFA nations have the additional opportunity to qualify via the "UEFA Nations League." All 55 UEFA member associations were initially divided into four *divisions* (i.e., A, B, C and D) according to their UEFA coefficients and further separated into four groups within each division. The UEFA Nations League has introduced two different ways into qualifying. First, in the group stage of the Qualifiers, the four teams which make the final round of the Nations League get placed into smaller Qualifier groups. Second, in the KO stage of the Qualifiers, the 10 group runners-up from the first stage are then joined by the two best Nations League *group* winners of the 2020–2021 season (based on Nations League overall rankings) that finished *outside* the top two of their Qualifying group. These 12 teams are then drawn into three different play-off groups. Two rounds of KO games are played in each group to determine the final three teams that qualify for the Finals in 2022.

This new qualification route has raised some concerns among scholars who examined its impact on the UEFA EURO 2020 qualification (Csato, 2019, 2021b; Haugen and Krumer, 2021). Although qualification process for the UEFA EURO is somewhat different than that for the FIFA World Cup, the arguable distortions introduced by Nations Leagues are common. These distortions include how in some situations, lower ranked teams in the Nations League have a significantly higher probability of qualifying for the World Cup or EURO Finals than higher ranked teams due to the combination of the Nations League qualifying route as well as the "usual" route. For example, in the 2020 UEFA European Championship it could be observed that being the top-ranked team in the lowest league (D) in the Nations League significantly improves the probability of qualifying compared to the lowest ranked team in the higher League C (Csato, 2021b). As argued, this alternative qualification route may also lead to a lack of incentive to win in the Qualifiers since nations can exert lower levels of performance and still be successful (Csato, 2021a; Dagaev and Sonin, 2018; Vong, 2017).

North and Central America and Caribbean (CONCACAF)

While the number of participating CONCACAF nations has doubled over time (17 in 1986, 35 in 2022), the number of representatives has only increased from two (in 1986) to three (in 2022). A reason for this might be the fact that 24 of the 35 CONCACAF nations belong to the bottom half of all nations in the FIFA World Rankings (as of January 2021).

The first stage is regularly organised as a KO round between the lowest ranked CONCACAF associations, with the highest ranked associations automatically qualifying for the second stage (an exception occurred in 1986 and 2006 Qualifiers, where all eligible nations took part in the first stage). Sorting out relatively weaker nations, CONCACAF group stage nations have the third highest HA amongst all confederations, with teams averaging about 1.80 points at home from 2006 to 2014 (Pollard and Armatas, 2017).

With nine different formats over the past ten years, CONCACAF Qualifiers are the second most susceptible to changes after CAF. These changes include Qualifiers with only three (1986, 1990, 2006 and 2022) and up to five stages (1994, 1998 and 2018). Within these different Qualifiers, there have been three editions with different *zones* (1994, 1998 and 2002), seven editions where only the lowest ranked teams started in the first stage, and an edition where all participating nations played in the first stage (2006). However, the Qualifiers' final round has been a single group, double round-robin structure with six teams since 1998. The three best teams make the Finals. Since 2006, the fourth-ranked team goes to the Inter-Confederation play-off.

In the most recent changes for the 2022 FIFA World Cup, seeding is ever more important. The top five seeded teams automatically move on to the final round without playing in any other stage. The other three teams are decided by the opening two stages. The Qualifiers' final round will then be eight teams playing each other twice. The three best teams make the Finals, while the fourth-ranked team advances to the Inter-Confederation play-off.

Oceania (OFC)

Oceania has very few participating nations (4 in 1984 and 11 in 2022) and by far the fewest representatives for the Finals. Three nations (New Caledonia, Niue and Tahiti) are affiliated with OFC but not with FIFA. Due to political conflicts with China, Chinese Taipei was a member of OFC from 1976 to 1978 and again from 1982 to 1989. Moreover, the Northern Mariana Islands have been considered an association member since 2009. These are not the only examples of teams entering OFC. For instance, in 1984, Israel competed in OFC qualifying due to exclusion from AFC. Every year, besides 1994, OFC has been allowed 0.5 representatives. This means that OFC nations are not competing for an automatic spot in the Finals, rather competing for a place in the Inter-Confederation play-off. As such, we omit an extensive discussion about the OFC Qualifiers in this chapter.

Importantly, however, Stone and Rod (2016) demonstrated concerns of how FIFA allocates qualification spots fairly among confederations particularly concerning the OFC. They observed that 50% of teams competing in CONMEBOL make the Finals while only around 30% (10%) [5%] of participating nations in UEFA (CONCACAF, AFC, CAF) [OFC] qualify for the Finals. The reduced probability to advance to the Finals led several times OFC nations entering and leaving the confederation.

South America (CONMEBOL)

With only ten FIFA-affiliated nations since 1986, the CONMEBOL Qualifiers are by far the most straightforward among all confederations. CONMEBOL has had some variation in World Cup Final representatives due to automatic bids (winning the previous World Cup or hosting), however, the confederation has also stayed consistent with total representatives in the World Cup (four since 1986, except for 1990 and 1994 (both three)).

Each Qualifier, the ten nations play one another home and away.[4] The four best ranked teams in the group directly advance to the Finals, while the fifth ranked team advances to the Inter-Confederation playoff. From 1998 through 2014, CONMEBOL used a mirrored double round-robin schedule for the qualifying tournament with a peculiarity in three tournaments (2002, 2006 and 2010) that the schedules were identical, that is the teams played their rivals in precisely the same order each time. This setup was perceived to unfairly benefit certain teams, as the number of home and away games per nation and round was unequal, as well as there were long breaks between games.

To tackle this issue, Duran, Guajardo, and Saure (2017) proposed fixtures be determined by random draw and the so-called French scheme, which allows the first and last rounds to be identical but the home-away status of the teams to be reversed. This format was implemented for the 2018 Qualifiers and constitutes CONMEBOL the only confederation using computational scheduling (Gasparetto and Barajas, 2018). Csato (2021a) focusing on Elo Ratings found that the new format promotes fairness as the probability of qualification for the 2018 FIFA World Cup for CONMEBOL relied solely on the strength of teams.[5] Moreover, similar to Duran et al. (2018), he showed that ever since the changes, CONMEBOL is the hardest confederation to successfully qualify for the Finals and far more balanced than it used to be.

CONMEBOL Qualifiers have the second highest HA among all confederations, with teams achieving on average about 1.84 points at home between 2006 and 2014 (Pollard and Armatas, 2017). While this points towards a certain degree of CB in the Qualifiers, the HA in CONMEBOL is also frequently associated with distortions caused by the geomorphology of the nations competing and especially the location of stadia in extreme high altitudes (Bogotá, Colombia: 2600 m; Quito, Ecuador: 2800 m; La Paz, Bolivia: 3600 m). Indeed, McSharry (2007) found that high altitude teams have a higher scoring rate and concede fewer goals when competing against teams from lower altitudes. Moreover, he found that for every additional 1000 m of altitude difference the goal difference is increased by about 0.5 goals.

---

4 Only 9 in 1990 and 1998 due to Argentina and Brazil, respectively, winning the previous WC, therefore gaining an automatic bid the next year. Only 9 in 1994 due to Chile being banned that tournament by FIFA. And only 9 in 2014 due to Brazil hosting the World Cup.

5 The World Football Elo Ratings depend on results of previous matches weighted on strength of team (see eloratings.net). These ratings have been widely used in academic research.

FIFA Men's World Cup Finals

The FIFA World Cup tournament began in 1930 and the format and scheduling of the Finals have changed many times throughout the history of the mega-event. This section discusses the format and schedule of the Finals with a special emphasis on the upcoming Finals in 2022 and 2026, followed by an overview of the seeding and draw systems examining how teams have historically been allocated into World Cup groups.

Format and Schedule

Thirteen nations participated in the inaugural FIFA World Cup in Uruguay 1930. For decades, nations outside of South America and Europe hardly participated in the tournament. Consequently, up until 1982, only 16 nations participated in the Finals. After this, however, the Finals expanded continuously to 24 teams (since 1986), 32 teams (since 1998) and 48 teams (in 2026).

The 1950 FIFA World Cup and every tournament thereafter has featured a group stage format in the first round. Although varying in number of groups (four groups of four from 1950 to 1978, six groups of four from 1982 to 1994, eight groups of four from 1998 to 2022), one thing remains common; each group plays in a single round-robin style tournament in the first stage. The last matches for each group are played simultaneously to prevent any possible collusion. However, although there might not necessarily be collusion, there are still some concerns about the fairness of this design.

Using data on all group stages from FIFA World Cups and UEFA EUROs from 1996 to 2014 and implementing propensity score matching to approximate random assignments, Krumer and Lechner (2017) found that a team playing in the first match of each round has a higher probability of qualifying for the following round. This scheduling type, on average, has a 17%-point effect on qualifying probability. In line with this, Krumer, Megidish and Sela (2017) found that a team competing in the first and third matches has the highest probability to win the entire round-robin tournament. Therefore, round-robin tournaments, specifically single round-robin tournaments, are considered intrinsically unfair for teams who do not participate in the first match of the group.

The distortion could be even greater for the 2026 FIFA World Cup with 16 groups of three teams, leading to potential collusion and an increased number of non-competitive games (Belam, 2018; Truta, 2018). Guyon (2019) addresses several fairness issues that arise from groups of three, including match fixing and imbalanced schedules. Overall, he concludes that the risk of collusion in at least one of the 16 groups is substantially high.

Krumer and Lechner (2017) discuss possible solutions of reducing tournament design and match scheduling effects on game outcome, especially in single round-robin tournaments. First, there should not be groups of odd numbers. Second, all games in a group stage should be played simultaneously. Likewise, Jian et al. (2017) provide evidence from an experimental study that simultaneous games are superior to sequential ones with regard to effort provision by each team, or efficiency. Therefore, a tournament design with simultaneous games, rather than sequential, where contestants have no information on other games in the group can mitigate the underlying scheduling effects of round-robin tournament structure. However, this could have a considerable impact on the broadcasting market with regard to the allocation of TV rights as well as the revenues generated by FIFA and broadcasters. For instance, Schreyer et al. (2017) report substantial substitution effects on the demand for games of the German national team when an alternative tournament game is scheduled concurrently.

Seeding and Draw

Up to the 2006 World Cup in Germany, the top seven ranked teams (according to a combination of their FIFA World Ranking and the team's performance in the last Finals) were seeded along with the host country into different groups. The remaining teams were drawn randomly from different pots ensuring geographic separation; aiming to have the minimum number of teams from the same confederation in the same group (Cea et al., 2020). The seeding and draw for the 2010 and the 2014 FIFA World Cup remained practically the same, besides that the past performance was only measured by the FIFA world rankings at the time of the draw, that is, eight months prior to the Finals (Cea et al., 2020).

Seeding policy relating to the draw can influence CB and uncertainty of outcome. Monks and Husch (2009) calculate that being one of these top eight seeded teams increases the nations probability of making the quarterfinals by 26%. Using two empirical models, Paul and Mitra (2008) examine how seeding of teams can affect the element of uncertainty. Despite the number of surprise upsets from the lower ranked teams, Paul and Mitra (2008) find evidence that results are strongly in favour for the higher ranked teams. Scarf and Yusof (2011) reveal that seeding policy in the Finals does, in fact, favour the stronger competitors in the tournament.

According to Guyon (2015), the main source imbalances stem from the enforced geographic constraints implemented to the Finals draw since some nations have a higher probability of ending up in a tougher group than others. Likewise, following Jones (1990), Rathgeber and Rathgeber (2007) and Guyon (2015), problems occurred for the 1990, 2006 and 2014 World Cups due to FIFA pre-allocating certain teams into groups. The pre-allocation while insisting that no South American unseeded teams be in the same group as seeded South American teams caused FIFA to enforce a group skipping policy, ultimately leading to overall distribution bias.

Guyon (2015) derives three simple suggestions to tackle these issues, that is, (i) to build the draw pots by level, (ii) to add an S-Curve constraint and (iii) to draw continents first and then the teams.[6] This would result in eight groups that are

6 An S-Curve, commonly used for the NCAA Basketball tournament, is implemented, and gets its name from "snaking" through seeding lists of teams based on groupings. In Guyon's suggested format, the S-Curve is imposed by creating eight pots of four by levels, where certain pots can be drawn against other specified pots. Example from Guyon's S-curve, Pot 1 would be drawn against pots 4, 5 and 8 only.

balanced for all teams, gives equal likeness to all outcomes, and facilitates geographically diverse groups.

Cea et al. (2020) also outlines issues with the Final draws that were used between 2006 and 2018. The authors detail a series of deficiencies including international friendlies, point depreciation and scheduling, and match result points. Since there is not a mandatory number of international friendlies each nation must participate in, there is a disadvantage for lower ranked teams. In some cases, if teams did not participate in as many international friendlies, they could have had a better seeding in the draw. Some higher ranked teams take advantage of this and do not play many friendlies in fear of losing and lowering their rank.

Regarding point depreciation and scheduling, Cea et al. (2020) outlines how cup games are worth more than friendlies, but since tournaments are played on different schedules for different confederations, the points earned in those cups matches depreciate differently. Thus, favouring countries whose confederations schedules cup matches closer to the Finals. Moreover, there might be disproportionate point differences in regard to the opponent's rank. For example, according to Cea et al. (2020), a draw in a friendly against a top-ranked team earns a maximum of 200 points toward rankings, however, a win against the 100th ranked team in the world could gain up to 255 points. As a consequence, Cea et al. (2020) proposes modified FIFA World Rankings by using a mixed integer linear programming model to balance out the difficulty levels of each group. His proposal and model suggest including home and away factor and omitting confederation strength, eliminating friendly matches, changing the number of points awarded for a win, and then omitting point depreciation by year.

FIFA Women's World Cup Qualifiers

With only eight different qualification tournaments having taken place so far, ever since the inaugural 1991 FIFA Women's World Cup Qualifiers, the qualification process for the Women's World Cup is relatively simpler than that of the Men's. However, both the number of eligible teams across confederations (49 in 1991 and 143 in 2019) and the number of spots in the Finals (12 in 1991 and 24 in 2019) tripled and doubled, respectively, signifying the rapid development of the competition and the closing of the gap between Women's and Men's football. Each of FIFA's six confederations determine their own qualification system to produce their rightful number of nations for the Final. This section will briefly discuss the qualifying formats for each confederation.

Africa (CAF)

The qualification process in CAF is determined by the African Women's Championship. This competition has witnessed a significant increase in the number of eligible nations (8 in 1991 and 24 in 2019) and in the number of representatives in the Finals (1 in 1991 and 3 in 2019). Similar to the Men's competition, however, and given the geopolitical and economic conditions in the continent, several nations withdrew their participation during the qualification phase (e.g., Congo, Senegal, Zambia and Zimbabwe in 1991).

Since the 1998 edition, the tournament remained fairly stable, with the qualification being staged as KO. The teams qualified in the African Women's Championship then compete in the first stage of the competition in groups with the two best placed teams of each group proceeding to the KO stage. The teams which succeed to participate in the finals, as well as the team winning the third-place playoff represent the continent in the Finals.

Asia (AFC)

The qualification process in Asia is determined by the AFC Women's Championship. Similar to all women's competitions, this competition has witnessed a significant increase in the number of eligible nations (9 in 1991 and 24 in 2018) and in the number of representatives in the World Cup Finals (3 in 1991 and 5 in 2019).

Since the 2006 edition and with the increase in the number of eligible nations, the entering to the tournament is decided upon a qualification phase. Identical to CAF the teams qualified in the AFC Women's Championship compete in the first stage of the competition in groups with the two best placed teams of each group proceeding to the KO stage. The four teams reaching the semi-finals, as well as the team winning the fifth-place playoff represent the continent in the Finals.

Europe (UEFA)

In contrast to the other five confederations, which use tournaments that double as the World Cup Qualification process, since 1999, UEFA organises a separate tournament designed specifically for the World Cup Qualification. Since the first edition of this tournament, UEFA has staged the highest number of eligible nations (18 in 1991 and 46 in 2017) among all confederations, therefore, it is not surprising to also have the most representatives in the Finals (5 in 1991 and 8 in 2019).

In contrast to the respective Men's competition of UEFA, the competition design of the women's' Qualifiers has undergone many changes. The most notable was the separation of teams between two different classes (class A and class B based on strength) in the 1999, 2003 and 2007 editions. In both classes, there was a group stage with the group winners of class A securing a spot in the Finals (in 1999 and 2003 also the second-placed teams could qualify through an extra play-off round). The group winners of class B played against the bottom placed teams of class A to decide promotion and relegation without having the opportunity to fight for a spot in the Finals.

From the 2011 edition onwards, UEFA cancelled the separation of teams into classes, following a format that resembles the Men's competition. In 2011, all eligible nations were drawn into groups, with group winners advancing to the play-off stage. The winners of the play-off stage advanced directly, while the play-off losers played KO rounds to determine a nation to play-off with the third-placed CONCACAF nation for a finals place. In the 2015 and 2019 tournament, the UEFA introduced a preliminary round to the qualifiers with the lowest ranked teams of the confederation (8 in 2015 and 16 in 2019) competing in groups and the best placed teams (two best placed in 2015; group winners and best second-placed in 2019) advancing to the Qualifiers.

North and Central America and Caribbean (CONCACAF)

The qualification process in North and Central America and Caribbean is determined by the CONCACAF Women's Championship (also known as Women's Gold Cup); besides in 1993 and 2000 when a separate tournament determined Final representatives. This competition has witnessed a significant increase in the number of eligible nations (8 in 1991; 30 in 2018) and in the number of representatives in the Finals (1 in 1991; 3.5 in 2019).

A separate qualification phase in three regions, North American, Central America and Caribbean determine the nations whom can compete in the CONCACAF Women's Championship. Identical to CAF and AFC, the eight teams (five in 1994 and six in 2006) qualified in the CONCACAF Women's Championship compete in the first stage of the competition in groups with the two best placed teams of each group proceeding to the KO stage.

Having an additional 0.5 spot from 1999 to 2019, second/third or fourth-placed CONCACAF nations had the opportunity to compete with their counterparts from the AFC (2003, 2007), the UEFA (2011) and CONMEBOL (1999, 2015, 2019) in inter-continental play-offs to secure a further spot in the Finals.

Oceania (OFC)

The Oceania Women's Nations Cup has served as the qualifying tournament for the Finals since conception in 1991. Ever since, the tournament has been inconsistent in number of competing teams; ranging from three in 1991 and 1994 to eight in 2018 and changing every year in between.[7]

OFC has also been inconsistent in the intervals of the Qualifiers; typically, the Qualifier is held quadrennially, however, there was a 5-year gap between 1998 and 2003, then only a three-year wait between 2007 and 2010. One consistency in the confederation, though, is the allocated representatives for the Final being one team from 1991 to 2018. As New Zealand is co-host in 2023, OFC will not have a qualifying tournament, as no other team can represent the confederation. In 1998, 2010 and 2018 the Oceania Women's Nations Cup followed a similar format like CAF, AFC and CONCACAF with the first stage being a group stage with the top

7 The inconsistency every year is as follows: three teams in 1991 and 1994, six teams in 1998, five teams in 2003, four teams in 2007, eight teams in 2010, four teams in 2014, eight teams in 2018.

two teams in each group qualifying for the second stage KO rounds. In all other years, however, OFC implemented a single round-robin tournament to determine the Final representative.

South America (CONMEBOL)

In South America, the Campeonato Sudamericano de Fútbol Femenino (South American Women's Football Championship) doubles as Qualifiers for the women's national teams of CONMEBOL. First being held in 1991, the initial two editions only had three and five teams, respectively, competing for one allocated spot in the Finals.

Since 1998 and staying consistent through the present tournament, similar to the Men's competition, all ten CONMEBOL nations compete in the South American Championship. In the 1998 edition, the runners-up of the CONMEBOL and CONCACAF qualification tournament competed in KO games for an additional spot in Finals. In the 2003, 2006 and 2010 editions of the tournament, CONMEBOL was allocated two representatives in the Finals, meaning the winner and runner-up of the tournament would advance. In the 2014 and 2018 editions, CONMEBOL nations were fighting for 2.5 spots, that is the third-placed team competed with the fourth-placed team from CONCACAF for an additional World Cup spot. Beginning in 2023, the confederation has three guaranteed representatives for the Final. As with the other confederations, besides UEFA, the first stage of their Qualifiers is a group stage, with the top two teams in each group advancing to KO stages.

Inter-confederation play-off

For the 2023 edition of the Finals, FIFA decided to expand the number of nations from 24 to 32. These eight additional nations are distributed as follows: plus three nations UEFA (total 11), plus one nation CAF (total 4), plus 0.5 nations CONMEBOL (total 3) and CONCACAF (total 4), while AFC remained at five plus Australia (host) and OFC is represented only by New Zealand (host). For the remaining three spots in the Finals, FIFA will implement for the first time an inter-confederation play-off as an additional qualifying route. In this competition, ten different nations from all six confederations (two from AFC, CAF, CONCACAF and CONMEBOL, one from OFC and UEFA) will compete in three groups, with the group winners advancing to the Finals. The selection criteria for the ten participants are still to be decided for five out of six confederations. UEFA, however, already decided to be represented in this competition by the team with worst combined record out of the four play-off winners (the other three secure directly a spot in the Finals).

FIFA Women's World Cup Finals

The FIFA Women's World Cup had its opening tournament in 1991 and has been played every four years since. A total of eight Finals have been played with the number participating nations growing three separate times (12 in 1991–1995, 16 in 1999–2011 and 24 in 2015–2019) and extending again in the upcoming Finals (32 in 2023). Format wise, the Women's Final is set up identical to the Men's with the first round consisting of a group stage of four teams per group and with more or less the same concerns regarding scheduling, seeding and draw flaws as discussed in the Men's section.

In years with 12 competing nations, the group winners and runners-up as well as the two best third-place teams would advance to the KO round. Tournaments with 16 teams had the group winner and runner-up of each group advance to the eight team KO rounds. Since 2015, with 24 nations competing, the two top teams in each group along with the four best third-place teams advance to the final 16 team KO stage.

The 2019 Finals seeding, and draw are identical to the 2018 Men's World Cup. Teams are allocated into four separate pots, with pot one including the host and the top-ranked teams, followed by pot two with the next best ranked teams. This is continued until all teams are in their designated pot. The rankings are solely based off the prior year's FIFA World Rankings.

Comparatively speaking to the Men's Finals, research on the Women's Finals is very limited. de Araújo and Mießen (2017) investigate the evolution of CB by comparing goal differences from the 1991 Final to the 2011 Final. The percentage of matches with a goal difference of more than three in the 1991 Finals was about 30% and only 6% in 2011. This improvement of CB over time could be ascribed to the players physical capacity growing (Krustrup et al., 2005) and the performance levels increasing (Mohr et al., 2008). Scelles (2021) goes a step further and examines how policy, political and economic determinants affected the evolution of CB in the Finals. Using data up to the 2019 edition, he confirms that CB has increased over time. Scelles (2021) argues that this is attributed to the growing participation of women in the sport which translates into an overall better quality for the different nations competing. The substantial rise of female athletes' participation in football is related to the different (sport) policies and politics across countries. Indeed, examining the determinants of goal difference between competing nations in the last eight tournaments (Scelles,2021) reports that nations performing better are those which implemented gender equality policies earlier, are well-populated, wealthier, have a successful men's national team and a higher number of expatriate players.

Conclusion

The overarching goal of the World Cup is to identify and celebrate the best team in the world. For this to be successful, competition design is of utmost importance. Hereof, this chapter examined the historical evolution of the structure, organisation, and format of the Men's and Women's FIFA World Cup Finals and Qualifiers.

With each of the six confederations, for both men and women, organising their own Qualifiers, it can be observed that competition designs are more susceptible to changes in less developed (in terms of football) continents. The Qualifiers underwent several modifications throughout the years to facilitate both the increasing number of eligible nations and spots for the Finals. With all confederations being concerned with finding the most fair and balanced competition design, CONMEBOL, seems to be particularly successful with recently adapting a computational scheduling.

For the Finals, researchers and scholars have raised concerns, as well as offered plausible solutions, on the matter of seeding and draw policy, as well as on inherent flaws of (single) round-robin tournaments. With the everchanging environment of football (e.g., the formation of new competitions such as the UEFA Nations League) and the growing knowledge and concerns of researchers and scholars, structure, format, and organisation will continue to adapt and adjust. Both FIFA and the confederations seem to be open to suggestions, as such researchers and scholars are advised to continue scrutinising the existing formats and suggest alternatives to promote fairness and competition in the king of all sports.

References

Armatas, V. & Pollard, R. (2014) Home Advantage in Greek Football, *European Journal of Sport Science*, 14(2), 116–122.

Belam, M. (2018) *Three hosts, 48 teams: How the 2026 World Cup will work.* [online]. The Guardian. Available at: https://www.theguardian.com/football/2018/jun/13/three-hosts-48-teams-how-the-2026-world-cup-will-work-united [Accessed 28 December 2020].

Cea, S., Durán, G., Guajardo, M., Sauré, D., Siebert, J. & Zamorano, G. (2020). An Analytics Approach to the FIFA Ranking Procedure and the World Cup Final Draw. *Annals of Operations Research*, 286(1-2), 119–146.

Csato, L. (2019) The Incentive (in) Compatibility of Group-based Qualification Systems, *International Journal of General Systems*, 49(4), 374–399.

Csato, L. (2021a) Quantifying the Unfairness of the 2018 FIFA World Cup Qualification. *arXiv preprint arXiv:2007.03412.*

Csato, L. (2021b) Fair Tournament Design: A Flaw of the UEFA Euro 2020 Qualification, *arXiv preprint arXiv:1905.03325.*

Dagaev, D. & Sonin, K. (2018) Winning by Losing: Incentive Incompatibility in Multiple Qualifiers, *Journal of Sports Economics*, 19(8), 1122–1146.

de Araújo, M.C. & Mießen, K.A. (2017) Twenty Years of the FIFA Women's World Cup: An Outstanding Evolution of Competitiveness, *Women in Sport and Physical Activity Journal*, 25(1), 60–64.

Duran, G., Guajardo, M. & Saure, D. (2017) Scheduling the South American Qualifiers to the 2018 FIFA World Cup by Integer Programming, *European Journal of Operational Research*, 262(3), 1109–1115.

Duran, G., Guajardo, M. & Saure, D. (2018) From O.R. to the World Cup Russia (With Love), *Impact*, 3(2), 7–12.

FIFA (2018) *Organising Committee takes important decisions on FIFA Women's World Cup*, viewed 28 March 2021, Available at: https://www.fifa.com/womensworldcup/news/organising- committee-takes-important-decisions-on-fifa-women-s-world-cup

Gasparetto, T. & Barajas, A. (2018) Leagues, tournaments, and competitions. In Chadwick, S., Parnell, D., Widdop, P., & Anagnostopoulos, C. (eds.), *Routledge Handbook of Football Business and Management.* London, UK: Routledge.

Guyon, J. (2019) Risk of Collusion: Will Groups of 3 Ruin the FIFA World Cup? *Journal of Sports Analytics*, 6(4), 259–279.

Guyon, J. (2015) Rethinking the FIFA World Cup Final Draw, *Journal of Quantitative Analysis in Sports*, 11(3), 169–182.

Haugen, K.K. & Krumer, A. (2021) On the importance of tournament design in sports management: Evidence from the UEFA Euro 2020 qualification. In Ratten, V. (eds.), *Innovation and Entrepreneurship in Sport Management.* Edward Elgar Publishing.

Jian, L., Li, Z. & Liu, T.X. (2017) Simultaneous Versus Sequential All-Pay Auctions: An Experimental Study, *Experimental Economics*, 20(3), 648–669.

Jones, M.C. (1990) The World Cup Draw's Flaws, *The Mathematical Gazette*, 74(470), 335–338.

Krumer, A. & Lechner, M. (2017) First in First Win: Evidence on Schedule Effects in Round Robin Tournaments in Mega-Events, *European Economic Review*, 100, 412–427.

Krumer, A., Megidish, R. & Sela, A. (2017) First-mover advantage in round-robin tournaments, *Social Choice and Welfare*, 48(3), 633–658.

Krustrup, P., Mohr, M., Ellingsgaard, H. & Bangsbo, J. (2005) Physical demands during an elite female soccer game: importance of training status, *Medicine and Science in Sports and exercise*, 37(7), 1242–1248.

McSharry, P.E. (2007) Effect of Altitude on Physiological Performance: A Statistical Analysis Using Results of International Football Games, *British Medical Journal*, 335(7633), 1278–1281.

Mohr, M., Krustrup, P., Andersson, H., Kirkendal, D. & Bangsbo, J. (2008) Match Activities of Elite Women Soccer Players at Different Performance Levels, *The Journal of Strength and Conditioning Research*, 22(2), 341–349.

Monks, J. & Husch, J. (2009) The Impact of Seeding, Home Continent, and Hosting on FIFA World Cup Results, *Journal of Sports Economics*, 10(4), 391–408.

Paul, S. & Mitra, R. (2008) How Predictable Are the FIFA World Cup football Outcomes? An Empirical Analysis, *Applied Economics Letters*, 15(15), 1171–1176.

Pollard, R. & Armatas, V. (2017) Factors Affecting Home Advantage in Football World Cup Qualification. *International Journal of Performance Analysis in Sport*, 17(1-2), 121–135.

Pollard, R. & Gómez, M.A. (2014) Components of Home Advantage in 157 National Soccer Leagues Worldwide, *International Journal of Sport and Exercise Psychology*, 12(3), 218–233.

Ponzo, M. & Scoppa, V. (2018) Does the Home Advantage Depend on Crowd Support? Evidence from Same-Stadium Derbies, *Journal of Sports Economics*, 19(4), 562–582.

Rathgeber, A. & Rathgeber, H. (2007) Why Germany Was Supposed to be Drawn in the Group of Death and Why It Escaped?, *Chance*, 20(2), 22–24.

Scarf, P.A. & Yusof, M.M. (2011) A Numerical Study of Tournament Structure and Seeding Policy for the Soccer World Cup Finals, *Statistica Neerlandica*, 65(1), 43–57.

Scelles, N. (2021) Policy, Political and Economic Determinants of the Evolution of Competitive Balance in the FIFA Women's Football World Cups, *International Journal of Sport Policy and Politics*, 13(2), 281–297.

Schreyer, D., Schmidt, S.L. & Torgler, B. (2017) Game Outcome Uncertainty and the Demand for International Football Games: Evidence from the German TV Market, *Journal of Media Economics*, 30(1), 31–45.

Stone, C. & Rod, M. (2016) Unfair Play in World Cup Qualification? An Analysis of the 1998-2010 FIFA World Cup Performances and the Bias in the Allocation of Tournament Berths, *Soccer and Society*, 17(1), 40–57.

Truta, T.M. (2018) FIFA Does It Right: 2026 FIFA World Cup Does Not Increase the Number of Non-competitive Matches, *arXiv preprint arXiv*:1808.*05858*

Vong, A.I. (2017) Strategic Manipulation in Tournament Games, *Games and Economic Behavior*, 102, 562–567.

7

AN INTEGRITY SYSTEM FRAMEWORK FOR THE FIFA WORLD CUPS

Géraldine Zeimers and Bram Constandt

Introduction

Integrity has been a long-standing issue for many international sports bodies (Pielke, 2016). FIFA, the international governing body of world football, represents no exception. For many commentators, FIFA has regularly indicated a lack of ethical and good governance practices over its past (Bason et al., 2018; Tomlinson, 2014). For instance, FIFA only introduced a code of ethics for the first time in 2004 and an independent ethical committee in 2006 after controversies with the company International Sport and Leisure (Bayle and Rayner, 2018; Tomlinson, 2014). In comparison, the IOC, forced by the Salt Lake City scandal, adopted substantial governance reforms in 1999 by setting up an ethics commission, drawing up a code of ethics to sanction unacceptable behaviours, limiting terms of office and stakeholders' representation (Chappelet, 2016). This led (Tomlinson, 2014, p. 1161) to note that "ethical issues have been peripheral to FIFA's concerns for most of its history" and "the culture of corruption and personal gain has long been endemic in the FIFA 'family" (p. 1162).

Throughout its history, FIFA has frequently been beset by allegations of corruption and flawed governance (Bayle and Rayner, 2018; Beans, 2018). The spotlight has been particularly strong on (the selection process regarding) the hosting of the World Cup, with allegations of bribery for the 2006 World Cup in Germany (Spiegel, 2016), the 2010 World Cup in South Africa (Harding, 2015), the 2014 World Cup in Brazil (Chade, 2017), and allegations of vote rigging in relation to the stunning double selection of Russia and Qatar to host the 2018 and 2022 World Cups in 2010 (Beans, 2018; Becker, 2013). Several critiques were formulated at that time. FIFA rated Russia "medium risk" and Qatar "high risk." Qatar did not have a football culture and is characterised by extreme weather conditions. Since 1984 the country selected to host the World Cup was

DOI: 10.4324/9781003121794-7

announced six years in advance. The bidding process was changed to jointly award both the 2018 and the 2022 World Cups for the 2010 occasion (Beans, 2018).

After the maelstrom generated by this double attribution, FIFA President Sepp Blatter adopted a first wave of "cosmetic reforms" toward more transparency and accountability (Beans, 2018). Between 2011 and 2014, FIFA commissioned governance evaluations with Pieth's "Governing FIFA" report (Pieth, 2011), Transparency International's "Safe Hands" Report (Schenk, 2011), and new Independent Governance Committee's reports recommending various governance changes. In the end, only a few proposals were accepted and implemented by FIFA and its continental confederations (Beans, 2018; Pielke, 2013). The appointment of Michael Garcia as the independent Chair of the Investigative Chamber of the remodelled Ethics Committee was one of them. In 2013 and 2014, Garcia investigated the selection of Russia and Qatar as World Cup hosts. FIFA initially refused to publish his report that revealed serious violations of bidding rules and the FIFA code of ethics. Six months after Garcia resignation, the so-called FIFAgate broke out. In 2015, FIFAgate culminated in the United States and Swiss criminal investigations which focused on allegations of corruption of media and marketing rights and vote trading when it comes to the 2018 and 2022 World Cups. These investigations caused the indictment and the arrest of leading officials for charges of racketeering, wire fraud conspiracies, money laundering conspiracies and bribery, the banning of its President and Secretary General, and major sponsors withdrawing their support (BBC, 2016, 2020; Beans, 2018; Cottle, 2019; Richau et al., 2019; Tomlinson, 2014).

In the aftermath of FIFAgate, FIFA adopted a second wave of substantial governance reforms recommended by the 2016 FIFA Reform Committee (Carrard, 2015) and elected Gianni Infantino as President. Notable governance changes included the separation of the governance (i.e., FIFA Council) and management (i.e., General Secretariat) roles, the adoption of FIFA statutes encompassing the commitment to good governance principles and human rights, a new code of conduct, the revision of its code of ethics (by the 68th FIFA Congress in June 2018), enhanced control and disclosure of development funds, confidential reporting mechanisms, FIFA Congress to vote on the award of the World Cup, salary disclosure, limit on president's term, revised presidency electoral regulation, enhanced eligibility, integrity checks, women representation in leadership positions, Football Stakeholder Committee, the creation of an independent Human Rights Advisory Board, with experts from the UN, trade unions, civil society and business partners, and the creation of the FIFA Integrity Department (FIFA Integrity) and related integrity programmes (FIFA, 2016, 2019).[1] These reforms implemented between 2016 and 2018 impacted the governance of bidding for and hosting World Cup tournaments. FIFA explicitly reported its intention to "build a

1 For a discussion of these reforms, please see (Bason et al. 2018).

stronger institution" with "no room for doubt" and pledged that "the selection of the host of the FIFA World Cup is no longer a synonym of scandal" (FIFA, 2019).

Despite these changes, recent scandals have continued to put FIFA's integrity and legitimacy into question [see e.g., (Constandt and Willem, 2021) about FIFA's code of ethics and (Richau et al., 2019) about FIFA's leadership legitimacy]. The 2018 World Cup was described as "sportswashing event" (The Guardian 2021) and FIFA admitted human rights abuses (Conn, 2017). In 2019, the Swiss authorities opened criminal proceedings against FIFA's President, Gianni Infantino, the man charged with restoring FIFA's reputation, over a secret meeting between Infantino and the former Swiss Attorney General Michael Lauber held in 2017 while Lauber investigated FIFA's alleged corruption. This meeting fuelled suspicions of collusion and is investigated on the grounds of breaching official secrecy, assisting offenders, indictment to break the law, and abuse of public office (Bonesteel, 2020). FIFA's Ethics Committee's decided to maintain Infantino despite several concerns raised by the ongoing investigation. The Committee justified its ruling on the basis that FIFA's code of ethics had not been violated and that some accusations towards Infantino were not covered by the provisions of the code (BBC, 2020; Constandt and Willem, 2021). Another voiced criticism was that the Committee applied a "double standard" as the same Committee had temporarily banned Sepp Blatter when the Swiss authorities opened a criminal investigation against him in 2015 (Dupré 2020). For (Richau et al., 2019, p. 1), "whether the way FIFA operates has changed since the election of its new president is questionable".

In addition to the above, deplorable labour conditions infringing workers safety, labour law and human rights provisions have been reported repeatedly regarding the situation in Qatar (Cohen, 2013; Kelly et al., 2019; Pattisson 2020). Following another article published by The Guardian stating that at least 6,500 migrant workers had died since Qatar won the bid (The Guardian, 2021a), the football world has started to speak up, later followed by more political and business actors. While these accusations were dismissed by the Qatari World Cup organiser, the Supreme Committee for Delivery and Legacy (SC) (The Guardian, 2021b), a Dutch company eventually refused to work for the 2022 World Cup (Courrier International, 2021). Ahead of the first round of World Cup qualifier matches in early 2021, national teams and FA's from Norway, Germany, the Netherlands, Denmark, and Belgium have protested against the working conditions and human rights in Qatar. For Stale Solbakken, Norway's manager, "It's about putting pressure on FIFA to be even more direct, even firmer with the authorities in Qatar, to impose stricter requirements" (Euronews, 2021). While the decision to boycott the tournament by some FA's and governments remain improbable, these events have shown that FIFA's stakeholders can make their "contribution to efforts to improve the plight of migrant workers in Qatar" (The Guardian, 2021b).

The aforementioned events are threats to the integrity of football and undermine FIFA's claims to act for the global public good (Tomlinson, 2014). These events are under a constant global scrutiny due to the exhaustive media coverage of the ongoing scandals. Furthermore, these scandals have eroded the public's trust in FIFA and in the bidding for and the hosting of World Cups (Hölzen and Meier, 2019; Pielke, 2016; Richau et al., 2019). As observed by Chris Graid in 2016:

> These [scandals] could have been avoided, or mitigated, by a more robust governance regime. It would appear that the checks and balances that have been in place at FIFA's management level have failed to appropriately regulate an organisation whose power and influence has multiplied exponentially as the commercialisation and globalisation of football continues to grow.

There are many reasons driving member associations to host the World Cup. The immense economic, industrial, commercial, political, and social interests at stake and FIFA's recent history and failures to prevent and convincingly deal with scandals have called upon transparent bidding and hosting processes and more generally appropriate governance responses in order to install a culture of integrity at FIFA and restore trust (Gardiner et al., 2017; Kihl, 2020).

In light of this background, the purpose of this chapter is to examine how the processes of bidding for and hosting of World Cup tournaments is governed. This will be underpinned by an analysis of ethical practices in both organisation and governance, as well as by focusing on the recent attempts to improve ethical standards applied to tournament decisions. Acknowledging the definitional ambiguity and the breadth of the constructs of governance, corruption, and ethics, we considered it is appropriate to synthetise these complementary constructs under the notion of integrity. This chapter uses – and argues the utility of applying – the lens of a sport integrity system framework as conceptualised by (Kihl, 2020) as a relevant governance approach to analyse FIFA's governance and integrity reforms. This chapter employs this framework to offer a number of critical points to take into consideration for future governance and integrity-enhancing initiatives in FIFA.

Governance and Integrity

The concepts of (good) governance, ethics and integrity are sometimes used interchangeably by academics as well as throughout the sport industry (Vanden Auweele et al., 2016). It is not within the remit of this chapter to analyse the synergies and the contradictions between these terms.[2] However, after defining and locating the concepts of sport event governance and good governance in the

2 Readers in search for a conceptual discussion on the overlap and commonalities between these concepts are encouraged to look into the work of – among others – (Gardiner et al. 2017), (Kihl 2020), (McNamee and Fleming 2007), and (Vanden Auweele et al. 2016).

literature, integrity is introduced and will be used throughout the present chapter to encapsulate a broader and holistic governance approach.

Sport Event Governance

Although governance has incrementally become part of the common vocabulary in sport organisations (Chappelet, 2016), an agreed definition remains elusive (Dowling et al., 2018; Parent, 2016). Henry and Lee categorised sport governance studies into three approaches (i.e., organisational, systemic or political) to illustrate that governance "is not simply about direction, management and power in the context of a single organisational form but also about the direction, management and power across an intricate multi-level network of organisations" (Pielke et al., 2020, p. 484).

Sport event governance explores the structures, ownership models, processes, stakeholders, and institutional dimensions of the given sport event (Leopkey and Parent, 2019). The majority of existing sport event governance research has investigated large and mega sports events, with a strong focus on the Olympic Movement (Dowling et al., 2018). Sport event governance focuses on both the governance of sport organisations and partners as well as on the governance of the sport event per se. In their sport governance review, Dowling et al. (2018) observed little attention paid to the organisational and political forms of sport event governance. The governance process of major event organising committee involves three modes: planning, implementation and wrap-up (Parent, 2016). Prior to that, the bid and transition are two important stages of the overall sport event governance process. Major sport events are a complex governance system surrounded by internal and external stakeholders influencing the work done by the organising committee and vice versa (Geeraert, 2017; Parent, 2016). These stakeholders include the event owners (e.g., the international sport federation), government bodies (local, regional, national government) and other-event-related stakeholders such as sponsors, media and the community (Parent, 2016). The host governments and the LOC should "ideally act in the ISO's [International Sport Organization] best interests, yet conflicting interests and information asymmetries give rise to agency problems" (Geeraert 2017, p. 27).

The governance debate is prescriptive, hence the global quest for "good governance" (Geeraert et al., 2014) and the considerable number of good governance codes, principles, and tools published (for a review see Parent and Hoye, 2018). Transparency, democracy, accountability, and social responsibility (also called integrity) are the four main principles consistently promoted across those codes (Chappelet, 2016; Geeraert, 2018; McLeod et al., 2021). Sport scholars have considered corruption as a symptom of widespread system failures in governance (i.e., systemic governance) (Dowling et al., 2018). In that regard, Geeraert et al. (2014) observed that "complying with good governance is also a means for making sure that an INGSO [International Non-Governmental Sport Organisations] is capable of steering its sport in an increasingly complex sporting world" (p. 283).

These principles apply just as much to sport event stakeholders as it does to international sport organisations owning the sport event. Despite the increased scrutiny by the media, the general public, and other stakeholders on sport event governance (Parent, 2016), limited studies have analysed this issue and specific sport event governance principles have not yet been proposed. Geeraert (2017) pointed that conflicts of interest and information asymmetries between principle and agent affected the event governance.

In this context, this chapter analyses both the governance of organisations involved as stakeholders in sport event hosting [e.g., FIFA and the Local Organising Committee (LOC)] and the governance of the sporting event (i.e., the governance of the FIFA World Cup). Leopkey and Parent (2020) noted little existing knowledge about the FIFA World Cup (beyond the event owner itself) in terms how the event is governed. We therefore aim to provide a better understanding in this regard.

The governance of FIFA

Various governance reports have been conducted to evaluate international sport governing bodies, described earlier as one of the key stakeholders in terms of sport event hosting. There is a small pool of research conducted on the governance of FIFA (Geeraert et al., 2014; Geeraert, 2017; Pielke, 2013; Tomlinson, 2014). For instance, (Geeraert et al., 2014) contended that international sport governing bodies (including FIFA) utilise flawed governance practices, which involved a lack of accountability, little transparency, a Eurocentric board leadership and a severe lack of female representation. The first Sport Governance Observer (SGO) report (Geeraert et al., 2015) "debunked the perception that FIFA's governance deficits are more severe than those of other international federations" (Geeraert, 2018, p. 6). In the second report, Geeraert (2018) observed that FIFA outperforms the other four surveyed international federations on good governance. "Yet although FIFA's scores reflect the positive impact of its most recent governance reforms, they also show that there is still room for improvement as they reveal a number of important deficits" (p. 26). These benchmarks demonstrated the need for governance improvements across international federations.

The governance of the FIFA World Cup

Like the IOC, when it comes to the Olympics (Leopkey and Parent, 2020), FIFA is the event owner of the World Cup tournaments [FIFA Club World Cup[3]; FIFA U20 World Cup; FIFA U17 World Cup; FIFA Woman World Cup; and FIFA

3 For the FIFA Club World Cup, another organisation is involved in the governance of the tournament in accordance with the FIFA regulations. The FIFA Organising Committee, appointed by the FIFA Council, is responsible for organising the World Cup (FIFA, 2020).

(Men) World Cup]. Each edition, FIFA appoints and delegates the hosting of the World Cup to an Organising Association (OA) (i.e., a national FA). The OA is responsible for the hosting and staging of the World Cup and sets up an LOC (FIFA 2017, 2018, 2019, 2020). The World Cup network also comprises host governments and local businesses. The bidding process is discussed first (but for more details see Chapter 3 in this *Handbook*), followed by the organisation process. Both processes entail different corruption risks (Zimbalist 2016).

The bidding process

Prior to 2016: To host the tournament, each interested nation (forming a bid committee) must submit a World Cup bid. Each bid committee needed to demonstrate how the country met and (ideally exceeded) FIFA's requirements for hosting the World Cup. For the first 12 World Cups, FIFA's Congress voted to determine which nation would host the World Cup. In 1966, it became the responsibility of the Executive Committee to vote (Becker, 2013). Although the voting criteria were imprecise, FIFA's requirements related to the presence of stadiums or the ability to build such stadiums in the host nation, stadium capacity and quality, and the potential to create a positive global change. No evaluation guidelines were specified. The votes took place in the form of a secret ballot; therefore, barring a leak or voluntary revealment (Becker, 2013).

This process reinforced "a pay to win mentality" and was highly criticised following the double attribution, with Becker (2013, p. 135) observing that "because of the large amounts of money surrounding the World Cup and FIFA's monopoly, it would behove FIFA to have strict and transparent standards in the bidding procedures. Unfortunately, under the current FIFA rules, such transparency is non-existent."

Post 2016: The revamped bidding process to select the hosts of the FIFA World Cup involved changes at four levels. First, *a transparent evaluation process*, with bid books, hosting requirements, bid evaluation reports and scores made public. Second, an *independent evaluation process* with a bid evaluation task force responsible for analysing the bids by delivering a bid evaluation report comprising the compliance, the risk (including adverse human rights impacts in connection with hosting the competition) and the technical assessment (involving infrastructure and commercial aspects), and an independent audit company acting as observer. Third, a *new open voting procedure* that puts the final decision in the hands of the 211 member associations at the FIFA Congress (as opposed to what was once a secret vote by the Executive Committee). Finally, *new bidding requirements* with a bid rules of conduct and the formal commitment to respect international human rights and labour standards according to the UN Guiding Principles by the bidders, a declaration of compliance to FIFA code of ethics, and the reporting of lobbying activities (FIFA, 2018; 2019). Despite these important regulatory changes which have already influenced the bidding process for the designation of the FIFA 2023 Women's World Cup and 2026 World Cup, more efforts could be made by considering integrity aspects – especially in relation to transparency – in the evaluation of the bid books.

The organisation process

Prior 2016: The organisation of the World Cup represents another opportunity for corruption which can arise from the capture of the host city by economic interests and reveals a lack of transparency. According to several studies, the 2010 and 2016 World Cup have particularly suffered from corruption behaviours such as in the awarding of contracts (Koval and Jvirblis, 2016; Müller, 2017; Zimbalist, 2016). As observed by Zimbalis (2016):

> In either democratic or authoritarian countries, the tendency is for event planning to hew closely to the interests of the local business elite. Construction companies, their unions (if there are any), insurance companies, architectural firms, media companies, investment bankers (who float the bonds), lawyers and perhaps some hotel or restaurant interests may get behind the Olympic or World Cup project. They stand to gain substantially from the massive public funding. Typically, these interests hijack the local organising committee, hire out an obliging consulting firm to perform an ersatz economic impact study, understate the costs, overstate the revenues and go on to procure political consent." (p. 202-203)

Analysing the 2018 World Cup in Russia, Koval and Jvirblis (2016) reported that the LOC only published the main official source on the preparation process using the FIFA website and Twitter account. They noted that

> Both sources focus on the news and very basic information on the stadiums and host cities. They do not provide documents or procedural or financial information on how the main actors are selected, nor do they provide information on how funds are allocated or spent, or even links to other sources containing this type of data. The sole annual report on the LOC's activities that is available on the FIFA website covers 2012 only.
>
> The report [from the Accounts Chamber of the Russian Federation] highlights overpricing, delays in construction and payments, conflicts over land rights, and non-delivery by subcontractors, and addresses governance-related problems, such as timely issuance of governmental decrees and the development of project evaluation methodologies (p. 225)

Post 2016: The reach of the reforms adopted to revise the governance of the World Cup seem to have less profoundly tackled the organising process. For the 2022 World Cup in Qatar, the abolition of the Kalifa system is explicitly presented by FIFA and the LOC as the legacy of the tournament (Qatar 2022a). Besides this achievement of which the actual implementation is at least doubtful according to *The Guardian*, other governance challenges remain such as the lack of in-depth information on the website [with a limited description of the management team and the board of the SC (Qatar 2022b), and the lack of a rotation system (Becker 2013)]. Moreover, the lack of transparency remains salient as reports disclosing comprehensive information about the budget, the use of public funding, the lobbying activities by companies, and more generally the preparation process are missing to diligently monitor these critical processes. Finally, in its effort "to safeguard the integrity of the process from the start to finish," FIFA stipulated that "the Bid Rules of Conduct continue to apply during the hosting phase, and FIFA reserves the right to terminate the hosting agreement if any unethical behaviour is detected" (FIFA 2018). The likelihood of FIFA using this statement remains uncertain. Despite the numerous critics directed toward Qatar, one could wonder if the legacy and the additional social responsibility initiatives (Zeimers et al., 2018) are sufficient to restore trust.

Integrity

Integrity[4] is commonly considered as the antithesis of corruption (Gardiner et al., 2017; Gardiner, 2018; Kihl, 2020). Integrity in sport "represents a range of moral values and norms that sport stakeholders and organisations should uphold in different contexts such as sporting and administrative behaviours, decision-making and governance systems" (Kihl, 2020, p. 397). The construct of integrity is used in this chapter for three main reasons. First, a conceptual one, as 'integrity' is a significantly under-theorised an under-conceptualised value within sport particularly in its use by a range of organisations fighting corruption in sport (Gardiner et al., 2017). Second, a practice based one. FIFA uses the construct of "integrity". In its policy document "Protect the Integrity of Football Practical Handbook for FIFA Member Associations" (FIFA n.a.), FIFA stated that:

> One of FIFA's core objectives is to protect the integrity of football. As stated in its Statutes, FIFA's objectives include "preventing all methods or practices, such as corruption, doping or match manipulation, which might jeopardise the integrity of matches, competitions, players, officials and member associations or give rise to abuse of association football.

Third and finally, governance and integrity management can both be viewed as means to enhance the integrity in and of sport on different levels (see e.g., Constandt, 2019; Gardiner et al., 2017). Sport integrity is a socially constructed, complex, and multifaceted concept that might relate to the integrity of people

4 In this chapter, the terms "integrity in sport" or "sport integrity" are used synonymously.

involved in sport (i.e., personal integrity), but also to the integrity of sport organisations (i.e., organisational integrity), sport competitions and events (i.e., procedural integrity), and the inherent integrity of sport itself (e.g., fair play) (Gardiner et al., 2017; Loyens et al., 2021).

This chapter includes viewpoints that mainly focus on the first three dimensions of sport integrity and argues that sport governance is an internal element of an overarching sport integrity system. Sport integrity violations encompass both corrupt and non-corrupt behaviours carried out by individuals, organisations and/or systems (Gardiner et al., 2017; Kihl, 2020). Integrity violations are generally facilitated through poor governance practices. These risks warrant an integrity system that can assist a sport organisation – in this case FIFA – in developing a coherent and consistent approach to create and maintain organisational integrity of FIFA itself, procedural integrity of their World Cup events, and the integrity of the sport competitions organised during these events.

Sport Integrity System Framework

Developing and sustaining a sound sport integrity system can be considered an important way of materialising integrity management intentions in sport organisations, which aims to both prevent and deal with integrity violations (Vanden Auweele, 2011). A successful sport integrity system involves both internal and external mechanisms that ensure integrity and accountability of and in a sport organisation (Kihl, 2020). Aiming to reach this goal, a sport integrity system consists of individuals, institutions, policies, practices, and agencies that contribute to safeguarding (public trust in) a sport organisation by mitigating integrity risks (Head et al., 2008; Huberts and Six, 2012; Kihl, 2020). More precisely, a sport integrity system "is responsible for monitoring, preventing and tackling integrity violations and minimising integrity risks. The central focus of an integrity system is outlining the elements and conditions necessary for preventing integrity violations and minimising integrity risks in governance and sports competitions" (Kihl, 2020, p. 400).

Drawing from the broader business ethics and integrity systems literature, Kihl (2020) outlines a sport integrity system framework comprised of three main components: (1) sport actors, (2) an internal environment and (3) an external environment, which reflect different but interrelated functions in terms of safeguarding integrity. The components of the sport integrity system framework outline the elements and conditions considered important for the integrity of a sport organisation and, in this context, of a sport event and the competitions organised during this event. After all, initially developed to be used in the context of national sport governing bodies, Kihl's (2020) sport integrity system framework can be applied to examine all kinds of sport organisations on different levels (e.g., local and regional). Hence, Kihl's (2020) framework is relevant for the purpose of this chapter because it is flexible to adapt to different contexts and types of sport organisations. We contend that this framework is thus also applicable to international sport organisations (e.g., FIFA) and sport events (e.g., World Cups).

Moreover, the framework offers a pertinent governance approach to ensure integrity in contrast to FIFA's widespread and long-standing corruption system and culture (Bayle and Rayner, 2018; Beans, 2018; Tomlinson, 2014; Pielke, 2020; Richau et al., 2018). Such governance approach that highlights the importance of a broad and holistic view on integrity is welcomed, as currently, "the governance of FIFA shows a narrow view of integrity" (Gardiner, 2018, p. 384).

Several reforms in relation to FIFA have been suggested by respected scholars and experts (e.g., Beans, 2018; Becker, 2013; Cottle, 2019). Nevertheless, current propositions have not adopted a systemic approach (Gardiner, 2018). Even in the face of reform, FIFA is still susceptible to more integrity violations due to "its own predominant control over internal reform, limitations for external review of its practices, and limited consequences for rule violations" (Cottle, 2019, p. 19). Instilling integrity through good governance practices is not sufficient and has revealed its limits. Creating an integrity system to achieve and sustain integrity of FIFA's World Cups represents a way for FIFA to take "responsibility for the representation of the 'self' and one's commitments" (Gardiner et al., 2017, p. 20). In the World Cup context, this means that FIFA, in collaboration with other stakeholders, should play a role in preventing integrity violations internally (in relation to e.g., its bidding process as well as its operations, employees, board members) and externally (when it comes to e.g., its organisation process and stakeholders including LOC, and respective confederations).

According to Kihl (2020, p. 405), "an effective system (consequence) should limit integrity breaches, as it contains sufficient capacity (e.g., resources, financial support, individuals), and involves coherent cooperation between the various components (actors, organisational governance practices, laws and regulations)." The following paragraphs review these components of the sport integrity system framework in the context of FIFA and the FIFA World Cups, thereby outlining the elements and conditions considered important to ensure integrity of the World Cup in particular.

Sport actors hold the responsibility of serving as generators and guardians of integrity in sport organisations (Huberts and Six, 2012; Kihl, 2020). They take charge of overseeing the entire system and integrity management infrastructure (Kihl, 2020). It is thereby important that each sport organisation determines which internal and external actors hold this responsibility at the club, regional, state, national and continental levels (e.g., governing board members, administrators, integrity officers and ethics committee members) as well as those external to the organisation (e.g., watchdog groups and media) for safeguarding integrity. When responsibilities to uphold integrity are not specified, the risk might be present that no-one feels responsible nor takes responsibility for integrity violations. Despite the inherent shared responsibility in this regard, the main accountability to promote integrity within FIFA's governance practices resides in FIFA's highest decision-making echelons. However, FIFA continues to indicate a lack of ethical leadership by failing to show credible role modelling that showcases the right way forward. Moreover, there is a risk to "hide behind experts" by allocating the integrity expertise mainly in the hands of specialists with a merely legal background and approach (Constandt and Willem, 2021). The constellation of FIFA stakeholders represents an opportunity as the recent boycott actions illustrate this capacity to voice (Hirschman, 1970).

The internal environment aims to develop a moral framework that guides and strengthens organisational decision-making processes and practices toward ethical behaviour, thereby limiting the likelihood that unethical practices and systemic failures take place (Kihl, 2020). Such moral framework is created through organisational characteristics [i.e., good governance structure and principles, ethical leadership, formal ethics policies, reward systems, socialisation mechanisms, and decision-making processes (Schein, 2010), cultural-behavioural norms, morals, myths, rituals, symbols, stories and language], as well as by integrity management instruments and processes (Constandt, 2019; Schein, 2010). Such strategies might focus on both rules-based (e.g., codes of conduct) and values-based (e.g., education) initiatives that outline the integrity standards sport stakeholders should accept and uphold (Constandt, 2019; Maesschalck and Vanden Auweele, 2010). In the recent years, FIFA has invested in an integrity tool kit relating to formal ethics policy measures such as a regularly revised code of ethics and an ethics committee which could be seen as textbook examples. However, as evidenced by continuing integrity scandals, these formal measures do not always perfectly capture the actual governance intentions and practices when it comes to allocating, planning and organising the World Cups.

The external environment serves as the checks and balance (guardians and accountability) to the system – who are peripheral to the sport organisation and consists of independent regulatory environments (i.e., laws, regulations and external regulatory oversight agencies such as the police, government and watchdog groups) and social environments (i.e., media, community members and fans) that ensure that local, regional and national sport governing boards and stakeholders operate within legal boundaries and social expectations (Kihl, 2020). These external stakeholders have been of fundamental importance concerning the exposure of integrity violations (e.g., vote rigging, bribery and human rights breaches) regarding the FIFA World Cups. NGO's like Human Rights Watch, Transparency International, and Play the Game; journals such as The Guardian; law enforcement agencies such as the FBI, lawyers and scholars; and even, to a lesser degree some multinational sponsors have directed public attention towards numerous scandals. Many of these external stakeholders have tried in vain to join forces with FIFA to be involved in the recent reform processes. They have once again highlighted that guardianship and pressure towards accountability is needed because of the failure of sport organisations to self-regulate (Geeraert et al., 2014).

Conclusions

Presently, the FIFA World Cups continue to face a clear lack of public trust in the governance strategies (e.g., tournament allocation) and practices (e.g., tournament planning and organisation) of FIFA and stakeholders. Drawing on the notion of a sport integrity system framework, this chapter has tried to outline the governance activities and reforms that have been implemented over the years to enhance people's trust in the integrity of the FIFA World Cups and in the institutions that organise these events. However, the governance reforms leave unclear how espoused improvements are to be achieved and monitored within FIFA's network. There seems to be a widely acknowledged difference between being formally adopted and becoming collectively accepted as a valid solution to a problem of societal concern (Haack et al., 2012). In the case of FIFA, it remains difficult to foresee a common ground across its multiple stakeholders' view, culture, values, and interests involved at the different levels of the governance of the World Cups.

Consequently, as scandals continue to highlight integrity failures and risks, the FIFA World Cups are in urgent need for a moral repair that enhances their credibility in the eyes of the millions that consume these sport entertainment products. The conceptual idea of moral repair outlines two conditions to restore trust: i.e., (1) the acknowledgement of past wrongdoings, and (2) the desire to re-install trust, indicated by a genuine investment in a better relationship with those who have been negatively impacted (Olukoya and Ogunleye-Bello, 2021). Considering the FIFA World Cups, both conditions do not seem to be successfully fulfilled. After all, despite its "promises-to-act story" (Haack et al., 2012, p. 830) and prevalent narratives separating yesterday's dark age from tomorrow's ideal, FIFA continues to downplay the scale and impact of several integrity issues related to organising the World Cups (e.g., the number of dying construction workers, the scale of taking bribes during the bidding process, and potential conflicts of interests), and largely fails to establish better relationships with those who have been hurt by their actions. However, no-one is actually successfully holding FIFA accountable and FIFA is not holding its stakeholders accountable. Hence, despite FIFA's recent reforms moving towards a positive governance direction, not that much seems to have changed eight years after (Tomlinson's, 2014) famous observation that FIFA is a "supreme leader that sails on."

References

Bason, T., Salisbury, P. & Gérard, S. (2018) FIFA. In S. Chadwick, D. Parnell, P. Widdop, and C. Anagnostopoulos (eds.), *Routledge Handbook of Football Business and Management* (pp. 423–440). London: Routledge.

Bayle, E. & Rayner, H. (2018) Sociology of a Scandal: The Emergence of 'FIFAgate', *Soccer and Society*, 19(4), 593–611.

BBC (2020) *Gianni Infantino: FIFA Closes Ethics Violation Case Against President, BBC.* Available at: https://www.bbc.com/sport/football/53838579

BBC (2015) Sepp Blatter: End of era for FIFA Boss, *BBC*. Available at: https://www.bbc.com/news/world-europe-32985553

BBC (2015) FIFA Corruption Crisis: Key Questions Answered, *BBC*. Available at: https://www.bbc.com/news/world-europe-32897066.

Beans, B. (2018) FIFA—Where crime pays. In M. Breuer and D. Forrest (eds.), *The Palgrave Handbook on the Economics of Manipulation in Sport* (pp. 279–314). Cham: Palgrave Macmillan.

Becker, R.J. (2013) World Cup 2026 Now Accepting Bribes: A Fundamental Transformation of FIFA's World Cup Bid Process, *The International Sports Law Journal*, 13, 132–147.

Bonesteel, M. (2020) FIFA President Facing Criminal Investigation in Switzerland, *The Washington Post*, July 31, Available at: https://www.washingtonpost.com/sports/2020/07/30/fifa-president-facing-criminal- investigation-switzerland

Carrard, F. (2015) Proposed Set of Principles for Reforms, FIFA, Available at: http://resources.fifa.com/mm/document/affederation/footballgovern-ance/02/74/17/96/exco_reformcommitteefinal_neutral.pdf

Chade, J. (2017) Stadium Deals, Corruption and Bribery: The Questions at the Heart of Brazil's Olympic and World Cup 'miracle', *The Guardian*, Available at: https://www.theguardian.com/sport/2017/apr/23/brazil-olympic-world-cup-corruption-bribery

Chappelet, J.L. (2016) Autonomy and governance: Necessary bedfellows in the fight against corruption in sport. *Global Corruption Report: Sport, Transparency International* (pp. 16–29), London and New York: Routledge.

Cohen, N. (2013) How many more must die for Qatar's World Cup?, *The Guardian*, Sept 21, Retrieved from: https://www.theguardian.com/commentisfree/2013/sep/21/qatar-human-rights-sport-cohen

Conn, D. (2017) "World Cup 2018: Fifa admits workers have suffered human rights abuses", *The Guardian*. Available at: https://www.theguardian.com/football/2017/may/25/fifa-world-cup-2018-workers-human-rights-abuses

Constandt, B. (2019) *Ethics management in football clubs* [Doctoral dissertation, Ghent University], Ghent University's Academic Bibliography. Available at: https://biblio.ugent.be/publication/8615197

Constandt, B. & Willem, A. (2021) Stimulating ethical behaviour and good governance in sport: The (non)sense of codes of ethics. In F. van Eekeren and A. Geeraert, *Critical reflections on good governance in Sport*. London: Routledge.

Cottle, A. (2019) A FIFA Soap Opera: Scandal, Corruption, Crime... and Reformation?, *North Carolina Journal of International Law*, 45(4), 1–25.

Le Courrier International (2021) Carton Rouge – Droits humains une entreprise néerlandaise refuse de travailler pour le mondial, *Le Courrier International*, Available at: https://www.courrierinternational.com/article/carton-rouge-droits-humains-une-entreprise-neerlandaise-refuse-de-travailler-pour-le-mondial

Dowling, M., Leopkey, B. & Smith, L. (2018) Governance in Sport: A Scoping Review, *Journal of Sport Management*, 32(5), 438–451.

Dupré, R., (2020) Affaire Infantino: la commission d'éthique de la FIFA sous pression, *Le Monde*. Available at: https://www.lemonde.fr/football/article/2020/08/01/affaire-infantino-la-commission-d-ethique-de-la-fifa-sous-pression_6047896_1616938.html

Euronews (2021) Norway's football team make Qatar protest ahead of qualifying match. Available at: https://www.euronews.com/2021/03/25/norway-s-football-team-make-qatar-protest-ahead-of-qualifying-match

FIFA (2015) 2016 FIFA Reform Committee Report, *FIFA*, Available at: https://img.fifa.com/image/upload/mzzxqw0dabgx8ljmhxwr.pdf

FIFA (2016) Governance Report 2016, *FIFA*, Presented to the 67th FIFA Congress, Manama, Bahrain, May 11. Available at: https://resources.fifa.com/image/upload/governance-report-2016-2878923.pdf?cloudid=gkpaxp18nq4kphki81gk

FIFA (2017) FIFA Regulations for the Selection of the Venue for the Final Competition of the 2026 FIFA World Cup, *FIFA*. Available at: https://img.fifa.com/image/upload/stwvxqphxp3o96jxwqor.pdf

FIFA (2018) Guide to the Bidding Process for the 2026 FIFA World Cup, *FIFA*. Available at: https://img.fifa.com/image/upload/hgopypqftviladnm7q90.pdf

FIFA (2018) Regulations FIFA U-20 World Cup Poland 2019, *FIFA*. Available at: https://resources.fifa.com/image/upload/fifa-u-20-world-cup-2019-regulations.pdf?cloudid=ujiwpedagooyxjvcwm89

FIFA (2019) Regulations for the FIFA U-17 World Cup, *FIFA*. Available at: https://resources.fifa.com/image/upload/fifa-u-17-world-cup-brazil-2019-regulations.pdf?cloudid=lldsqmeb9e1lpkjuw8hq

FIFA (2019) FIFA's key achievements: 2016-2019, *FIFA*. Presented to the 69th FIFA Congress, Paris, France, June 5. Available at: https://resources.fifa.com/image/upload/fifa-s-key-achievements-2016-2019.pdf?cloudid=qyxnjzjfwwv5wcpnfugp

FIFA (2020) Regulations FIFA World Cup 2022, *FIFA*. Available at: https://img.fifa.com/image/upload/ytkbpnxyvcghx6bebesv.pdf

Gardiner, S. (2018) Perspectives on Ethics and Integrity in Football. In S. Chadwick, D. Parnell, P. Widdop, and C. Anagnostopoulos (eds.) *Routledge Handbook of Football Business and Management* (pp. 376–387). London: Routledge.

Gardiner, S., Parry, J., & Robinson, S. (2017) Integrity and the corruption debate in sport: Where is the integrity? *European Sport Management Quarterly*, 17(1), 6–23.

Geeraert, A. (2018) *Sports Governance Observer 2018. An assessment of good governance in five international sports federations, Aarhus: Play the Game / Danish Institute for Sports Studies*, Retrieved from http://playthegame.org/knowledge-bank/downloads/sports-governance-observer- 2018/205c4aa7-4036-4fe1-b570-a99601700e5d.

Geeraert, A. (2017) Theorizing the governance of sport mega-events a principal-agent perspective, In S. Frawley (ed.), *Managing Sport Mega-Events* (pp. 24–36). New York: Routledge.

Geeraert, A., Alm, J., & Groll, M. (2014) Good Governance in International Sport Organizations: An Analysis of the 35 Olympic Sport Governing Bodies. *International Journal of Sport Policy and Politics*, 6(3), 281–306.

Geeraert, A., Mrkonjic, M., & Chappelet, J.L. (2015) A Rationalist Perspective on the Autonomy of International Sport Governing Bodies: Towards a Pragmatic Autonomy in the Steering of Sports, *International Journal of Sport Policy and Politics*, 7(4), 473–488.

Graid, C. (2016) A Legal Analysis of FIFA's Governance Reforms: Do They Meet the Standards of Best Global Practice?, *Law in Sport,* May 18, Available at: https://www.lawinsport.com/topics/anti-corruption/item/a-legal-analysis-of-fifa-s-governance-reforms-do-they-meet-the-standards-of-best-global-practice?category_id=114

The Guardian (2021) 6,500 Migrant Workers Have Died in Qatar since World Cup awarded, *The Guardian*. Available at: https://www.theguardian.com/global-development/2021/feb/23/revealed-migrant-worker-deaths-qatar-fifa-world-cup-2022

The Guardian (2021) Germany Players Add Support Over Human Rights Before Qatar World Cup, *The Guardian*. Available at: https://www.theguardian.com/football/2021/mar/26/germany-players-add-support-over-human-rights-before-qatar-world-cup

Haack, P., Schoeneborn, D., & Wickert, C. (2012) Talking the Talk, Moral Entrapment, Creeping Commitment? Exploring Narrative Dynamics in Corporate Responsibility Standardization, *Organization Studies*, *33*(5-6), 815–845.

Harding, A. (2015) Fifa Corruption: South Africa Cash 'worrisome', *BBC*, Available at: https://www.bbc.com/news/world-africa-33127146

Head, B., Brown, A.J., & Connors, C. (eds). (2008) *Promoting Integrity: Evaluating and Improving Public Institutions*. Ashgate Publishing, Ltd.

Hirschman, A.O. (1970) *Exit, Voice, and Loyalty: Responses to Decline in Firms, Organizations, and States*. Cambridge: Harvard University Press.

Hölzen, M. & Meier, H.E. (2019) Do Football Consumers Care About Sport Governance? An Analysis of Social Media Responses to the Recent FIFA Scandal. *Journal of Global Sport Management*, 4(1), 97–120.

Huberts, L.W. & Six, F.E. (2012) Local Integrity Systems: Toward a Framework for Comparative Analysis and Assessment, *Public Integrity*, 14(2), 151–172.

Kelly, A., McIntyre, N. & Pattisson, P. (2019) In Doha Hundreds of Migrant Workers Dying of Heat Stress in Qatar Each Year, *The Guardian*. Available at: https://www.theguardian.com/global-development/2019/oct/02/revealed-hundreds-of-migrant-workers-dying-of-heat-stress-in-qatar-each-year

Kihl, L. (2020) Sport Integrity Systems: A Proposed Framework. In D. Shilbury and L. Ferkins (eds.). *Routledge Handbook of Sport Governance* (pp. 395–409). London: Routledge.

Koval, A. & Jvirblis, A. (2016) The Need for Transparency and Monitoring Ahead of the 2018 World Cup in Russia (pp. 250–259). *Global Corruption Report: Sport, Transparency International*. London and New York: Routledge.

Leopkey, B. and Parent, M. (2019) *Sport event governance models*. In D. Shilbury and L. Ferkins (eds.). *Routledge Handbook of Sport Governance* (pp. 226–239). London: Routledge.

Loyens, K., Claringbould, I., Heres, L. & van Eekeren, F. (2021) The Social Construction of Integrity: A Qualitative Case Study in Dutch football. *Sport in Society* [Advance online publication] 10.1080/17430437.2021.1877661

Maesschalck, J. & Vanden Auweele, Y. (2010) Integrity Management in Sport, *Journal of Community and Health Sciences*, 5, 1–9.

McLeod, J., Shilbury, D. & Zeimers, G. (2021) An Institutional Framework for Governance Convergence in Sport: The Case of India, *Journal of Sport Management*, 35(2), 144–157.

McNamee, M. & Fleming, S. (2007) Ethics Audits and Corporate Governance: The Case of Public Sector Sports Organizations, *Journal of Business Ethics*, 73, 425–437.

Müller, M. (2017) How Mega-events Capture Their Hosts: Event Seizure and the World Cup 2018 in Russia, *Urban Geography*, 38(8), 1113–1132.

Olukoya, B. & Ogunleye-Bello, A. (2021) Restoring Trust in football Through Behavioural Advocacy: A Case Study from Nigeria. In Ordway C. (ed.), *Restoring Trust in Sport. Corruption Cases and Solutions* (pp. 176–189). London: Routledge.

Parent, M.M. (2016) Stakeholder Perceptions on the Democratic Governance of Major Sports Events, *Sport Management Review*, 19(4), 402–416.

Parent, M.M. & Hoye, R. (2018) The Impact of Governance Principles on Sport Organisations' Governance Practices and Performance: A Systematic Review, *Cogent Social Sciences*, 4(1), 1503578.

Pattisson, P. (2020) Qatar World Cup: Report Reveals 34 Stadium Worker Deaths in Six Years, *The Guardian*, March 16, Available at: https://www.theguardian.com/global-development/2020/mar/16/qatar-world-cup-report-reveals-34-stadium-worker-deaths-in-six-years

Pielke, R. (2013) How Can FIFA Be Held Accountable?, *Sport Management Review*, 16(3), 255–267.

Pielke, R. (2016) Obstacles to Accountability in International Sports Governance, *Global Corruption Report: Sport, Transparency International* (pp. 29–38). London and New York: Routledge.

Pielke, R., Harris, S., Adler, J., Sutherland, S., Houser, R. & McCabe, J. (2020) An Evaluation of Good Governance in US Olympic Sport National Governing Bodies, *European Sport Management Quarterly*, 20(4), 480–499.

Pieth, M. (2011) Governing FIFA, *FIFA*. Available at: http://www.fifa.com/mm/document/affederation/footballgovernance/01/54/99/69/fifagutachten-en.pdf

Qatar (2022a) Workers Welfare, Qatar 2022. Available at: https://www.qatar2022.qa/en/opportunities/workers-welfare

Qatar (2022b) Frequently Asked Questions, Qatar 2022. Available at: https://www.qatar2022.qa/en/about/faq

Richau, L., Emrich, E., & Follert, F. (2019) Quid Pro Quo! Organization Theoretical Remarks about FIFA's Legitimacy under Blatter and Infantino, *The Economists' Voice*, 16(1), 1–9.

Schein, E.H. (2010) *Organisational Culture and Leadership* (4th Ed.). San Francisco: Jossey-Bass.

Schenk, S. (2011) *Safe Hands: Building Integrity and Transparency at FIFA*, Transparency International. Available at: https://www.transparency.org/whatwedo/publication/safe_hands_building_integrity_and_transparency_at_fifa.

Spiegel (2016) World Cup Scandal: Germany Appears to Have Bought Right to Host 2006 Tournament, *Spiegel Online*. Available at: http://www. spiegel.de/international/world/documents-indicate-slush-fund-used-in-german- world-cup-bid-a-1058212.html

Tomlinson, A. (2014) The Supreme Leader Sails on: Leadership, Ethics and Governance in FIFA, *Sport in Society*, 17(9), 1155–1169.

Transparency International (2009) Corruption and Sport: Building Integrity and Preventing Abuses, Working Paper no. 03/2009, Berlin.

Transparency International (2011) *Safe Hands: Building Integrity and Transparency at FIFA*, Berlin.

Vanden Auweele, Y. (2011) Implementation of Panathlon Declaration on ethics in youth sport and 'integrity plans'. In A. Aledda and M. Monego (eds.), *The primacy of ethics. Also in sports?* (pp. 63–73). Milano: Franco Angeli.

Vanden Auweele, Y., Cook, E. & Parry, J. (2016) *Ethics and Governance in Sport. The Future of Sport Imagined*. London: Routledge.

Zeimers, G., Anagnostopoulos, C., Zintz, T. & Willem, A. (2018) Corporate social responsibility (CSR) in football. In: Chadwick, S., Parnell, D., Widdop, P., and Anagnostopoulos, C. (eds.), *Routledge Handbook of Football Business and Management* (pp. 114–130). London: Routledge.

Zimbalist, A. (2016) Corruption and the Bidding Process for the Olympics and World Cup, *Global Corruption Report: Sport, Transparency International* (pp. 178–182). London and New York: Routledge.

Zimbalist, A. (2020) *Circus Maximus: The Economic Gamble behind Hosting the Olympics and the World Cup*. Washington: Brookings Institution Press.

8

ENVIRONMENT AND SUSTAINABILITY IN FIFA WORLD CUPS

Madeleine Orr, Jessica R. Murfree, Austin Anahory, and Rony Epelbaum Edwabne

Introduction

In one of the hottest years ever recorded, the 2019 FIFA Women's World Cup was played in France through searing temperatures (NOAA, 2020). The heat wave coinciding with the tournament saw game-time temperatures exceed 38°C (100°F; Cutler, 2019), well above the recommended thresholds for safe sport. As a result, athletes, coaches and officials were exposed to a range of heat and humidity-related concerns, including dehydration, cognitive impairment and declining physical skills (Houssein et al., 2016). This was not an isolated case of environmental conditions adversely affecting a sport event.

Globally, environmental conditions such as air quality, temperature and precipitation, dictate how football is played and consumed (Taylor, 2019; Watanabe et al., 2017). In many cases, climate change is worsening the environmental conditions and rendering sport uncomfortable, and in some cases dangerous and untenable. Due to sport's reliance on particular environmental conditions, for example, reasonably warm (but not too hot) temperatures for summer sports, and sufficient cold for snow sports, the environmental conditions determine when and where games and tournaments take place, effectively controlling the sport's existence.

In the context of FIFA World Cups, a policy precedent was set during the 2014 Men's FIFA Men's World Cup in Brazil when the courts ordered alterations to game delivery in the interest of player safety (Blount, 2014). Specifically, the courts mandated extra water breaks when Wet Bulb Globe Temperatures (WBGT) reached or exceeded 32°C (Houssein et al., 2016), consistent with the latest research on heat-related illness in sport.

In addition to heat, mounting climate impacts threaten the feasibility of FIFA's future mega-events. For example, the 2022 FIFA World Cup in Qatar was

DOI: 10.4324/9781003121794-8

rescheduled from mid-Summer to late-Fall and will feature stadium and playing surface cooling technology to protect fans and players from the heat (Chad, 2019). At the 2026 FIFA World Cup, projected extreme heat in the U.S. South and Mexico introduce yet another challenge for organisers (Ross and Orr, forthcoming). Conversely, the world's largest football governing body detrimentally affects the natural environment through the production and delivery of its events. The bidirectional relationship where sport both *impacts* and is *impacted by* the natural environment has been dubbed "sport ecology" (McCullough et al. 2020) and is emerging as a new and important area of research in sport management. While sport ecology research is relatively nascent, the relationship it explores has existed since sport's inception. Consider, for example, that most sports were conceived of unique person–environment interactions in a given place: for instance, surfing emerged from indigenous traditions and culture in Polynesia, golf grew in the rolling hills of Scotland and ice hockey was born on Canada's frozen ponds. Each of these sports responded to desires for play (or in some cases, transport) in a specific place, given the environmental conditions and available resources. Further and importantly, sports are dependent on the natural environment for clean air, water, weather, and the natural resources that produce the sporting goods we use to play the games we love (e.g., rubber for balls, cotton for shirts, wood and steel for stadium construction). However, environmental issues have only recently gained the attention of sport managers and researchers as climate change poses greater, more expensive, and increasingly severe risks to the sport sector (Murfree and Moorman, 2021).

Similarly, environmental sustainability initiatives are growing in number and scope across the football world. Following a heated contest between Japan and Columbia at the 2018 FIFA Men's World Cup in Russia, Japanese fans demonstrated strong environmental stewardship by cleaning the stadium of litter and food waste (Illmer, 2018). Two years later in 2020, ahead of the 2022 Qatar tournament, FIFA and the Supreme Committee for Delivery and Legacy (SC) developed the first joint strategy for environmental sustainability between the Federation, host nation and local organising committee (FIFA, 2020).

The UNFCCC's Sport for Climate Action Framework, launched in 2018, serves as a call to action to address climate change, the "defining crisis of our time" (United Nations, 2018, 2019, para. 1). The urgency of addressing environmental sustainability in and through sport was echoed by former U.S. President Barack Obama's declaration of Green Sports Day in 2016 and the Commonwealth Secretariat's Kazan Action Plan (Stone, 2016; UNESCO, 2017). As one of the largest sport entities in the world, FIFA's global social and environmental footprint can serve as an influential vehicle for improved environmental management in sport, with potential to influence sponsors, partners, fans, and the sport sector.

This chapter first explores the impacts of climate change on FIFA, introducing concepts associated with climate vulnerability and adaptation. The chapter then moves onto unpacking the many ways FIFA and its events impact the natural environment, with a focus on measuring the environmental footprint, then reducing it. We conclude the chapter with a review of FIFA's past and current efforts to communicate about their environmental efforts.

Impacts of Climate Change on FIFA

Most sport organisations are vulnerable to climate-related disruptions. Research has demonstrated the outdoor sports, in particular, are vulnerable to climate hazards. However, there is perhaps no better setting in which to examine climate change in the context of sport than at mega multi-sport events like the Olympic Games and FIFA World Cups. What makes mega-events particularly vulnerable to the impacts of climate change is that they move locations for each iteration of the event, introducing a new set of environmental conditions for which event organisers must plan.

Climate vulnerability in sport

Vulnerability to climate change is the degree to which an entity – such as a person, an organisation, a building or a community – is at risk of experiencing negative outcomes from climate change, such as warmer weather, droughts, fires, floods and storms The United Nations Office for Disaster Risk Reduction provides a framework to assess vulnerability based on three key factors:

- Exposure – How likely is X to happen?
- Sensitivity – How bad would it be if X happened?
- Adaptive capacity – How ready is the entity to cope with X, with minimal disruption or losses?

There exist several free and easily accessible resources to assess the exposure of sport events to climate hazards. For instance, the Intergovernmental Panel on Climate Change produces reports every five years which detail the expect climate impacts on each region of the world, and Climate Central maintains a global map of flooding risk on their website.

Sensitivity can be assessed through a review of the sport medicine research. As with all summer sports, the health and athlete performance issues facing football as a consequence of heat (heat-related illnesses), air quality (breathing issues, visibility issues; Duda et al. 2020; Lippi, Guidi and Maffuli, 2008; Marr and Ely, 2010) and natural disasters (flooding, drought, storms) are well documented. It is also possible to review past cases of sport events being impacted by climate hazards to determine how severe the impacts can be. For instance, the 2019 Rugby World Cup in Japan was impacted by Super Typhoon Hagibis which caused off-field flooding, including through the lower levels of stadiums, and created challenging playing conditions (ABC News, 2019; NASA, 2019).

What is less clear from the extant research is how best to respond to climate hazards, leaving managers largely unprepared to address climate-related challenges.

A new line of research (Kellison and Orr, 2020; Orr, 2021) offers initial insight into the factors that make a sport event or organisation resilient in the face of climate hazards. These include, among others, advanced planning for climate response, the development of emergency response policies and procedures, adequate training for staff on how to carry out emergency procedures, access to insurance plans which cover the losses in the case of cancelled events due to climate hazards, and adequate support for flexible scheduling from the media, leagues, local authorities and governing bodies (Orr, 2021). To date, little is known of the emergency planning that happens at FIFA due to limited access and interest among reporters on this topic.

Encouragingly, the International Football Association Board (IFAB), which governs the rules of the game for international competition, has developed flexible policies that allow for cooling breaks in the case of high temperatures and humidity, and weather delays for storms (IFAB, 2020). However, these may need to be extended in future to accommodate additional environmental challenges, such as air quality issues.

At the host committee level, the Supreme Committee for Delivery and Legacy, the Qatari organisation charged with hosting the 2022 Men's World Cup, has shown some consideration for climate challenges at their event, making this the first event with a publicly accessible climate plan. This comes on the heels of over 30 worker deaths in the construction phase of the event, attributed to heat-related heart attacks (Gangi, 2018; Pattison et al. 2021) in otherwise healthy men. To minimise the potential negative impacts of heat at the event, several innovative strategies have been adopted for air conditioning outdoors. All indoor spaces in the host cities are air conditioned using environmentally friendly cooling technologies such as evaporative cooling techniques and misting (Sofotasiou, Hughes and Calautit, 2015) to ensure the comfort and safety of players, officials and fans.

To avoid moving all football games indoors, FIFA host committees must follow the lead of the Qataris and ensure a thorough climate vulnerability assessment is conducted to identify all possible hazards and the exposure and sensitivity of each venue. Then, policies for flexible scheduling and climate-adaptive strategies must be developed and deployed. This might include a heat and air quality policy to govern possible game postponements or delays in bad conditions, and climate-adaptive technologies such as misting machines, the use of cooling towels, and shaded rest areas on the sidelines (Kakamu et al., 2017). Of course, these efforts must not go so far as to have a trade-off effect. That is to say, organisers must be careful to ensure their climate adaptation efforts do not increase (i.e., worsen) the environmental footprint of the event.

The Environmental Footprint of the FIFA World Cup

Based on the adage that "what gets measured gets managed," the first step in addressing (i.e., reducing) the environmental impacts of a sport event is to measure the expected footprint of the event. Considerable research attention has been directed at conducting environmental footprint analyses of FIFA events and other mega-events. Indeed, mega-events are the most studied sport events when it comes to the environmental impact of sport. However, environmental footprints are inconsistently measured (McCullough et al. 2020). For instance, some events include the legacy period of the event in the calculation of overall impact, while others do not. This can be partially explained by the fact that sports events have poorly defined lifecycles compared with consumer goods such as a pair of cleats or a football, which have initial materials, manufacturing processes, transport, sale, use and disposal stages that can be clearly delineated and measured (McCullough et al. 2020). It can also be partially explained by the lack of training made available to sport managers for environmental management and the lack of resources devoted to sustainability by public sports venues and events (Ross and Mercado, 2020). Nonetheless, measurement of current environmental impacts remain the most important first step in addressing and reducing the impacts of an event (McCullough, Orr and Watanabe, 2020).

The environmental footprint of sport events can be conceptualised and addressed using the direct and external environmental impacts (DEEI) framework (Figure 8.1; McCullough, Orr and Watanabe, 2020). The DEEI framework has four quadrants representing the direct and indirect environmental impacts of both event production (i.e., the organisers' footprint, the venues and construction, event delivery, back-of-house) and consumption of events (i.e., ticket purchasing, travel to the event, hotel stays, restaurant meals and local tourism activities) For the production items, the organisers or their suppliers and partners have direct access to the information needed to calculate the footprint. For instance, the organisers would be able to get information about energy use in the venues by asking the venue managers directly. Similarly, information about the travel footprint of the media teams can be attained by asking about travel plans through the registration platforms for media credentialling, and through direct consultation with onsite broadcasting teams. In comparison, the environmental footprint associated with consumption of the event is less clear and requires collecting information directly

	Production	**Consumption**
Direct impacts	Venue operations Event planning Event production Staffing and staff impacts	Ticket purchase Transportation to/from event On-site purchases Tailgating activities
Externalities	Impacts of suppliers Impacts of sponsors Impacts of host city Hosting activities, off-site	Restaurant meals off-site Hotel stays Out-of-town transport Purchases off-site

FIGURE 8.1 The direct and external environmental impacts of sport events framework

from fans, or inferring this information from economic impact analyses of the event. Consequently, it can be much easier for organisers to measure and manage the environmental footprint of event production, compared with event consumption. In the following sections, we detail what goes into each quadrant of the DEEI framework.

Direct impacts of consumption

Consistently, the research bears out the notion that the largest contributor to overall environmental footprint at mega-events is travel to-and-from the event, ground transport, and the consumption behaviours of athletes, staff, media, various service providers and fans (Collins, Jones and Munday, 2009). Consequently, this should form the main focus of most environmental impact efforts. The massive crowds at FIFA World Cup events and the multi-city hosting model exacerbate the environmental impacts in this category. In 2016, FIFA commissioned reports on the expected environmental impacts of the 2018 Men's World Cup event in Russia which indicated that travel would account for upwards of 73% of the overall greenhouse gas (GHG) emissions of the event.

Other factors, such as the number of teams competing and the number of matches in each tournament, also contribute to the overall environmental impact of the event. Generally, the more games and the more teams involved, the higher the environmental impact will be. One study aimed at projecting the 2030 FIFA World Cup emissions showed that an increase from 32 to 48 teams would increase the GHG emissions by 36%, or 557 tCO_2-eq (Pereira, Filimonau and Ribeiro, 2020). However, it is possible that COVID pandemic-related policies that limit fans at events may reduce the impacts of travel in near-future events (e.g., 2020–2025).

For the Qatar 2022 FIFA World Cup™, major public transport projects such as the Doha Metro and Lusail Tram will aim to reduce overall carbon emissions and encourage fans to use public transport through initiatives such as free public transport access with a FIFA World Cup 2022™ ticket and a journey planner. Both the metro and the tram will have stations within a short walk of most stadiums, with the remaining tournament venues reachable via a combination of metro and fuel-efficient buses (FIFA, 2020).

Direct impacts of production

The next biggest contributor to overall environmental impacts of FIFA sport events is the sports facilities, as they produce waste and pollution at every stage of their lifecycle: planning, construction, use phase and demolition (Wesstrom, 2016).

One example of a FIFA football stadium with a particularly egregious environmental footprint is the Arena de Amazônia in Manaus, Brazil. Built in the heart of the Amazon, one of the most biodiverse and ecologically sensitive regions in the world, construction of the Arena relied on clearcutting a heavily forested area and importing supplies from Portual on cargo ships that navigated first the Atlantic Ocean, then the Amazon River, because of a lack of truck-accessible roads to Manaus. Each of the cargo ships took roughly 17–20 days to cross the Atlantic Ocean, then navigate the Amazon River and its tributaries to arrive in Manaus. Overall, the construction phase of the event caused environmental damage through forest degradation, cargo transport emissions and disruption in the region of the build. Further, plans for powering the stadium with solar energy, which would have limited its environmental footprint in the use phase, had to be abandoned amid construction delays. In the end, the facility was only used for the FIFA World Cup event and has been left largely empty and unused since (Powell, 2016).

Not all FIFA facilities are built to have detrimental impacts, some are far more environmentally friendly by design. For instance, in some cases, FIFA World Cup host committees have endeavoured to supplement existing sports facilities with innovative environmental initiatives nearby. One example is Green Point Park in Cape Town, South Africa. Ahead of the 2010 Men's World Cup, organisers partnered with city officials to develop the 12.5 hectares of Green Point Park into the Biodiversity Showcase Garden as an extension of Cape Town Stadium. The main goal of this garden was to highlight the unique Cape Flats Sand Fynbos habitat, which historically could be found throughout the Cape Town region (Peterson, Husted, Rebelo and Holmes, 2007). The rich biodiversity found within this habitat is threatened by pressures such as urbanisation. Three thematic areas in the garden include people and plants, the discovering biodiversity trail and the wetland walk. Displays hidden in and amongst the plants feature original artworks and interpretive boards with illustrations and photographs for people to explore this learn about the city's remarkable native biodiversity (Krasny, Lundholm, Shava, Lee and Kobori, 2013). This park serves not only as a biodiversity preservation effort, but also as a carbon sink for local emissions as the carbon-capture potential of its diverse flora is significant.

Other environmental impacts that would fit under the Direct Impacts of Production category of the DEEI framework include energy and resources consumed by offices and staff activities in the planning stages of the event, and the wrap-up post-event.

Externalities of production

The production of major and mega-sporting events such as FIFA World Cups requires significant investments and involvement of local governments, the media, and the private sector in the form of sponsorships, as discussed elsewhere in this book. Each of those parties contributes to the overall environmental footprint of the event's delivery and thus, ought to be considered in a holistic tabulation of overall event impacts. For instance, at the 2018 Men's World Cup in Russia, 11 media centres accommodated over 2,000 accredited journalists who travelled domestically and internationally to attend and report on the event, in addition to several hundred more unaccredited journalists. This formed only one component of the event (i.e., media coverage and broadcasting) and does not include the footprint of production centres outside the country that produced the event, or those of other partners such as sponsors.

FIFA's network of global partners, which have a presence and footprint at each FIFA World Cup event, includes Coca-Cola, Adidas, Wanda Group, Visa and Qatar Airways. To align with the expectations of their clients and partners, including FIFA, each of these brands has incorporated sustainability into their corporate social responsibility portfolios. For example, Adidas' sustainability strategy includes targets for managing energy, water, and waste, with a primary focus of ending plastic waste for ocean conservation (Adidas, n.d.). In 2020, Qatar Airways launched a partnership to support their carbon offset goals with the International Air Transport Association (IATA), ClimateCare and India's Fatanpur Wind Farm project (Qatar Airways, 2020). The engagement of these partner organisations enhances and aligns with FIFA's environmental efforts and those of host committees. Unfortunately, the independent environmental initiatives of FIFA's partners does not always manifest in reduced emissions, waste and pollution at the event sites. Extending sustainability into the sponsorship activation efforts on site (e.g., eliminating giveaways of plastic cups, eliminating paper, using the same branding materials at each event and offsetting the travel of staff) will be the next step in measuring and reducing the overall footprint of FIFA events.

Externalities of consumption

The externalities of consumption associated with attending a FIFA World Cup as a consumer (i.e., a sport tourist) can be substantive. Tourism activities associated with attending a FIFA event may include air travel to-and-from the event, multiple nights of hotel stay, several meals in restaurants, ground travel, and other purchases of merchandise and other goods in the host cities (Pereira, Camara, Ribeiro and Filimonau, 2017). This category can be the most challenging for event managers to measure as it requires third parties such as hotels, restaurants and other independent businesses to accurately report the environmental footprint of their operations for the period of the event, and share these figures with the event organisers (McCullough et al. 2020). An alternative mechanism for measuring and reducing the externalities of consumption is to survey attendees on their travel behaviours and invite the fans to offset their own consumption-related footprint.

Environmental Initiatives at FIFA Events

In its capacity as a global organisation with massive influence, FIFA can capitalise on the increasing discussion of climate change and awareness to inspire football organisations and fans to engage in climate action. FIFA has the potential to address issues as well as promote positive responses to the climate crisis that threatens the future of the game. Young athletes and footballers around the world look to mega-events like the FIFA World Cup with admiration and aspiration. The potential of the FIFA platform to serve as a leader in the sustainability space is significant and should not be overlooked.

The potential was initially recognised by FIFA when it initiated its first major environmental programme in 2006, a series of initiatives called 'Green Goals'. The programme took aim at reducing the environmental impacts of the 2006 and 2010 Men's World Cups in Germany and South Africa, and the 2011 Women's World Cup, also in Germany. The environmental campaign was a first-of-its-kind carbon reduction-and-offsetting programme (City of Capetown, 2009). A few years later, in 2016, FIFA became the first international sports organisation to join the Climate Neutral Now initiative, pledging to become greenhouse gas emission neutral by 2050.

More recently, in December 2018, FIFA became an early signatory of the UN Sports for Climate Action Framework, which provides support and guidance to sport organisations for climate action, along five principles. The principles of the framework are as follows: 1) undertake systematic efforts to promote greater environmental responsibility, 2) reduce overall climate impact, 3) educate for climate action, 4) promote sustainable and responsible consumption and 5) advocate for climate action through communication. By signing onto this framework, FIFA has asserted a high level of dedication to addressing the climate issue. As FIFA is one of the largest sport organisations and is head of the World Cup, a mega-sporting event, this decision reflects a long-term plan for sustainability and signals to the rest of the football community globally that environmental sustainability is worth addressing. To fulfil the principles of the framework, FIFA has hired several full-time staff who are working to advance FIFA's environmental agenda internally and across the World Cups portfolio, offering support to organising committees. Implementing the five principles into each event will lead to a more environmentally conscious mega event and allows FIFA to redefine the norms of sporting tournaments.

Individual host committees have similarly taken up the mantle of environmental efforts. From the 2006 Men's World Cup in Germany, each host committee has developed a sustainability plan to comply with first the Green Goals, and now with FIFA's sustainability requirements for hosting. As noted earlier, the Supreme Committee for Delivery and Legacy of the 2022 Men's World Cup in Qatar also has an ambitious sustainability agenda linked mainly to building sustainable venues.

Other parties in the sport of football have stepped up to engage in sustainable efforts, following FIFA's lead. Arsenal Football Club is one example of a football team leading in this space. Arsenal made it clear they are committed to tackling climate change, and Arsenal's Hector Bellerin has been front and centre in his dedication to addressing this issue. Vowing to donate 6,000 trees through One Tree Planted, for every team win, Bellerin garnered the support of English football fans and environmentalists alike (Chaplin, 2020). Arsenal fans helped Bellerin contribute trees with one-pound donations per tree. Arsenal competitor Paddy

Power opted to siege this opportunity to donate 6,000 trees for every time Arsenal did not win. This idea and announcement from Bellerin resulted in 58,617 trees to be planted in the Amazon (Chaplin, 2020). In addition to his work with One Tree Planted, Hector Bellerin also contributed financially into Forest Green Rovers, a football club that is run by Dale Vince an environmentalist.

Forest Green Rovers Football Club, a member-owned club that competes in the fourth tier of English Football, was described by FIFA as one of the world's most sustainable football teams due to their recent actions on and off the pitch (FGR, 2020). The environmental efforts of this previously little-known club have attracted attention across the sports world. Forest Green Rovers has implemented an all-vegan menu for players and fans, jerseys that implement a construction of half bamboo textile, and fully renewable energy to power the team (FGR, 2020). The club has been climate neutral for several years and has ambitious plans to build the world's greenest sporting stadium surrounded by trees and powered by renewable energy. Dale Vince, majority owner of Forest Green Rovers and Ecotricity CEO, said he believes in doing the right things for the right reasons, trusting that good karma will follow.

A final example of best practice in the sustainable management of football can be found in Germany where teams and fans are addressing climate change at every game. A "Climate Ticket" was introduced by TSG Hoffenheim, a Bundesliga football team (Hoffenheim, 2019). This ticket allows fans to donate one euro on top of the purchase of their matchday ticket. This one-euro donation is directed to a farm in Uganda when each euro goes towards the planting of a tree sapling (Hoffenheim, 2019). Fans are encouraged to donate for as many saplings as they would like. Although the planting of trees is not an immediate impact, it raises the issue of climate change every ticket transaction. This spurs conversation among fans and opens discussions to address the climate issue on a larger scale.

Conclusion

Research continues to demonstrate the considerably environmental impact of FIFA events, and evidence of the impacts of climate change on FIFA events is growing. Moving forward, it will be important for academics and practitioners pay close attention to environmental issues to avoid major damages and losses from climate hazards, and the potential negative public relations fallout of failing to reduce environmental impacts.

Increasingly, the public is taking notice of environmental issues in sport. Since 2016, media coverage of climate issues in sport has increased annually (Muehlbauer and Orr, 2020), the United Nation's Sport for Climate Action Framework was launched, and several conferences and consulting firms have emerged to guide sport managers in their environmental efforts. Regional industry associations such as Green Sports Alliance (North America), Sport Positive (global scope), Sport and Sustainability International (Europe), British Association for Sustainable Sport, and Sport Environment Alliance (Australia and New Zealand) are just some of the organisations providing resources to drive climate action in the sport sector.

With FIFA's 100 year anniversary of World Cup tournaments fast-approaching in 2030, the impact of FIFA on the environment and the impact of the environment on FIFA must be a focus in the next century.

References

ABC News (2019) *Typhoon Hagibis: Japan-Scotland Rugby World Cup game to go ahead despite rain, flooding*. Available at: https://www.abc.net.au/news/2019-10-13/japan-scotland-rwc-go-ahead-despite-typhoon-hagibis-lashing/11597888

Adidas (n.d.) *Sustainability: General Approach*. Available at: https://www.adidas-group.com/en/sustainability/managing-sustainability/general-approach/#/successful-completion-of-2020-targets/

Blount, J. (2014)Judge Orders World Cup Water Breaks if Heat Reaches 32 degrees C. Reuters. Available at: https://www.reuters.com/article/soccer-world-water-injunction/judge-orders-world-cup-water-breaks-if-heat-reaches-32-degrees-c-idUSL2N0P11AE20140620

Chad, N. (2019) *At 2022 World Cup, the Global Game Will Meet Global Warming. The Washington Post*. Available at: https://www.washingtonpost.com/sports/soccer/at-2022-world-cup-the-global-game-will-meet-global-warming/2019/11/10/bfd348d2–0277-11ea-8501-2a7123a38c58_story.html

Chaplin, D. (2020) *Arsenal's Hector BELLERIN is planting 58,617 trees in the Amazon*. Available at: https://onetreeplanted.org/blogs/stories/arsenal-hector-bellerin-amazon [Retrieved 7 March 2021].

City of Capetown (2009) *2010 FIFA World Cup, Host City Cape Town: Green Goals Progress Report*. Available at: https://www.kas.de/c/document_library/get_file?uuid=046c1e85-e4df-837d-c1fb-6818b11e910bandgroupId=252038 [Accessed 30 March 2021].

Cutler, V. (2019) *Soccer and Extreme Heat: A Potentially Dangerous Mix for US-France World Cup match. ABC News*. Available at: https://abcnews.go.com/Health/soccer-extreme-heat-potentially-dangerous-mix/story?id=64007843

Duda, H., Rydzik, Ł., Czarny, W., Błach, W., Görner, K., & Ambroży, T. (2020) Reaction of the Organisms of Young Football Players to City Smog in the Sports Training, *International Journal of Environmental Research and Public Health*, 17(15), 5510. 10.3390/ijerph17155510

FGR (2020) *Another Way*. Available at: https://www.fgr.co.uk/another-way[Retrieved 7 March 2021].

FIFA (2020) FIFA World Cup Qatar 2022 Sustainability Strategy (version 1.1). *FIFA*. Available at: https://resources.fifa.com/image/upload/fifa-world-cup-qatar-2022tm-sustainability-strategy.pdf?cloudid=u25obd7303tdxupsjysn

FIFA.com (2018) 2018 FIFA WORLD Cup™ - news - more than half the world WATCHED RECORD-BREAKING 2018 World Cup. Available at: https://www.fifa.com/worldcup/news/more-than-half-the-world-watched-record-breaking-2018-world-cup#:~:text=A%20combined%203.572%20billion%20viewers,the%202018%20FIFA%20World%20Cup [Retrieved 7 March 2021].

Gangi, S.K. (2018) Leveraging the World Cup: Mega Sporting Events, Human Rights Risk, and Worker Welfare Reform in Qatar. *Journal on Migration and Human Security, 4*(4), 221–259.

Hoffenheim, T. (2019) TSG Hoffenheim launches "CLIMATE TICKET". Available at: https://www.tsg-hoffenheim.de/en/news/overview/2019/10/tsg-hoffenheim-launches-climate-ticket/ [Retrieved 7 March 2021].

Houssein, M., Lopes, P., Fagnoni, B., Ahmaidi, S., Yonis, S.M., & Leprêtre, P.-M. (2016) Hydration: The New FIFA World Cup's Challenge for Referee Decision Making?, *Journal of Athletic Training*, *51*(3), 264–266. 10.4085/1062-6050-51.3.04

IFAB (2020) *Laws of the Game 2020-21*. Available at: https://resources.fifa.com/image/upload/ifab-laws-of-the-game-2020-21.pdf?cloudid=d6g1medsi8jrrd3e4impRetrieved 1 April 2021.

Illmer, A. (2018) World Cup: Japan Fans Impress by Cleaning Up Stadium. *BBC News*. https://www.bbc.com/news/world-asia-44492611#:~:text=But%20after%20the%20team%20swept,as%20they%20had%20found%20it.

Kakamu, T., Wada, K., Smith, D.R., Endo, S., & Fukushima, T. (2017) Preventing heat illness in the anticipated hot climate of the Tokyo 2020 Summer Olympic Games, *Environmental Health and Preventive Medicine*, *22*(1), 68. 10.1186/s12199-017-0675-y

Krasny, M.E., Lundholm, C., Shava, S., Lee, E., & Kobori, H. (2013) Urban landscapes as learning arenas for biodiversity and ecosystem services management (pp. 629–664). In Elmquist, T., Fragkias, M., Goodness, J., Güneralp, B., Marcotullio, P., McDonald, R., …et al. (eds). *Urbanization, Biodiversity and Ecosystem Services: Challenges and Opportunities*. London: Springer.

Lippi, G., Guidi, G., & Maffuli, N. (2008) Air Pollution and Sports Performance in Beijing, *International Journal of Sports Medicine*, *28*(2), 696–698. 10.1055/s-2008-1038684

Marr, L.C., & Ely, M.R. (2010) Effect of Air Pollution on Marathon Running Performance, *Medicine and Science in Sports and Exercise*, *42*(3), 585–591. 10.1249/MSS.0b013e3181b84a85

Murfree, J.R. & Moorman, A.M. (2021) An Examination and Analysis of Division I Football Game Contracts: Legal Implications of Game Cancellations Due to Hurricanes, *Journal of Legal Aspects of Sport*, *31*(1), 123–146. 10.18060/24922

McCullough, B.P., Orr, M. & Kellison, T. (2020) Sport Ecology: Conceptualizing an Emerging Subdiscipline within Sport Management, *Journal of Sport Management*, *34*(6), pp. 509–520.

McCullough, B.P., Orr, M. & Watanabe, N.M. (2019) Measuring Externalities: The Imperative Next Step to Sustainability Assessment in Sport, *Journal of Sport Management*, *34*(5), 393–402.

NOAA (2020) *2019 was 2nd-hottest year on record for Earth say NOAA, NASA*. Available at: https://www.noaa.gov/news/2019-was-2nd-hottest-year-on-record-for-earth-say-noaa-nasa#:~:text=NASA%20also%20found%20that%202010,second%20warmest%20for%20the%20globe.

NASA (2019) *Hagibis floods Japan*. NASA Earth Observatory. Available at: https://earthobservatory.nasa.gov/images/145736/hagibis-floods-japan

Pattison, P., McIntyre, N., Mukhtar, I., Eapen, N., Bhuyan, M.O.U., Bhattari, U. & Piyari, A. (2021) Revealed: 6,500 Migrant Workers Have Died In Qatar Since World Cup Awarded. Available at: https://www.theguardian.com/global-development/2021/feb/23/revealed-migrant-worker-deaths-qatar-fifa-world-cup-2022 [Retrieved 30 March 2021].

Pereira, R.P.T., Camara, M.V.O., Ribeiro, G.M., & Filimonau, V. (2017) Applying the Facility Location Problem Model for Selection of more Climate Benign Mega Sporting Event Hosts: A Case of the FIFA World Cups, *Journal of Cleaner Production*, 159, 147–157.

Pereira, R.P., Filimonau, V., & Ribeiro, G.M. (2020) Projecting the Carbon Footprint of Tourist Accommodation at the 2030 FIFA World CUPTM, *Cleaner and Responsible Consumption*, 1, 100004. 10.1016/j.clrc.2020.100004

Peterson, N., Husted, L., Rebelo, T., & Holmes, P. (2007) Fynbos wake up call, *Veld and Flora*, *93*(2). https://hdl.handle.net/10520/EJC113057

Powell, M. (2016) In the Brazilian Rain Forest, 'A White Elephant, A Big One'. *The New York Times*. Available at: https://www.nytimes.com/2016/08/17/sports/manaus-brazil-amazon-rain-forest-stadium.html

Qatar Airways (2020) *Qatar Airways Partners with IATA and ClimateCare to Launch Voluntary Carbon Offset Programme for Passengers*. Available at: https://www.qatarairways.com/en/press-releases/2020/November/CarbonOffset.html

Ross W.J., & Mercado, H.U. (2020) Barriers to Managing Environmental Sustainability in Public Assembly Venues, *Sustainability*, 12(24), 10477.

Ross, W.J. & Orr, M.(Forthcoming) Predicting Climatological Impacts to Mega-Events in the 2020s, *North American Society for Sport Management*.

Sofotasiou, P., Hughes, B.R. & Calautit, J.K. (2015 Qatar 2022: Facing the FIFA World Cup Climatic and Legacy Challenges, *Sustainable Cities and Society*, 14, 16–30.

Stone, A. (2016) New actions to tackle climate through sport. *Obama White House Archives*. Available at: https://obamawhitehouse.archives.gov/blog/2016/10/06/new-actions-tackle-climate-through-sports

Taylor, L. (2019) Cancelled races, fainting players: How climate change is affecting sport. *World Economic Forum*. Available at: https://www.weforum.org/agenda/2019/08/climate-change-turns-up-heat-on-sports/

UNESCO (2017) Kazan Action Plan. *Sixth International Conference of Ministers and Senior Officials Responsible for Physical Education and Sport*. pp. 1–26. Available at: https://unesdoc.unesco.org/ark:/48223/pf0000252725

United Nations (2018) *Sports for climate action framework*. United Nations Climate Change. Available at: https://unfccc.int/climate-action/sectoral-engagement/sports-for-climate-action

United Nations (2019) *The Climate Crisis – A Race We Can Win*. Available at: https://www.un.org/en/un75/climate-crisis-race-we-can-win

Watanabe, N., Wicker, P., & Yan, G. (2017) Weather Conditions, Travel Distance, Rest, and Running Performance: The 2014 FIFA World Cup and Implications for the Future, *Journal of Sport Management*, 31, 27–43. 10.1123/jsm.2016-0077

9

FINANCE OF THE FIFA WORLD CUP

Daniel Plumley and Rob Wilson

Introduction

They call football the "beautiful game" but hosting the FIFA World Cup can often be an ugly prospect for a nation's economy. Russia's hosting of the tournament, in 2018, delivered the accolade of being the most expensive ever, an official staging cost of just over US $14 billion (The Moscow Times, 2018). Qatar 2022 will undoubtedly surpass this figure, although we are yet to know by how much exactly. When Qatar was chosen as the host for the 2022 competition back in 2010, early estimates of total cost were cited as being around $65 billion at least (Arabian Business, 2010).

This chapter seeks to examine these staggering numbers, explaining what the numbers correspond to and why countries fall over themselves to earn the right to host the tournament against a backdrop of such significant costs. While some commentators may express the view that it is not about the money, others will question the return on investment for mega-events of this type. For many host nations, generating a profit might barely be on the radar. For these, it might well be about the prestige, the political associations, and the pursuit of "soft power" through sport.

For FIFA, the narrative is much more straight forward. For them, the World Cup is about the monetary gain and revenue generation to fund its operations across each four-year cycle. Indeed, following the success of the tournament in Russia in 2018, FIFA's revenue reached a new high of $6.42 billion, of which $5.36 billion (83%) was directly attributable to Russia 2018 (FIFA Financial Report, 2018). Hosting a tournament may come at a significant cost to the host nation but it is in FIFA's interests to make sure the event is a success, and of course, they need not worry about the costs.

DOI: 10.4324/9781003121794-9

Against this context, this chapter considers the role that finance plays in shaping the world's biggest football tournament, incorporating key themes including the business of FIFA, regulatory accounting frameworks and legal requirements covering the income statement and balance sheet, FIFA's finances, the Women's World Cup, the business model of hosting the FIFA World Cup and future financing of the World Cup.

The Business of FIFA

As the governing body of the world's most popular sport, FIFA is naturally a large organisation. It employees over 800 people from 50 nations and is responsible for supporting 211 affiliated associations (countries) both financially and logistically through various programmes. The vision of FIFA (taken from the strategy section on their website) is "to promote the game of football, protect its integrity and bring the game to all." Part of realising this vision involves a strong narrative around "growing the game." It is within this narrative that the importance of the World Cup becomes clear to FIFA. To grow the game, they must invest in the game. To invest in the game, they need to generate significant finance. To generate significant finance, they need a successful World Cup tournament. In generating such finance, much like any large organisation, it is subject to the regulatory accounting frameworks and legal requirements. Every year, FIFA files its annual report and financial statements in line with the International Financial Reporting Standards (IFRS), which must be approved by an auditing firm. The report must also receive approval internally, through FIFA's Financial Committee, the FIFA council and, finally, the FIFA congress. The structure of FIFA is not the easiest to map from a hierarchical perspective. There is a president at the top, but presidents are elected by the FIFA congress and FIFA council. Once elected, the president controls and oversees both the FIFA congress and council. There is also a secretary general who works closely with the president. Underneath these councils and individuals are nine separate standing committees that report to the FIFA council and 211 affiliated associations across six confederations (the AFC in Asia, CAF in Africa, CONCACAF in North and Central America and the Caribbean, CONMEBOL in South America, UEFA in Europe and the OFC in Oceania) that FIFA supports financially and logistically through various programmes. More information on this structure can be found on the FIFA website. Irrespective of the uniqueness of their governance structure, FIFA, like all sporting organisations (including professional football clubs themselves) must conform with IFRSs that have been established by The International Accounting Standards Board (IASB). Companies have been required to publish their financial statements using IFRSs rather than domestic standards since January 2005.

Financial statements are the accountant's summary of the performance of a company over a particular period and of its position at the end of that period. Performance providing details of what money has been generated and what has been spent, leaving behind a profit or loss, and position establishing the net worth of an organisation once all the items that it owns and all the items that it owes have been calculated. Such financial statements are prepared using several basic principles as defined by the IASB and are mandatory for all listed companies. A more detailed overview of the statement of principles and the impact that financial regulatory frameworks have had on football can be found in a chapter on finance and accounting in football by (Wilson and Plumley, 2018) in the *Routledge Handbook of Football Business and Management*.

The use of the word period in the context of financial performance is especially relevant in the context of an organisation like FIFA. Normally, a company would define a financial period as one year, yet FIFA operates on a four-year cycle (centred around the World Cup) and their financial statements are defined in a way that refers to periods (e.g., 2015–2018) rather than singular years. To unpick this further, let us focus on the most recent completed cycle for FIFA (2015–2018) and outline the relevant components of income and costs linked to the regulatory framework for accounting statements as prescribed by IFRS.

Income Statements and Balance Sheets

All sport organisations have a responsibility to produce financial statements: the legal requirements for which, will be determined by the nature of the company (i.e., whether they are a sole trader or a public company). There are two main financial statements that need to be drawn up by financial accountants: the balance sheet and income statement. The *Balance Sheet* provides a list of all assets owned by the business and all the liabilities owed by a business. It is often referred to as a "snapshot" of the financial position of the business at a specific moment in time (normally at the end of a financial year) and therefore is only really useful on the day on which it is produced.

The *Income Statement* provides a statement showing the profits (or losses) recognised during a period (normally 12 months as per the *Balance Sheet*). The profit is calculated by deducting expenditure (including charges for capital maintenance) from the income generated during the accounting period. In simple terms, these documents help define a company's operations against the key financial equation:

$$Assets - Liabilities = Capital$$

Assets are resources that the business owns, for example, buildings, machinery and vehicles. Such resources will be used by the business in its operations. There may also be bank balances and cash. These will hold the funds that the business needs to operate. However, the business may also owe money to its owners, other people or organisations – these are called liabilities. A limited company will produce an income and expenditure statement for the period of one year. However, it is not uncommon for internal users to produce income statements on a quarterly or even monthly basis. Income statements that you come across externally are likely to be in annual reports and will therefore be for a 12-month period.

FIFA's Finances

When analysing the income statement of FIFA, we can see that their revenue reached a new high of $6.42 billion during the 2015–2018 cycle. $4.64 billion of this was revenue generated in 2018 alone, showing the importance of the final year (World Cup year) of the cycle in the four-year business model. Interesting, the figure of $4.64 billion showed an increase of 16% against FIFA's budgeted target, meaning that the World Cup in Russia exceeded financial expectations. Additionally, the 2015–2018 cycle showed revenue growth of $888 million against the previous cycle (2011–2014).

Many might ask at this point where the money comes from? This is quite straight forward: FIFA has five core revenue categories: hospitality rights and ticket sales, licensing rights, marketing rights, television broadcasting rights and other revenue. Most of the revenue continues to be driven by television broadcasting rights, although FIFA also saw the biggest growth come from licensing rights based on previous cycles. In terms of the former, the rights to the 2018 FIFA World Cup Russia contributed 95% of all income from TV broadcasting rights relating to all FIFA tournaments and events hosted in 2015–2018. The number of unique viewers of the 2018 tournament exceeded three billion across all viewing methods and more than one billion people watched the final. In relation to the latter, FIFA attributes the growth to a strong performance in brand licensing citing the delivery of the FIFA eWorld Cup™ Grand Final 18. This is perhaps a sign of future growth also in relation to the presence of eSports and their global reach. A detailed breakdown of FIFA's $6.42 billion revenue for the 2015–2018 is provided by categories and items in Figure 9.1 and Table 9.1 for reference.

Unsurprisingly, the biggest cost element of the cycle also occurred in 2018 with total expenses being $2.89 billion in 2018 against a total expense of $5.37 billion for the cycle. After operating at a loss for the years 2015–2017, a profit (before tax) of $1.75 billion in 2018 led to an overall surplus for the cycle of $1.05 billion. Most of FIFA's expenses relate to football-related activities ($4.36 billion for the 2015–2018 cycle) including a substantial amount of cost relating directly to the World Cup itself ($1.82 billion for Russia 2018).

The Women's World Cup

The men's World Cup will undoubtedly continue to dictate the strategic direction of FIFA's four-year business cycle, but the organisation will also benefit in future from the significant growth (and growth potential) of the women's game. Indeed, there are already early signs that this is starting to generate further revenue for FIFA following the success of the Women's World Cup in France in 2019. That tournament had a total combined global audience of 1.12 billion people across 205 territories worldwide, shattering many national audience records along the way (FIFA Annual Report, 2019). Additionally, FIFA's revenue in 2019, the first year

TABLE 9.1 FIFA Revenue 2015–2018 ($m) by category and item

Category	*Item*	*Value ($m)*
Hospitality and ticket rights	Hospitality/accommodation	148
	Ticket Sales	564
Total		**712**
Licensing rights	Brand licensing rights	575
	Other licensing rights	25
Total		**600**
Marketing rights	FIFA Partners	1,118
	FIFA World Cup Sponsors	363
	FIFA Regional Supporters	153
	FIFA National Supporters	26
Total		**1,660**
TV Broadcasting rights	Europe	920
	Asia and North Africa	974
	South and Central America	452
	North America & Caribbean	522
	Rest of World	104
	Other broadcasting & events	155
Total		**3,127**
Other Revenue	FIFA Club World Cup	123
	Penalties/appeals	27
	FIFA Quality Programme	44
	FIFA World Football Museum	12
	Income from sales of film/video rights	22
	Other events and areas	94
Total		**322**
Cumulative Total		**6,421**

Source: Adapted from FIFA Annual Report, 2019.

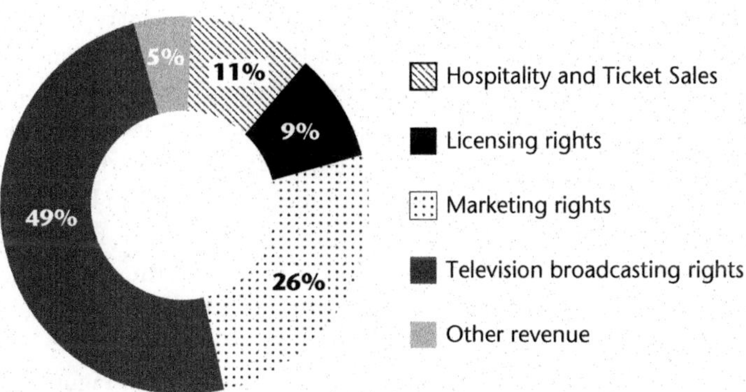

FIGURE 9.1 FIFA Revenue 2015–2018 by category. Adapted from FIFA Annual Report, 2019

of the 2019–2022 cycle, totalled $766 million, a figure that was 41% higher than the same period in the previous cycle (2015). As the women's game is expected to grow in commercial value in future years so too will FIFA's revenue and the women's game will help them generate future surpluses in the early stages of cycles given that the tournament takes place one year after the men's tournament and that the two will never clash from a scheduling perspective. There are further positive signs for FIFA in relation to the women's tournament. The French Football Federation (FFF) cited that the 2019 tournament contributed roughly €284 million to France's GDP with the average financial contribution of each spectator estimated to be €142. This is almost double the economic activity recorded at the 2015 tournament in Canada, adding more weight to the argument that women's football is transitioning into a serious economic and cultural product. Good financial news for host countries means good financial news for FIFA. They have developed a business model that involves selling the greatest sporting product to the highest bidder at minimal cost (from a hosting perspective). With the growth potential of the women's game in the future, they may have just added another significant cash cow to their arsenal.

In this section, we have seen where FIFA makes its money and where its biggest costs are. However, it is also clear here that FIFA do not directly cover the cost of hosting a World Cup. That cost is laid solely at the door of the host nation. Additionally, FIFA take all the revenue generated from broadcasting and ticket sales etc. This begs the question as to what the benefits of hosting a FIFA World Cup are for the host nation. Put simply, why are so many countries so desperate to host it?

The Business Model of Hosting a FIFA World Cup

Before we cover the actual technical aspects of bidding for and hosting a FIFA World Cup, let us briefly consider the earlier-mentioned question as to why countries want to host major sporting events. The main benefits associated with this are mostly split into monetary and non-monetary benefits. Monetary benefits can include, but are not limited to, economic impact (for the cities and country), direct and indirect spend and, most crucially, out-of-town attendees. Non-monetary benefits often cited include social, environmental and cultural impacts as well as the age-old argument of the creation of a "legacy" from the event. Figure 9.2 outlines the role that individual citizens of the country play in hosting a major sporting event and why they should be "happy" to do so. We begin the figure at "residents pay taxes" and then move through the rest of the cycle. The right-hand side of the cycle depicts outflows of revenues whilst the left-hand side depicts inflows of revenues.

Whether all residents in any given country buy into the narrative of Figure 9.2 is part of a wider debate, and certainly beyond the scope of this chapter, but there is little doubt that governments of host nations, looking to secure a World Cup, play hard on the benefits of hosting a tournament and look to sell it to their

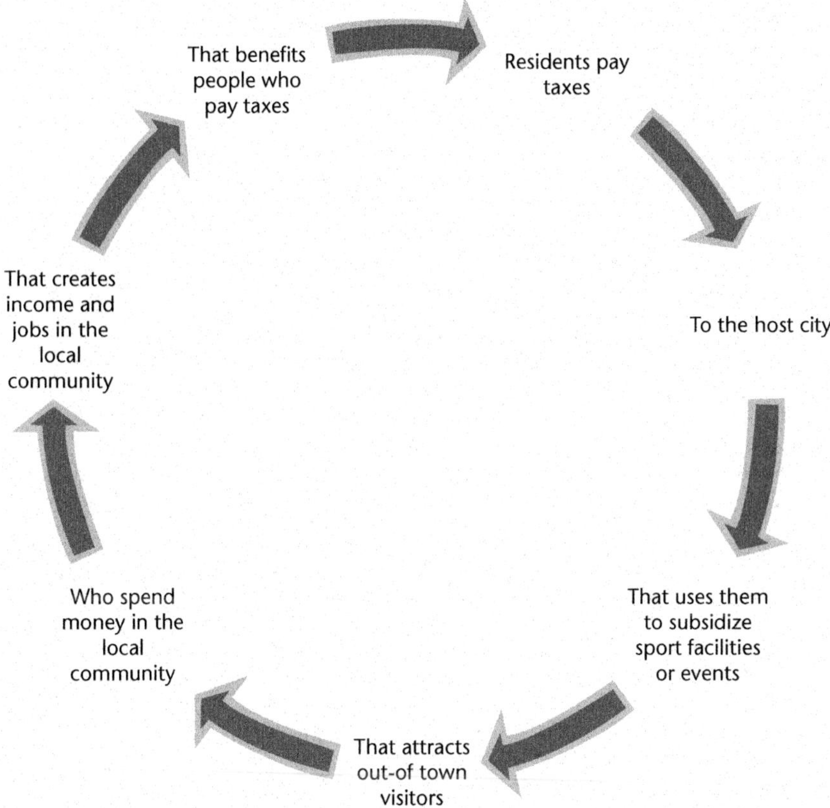

FIGURE 9.2 The role of the taxpayers in hosting major sporting events. Adapted from (Stewart, 2017)

citizens on the wider benefits it can have to cities, regions and nations. Unfortunately, it is not just the citizens of their own country that the bidders must convince. Any bid to host the World Cup requires significant financial investment to meet the technical evaluation criteria outlined by FIFA as part of their bidding process. This cost is incurred before the host is even decided so it does come with financial risk for host nations. Indeed, when England failed in their bid to host the 2018 tournament, securing only 2 votes out of a possible 22 and being eliminated in the first round of voting, they spent £21 million in doing so. The cost is high because the technical evaluation is complex. For example, the overview of the scoring system for the technical evaluation of the 2026 World Cup is a document that stretches 50 pages. Countries bidding must demonstrate how they hit the nine criteria for the technical evaluation which is broadly categorised into two areas of "Infrastructure" and "Commercial." A more detailed overview of these criteria is discussed next (see also Tables 9.2 and 9.3).

TABLE 9.2 Key Criteria for the Bidding Process of a FIFA World Cup

Technical Evaluation	
Infrastructure Criteria (70%)	
1. Stadiums	The proposed stadiums
2. Teams and Referee Facilities	The facilities proposed for participating teams and referees
3. Accommodation	The secured accommodation
4. Transport (including airports)	The transport infrastructure and concept for general mobility, including the proposed airports
5. IT&T and IBC	The IT&T fixed and mobile network and infrastructure in the host country/host countries as well as the proposed locations for the International Broadcast Centre
6. FIFA Fan Fest™ and Event Promotion	The proposed locations to be used for the staging of the FIFA Fan Fest™ and for event promotional purposes
Commercial Criteria (30%)	
7. Organising Costs	The predicted costs of the tournament, including the predicted direct costs of FIFA, the predicted costs related to the performance of the obligations of the member association(s) as well as third-party stakeholder costs predicted for the hosting of the tournament in the host country/host countries
8. Ticketing and Hospitality Revenues	The estimated revenues that may be generated by FIFA from the sale of tickets and hospitality packages for the tournament
9. Media and Marketing Revenues	The estimated revenues that may be generated by FIFA from the sale of media and marketing rights for the tournament inside the host country/host countries and on a global basis

Source: FIFA 2026 Technical Bid Specification Document.

Key criteria for the bidding process of a FIFA World Cup

Technical evaluation part 1: infrastructure criteria (weighted at 70% of overall total)

- **Stadiums**
  - This area relates to the proposed stadiums that are planned on being used to host the event. This includes both existing stadia and proposed new stadia.

TABLE 9.3 Sub-criteria and weightings for "Stadiums"

Stadiums		
Sub-criteria	*Explanation*	*Weight (%)*
Stadium costs and planning milestones	Key construction milestones, total investments and cost per seat	10
Stadium orientation and space requirements	Site maps and floor plans analyses	10
Stadium capacity	Gross capacity, VIP tribune capacity and seat kills	22.5
Pitch	Pitch type and dimensions	10
Technical installations	TV, power, infotainment and IT installations	20
Accessibility and sustainability	Sanitary facilities and infrastructure for disabled spectators	7.5
Roof, residents and overlay	Roof and overlay cost estimates	20

Source: FIFA 2026 Technical Bid Specification Document.

- **Teams and referee facilities**
  - This area relates to the facilities proposed for participating teams and referees. Again, this includes both existing facilities and proposed new facilities.
- **Transport**
  - The transport infrastructure and concept for general mobility, including the proposed airports and any other necessary transfer links regarding travel options from airports to cities and between cities linked to proposed stadia arrangements.
- **Accommodation**
  - Any proposed accommodation for any relevant party associated with the hosting of the competition. Normally relates to secured accommodation.
- **Information Technology and International Broadcast Centre**
  - This relates to IT and broadcasting infrastructure. It includes the IT&T fixed and mobile network and infrastructure in the host country/host countries as well as the proposed locations for the International Broadcast Centre. This is particularly important given the global commercial nature of the event.
- **FIFA Fan Fest™ and event promotion**
  - This relates to the proposed locations to be used for the staging of the FIFA Fan Fest™ and for event promotional purposes. Fan zones are now an integral part of any technical bid criteria and an important component of the infrastructure criteria.

Technical evaluation part 2: commercial criteria (weighted at 30% of overall total)

- **Organising costs**
  - This relates to the predicted costs of the tournament, including the predicted direct costs of FIFA, the predicted costs related to the performance of the obligations of the member association(s) as well as third-party stakeholder costs predicted for the hosting of the tournament in the host country/host countries. It is important that these costs are as detailed as possible at the bid stage.
- **Ticketing and hospitality revenues**
  - This relates to any estimated revenues that may be generated by FIFA from the sale of tickets and hospitality packages for the tournament. This covers all range of tickets from basic attendee tickets all the way up to the highest level of corporate hospitality tickets.
- **Media and marketing revenues**
  - This relates to any estimated revenues that may be generated by FIFA from the sale of media and marketing rights for the tournament inside the host country/host countries and on a global basis. Again, it is important that these revenues, as with ticket and hospitality, are as detailed as possible at the bid stage.

Source: Adapted from FIFA 2026 Technical Bid Specification Document)

Each of the nine criteria also have their own respective weighting within their sub-section. For example, all commercial criteria are split equally at 10% each, but in the "Infrastructure" criteria stadiums have a weighting of 35%. Facilities and accommodation are weighted 6% each, transport is weighted 13% with IT&T and IBC (7%) and Fan Fest locations (3%) making up the remainder of that criteria. Additionally, each individual criterion has its own sub-criteria and weighting that make the bidding process even more technical. An example of the sub-criteria and weighting for stadiums is provided later as a worked example.

Sub-criteria and weightings for "Stadiums" (weighting total 100%)

Relevant stadium costs and estimated planning milestones

- Any key construction milestones should be explained here along with total investments and estimations such as cost per seat etc.
- Weighted at 10% of overall total.

Proposed stadium orientation and estimated space requirements

- This should include relevant space requirements such as site maps and plans and relevant analysis of floor plans.
- Weighted at 10% of overall total.

Proposed stadium capacities

- This should include relevant space requirements such as site maps and plans and relevant analysis of floor plans.
- Weighted at 10% of overall total

Pitch specifications

- Stadium capacity data including gross capacity, VIP tribune capacity and seat kills.
- Weighted at 22.5% of overall total.

Proposed technical installations

- Proposed technical installations included items such as television, power, infotainment and IT installations.
- Weighted at 20% of overall total.

Accessibility and sustainability

- This aspect focuses on relevant provisions for different groups of people such as the inclusion of sanitary facilities and infrastructure for disabled spectators.
- Weighted at 7.5% of overall total.

Roof, residents and overlay

- Any relevant costs associated with items such as roof and overlay cost estimates (if applicable based on certain stadiums).
- Weighted at 20% of overall total.

Source: Adapted from FIFA 2026 Technical Bid Specification Document.

Further weighting criteria and individual section scores for each criterion are then computed before an overall score is eventually arrived at. The devil, as always, is in the detail and many countries have fell short at the bidding stage because their bid was not upto scratch not necessarily because they could not feasibly host the tournament.

If we look at the list of key criteria for the bidding process of a FIFA World Cup above, however, there is a significant cost to a host country before any of the benefits can be realised. The reason for citing the importance of the stadium criteria in the above list is because that is often where the biggest costs lie. A host country must have the stadiums that are fit for mega-events. If not, they must build them. And they are not cheap to build. That cost, alongside the wider transport and infrastructure costs of accommodating and transporting a significant number of visiting fans around your country, is more easily absorbed in developed countries. Countries that already have good transport links and stadia in place tend to have lower costs in relation to bids. However, some countries still use the World Cup to build new stadia or redevelop existing ones, with such projects being funded by the public purse. The question of legacy and stadium "white elephants" is important here and some recent examples portray an alarming picture about the potential long-term perils of hosting a World Cup when the show is over and the tourists head home.

It is still too early to measure the impact of Russia 2018, although state officials in the country have claimed that the tournament will add $26–$31 billion to the national economy in the longer-term, against an estimated cost of $12 billion to stage the tournament. Russia did, however, use the World Cup to build six new stadia (out of a total of 12 used) from scratch. The other six all required some form of renovation costs and all but one of which were built using public finances. In 2014, Brazil spent an estimated $15 billion to build stadiums and transportation, among other things when they hosted the World Cup. The most expensive of those stadiums, Mane Garrincha Stadium, cost $550 million and was only used a handful of times in the months after the tournament. In 2015, it was being used as a parking lot for buses. A further stadium used in Brazil, at a cost of $215 million, has since been closed down because of faulty construction and reports of homeless people squatting in its unused locker rooms. South Africa's World Cup in 2010 has been described as "a blessing and a curse" by legendary South African footballer Benni McCarthy ten years on, citing examples of "missed opportunities" when it came to the generating a true legacy from the tournament linked to infrastructure and the development of the national South African football team.

A further cost is linked to tax exemptions. In essence, FIFA requires bids to host the World Cup to include massive tax exemptions for the association. Germany offered FIFA an estimated $272 million in tax exemptions when it hosted the 2006 World Cup, with South Africa and Brazil following suit in 2010 and 2014, respectively. The agreements establish tax-free zones for the World Cup venues, with FIFA's corporate partners being exempt from income and sales taxes.

The most recent iteration of the tournament, to be hosted by Qatar in 2022, is on a different planet financially. The estimated spending for this tournament could potentially top $200 billion having been initially projected around the $65 billion mark. However, just a fraction of this is for direct costs relating to the World Cup, with the majority being allocated to projects that may go ahead independently of the football competition. Indeed, many have argued that making money from the World Cup is merely a "secondary driver" for Qatar. James Dorsey, a prominent author on Middle East Soccer, argued that it is not about economic viability for

Qatar. The 2022 World Cup is likely to be loss making in commercial terms. The primary gains Qatar is seeking are non-commercial. International relations are the key motivation for hosting the tournament and it is also about soft power as a defence and security strategy. Money is clearly no object to Qatar. The country can clearly afford to host a World Cup and is willing to absorb the losses attached. It is unrealistic, therefore, to compare the economic and financial power of Qatar to other countries that have hosted past World Cups such as Brazil and South Africa. In many ways, the 2022 World Cup is a financial anomaly.

What is clear from the above is that there is only one winner when it comes to hosting a World Cup; FIFA themselves. The business of hosting a FIFA World Cup simply does not appear to pay from a host country perspective. Which brings us back to the reason for hosting this tournament centring on a wider benefit for the country linked to economic and social aspects, or, more crudely, putting your country in the shop window and making yourself look good to the outside world. It is all a vanity project, creating a beautiful show for the beautiful game with the sanity of financial prudence cast aside. So where does the show move to next? What might we see in the future related to the financing of the biggest footballing event on the planet?

Future World Cup Financing

As previously stated, the Qatar tournament in 2022 is perhaps not the best comparison, or future marker, of a World Cup from a financial perspective. It will no doubt be unlike anything we have ever seen before, given the nation's financial power and resources, but it is unlikely to show us what might happen to the future of World Cup financing beyond 2022. In fact, we are suited to focusing our thoughts further ahead, to the World Cup of 2026 and beyond. The 2026 tournament has already been branded as "United 2026" in the official logo. It will be jointly hosted by the United States, Canada and Mexico. It will be the first co-hosted tournament since 2002 (co-hosted by Japan and South Korea) and the first to have more than two countries as co-hosts. The United States will host most of the matches, including the quarterfinals, semi-finals and final, but both Canada and Mexico are guaranteed to host 10 matches each. Co-hosting of tournaments was actually banned by FIFA following the 2002 World Cup, but this ban has now been removed and it may open the door for more countries to consider this method in the future. Indeed, there has already been a suggestion of a United Kingdom bid for the tournament in 2030 which would include England, Scotland, Wales, Northern Ireland and the Republic of Ireland all as co-hosts. There have been further rumours of joint bids from other countries for the 2030 tournament including South America (Chile, Argentina, Paraguay and Uruguay) and Europe/North Africa (Spain, Morocco and Portugal).

This is also an approach that UEFA have taken recently with the hosting of the European Football Championships (Euros). The 2020 version of that tournament (delayed until 2021 because of the COVID-19 pandemic) is due to take place across 12 different European cities. Multi-country hosting might become the future of hosting the greatest show on earth. Given the extortionate costs attached with hosting the World Cup, you can see the appeal to the host nation(s). It presents an opportunity to limit financial cost and risk whilst still being able to generate some of the intangible benefits of hosting a major sporting event. For FIFA, the scenario remains win–win. In fact, it may even deliver a bigger windfall; more host countries means a bigger target audience to sell tickets to. It means more fan parks in more places and more opportunity to generate revenue from fan activities. It means more opportunity for unique commercial partnerships and sponsorships. It also increases the potential number of bidders to host, providing FIFA with a relentless chain of successors all scrambling to welcome them and the World Cup with open arms.

Conclusion

This chapter has introduced the concepts surrounding the finances of the FIFA World Cup, the business of FIFA and the cost of hosting a tournament to the public purse. Following the completion of this chapter, the reader should now understand and appreciate the importance of financing the World Cup in the four-year business cycle that FIFA operate under and the uniqueness of football compared to other mainstream businesses.

The financing of major sporting events, including the FIFA World Cup will continue to be a challenge for sport managers and researchers to leverage and secure benefit, while operating in a spirit that delivers participation. Any mention of prospective benefits should also consider the role that finance plays in hosting a World Cup and the wider objectives and strategy of a host nation and preparing a bid. Critically, it should look to examine whether "legacy" is a real concept and whether hosting a World Cup is in fact detrimental to a country's economy in the longer term. The role of FIFA in all of this is clear. Sell the World Cup to the highest bidder. There is nothing wrong with this from a business point of view. Indeed, one of the fundamental rules of finance is to make sure your selling price is higher than the cost. It is merely that, in this instance, the cost is borne by somebody else. The business model of the FIFA World Cup is indeed unique. However, it remains a lucrative one for FIFA and its commercial partners.

References

Arabian Business (2010) *Qatar makes $65bn Bet to Transform Economy for World Cup*. Available at: https://www.arabianbusiness.com/qatar-makes-65bn-bet-transform-economy-for-world-cup-368140.html

FIFA (2018) 2026 Technical Bid Specification Document. Available at: https://resources.fifa.com/image/upload/overview-of-scoring-system-for-the-technical-evaluation-of-2026-fifa-world-cup-b.pdf?cloudid=eg1fnzj6q9ik5gmggkwi

FIFA Annual Report (2019) Available at: https://img.fifa.com/image/upload/ksndm8om7duu5h8qxlpn.pdf

FIFA Financial Report (2018). Available at: https://resources.fifa.com/image/upload/xzshsoe2ayttyquuxhq0.pdf

Stewart, B. (2017) *Sport Funding and Finance.* London, UK: Routledge.

The Governance of FIFA. Available at: https://www.fifa.com/what-we-do/governance/finances/

The Moscow Times (2018) *Russia's World Cup Costs to Exceed $14bn.* Available at: https://www.themoscowtimes.com/2018/06/08/Russias-World-Cup-Costs-to-Exceed-Record-Setting-14Bln-a61732#:~:text=The%20cost%20of%20hosting%20the,expensive%20football%20competition%20in%20history.

Wilson, R & Plumley, D. (2018) Finance and Accounting in Football. In S. Chadwick, D. Parnell, P. Widdop & C. Anagnostopoulos (eds), *Routledge Handbook of Football Business and Management.* London: Routledge.

10

PLANNING AND ORGANISING FIFA WORLD CUPS

Sebastian Merten and Mathieu Winand

Introduction

FIFA World Cups are considered mega-sporting events, which according to Getz (2007, p. 25) are those that "by way of their size of significance, are those that yield extraordinarily high levels of tourism, media coverage, prestige, or economic impact for the host community, venue or organization." FIFA has projected that the 2026 World Cup to be held across Canada, Mexico and the United States will generate a revenue of US $11 billion (Statista, 2020). The economic, but also the political and social magnitude of this mega-event has grown considerably since the first World Cup was hosted more than 90 years ago. The event is now the most popular team sports tournament in the world. The FIFA World Cup as we currently know it can be traced back primarily to the commitment of Jules Rimet, FIFA President from 1921 to 1954 (FIFA, 1998). Jules Rimet recognised the potential of the sport and it was at his instigation that the decision was taken to organise an independent tournament separate from the Olympic Games which made its debut in Uruguay in 1930 (FIFA, 1998). According to FIFA official terminology, the FIFA World Cup refers to men's football only. It would take another 61 years before the first official FIFA Women's World Cup would take place in China in 1991 (FIFA, 2015b). Overall, FIFA is now responsible for a whole range of events for men and women, across multiple different age groups (see Table 10.1). In terms of revenue and reach, however, the Men's World Cup remains by far FIFA's most important event. As a major global sporting event, the FIFA World Cup is ever omnipresent in the media and various platforms that it is almost impossible not to notice the event. The 2018 tournament in Russia was watched by more than half of the world's population. This was also the most profitable edition of the World Cup to date, contributing a total of 83% of FIFA's revenue for the 2015–2018 cycle (FIFA, 2019a). These figures illustrate the stature

DOI: 10.4324/9781003121794-10

TABLE 10.1 Events organised by FIFA

Men	*Women*
FIFA World Cup	FIFA Women's World Cup
FIFA Confederations Cup (until 2017)	FIFA U20 Women's World Cup
FIFA U20 World Cup	FIFA U17 Women's World Cup
FIFA Club World Cup	Women's Olympic Football Tournament
FIFA Beach Soccer World Cup	Girl's Youth Olympic Football Tournament
FIFA Futsal World Cup	
Men's Olympic Football Tournament	
Boy's Youth Olympic Football Tournament	
FIFA eWorld Cup	

of the event and the attention it attracts worldwide. It also provides a glance of how complex the planning phase and the operational implementation of an event of this magnitude is.

The successful organisation and operation of mega-sporting events requires strategic management and sustainable planning to maximise the chances of success. Hosting an event on the scale of a World Cup brings global attention and puts the hosting management, as well as the hosting country, under the international spotlight. It is therefore important for the organiser to formulate clear objectives already in the planning phase and to have them in mind together with the stakeholders involved. This is the only way to ensure proper event planning, implementation and sustainable results, a legacy. Well-defined objectives provide concrete information for the reviewing processes throughout in the planning phase and the associated feasibility analysis, which also plays an important role in the bidding process conducted by FIFA. Event objectives must be formulated as clear KPIs (Key Performance Indicators) and thus be as specific and measurable as possible. Without effective indicators, it is difficult to design an event, have a smooth planning phase and a successful delivery of the World Cup, not to mention an objective evaluation of the tournament afterwards. To meet these requirements, event management for FIFA events usually comprises of five partly overlapping phases: design, development, implementation, operations and evaluation (FIFA, 2018b). These are described in the following sections.

Planning Phase: Event Design and Development

How the start of an event's planning phase is conducted is, of course, heavily dependent on the event in question. In the case of the FIFA World Cup, it is a pre-existing event that has some repetitive aspects but takes place in different host nations every four years and therefore needs to be customised for each edition. This constant change of host means that knowledge transfer is an essential and challenging element of event design and organisation (Parent and Smith-Swan, 2013).

The tournament is awarded to the host in the form of a bidding procedure. The planning phase thus already begins with the decision to bid for hosting the World Cup and the subsequent preparation of the formal bid for the bidding process. In the decision-making process of applying to host an event, it is important to reach agreements with key stakeholders and discuss important programme elements that will make the event unique and special (Bowdin et al., 2011). However, to participate in the bidding process for a FIFA World Cup, interested federations must first express their interest to FIFA in hosting the tournament within a specified period of time in order to receive all the necessary bidding and hosting documents (FIFA, 2018a). The example of the 2026 World Cup and the approximately eight months allowed between the declaration of interest in hosting the event and the submission of the formal bid indicates how high the requirements are for the final bid documents (FIFA, 2018a).

To increase the chances of a successful bidding process, Bowdin et al. (2011) have formulated key elements such as the identification of resources that can be used to support the event (e.g. venues and government grants), a plan for the composition of the delivery organisation, a concept for the event, an analysis of key elements of past successful bids for the preparation of one's own bid document and the bid presentation to the rights holder, as well as lobbying to support the bid. One of the most important aspects of the World Cup bidding process for FIFA is the support from the government of the respective bidder (FIFA, 2018a). Bidding associations, but also governments and all organisations involved in the organisation of the tournament, such as those responsible for any construction work (e.g. stadiums, training facilities, hotels and airports), must guarantee the implementation of and compliance with human rights and labour standards. The basis for this is the ISO 20121 standard and the international human rights and labour standards in accordance with the United Nations Guiding Principles on Business and Human Rights (FIFA, 2018a).

The documents provided by FIFA form the framework for creating the event concept for the formal bidding process. Once the event concept is sufficiently developed, it can be subjected to a more detailed review. Once completed, a preliminary assessment can be made as to whether they fit the potential host's capabilities and the local conditions. This is followed by a detailed feasibility study that examines the concept in more detail (Bowdin et al., 2011). Even the preparation of a bid and the bidding process associated with it can create high costs for the applicants, without the guarantee that the rights to host the desired event will be granted. Australia, for example, invested the equivalent of about US$ 46,000,000 of taxpayers' money (based on the year-end exchange rate AUS$/US$ 2010) in its 2022 World Cup bid and was unsuccessful, leading to public criticism of its spending (Cannane, 2018). By comparison, for their successful 2022 World Cup bid, Qatar reportedly invested more than US$ 80,000,000 (Chalip and Heere, 2014).

Since the 2000s, it can be observed that more and more developing and emerging countries are also competing in the bidding process to host sports mega-events (e.g., BBC, 2009; Dove, 2018; FIFA, 2003). This development is also reflected in the organisers of the past three World Cups in South Africa (2010), Brazil (2014), Russia (2018) and the upcoming tournament 2022 in Qatar.

Bowdin et al. (2011) recommend that each event should have a clear statement of purpose and a vision that is aligned with the different stakeholders (e.g., potential visitors, government, sponsors and volunteers), as this helps to ensure a clear direction and focus for the event. In the case of the 2018 FIFA World Cup, the Local Organising Committee's (LOC) vision was to distinguish it from previous World Cups. LOC CEO Alexey Sorokin elaborated: "On the one hand, the vision must articulate values that are clear and familiar to the people of this country, and on the other hand, it must be accessible to every football fan around the world" (FIFA, 2012). The Russian LOC used experts, journalists and other members of the football family to identify four key areas:

- stage an unforgettable festival for the football community,
- project a positive image of a modern Russia and improve relationships with one another through real achievements and the interplay between cultures
- use football's inspirational power to promote a healthy lifestyle, and
- realise the potential of different regions in Russia by creating a sustainable world-class legacy.

One of the most important decisions in the design phase is the selection of the World Cup venues, as often a number of cities are interested in being one of the required venues. This was also the case for the 2018 World Cup in Russia, which is why the LOC developed a selection process that used a system of five main evaluation criteria: the current standard of infrastructure, the level of socio-economic development, the nature of the investment programmes for the 2018 World Cup, the concepts for the 2018 World Cup and how the host cities will effectively use the legacy of the tournament (FIFA, 2012). The LOC then visited the candidate cities together with FIFA experts and selected the 12 World Cup venues about four years before the start of the tournament. Legacy is becoming more and more important, already in the planning and bidding phase, to increase the chance of sustainable positive effects of mega-events for the host. "Irrespective of the time of production and space, legacy is all planned and unplanned, positive and negative, tangible and intangible structures created for and by a sport event that remain longer than the event itself (Preuss, 2007, p. 211)." Although Preuss (2007) identifies the intangible effects as the most important legacy of major sporting events, it is often the oversized infrastructure of the hosts that subsequently poses problems. More sustainability in the requirements for major sporting events is therefore necessary to reduce the demands on host cities, as they increasingly have problems providing the required infrastructure. Examples from past tournaments can also be found in oversized and/or unsustainable facilities in various cities of the World Cups 2002 in Japan (Preuss, 2007), 2010 in South Africa (Bladen et al., 2018) or 2014 in Brazil (Boadle, 2014).

While a World Cup itself lasts only a few weeks, the changes brought about by such an event can have important consequences for the host cities for much longer. Preuss (2015) distinguishes five superordinate event structures, namely infrastructure, knowledge, policy, networks and emotions, to which the different legacies can be subordinated. They are often triggers and accelerators for change at the political, economic and social levels that are otherwise difficult to break down due to the presence of established, sometimes outdated patterns (Preuss, 2015). However, in the context of major sporting events, there have recently been more critical voices about investments in connection with these events. Especially in the context of the 2014 World Cup in Brazil, citizens have expressed their displeasure about the costs of the World Cup to the public purse (Watts, 2014). This led to social unrest in Brazil, as the population was unhappy about the distribution of public spending on infrastructure for the mega-event. Protesters were unfortunate with the prioritisation of spending, to the detriment of health, education and public safety, as they saw their basic needs unmet. From their point of view, the money for the construction of stadiums and highways was spent to please the tourists and not to benefit the local population.

This trend has also contributed to the fact that FIFA's bidding guide now lists sustainability as one of the priority areas in its criteria for potential hosts (FIFA, 2018a). The main criteria for hosting the tournament are divided into five pillars:

- Hosting vision and strategy,
- Host country information,
- Technical matters,
- Other event-related matters, and
- Sustainable event management, human rights, environmental protection

However, the importance of government support and sustainability and human rights is particularly emphasised in FIFA's bidding guide (Figure 10.1).

Implementing and Operating a World Cup

After the FIFA Congress has decided on a host, the operational planning enters the decisive phase. Based on the strategic plans created for the bidding process, the operational plan is implemented.

As FIFA World Cups are very complex and each tournament is individually different due to local circumstances, not all processes can be replicated exactly from previous World Cups. However, FIFA (2019c) has launched a sustainability strategy and created a knowledge base to use lessons learned from previous tournaments and to safeguard them for the event management of future tournaments. The focus on sustainability also aims to ensure that the tournament contributes to the well-being of people, economic development and environmental protection, and maximises these benefits. Both in the short and long terms. This is reflected in the five pillars to which FIFA subordinate all objectives

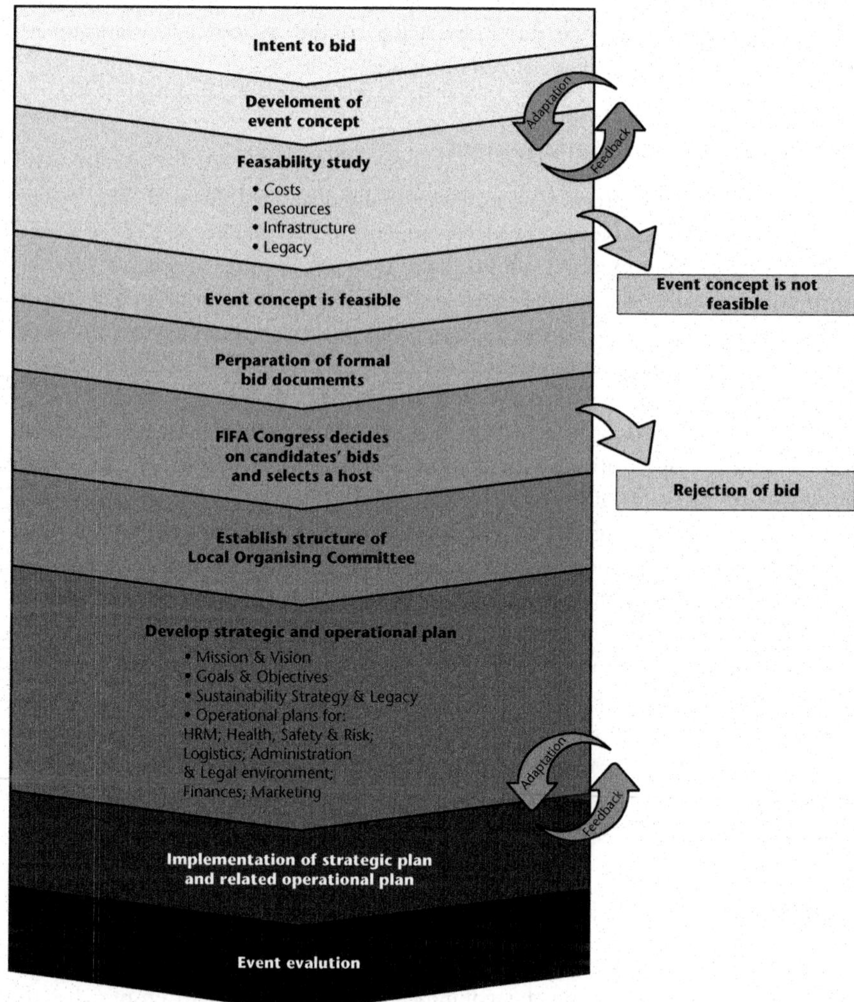

FIGURE 10.1 Planning phases of a FIFA World Cup. Adapted from Bowdin et al. (2011)

in connection with the tournament: Economic, Environmental, Human, Social and Governance.

Bladen et al. (2018) have categorised event operations management into six overarching areas: Human Resources; Health, Safety and Risk; Logistics; Legal Environment; Finance and Marketing. To ensure the smooth running of event operations management, it is important to successfully orchestrate the skills and resources needed to deliver an event (Bowdin et al. 2011). This requires a functional structure that promotes specialisation of the workforce. As a result, areas of responsibility can be assigned to individual persons or groups (e.g., committees), thus eliminating redundancies of responsibilities.

Human Resources Management

Mega-events like the World Cup pose very individual needs for staff. This creates challenges for Human Resources Management (HRM), also because of the special dependency on volunteers. Volunteer management requires specialised knowledge, event-specific policies and practices within the human resources department (Getz, 2007). Volunteers, however, do not offer the only special feature for HRM at events. As event organisations are more "project-oriented" than functional, this also has implications for the associated workforce requirements (Bladen et al., 2018). They differ from traditional business organisations in their demands on staff and leadership, which means that traditional functional structures and associated processes are often less effective when it comes to the ideal composition of staff and how they are managed. Challenges for leadership and event staff often result from stakeholder demands, limited resources, tight schedules and deadlines, and the ongoing and constant changes and influences from the environment (Bladen et al., 2018).

HRM for the upcoming 2022 FIFA World Cup requires that FIFA and the local delivery partners together employ tens of thousands of people over the cycle of the tournament. These are spread across services in areas such as construction, food and beverage, cleaning, event management, hospitality, transport and security; divided into full-time and temporary staff, contractors, supplier staff and volunteers (FIFA, 2019c).

Volunteers

One of the most important pillars to guarantee the successful running of events like a FIFA World Cup are the volunteers. Volunteers help to ensure that the numerous event components function. At the 2018 World Cup in Russia, a total of 17,000 volunteers were deployed in 20 key functional areas (FIFA, 2018c). These areas were (FIFA, 2016b): spectator services, marketing, catering, arrivals and departures, protocol, broadcasting operations, volunteer management, accommodation, ticketing, medical services and doping control, information technologies, accreditation, transport, sustainability, ceremonies, media operations, venue management, language services, hospitality and team services.

Volunteer programmes in the context of mega-events usually offer interesting opportunities for citizens to broaden their skillset and gain basic qualifications and work experience (Bladen et al., 2018). This should also contribute to local economic development in the host community. Employment growth is one of the key elements in the justification of applicants for hosting mega-events (Bladen et al., 2018). But especially for international events on the scale of a football World Cup, volunteers are not limited to the host's citizens.

One challenge for the organiser is to keep the volunteers satisfied to prevent them from churning (Getz, 2007). It is therefore important for event organisers to understand the motivations of volunteers. According to an analysis by Getz (2007), motivations to volunteer for events include altruism, networking, career benefits, challenging oneself, belonging and participation, as well as the desire for serious leisure. Of course, the fame of an event also plays a role, which is reflected in the high number of applicants for volunteer positions at FIFA World Cups. More than 150,000 volunteers signed up for the 2018 World Cup in Russia, a number that will be significantly exceeded by the so far 265,000 applicants for the 2022 World Cup (FIFA, 2018c; AS, 2021).

Health, Safety and Risk

Since every football World Cup is different, risk management has also to be planned and adapted individually. Health, Safety and Risk management needs to be people oriented and includes crowd management, which is about preventing problems and facilitating good experiences (Getz, 2007). A wide range of factors must be included in risk management planning and these need to be properly weighed up (Tarlow, 2002, p. xii):

- Size and age of crowd
- Size and nature of the event site
- Time of day
- Nature of the event
- Consumables (food, water, alcoholic beverages)
- Weather conditions
- Location of the event venue (urban, rural, etc.)

In conjunction with these factors, each event requires its own specific protocols, which are designed for emergency procedures as part of the logistical planning of events. These range from evacuation procedures, the extent of onsite first aid, to disaster planning (Bladen et al., 2018). The obligations for the different aspects of the security requirements at FIFA World Cups are determined by the respective LOC in accordance with FIFA's explicit specifications (e.g., FIFA Stadium Safety and Security Regulations; FIFA, 2014b). FIFA provides various guidelines for new constructions and stadium renovations in order to strike a healthy balance between stadium design and stadium management, ensuring effective stadium security (FIFA, 2014b). These documents also serve to educate FIFA event organisers about their duties and responsibilities, as they are responsible for the safety of spectators for the duration of the event. The host assumes this responsibility by signing the Host Agreement. This includes full responsibility for the conduct of all security matters relating to the competition and applies to all sites and venues (including airports and main railway stations of the host country). In addition, it includes responsibility for the security of representatives of national governments, the FIFA delegation, teams and match officials during the time that members of these groups are in the host country for purposes directly related to the World Cup, whether in preparation for the tournament or during the competition (FIFA, 2014b). However, this does not usually mean that LOCs also take control of the security of the event, but that they have to coordinate it (Frawley and Adair, 2014).

The host is responsible for employing professionally competent and trained persons (e.g., national security officers, stadium & venue security officers, stadium stewards and private security services) to perform the tasks required for the security management and operation of the event (FIFA, 2014b). For the more than 3,000,000 fans in the stadiums (Statista, 2018) and the 32 national teams participating in the FIFA World Cup in Russia 2018 a total of 19,000 stewards were on duty during the tournament to provide a safe environment (FIFA, 2018d). To ensure the best possible security, FIFA organised a three-day training workshop prior to the event, with the aim of consolidating the experience and knowledge of current FIFA security officers and identifying those who have what it takes to represent FIFA (FIFA, 2018d). To support the respective hosts, FIFA has set up the "FIFA Security Division," which offers professional advice on security at major events (FIFA, 2014b).

One of the main aspects of steward services at events like the FIFA World Cup is to ensure that the right people (e.g., Press, VIP guests, Members and staff of the football teams, Hospitality staff) have access to certain areas during build-up, the event itself and during the dismantling process. This is usually organised by issuing laminated badges or colour-coded wristbands signalling access authorisation to the individual groups (Bladen et al., 2018). Another aspect is that mega-events such as the World Cup are a potential target for protests, riots and even terrorist attacks due to the high level of international media attention, the large number of visitors onsite, their stadiums and fan festivals usually located on major transport routes and in highly populated areas, in addition to their economic importance (Tarlow, 2002). This places high demands on tournament hosts, as they are responsible for the safety of fans, players and staff.

For the 2018 World Cup in Russia, the tournament organisers, in partnership with the World Health Organisation (WHO) as part of this aspect of tournament planning, designed a campaign targeting football fans to promote healthy lifestyles (including topics such as tobacco use, excessive salt intake and physical inactivity). WHO is committed to making major international events as safe as possible from health risks and to using these events as a platform to communicate health issues and promote healthy choices (WHO, 2018). Mass events such as the World Cup bring together large numbers of people from different parts of the world, with the potential for the spread of infections and the adoption of risky and unhealthy behaviours, which WHO aims to counteract (WHO, 2018).

Event Logistics

Management logistics literature is about the flow of goods, resources and information and their effective orchestration. However, event logistics faces the challenge that the customer must be brought to the product, as this is not feasible the other way round for mega-events (Bladen et al., 2018). Event logistics is usually about a project or campaign, such as a football World Cup, and less about ongoing management, as is the case in classic business logistics. According to Bowdin et al. (2011) events can be divided into the following phases: definite preparation, lead up, execution and shutdown.

These phases also affect the main areas of event logistics which Bowdin et al. (2011) break down into the following: Supply, Transport, Linking, Flow Control, and Information Networks.

Supply concerns the areas of customers, product and facilities. Customer supply mainly refers to the areas of marketing, ticketing, queuing and transport, the importance of which varies over time before, during and after the event.

At FIFA World Cups, the focus on marketing is mainly achieved before and during the tournament to generate attention for the upcoming event, attract sponsors, sell tickets and get the best possible broadcasting deals. Similarly, the majority of tickets are usually sold well in advance of the events (e.g., FIFA, 2014a). For FIFA, it has been common practice in recent editions to start ticket sales approximately one year before the start of the tournament (e.g., FIFA, 2017).

Although the necessary transport infrastructure must be planned and created well in advance of the tournament and is ideally designed to be of use to the legacy of the event, the focus of its use is during the event. The organisation of queuing is partly linked to transportation and focuses on the phase during which the event takes place. In many cases, queuing is the first experience that fans have when they enter the venue. In the stadium itself, however, there may be queues again afterwards on the way to the seat, for food, drinks or visit restrooms. When leaving the stadium or the subsequent departure by car or public transport, a queue can often also be the last experience for fans and thus effect a negative memory associated with the event. This illustrates the importance of this aspect of event logistics in terms of customer satisfaction, but it is also closely linked to the ticketing, transport and security concepts. FIFA's ticketing strategy, with a centralised ticket shop and focus on pre-sales, allows for forward planning of the resources and logistics required at the venue to minimise queuing.

If not planned ahead, this can quickly lead to a logistical issues and associated security risks at events. In addition to reducing other hazards, it eliminates the possibility of too many visitors and reduces the risk of blocked escape routes. During the event, the flow of materials and people along with the communication networks are the most important areas of logistics at the venue (Bowdin et al., 2011). Here, it is also important to be prepared for the flow of equipment and people during an emergency. Logistics is also crucial in relation to the teams and referees, the producers of the core product of FIFA World Cups, football matches. This is already reflected in the criteria formulated by FIFA for the evaluation of bids for hosting a tournament. These criteria provide the framework to quantify and evaluate the infrastructural and commercial aspects of each bid. Applications that do not achieve the minimum overall score required or the requirements of the key criteria will be excluded from the bidding process.

Infrastructure criteria in which a minimum score must be achieved include different needs of the teams and referees onsite: stadiums, facilities for teams and referees, accommodation and transport and mobility (including airports; FIFA, 2018a).

Legal Environment

FIFA itself is the owner and ultimate decision-maker of the event, setting the technical requirements, coordinating the delivery of the competition and managing the key stakeholders. In the case of the FIFA World Cup 2022, they are supported by two local delivery partners, FIFA World Cup Qatar 2022 LLC (Q22) and the Supreme Committee for Delivery & Legacy (SC). The SC is the lead government agency whose main purpose is to provide the necessary infrastructure. It is responsible for the planning and implementation of services and the legacy programme in the host country, ensuring that they are in line with overall national development objectives and the creation of a sustainable legacy (Government Communications Office, 2020). In early 2019, Qatar and FIFA communicated the newly formed joint venture Q22 to enable a more efficient organisation of the 2022 FIFA World Cup™. The newly established non-profit organisation is the body responsible for the planning and implementation of the tournament and related projects (FIFA, 2019c). This includes the implementation of the competition, tournament operations and services for the tournament's participant groups, as well as the operation of the official FIFA World Cup venues. They are also responsible for various team services, training facilities, event volunteers, guest management, logistics, catering and accreditations. This legal entity is a limited liability company established by FIFA, which holds 51% of the shares, and the Qatar 2022 Local Organising Committee, which holds 49% of the shares. The organisation will benefit from the knowledge Qatar has built up since winning the bid in 2010, as well as FIFA's extensive experience in staging tournaments (FIFA, 2019d).

Finances of the FIFA World Cup

In the recent decades, there has been an exponential increase in FIFA's revenue from the Men's World Cup (Statista, 2020). This has been accompanied by an increase in the competition to host this mega-sporting event, as it can potentially fulfil versatile social and political objectives in addition to economic ones. Due to the huge reach and public interest in the FIFA World Cup, it is also very interesting as an advertising platform for sponsors.

Revenues are generated from the event through the sale of television rights, marketing rights and licensing rights, as well as income from ticket sales. FIFA's costs are minimal in comparison, which allows FIFA, which is registered as a non-profit organisation, to reinvest much of this money in the development of football.

The low costs are made possible by the fact that infrastructure costs for World Cups are left to the host countries. In 2018, FIFA generated more than $4.6 billion in revenue (FIFA, 2019a). All revenue sources combined, 90% of FIFA's turnover is attributable to the World Cup (Statista, 2018). While revenues between 2002 and 2018 have been relatively constant between US$ 2.3 billion (2002 Japan/South Korea) and US$ 2.8 billion (2018 Russia) and have steadily increased slightly except for 2010 in South Africa, revenues are projected to increase sharply to US$ 3.9 billion in 2022 (Qatar). However, this is significantly dwarfed by the forecast for 2026 (Canada/USA/Mexico) at US$ 11 billion (Statista, 2020). The reasons for this are, among others, the host countries and the marketing opportunities there, and the largest field of participants in a World Cup to date with a total of 48 teams.

Marketing Planning

Event marketing is often mistakenly considered to be the equivalent of event promotion, advertising and sales (Bowdin et al., 2011; Getz, 2007). However, it is rather the structured and coherent approach of planning and delivering an event, aiming for ticket sales, bringing about visitors' satisfaction with the event and generating profits or increased understanding of a cause. It is important for event organisers to carry out marketing activities already in the run-up to the actual event. Generally speaking, marketing is a discipline that is used before and during the event as well as after it has ended (Bladen et al., 2018). In marketing management, communication is key for event organisers to establish a connection between the event and its stakeholders in the ongoing process of achieving the goals set for the event (Getz, 2007).

Due to the great challenges, the ever-changing environment and the constant alteration of host that FIFA World Cup organisers face, there is little doubt how imperative marketing planning is for the organisers to be successful (McDonald and Wilson, 2016).

In line with McDonald and Wilson (2016, p. 57), the four phases of marketing planning are as follows:

- Goal setting
- Situation review
- Strategy formulation
- Resource allocation and monitoring

Marketing planning is an iterative process with continuous measurement and review of the individual steps. An important baseline for the development of the event marketing concept are vision, mission and long-term objectives of an event (Bowdin et al., 2011). This ensures that marketing activities are in line with the overall goals of the event and requirements of the different stakeholders. Successful (event) marketing results from a complete understanding of its target consumers and strategies and tactics based on this understanding, encompassing the event product (including programme, look and feel), the venue, processes, staff and partnerships, as well as integrated marketing communications (Bowdin et al., 2011). Close coordination with its stakeholders (partners, sponsors and other business partners) is also what FIFA highlights as a key success factor of its World Cup marketing programmes (FIFA, n/a).

Event Evaluation

Post-event evaluation allows to determine how successful or unsuccessful the organisers were in achieving the goals and objectives set for the event. This often involves indirect, often subtle effects that can only be evaluated in the long term, the so-called legacy of events (Getz, 2007). Event evaluation is also important to identify problems and shortcomings of the planning process and learn from them for future events (FIFA, 2018b). The FIFA Women's World Cups have gone from strength to strength. The FIFA Women's World Cup has surpassed 1 billion viewers across all platforms combined, with the average global live match viewership doubling compared to Canada 2015 (FIFA, 2019b). This trend has also been made possible by the constant evaluation of the tournaments and the resulting learnings which lead to steadily increasing professionalism in women's football. Now, it is the world's fastest growing sport (Dunn, 2016) with an estimated 26 million female players worldwide (Williams, 2013).

As FIFA is not only limited to the event management of the tournament, but also the global governing body of football, not only the event management key performance indicators are evaluated after each World Cup (e.g., FIFA, 2015a, 2019b), but also the sporting performance achieved in the tournament (e.g., FIFA, 2016a, 2020a).

In addition to the usual KPIs such as TV coverage, ticket sales, stadium utilisation and sponsorship revenues, a detailed sustainability strategy with clearly formulated goals was developed for the FIFA Women's World Cup 2019 in France. A consistent and iterative evaluation process was also carried out for this strategy (e.g., Carbon footprint; FIFA, 2020b), in which processes and target achievement were reviewed in the planning phases, during the event and at the end of the tournament, to generate learnings for future tournaments. FIFA's involvement in the organisation of women's football tournaments also led to improvements in the operation of qualifying competitions in the individual continents and helped the sport to achieve a higher status. As a result, a continuous growth, especially in the youth sector, analogous to men's football, could be observed (de Araújo and Mießen, 2017).

Internal and external evaluations are crucial for improvement and learning. For those responsible for events, it is therefore important to be a learning organisation and, to this end, to establish an overall process for gathering information, conducting research and evaluate data to determine how best to analyse, disseminate and use it in an evidence-based manner (Getz, 2007).

Conclusion

This chapter highlighted the elements and processes required to take a World Cup from conception to victory. It has highlighted how mega-events are operationalised in terms of planning and organisation. The formation of organising committees and their close collaboration with government and FIFA, the challenges of human resources management, health, safety and risk requirements and projects, and the importance of marketing planning were explored and explained.

References

AS. (2021) *Qatar 2022: 265,000 Volunteers Have Signed up for the World Cup*. Available at: https://en.as.com/en/2021/01/08/football/1610127646_892501.html [Accessed 10 April 2021].

BBC (2009) *England 2018 Cup Rivals Confirmed*. Available at: http://news.bbc.co.uk/sport2/hi/football/internationals/7863406.stm [Accessed 29 March 2021].

Bladen, C., Kennell, J., Abson, E. & Wilde, N. (2018) Mega-Events .*Events Management: An Introduction. 2nd edition*. London, UK: Routledge.

Boadle, A. (2014) World Cup Leaves Brazil Costly Stadiums, Poor Public Transport. Available at: https://www.reuters.com/article/uk-brazil-worldcup-infrastructure-idUKKBN0EG24F20140605 [Accessed 25 March 2021].

Bowdin, G., Allen, J., O'Toole, W., Harris, R., McDonnell, I. (2011) *Events Management*, Vol. 3. London, UK: Routledge.

Cannane, S. (2018) Australia's $46 million 2022 World Cup bid 'never had a chance', says former FIFA boss Sepp Blatter. Available at: https://www.abc.net.au/news/2018-01-25/australia-world-cup-bid-never-had-a-chance2c-says-sepp-blatter/9360472 [Accessed 29 March 2021].

Chalip, L. & Heere, B. (2014) Leveraging sport events: Fundamentals and application to bids. In I. Henry and L.-M. Ko (Eds.), (pp. 183–193). New York: Routledge.

de Araújo, M.C. & Mießen, K.A. (2017) Twenty Years of the FIFA Women's World Cup: An Outstanding Evolution of Competitiveness, *Women in Sport and Physical Activity Journal*, 25(1), 60–64.

Dove, E. (2018) *Another Chapter in Morocco's History of World Cup Bidding Failure*. Available at: https://www.espn.com/soccer/blog-football-africa/story/3524440/another-chapter-in-moroccos-history-of-world-cup-bidding-failure [Accessed 29 March 2021].

Dunn, C. (2016) *Football and the Women's World Cup: Organisation, Media and Fandom*. Springer.

FIFA (1998) *Jules Rimet: The Father of the World Cup*. Available at: https://www.fifa.com/news/jules-rimet-the-father-the-world-cup-71489 [Accessed 26 March 2021].

FIFA (2003) *2010 FIFA World Cup™ Bid Dossiers Submitted to FIFA Today*. Available at: https://www.fifa.com/worldcup/news/2010-fifa-world-cuptm-bid-dossiers-submitted-fifa-today-89025 [Accessed 29 March 2021].

FIFA (2012) *Russia 2018 LOC Sets Out Vision*. Available at: https://www.fifa.com/worldcup/news/russia-2018-loc-sets-out-vision-1603617 [Accessed 12 April 2021].

FIFA (2014a) *Over 3.5 Million Tickets Requested in Second Sales Phase*. Available at: https://www.fifa.com/worldcup/news/more-than-million-tickets-for-brazil-2014-requested-second-sales-phase-2267462 [Accessed 11 April 2021].

FIFA (2014b) *Stadium Safety and Security*. Available at: https://www.fifa.com/news/stadium-safety-and-security-fifa-tournaments-2261044 [Accessed 15 April 2021].

FIFA (2015a) *Key Figures from the FIFA Women's World Cup Canada 2015™*. Available at: https://www.fifa.com/womensworldcup/news/key-figures-from-the-fifa-women-s-world-cup-canada-2015tm-2661648 [Accessed 13 April 2021].

FIFA (2015b) *USA Triumph as History Made in China PR*. Available at: https://www.fifa.com/womensworldcup/archive/chinapr1991/ [Accessed 15 January 2021].

FIFA (2016a) *Physical Analysis of the FIFA Women's World Cup Canada 2015™*. Available at: https://resources.fifa.com/image/upload/canada-2015-physical-analysis-2812487.pdf?cloudid=agoxuqlps0zbiuyudcv0 [Accessed 13 April 2021].

FIFA (2016b) *Volunteers' Functions*. Available at: https://www.fifa.com/news/volunteers-functions-2783163 [Accessed 18 April 2021].

FIFA. (2017) *Ticket Sales for 2018 FIFA World Cup™ to Start from 14 September 2017*. Available at: https://www.fifa.com/worldcup/news/ticket-sales-for-2018-fifa-world-cuptm-to-start-on-14-september-2017–2907645 [Accessed 11 April 2021].

FIFA (2018a) *Guide to the Bidding Process for the 2026 FIFA World Cup™*. Available at: https://img.fifa.com/image/upload/hgopypqftviladnm7q90.pdf [Accessed 26 March 2021].

FIFA (2018b) *Sustainability Strategy FIFA Women's World Cup France 2019™*. Available at: https://resources.fifa.com/image/upload/sustainability-strategy-for-the-fifa-women-s-world-cup-france-2019.pdf?cloudid=r2sks010xbbqhhobnkq1 [Accessed 11 April 2021].

FIFA (2018c) *Volunteering at the FIFA World Cup: A Unique Experience*. Available at: https://www.fifa.com/worldcup/news/volunteering-at-the-fifa-world-cup-a-unique-experience#the-volunteer-programme-launching-ceremony-which-took-place-in-moscow--2799376 [Accessed 10 April 2021].

FIFA (2018d) *Working the Crowd: FIFA Safety & Security Officers Gather in Zurich*. Available at: https://www.fifa.com/who-we-are/news/working-the-crowd-fifa-safety-security-officers-gather-in-zurich [Accessed 10 April 2021].

FIFA (2019a) *FIFA Financial Report 2018*. Available at: https://resources.fifa.com/image/upload/fifa-financial-report-2018.pdf?cloudid=xzshsoe2ayttyquuxhq0 [Accessed 8 April 2021].

FIFA (2019b) *FIFA Women's World Cup France 2019™Facts and Figures*. Available at: https://resources.fifa.com/image/upload/fifa-women-s-world-cup-france-2019tm-facts-and-figures-up-to-and-including-4-jul.pdf?cloudid=ugj0a1np8yovf3mrqzhb [Accessed 13 April 2021].

FIFA (2019c) *FIFA World Cup Qatar 2022™ Executive Summary*. Available at: https://resources.fifa.com/image/upload/fifa-world-cup-qatar-2022tm-sustainability-strategy-executive-summary.pdf?cloudid=bl0bgeroqdmxjme4sy7h [Accessed 7 April 2021].

FIFA (2019d) FIFA World Cup Qatar 2022 LLC. Available at: https://www.fifa.com/worldcup/organisation/llc/ [Accessed 15 February 2021].

FIFA (2020a) *Physical Analysis of the FIFA Women's World Cup France 2019™*. Available at: https://img.fifa.com/image/upload/zijqly4oednqa5gffgaz.pdf [Accessed 12 April 2021].

FIFA (2020b) *Study on the Environmental and Socio-economic Impact of the FIFA Women's World Cup France 2019™*. Available at: https://resources.fifa.com/image/upload/study-on-the-environmental-and-socio-economic-impact-of-france-2019.pdf?cloudid=l1gppgwfk8frtxs9av4f [Accessed 15 April 2021].

FIFA (n/a) *FIFA Marketing Programmes*. Available at: https://www.fifa.com/what-we-do/marketing/programmes/ [Accessed 16 April 2021].

Frawley, S. & Adair, D. (2014) *Managing the World Cup*. London, UK: Palgrave Macmillan.

Getz, D. (2007) *Event Studies: Theory, Research and Policy for Planned Events*. Elsevier.

Government Communications Office (2020) *2022 FIFA World Cup*. Available at: https://www.gco.gov.qa/en/focus/2022-fifa-world-cup-qatar/ [Accessed 15 February 2021].

McDonald, M. & Wilson, H. (2016) *Marketing Plans: How to Prepare Them, How to Profit from Them*. John Wiley & Sons.

Parent, M. & Smith-Swan, S. (2013) *Managing Major Sports Events*. New York: Routledge.

Preuss, H. (2007) The Conceptualization and Measurement of Mega Sport Event Legacies. *Journal of Sport & Tourism*, 12, 207–227.

Preuss, H. (2015) A Framework for Identifying the Legacies of a Mega Sport Event. *Leisure studies*, 34(6), 643–664.

Statista (2018) *Average and Total Attendance at FIFA Football World Cup Games from 1930 to 2018*. Available at: https://www.statista.com/statistics/264441/number-of-spectators-at-football-world-cups-since-1930/ [Accessed 10 April 2021].

Statista (2020) *Einnahmen der FIFA durch die Fußball-Weltmeisterschaften bis 2026*. Available at: https://de.statista.com/statistik/daten/studie/872296/umfrage/einnahmen-der-fifa-fussball-weltmeisterschaften/ [Accessed 28 December 2020].

Tarlow, P.E. (2002) *Event Risk Management and Safety* (Vol. 4). John Wiley & Sons.

Watts, J. (2014) *Anti-World Cup Protests in Brazilian Cities Mark Countdown to Kick-Off*. Available at: https://www.theguardian.com/football/2014/jun/12/anti-world-cup-protests-brazilian-cities-sao-paulo-rio-de-janeiro [Accessed 4 January 2021].

WHO (2018) *2018 FIFA World Cup: Protect Your Health and Score!*. Available at: https://www.euro.who.int/en/health-topics/disease-prevention/pages/news/news/2018/6/2018-fifa-world-cup-protect-your-health-and-score! [Accessed 15 April 2021].

Williams, J. (2013) *Globalising Women's Football: Europe, Migration and Professionalisation*. Oxford: Peter Lang.

11

PLANNING, SOURCING AND MANAGING RESOURCES FOR FIFA WORLD CUPS

Eric C. Schwarz and Michael M. Goldman

Introduction

The resources required to successfully host a FIFA World Cup are substantial, and the management of this event is extremely complex. For example, over 30,000 full-time, temporary and volunteer staff were involved in delivering the 2014 FIFA World Cup in Brazil, a tournament which included, among others, 12 stadiums and 32 team base camps, over 2,000 printed accreditations, more than 300 tons of team equipment, 748 live Fan Fest performances, 70 official merchandise licensees, 1,210 newly issued laptops, and 3,240 Adidas balls (FIFA, 2014b).

This chapter is based on a model of sourcing and managing resources for FIFA World Cups that considers the types of typical resources required to successfully deliver a World Cup, as well as the processes involved in managing the resources. Resources are categorised into three main types: *services*, *materials* and *staffing*. The management processes of planning, sourcing, deploying, controlling and disposing of are detailed for each of these resource categories.

It is important to remember that there are many World Cup tournaments hosted by FIFA (see Chapters 2 and 3 in this *Handbook* for more detailed accounts about them). Briefly, and beyond the Men's and Women's World Cup, FIFA also is responsible for organising international tournaments at the youth level (Under-20 and Under-17 for both men and women), clubs (the FIFA Club World Cup) and modified versions of the sport (futsal and beach soccer) (FIFA, 2021). Regardless of the type of FIFA World Cup, the management processes and resources needed are relatively the same, but the different sizes and scope of the events will directly influence the amount and types of sourcing and managing resources needed to effectively implement the event.

DOI: 10.4324/9781003121794-11

Relevant Core Concepts

The disciplines that underpin sourcing and managing resources for FIFA World Cups are resource management, project management and logistics. The following sections briefly introduce each of these disciplines.

Resource management

Organisational theorists have argued since the 1980s that the resources that organisations have access to, and that they can use to achieve a competitive advantage, allow some of them to sustainably perform better than their competitors. These resources have been described as both tangible and intangible assets, which are categorised as physical, financial, human or organisational (Badrinarayanan et al., 2019). The resource-based view of the firm, or more formally resource-based theory (RBT), explains how strategic resources that are valuable, rare, inimitable, non-substitutable, and organised can provide long-term competitive advantage (Bhandari et al., 2020). Resources are valuable when they increase differentiation and decrease production costs, and in this way help the organisation to "conceive or implement strategies that improve its efficiency and effectiveness" (Barney and Clark, 2007, p. 57). Rare resources exist when one or only a few organisations have access to them. Resources categorised as inimitable are unique, difficult to imitate, or expensive to replicate, and therefore cannot be easily substituted by competitors. Resources need to be well organised and managed so that they can be exploited to provide a competitive advantage, including issues of reporting structures, management control systems and compensation policies (Barney and Clark, 2007). Managerial action, therefore, plays an important role in structuring (sourcing and disposing of), bundling (planning), and leveraging (controlling and deploying) resources (Badrinarayanan et al., 2019).

Project management

Project management has been defined as the "management discipline that plans, organizes and controls people, money and cash" to ensure successful completion of a project while mitigating the relevant risks (Lock, 2017, p. 1). A project exists to produce specific deliverables and is therefore temporary and not part of the ongoing operations of an organisation (Marion, 2018). Project management guides the processes involved in delivering the project, from conceptualising the idea and developing the plan, to executing the plan and closing out the project. The Project Management Institute's Project Management Body of Knowledge (PMBOK) details 47 processes, which are organised into five process groups: initiating, planning, executing, monitoring and controlling, and closing (Marion, 2018). The initiating processes include developing a project charter and identifying stakeholders. The planning process group includes scoping, defining, scheduling and costing activities, as well as considering issues of quality, risk, resourcing and stakeholders. The executing process group is focused on managing the activities and people for all project actions. The monitoring and controlling processes involve tracking performance and considering potential changes in the plan. Finally, the closing process group includes completing the deliverables as agreed, managing the reallocation or disposal of resources, and reporting on the project.

The PMBOK process groups are similar to an alternate project management methodology, PRINCE2 (PRojects IN Controlled Environments), which is more common in the United Kingdom. The PRINCE2 framework includes directing a project, starting up a project, initiating a project, managing stage boundaries, controlling a stage, managing product delivery, and closing a project (Axelos, n.d.). Recent research found strong evidence of the effectiveness of a project management methodology, such as PMBOK and PRINCE2, while highlighting important organisational conditions that contribute to successful project management. These conditions included the difficulty of sticking to a method, creating internal silos, creating proprietary method rivalries, adopting common organisational formats, having flexibility and customisation, and distinguishing project management content from the process (McGrath and Whitty, 2020).

Logistics

Logistics involve the movement and storage of inventory, including order processing, purchasing, transportation, production, inventory management, distribution, and related systems (Sadler, 2007). In this way, logistics manage and optimise the movement of resources from the point of origin to the final destination. Managers need to consider inbound logistics, which focus on purchasing and coordinating the movement of resources into an organisation, as well as outbound logistics, which involve the storage and movement of resources from the organisation to the customer or end-user. Importantly, logistics also consider the disposal of resources and waste products. More recently, Rogers et al. (2020) pointed to several ways in which the logistics paradigms of the past decades need to be challenged, including technological change, increased service expectations, and changing consumer purchasing behaviour online. Specifically, the authors demonstrated the role of shared warehousing as part of a portfolio approach to omni-channel distribution. Similarly, Matusiewicz (2020) demonstrated how the global logistics system can be further optimised by using the Physical Internet approach, which involves transporting resources or products in "standardised, modular containers as efficiently and seamlessly between continents as in the case of Digital Internet transferring information between servers" (p. 201).

Planning and Sourcing Resources for FIFA World Cups

Planning and sourcing resources are the first crucial steps in effectively implementing a supply chain management process for any FIFA World Cup. The complexity in terms of the size, scope, and global prominence of the FIFA World

Cup requires the supply chain to operate efficiently to deliver all aspects of this mega-event. The planning part involves developing a strategy to manage the services, materials, and human resources efforts necessary for meeting the demands related to a FIFA World Cup through monitoring the supply chain for efficiency, reduce costs, and delivery of quality and value to end-users (Schwarz and Hunter, 2018). This then leads to the sourcing of services, materials, and human resources from suppliers to meet the supply chain needs. The purchasing processes inherent to sourcing may be through long-established partnerships with similar objectives that seek to maximise capabilities, or when partners cannot meet the needs look to competitive sourcing to find the best suppliers that can. Again, considering the size and scope of a FIFA World Cup and the need for global sourcing of services, materials, and human resources, sourcing can become challenging, to say the least, due to several factors. These include, but are not limited to, uncontrollable and unpredictable tariff barriers, trade regulations and agreements, currency exchange rates, ethical and quality standards, and immigration issues.

Services

The planning and sourcing of services associated with the delivery of a FIFA World Cup involve three major logistics groups. The first is comprised of the functional areas of the organising committee in the nation(s) where the FIFA World Cup will take place. The main functional areas include the delivery of matches, the integration of information technology, and the overlays related to venues in terms of new construction and the alteration or renovation of existing facilities (Minis et al., 2006).

The second logistical group includes the external clients that are integral to the successful implementation of a FIFA World Cup. These parties are not part of the organising committee and include both football-focused and non-football-focused clients. In terms of football-related clients, these include the national football federations of the teams competing in the event, as well as the global media covering it. Non-football-related clients include vendors and suppliers from around the world that provide products and services to a FIFA World Cup. For all, this includes implementing an efficient transportation infrastructure within the host nation(s) that includes streamlined customs clearance procedures and efficient freight forwarding of materials from the point of origin anywhere in the world to the host nation, then on to the appropriate World Cup venue, and reversing back to the origin after the event has concluded (Minis et al., 2006). For the 2014 FIFA World Cup in Brazil, a local company, Globo Marcas, was appointed as Master Licensee, with the exclusive production and distribution rights for the territory of Brazil, while the rest of the world was managed by FIFA's in-house team and three licensing agents in Asia (FIFA 2014a).

The final logistical group encompasses the venues hosting FIFA World Cup matches. A FIFA World Cup encompasses numerous venue logistics challenges resulting from the large flow of users (spectators, participants and clients) to several venues across one or more nations over a relatively short time. Hence, this requires a substantial concentration of logistics implementations that may only be needed once and must work right the first time (Creazza et al., 2015, Minis et al., 2006). These services range across numerous operational and service areas, including plant and field operations, maintenance and cleaning, waste and recycling, utilities, inventory management, safety and security, ticketing, parking, and transportation, merchandising, food service, customer service, and pre-/on/post-event management (Schwarz et al., 2019). For example, it was expected that Qatar 2022 would create over $380 million in business opportunities for Qatari small- and medium-sized enterprises (De La Cerna, 2017).

Products, equipment and materials

As with services, the planning and sourcing of products/goods, equipment, and materials focus on three logistics groups – the functional areas of the organising committee (internal clients), external clients and venue logistics. Appropriate planning and sourcing of tangible goods for a FIFA World Cup requires an extensive understanding of logistics operations and management in terms of receiving, tracking, storing, transporting, distributing, installing and recovering all materials (Minis et al., 2006).

The challenges of planning and sourcing tangible goods to deliver a global mega-event are immense, especially one that is transient in nature, has large-scale logistics that are diverse and sometimes uncertain, must be delivered with tight schedules and milestones, and must work right the first time (Minis et al., 2006). It is critical that the entire operation related to a FIFA World Cup, whose planning and sourcing processes often extend to 5–6 years to deliver an event that is held over 30–45 days, has effective capacity planning, service quality and control, supply chain management, and process designs (Kauppi et al., 2013). Most host nations will work to establish an internal logistics command centre to manage the standardisation of materials and administration functions related to products and equipment acquisition. Additionally, there is also a need to work with outsourced vendors, coordinate just-in-time (JIT) deliveries, and coordinate with third-party logistics (3PL) companies to ensure that all tangible goods are sourced and delivered as needed (Minis et al., 2006, Schwarz and Hunter, 2018). For example, FIFA announced in March 2015 that Hawk-Eye, a camera-based goal-line technology, would be used for the Women's World Cup in Canada that kicked off in early June that year (Doherty, 2015).

Staffing

Another integral function of a FIFA World Cup that must be appropriately planned for and requires significant sourcing is staffing; the human resources function is vital to ensuring the smooth delivery of a FIFA World Cup. A FIFA World Cup will need to hire a mixture of executive, administrative, supervisory, and general staff to plan, organise, lead, and evaluate the event. The executive-level staff and some administrative staff will be associated with FIFA as the owner of the tournament and the local organising committee as the host of the event, while the remaining administrative-level staff, along with supervisors and general staff, will either need to be hired as paid employees or by volunteers. In general, there is normally a balance between the number of professional staff hired and the number of volunteers sourced (Herold et al., 2019, Minis et al., 2006).

To start with the planning and sourcing of staff, the local organising committee will often hire a human resources manager to oversee this function. This manager will need to conduct a full job analysis to determine the specific tasks that need to be completed across all venues and locations for the entire mega-event, create an organisational structure to meet those needs in terms of the work activities to be completed, develop job descriptions for paid and volunteer positions, and then recruit and select personnel (Schwarz et al. 2019). The sourcing of staff and volunteers for a FIFA World Cup is a massive undertaking, as the majority of individuals recruited and selected are newly hired to the organisation and often have little or no experience working at a mega-event (Herold et al., 2019, Minis et al., 2006). As there is a need for securing thousands of staff and volunteers, there will be a combination of efforts enacted to secure these employees. Some will be filled through traditional application and interview processes overseen by the human resource manager. Other positions, especially volunteers, will be managed through a dedicated website where individuals can apply to become a part of delivering the event – either for altruistic reasons or to give back to the sport or nation. Finally, some recruitment and selection processes will be outsourced to third parties that specialise in sourcing staff and volunteers for sporting events. For example, over 2,500 volunteers from 75 countries were involved in organising the FIFA Women's World Cup in France (FIFA, 2019).

Managing Resources for FIFA World Cups

The sourcing of resources is only the first part of an elaborate process to deliver a large-scale event such as a FIFA World Cup. Once products, equipment, materials, services, and staffing have been sustainably sourced, next is the process of managing those resources effectively to ensure the optimal delivery of an event that meets the needs and wants of all stakeholders. Considering the size and scope of a FIFA World Cup and the global reach of the stakeholders, the strategic management of resources can be a complex and elaborate process across a multitude of logistical, allocation, and control processes. Furthermore, once the final whistle blows on a FIFA World Cup and the organising committee begins the process of closing out the event, management needs to ensure that the resources from the event are responsibly and sustainably disposed of as part of the lasting impact and legacy of the event.

Services

As noted earlier in the chapter, services related to delivering a World Cup focus on three categories of clients: external clients including national federations and media; functional areas of the organising committee within the host nation(s); and the operation of World Cup venues (Minis et al., 2006). The managing of services for all clients focuses on not only quality and control but also the value perceptions of those clients. According to Biscaia et al. (2017), the individuals that benefit from the appropriate management of services at a FIFA World Cup are the teams, the referees, the event employees, and the crowd in terms of safety and security at venues and the location of the matches, the event atmosphere, and the experience in the stands.

Therefore, the effective delivery of events, informational technology, and venue amenities and overlays need to be managed back-of-house by an efficient purchasing and supply chain management system that ensures quality logistical, allocation, and control processes across all operational and service areas. The overall goal of the management of services is to provide hedonic and utilitarian value for all who have experienced a World Cup. The goal of creating hedonic value is to ensure that all involved have a positive experience in terms of fun, enjoyment, and positive emotions. As far as utilitarian value, the goal is to justify partaking in the consumptive behaviour of engaging with a World Cup in terms of quality delivery of the event and its amenities, value for money, and overall satisfaction of involvement.

From a service delivery standpoint, it is important to create an engaging atmosphere for all participants and spectators (Biscaia et al., 2017). This is often articulated through the individual FIFA World Cup marketing plan and the specific marketing plans of the organising committee and each venue. These plans create a blueprint for delivering memorable stakeholder experiences through multiple interactive moments before, during, and after the event by providing service quality that translates into positive emotional encounters and creates both customer satisfaction and positive impressions (Schwarz et al., 2019).

Once the event has concluded, management must engage in service contract terminations, reconciliations, and reallocations. Given the temporary nature of World Cup events, service contract termination provisions can be expected to be detailed in the initial contract terms. A contract can be terminated when both parties have fully performed, by mutual agreement, by written contract provisions, or when one party has committed a material breach (Stim, 2016). Certain obligations may continue after the termination of a contract, such as provisions related to confidentiality and the responsible disposal of resources. Service contracts may also be reallocated from an organising committee to another entity, such as a national government, legacy organisation, FIFA, or a subsequent host committee. An example of this is the Supreme Committee of Delivery and Legacy for Qatar 2022 imposed a high level of confidentiality on consultants and contractors related to the event and required international contractors to form partnerships with Qatari entities to perform work (Alkarimi, 2016).

Products, equipment and materials

The management of tangible goods for a FIFA World Cup is driven by the capacity planning and demand planning implemented during the planning and sourcing processes. Hence, it is vital to ensure that the host nation(s) and associated venues have the production capacity and workforce needs to make certain the supply chain can forecast and meet the demand for products, equipment, and materials. This then drives the procurement process in coordination with both the local and global supply chains. For example, many players challenged the use of artificial turf as the playing surface for the 2015 FIFA Women's World Cup in Canada, although that country's bid had proposed a majority of artificial pitches. As part of the negotiations before the tournament, FIFA promised that artificial turf would not be used at a Women's World Cup again (Payne, 2015).

In consideration of a FIFA World Cup being an event with a global reach that needs the coordination of products, equipment, and materials for internal clients (functional areas of the organising committee, venues) and external clients (national football federations, media/broadcasters, vendors/suppliers), there are massive logistical challenges to implement and manage the receiving, tracking, storing, transporting, distributing, installing, and recovery of these tangible goods (Minis et al., 2006). This requires the development of quality procedural decision-making and problem-solving processes, as well as a product management plan focused on time management issues ranging from appropriate lead times to match-time deliveries. Areas of importance to efficiently coordinate include freight forwarding, security screening, customs clearances, warehousing, and delivery to various locations across multiple locations. This becomes even more complex when multiple nations are hosting a FIFA World Cup, which then requires the coordination of potentially different logistical, allocation and control procedures in each nation.

There are also the considerations associated with recycling, reusing and disposing of products, equipment, and materials. Recycling can be described as the "creation, recovery and the re-creation of value" (Alexander and Reno, 2012), although the idea of a closed system where materials continue to be reused or recycled forever is not yet true. As organising committee offices close, and ownership or usage of facilities are transferred after a World Cup, all materials need to be responsibly allocated. The Qatar 2022 Sustainability Strategy includes a post-tournament asset distribution programme, which promotes procuring shared or leased equipment that can be reused after the tournament. By October 2020, 65% of the waste (by weight) from stadium construction for Qatar 2022 had been diverted from landfills, while an extension of Qatar's national recycling industry was underway to managed tournament-related waste (FIFA, 2020b). Accurate management of materials during the event should limit the resources that need to be managed at the end of the tournament. For example, FIFA's retail and merchandising campaign for Brazil 2014 included a sustainable business pillar, which included working with retailers and licensees to "avoid market over-saturation".

Qatar's Al Rayyan Stadium reportedly reused approximately 90% of the materials from the previous Ahmed Bin Ali Stadium, and the upper tier will be dismantled after the tournament and donated to other countries for continued use (Rosenfield, 2015). Perhaps most creatively and sustainably, the Ras Aboud Stadium for Qatar 2022 is the first fully demountable stadium in the history of the World Cup, being constructed with 949 shipping containers. It is expected that the 40,000-seater stadium will be converted into approximately 30 smaller community venues after the tournament as if the containers were Lego cubes. The former industrial site needed to be decontaminated before use, including removing and safely disposing of over 65 tons of asbestos-containing materials, and reusing or recycling over 80% of the materials from the demolished buildings (Local Organising Committee for the 2022 FIFA World Cup™ 2020). To address the risk of not planning for the sustainable reusing of materials after the event due to reduced organising committee capacity and more immediate priorities, Preuss (2013) called for governments of host nations to take responsibility for controlling and directing these activities.

Staffing

As noted earlier, the sourcing of thousands of employees and volunteers to deliver a FIFA World Cup is an immense challenge, however, that is only the starting point. The management of the workforce plan for a FIFA World Cup is another daunting task. To start, the human resources manager will need to ensure that the individuals selected for employment have all the appropriate work visas, visitor visas, and exit permits. If not, then there will likely need to be a backfilling of positions to meet the needs of the event. This will be an ongoing process throughout the delivery of a World Cup until the final game is played, so flexibility in the allocation and control of staffing is needed.

In terms of logistics and the coordination of human resources, the overall goal is to ensure that the staffing can meet the service level expected of FIFA, the organising committee, the national federations participating in the event and the spectators. This requires the development of an integrated human resource management system that can address all key stakeholders while implementing a flexible and efficient structure. It also must address issues that are vital to the successful implementation of any sporting event including ethics, conduct, expectations of employees and volunteers, creation of an environment demonstrating pride of ownership in delivering a World Cup, efficient scheduling, standardised routines, and clear policies and procedures.

The biggest challenges with managing human resources for a FIFA World Cup are that the majority of the staff are new to working this type of a mega-event, they often come from a wide geographic spread and may not arrive into the host nation(s) until immediately before or even during the event, and their experience and availability vary greatly (Herold et al., 2019, Robinson et al., 2010). This requires an effective orientation, training and performance management process that has to be managed across multiple locations, potentially in multiple nations. A focused orientation introduces new employees to the event, venues, and areas of responsibility. This is an integral process to integrating the new individuals into the organisational culture, helping them adjust to a potentially new and foreign environment, enabling them to understand their roles and responsibilities, and creating a positive working relationship (Schwarz et al., 2019). In terms of training, it is important to understand that the education and experiences of the employees will vary greatly, but extensive training is not always possible due to the short time between orientation and starting the job. For this reason, the human resource managers and individual location managers need to quickly identify those with some level of experience to help oversee those with less experience.

The recruitment, selection, and management of volunteers is an additional challenge. A volunteer is someone who contributes their experience, skills, and time for no compensation or minor reimbursement of expenses to benefit the community or a specific industry. Volunteers are a vital human resource for any event as without volunteers, an event likely could not afford the employment costs associated with running an event safely and securely. Volunteer recruitment and selection requires a strategic approach that is fair, efficient, effective and prioritises the short-term goals and needs of the sporting event (Cuskelly et al., 2020). While the goal would be to have as much community involvement as possible since locals have a vested interest in an event within their community and often have greater availability because of their proximity to the event, the reality of a global mega-event such as a FIFA World Cup is that volunteers will be drawn from around the world. So, many of the same human resource processes implemented for hiring employees will need to also be followed when securing volunteers. Also, determining the skills and qualifications mix of volunteers, as well as at what stages of the event they are required, are substantial management issues that need to be addressed. Finally, ensuring that volunteers stay motivated throughout the event is crucial. Since they are unpaid and giving of their time and energy either for an altruistic reason or the desire to give back to the sport or community, the moment their motivation wanes they will cease being an asset to the event. Hence, sport event managers must understand and implement processes to ensure maximum motivation of volunteer involvement during a FIFA World Cup across multiple factors including "expression of values, patriotism, personal contacts, career orientation, personal growth, and extrinsic rewards" (Bang and Chelladurai, 2009).

Beyond recruitment and selection, the management of human resources comes with the additional possibility of needing to terminate an employee or volunteer for cause before or during the event. This could include not showing up for a shift, leaving during a shift without permission, or dereliction of duty. This requires good record-keeping by staffing managers and making sure that all efforts have been made to remedy poor performance. The added challenge for human resource managers of a FIFA World Cup is that termination may also result in the cancellation of work or visitor visas, hence requiring coordination with government immigration officials since the purpose of receiving the visa has been breached.

This may also result in the potential removal of the employee or volunteer from the country.

Further to this is the requirement for post-event contract terminations and reallocations. Unlike a typical employment context, where the end of one's contract may be unplanned or unexpected, the end of FIFA World Cup staffing contracts are typically clearly understood and are linked to the wrap-up schedule at the end of the tournament. Staff who have worked in sports events can suffer post-event hangover and burnout due to the fast-paced and high-performance nature of mega-event delivery (Parent and Ruetsch, 2020). It is the responsibility of management, therefore, to help prepare paid and volunteer staff for transition after the event. Management can facilitate individual or group feedback sessions, host career development workshops, connect staff with job opportunities with World Cup partners and stakeholders, officially recognise and reward staff, and organise celebrations and social events. For example, the human sustainability strategy for Qatar 2022 includes outplacement support including assistance with job searches and professional reorientation, and facilitating potential transitions to roles within associated sectors in Qatar and abroad (FIFA, 2020a). By October 2020, over 24,000 staff involved in Qatar 2022 had also received hard and soft skills training in more than five languages by the Qatar International Safety Centre and Josoor Institute (FIFA, 2020b).

Conclusion

Establishing coordinated systems through managing and sourcing of products and services is integral to the effective flow of information and the distribution of resources to meet stakeholder needs. This is an especially large challenge when delivering a large-scale sporting event such as a FIFA World Cup. The disciplines of resource management, project management, and logistics were first introduced to provide a foundational understanding of the disciplines underpinning the planning, sourcing and managing resources. This was followed by an exploration into the complex systems and processes inherent to the planning, sourcing, and managing of resources for a FIFA World Cup including services; products, equipment, and materials; and staffing efforts. It is important to note that regardless of the type of FIFA World Cup to be implemented (senior Men's or Women's, youth Men's or Women's at the U-20 and U-17 levels, the FIFA Club World Cup, or variations for futsal and beach soccer), the efficient planning, sourcing and managing of resources is vital to each event's success. What would be different for each event will be the scope of resources needed based on the size of the event.

References

Alexander, C. & Reno, J. (2012) Introduction. InAlexander, C. & Reno, J. eds. *Economies of Recycling: The Global Transformation of Materials, Values and Social Relations*. London: Zed Books Ltd.

Alkarimi, A. (2016) The road to Qatar's construction of the 2022 FIFA World Cup stadiums [Paper Presentation]. *IBA Annual Conference*, Washington, D.C.

Axelos, n. d. *What is Prince 2®?* [online]. Available at: https://www.axelos.com/best-practice-solutions/prince2/what-is-prince2 [Accessed 14 March 2021].

Badrinarayanan, V., Ramachandran, I. & Madhavaram, S. (2019) Resource Orchestration and Dynamic Managerial Capabilities: Focusing on Sales Managers as Effective Resource Orchestrators, *Journal of Personal Selling and Sales Management*, 39(1), 23–41.

Bang, H. & Chelladurai, P. (2009) Development and Validation of the Volunteer Motivations Scale for International Sporting Events (VMS-ISE), *International Journal of Sport Management and Marketing*, 6(4), 332–350.

Barney, J.B. & Clark, D.N. (2007) *Resource-Based Theory: Creating and Sustaining Competitive Advantage*. Oxford, UK: Oxford University Press.

Bhandari, K.R., *et al.* (2020) Relative Exploration and Firm Performance: Why Resource-theory Alone Is Not Sufficient?, *Journal of Business Research*, 118, 363–377.

Biscaia, R., *et al.* (2017) Service Quality and Value Perceptions of the 2014 FIFA World Cup in Brazil, *Event Management*, 21(2), 201–216.

Creazza, A., Colicchia, C. & Dallari, F. (2015) Designing the Venue Logistics Management Operations for a World Exposition, *Production Planning and Control*, 26(7), 543–563.

Cuskelly, G., Fredline, L., Kim, E., Barry, S., & Kappelides, P. (2020) Volunteer Selection at a Major Sport Event: A Strategic Human Resource Management Approach, *Sport Management Review*, 24(1), 116–133. DOI: 10.1016/j.smr.2020.02.002

De La Cerna, F. (2017) Qatar: $380m FIFA-Related Opportunities for SMEs. *Construction Week* [online]. Available at: https://www.constructionweekonline.com/article-43824-qatar-380m-fifa-related-opportunities-for-smes [Accessed 26 March 2021].

Doherty, K. (2015) Goal-line technology to debut at Women's World Cup in Canada. *The Globe and Mail* [online]. Available at: https://www.theglobeandmail.com/sports/soccer/goal-line-technology-to-debut-at-womens-world-cup-of-soccer/article 23702240 [Accessed 31 March 2021].

FIFA (2014a) The 2014 FIFA World Cup Brazil™ retail and merchandising highlights. [online]. Available at: https://img.fifa.com/image/upload/uw6dcn4ep5cpohfktc6s.pdf [Accessed 25 March 2021].

FIFA (2014b) *The 2014 FIFA World Cup™ in Numbers*. [online]. Available at: https://img.fifa.com/image/upload/re9rlmc6uzlvazsqj1m8.pdf [Accessed 25 March 2021].

FIFA (2019) *FIFA Women's World Cup France 2019™ Facts and Figures*. [online]. Available at: https://resources.fifa.com/image/upload/fifa-women-s-world-cup-france-2019tm-facts-and-figures-up-to-and-including-4-jul.pdf?cloudid=ugj0a1np8yovf3mrqzhb [Accessed 25 March 2021].

FIFA (2020a) *FIFA World Cup Qatar 2020™ Sustainability Strategy*. [online]. Available at: https://resources.fifa.com/image/upload/fifa-world-cup-2022tm-sustainability-strategy.pdf?cloudid=o2zbd8acyiooxyn0dwuk [Accessed 25 January 2021].

FIFA (2020b)*FIFA World Cup Qatar 2022™ First Sustainability Progress Report*. [online]. Available at: https://img.fifa.com/image/upload/qlsdbl7ipsax0ndjqyup.pdf [Accessed 28 January 2021].

FIFA (2021) *FIFA Tournaments*. [online]. Available at: https://www.fifa.com/fifa-tournaments [Accessed 29 March 2021].

Herold, D.M., *et al.* (2019) Sport Logistics Research: Reviewing and Line Marking of a new field, *The International Journal of Logistics Management*, 31(2), 357–379.

Kauppi, K., Moxham, C. & Bamford, D. (2013) Should We Try Out for the Major Leagues? A Call for Research in Sport Operations Management, *International Journal of Operations and Production Management*, 33(10), 1368–1399.

Local Organising Committee for the 2022 FIFA World Cup™ (2020) *The Green Legacy of Ras Abu Aboud Stadium*. [online]. Available at: https://www.fifa.com/worldcup/news/the-green-legacy-of-ras-abu-aboud-stadium [Accessed 25 March 2021].

Lock, D. (2017) *Project Management*. 7th ed. Oxford, UK: Routledge.

Marion, J.W. (2018) *Project Management: A Common Sense Guide to the PMBOK, Part One—Framework and Schedule*. New York: Momentum Press.

Matusiewicz, M. (2020) Logistics of the Future—Physical Internet and its Practicality, *Transportation Journal*, 59(2), 200–214.

McGrath, S. & Whitty, J. (2020) Practitioner Views on Project Management Methodology (PMM) Effectiveness, *Journal of Modern Project Management*, 8(1), 188–215.

Minis, I., Paraschi, M. & Tzimourtas, A. (2006) The Design of Logistics Operations for the Olympic Games, *International Journal of Physical Distribution and Logistics Management*, 36(8), 621–642.

Parent, M.M. & Ruetsch, A. (2020) *Managing Major Sports Events: Theory and Practice*. Oxford, UK: Routledge.

Payne, M. (2015) The Artificial Turf at the Women's World Cup Was Reportedly 120 degrees at Kick Off, *Washington Post*, June 6, p. 1.

Preuss, H. (2013) The Contribution of the FIFA World Cup and the Olympic Games to Green Economy, *Sustainability*, 5(8), 3581–3600.

Robinson, P., Wale, D. & Dickson, G. (2010) *Events Management*. Oxford, UK: CABI.

Rogers, Z.S., Golara, S., Abdusalam, Y., & Rogers, D.S. (2020) A Sharing-enabled Portfolio Approach to Distribution, *Transportation Journal*, 59(2), 99–128.

Rosenfield, K. (2015) *Qatar Unveils Fifth World Cup Venue: Al Rayyan Stadium by Pattern Architects*. [online]. Available at: https://www.archdaily.com/623220/qatar-unveils-fifth-world-cup-venue-al-rayyan-stadium-by-pattern-architects [Accessed 25 March 2021].

Sadler, I. (2007) *Logistics and Supply Chain Integration*. Thousand Oaks, CA: Sage.

Schwarz, E.C., Hall, S.A. & Shibli, S. (2019) *Sport Facility Operations Management: A Global Perspective*. 3rd ed. Oxford, UK: Routledge.

Schwarz, E.C. & Hunter, J.D. (2018) *Advanced Theory and Practice in Sport Marketing*. 3rd ed. ed. Oxford, UK: Routledge.

Stim, R. (2016) *Contracts: The Essential Business Desk Reference*. 2nd ed. Berkeley, CA: Nolo.

12

ENGAGING FANS AT FIFA WORLD CUPS

André Bühler

Introduction

A decade ago, Bühler and Nufer (2010) wrote:

> Imagine the business of sports without fans. No spectators at sports matches, no buyers of merchandising, no potential customers for sponsoring companies, no recipients for the sports media. Such a scenario would be unthinkable (p. 63).

During the 2020/2021 COVID-19 pandemic, the unthinkable somehow became reality as spectators were banned from sports matches all over the world. Large sporting events such as UEFA Euro 2020 as well as the Tokyo Olympic Games 2020 had to be postponed because the organising committees feared that their premium products would suffer without fans in the stadiums. Of course, there were still millions of people watching live streams of sports events or buying replica shirts of their favourite teams during those difficult times. The pandemic, however, proved once more a basic rule in the business of football: The football business in general (and professional football organisations in particular) need fans who are willing to spend their time, their emotions and their money for their favourite football team. Supporters are the primary – and arguably most important – customers of a sports entity. Therefore, it is essential for every professional football organisation to establish and maintain a healthy relationship with their fans and to engage them in any possible way.

Fan engagement can be viewed from two perspectives: one is from the football business' point of view, where professional football enterprises (such as clubs, associations, agencies, marketing companies) are trying to engage fans. The aim here clearly is to attract a larger and more loyal audience and ultimately to increase

DOI: 10.4324/9781003121794-12

the revenue streams coming from fans as customers. However, fan engagement can also be viewed from the fans's perspective. Here, the simple question is: How do fans themselves engage with football and their favourite club – or in the context of this Handbook – with the FIFA World Cup™ in general and their favourite national team in particular? However, the basic of both perspectives is a deep understanding of what a football fan is.

This chapter combines both perspectives of fan engagement. It kicks off by describing the nature of fans and therefore answering two questions: What is a fan and which types of football fans are there? The second part of this chapter addresses the concept of fan engagement. It analyses the status quo of empirical research in this field and also provides examples of how to engage fans from a sports entity's perspective. The third part will then look at fan engagement at different FIFA tournaments, with special focus on the FIFA World Cup™. Here, the distinction between fan engagement at the sporting venues, at the so-called FIFA Fan Fests and in the context of social media will be made. Finally, this chapter concludes with a word of warning when it comes to fan engagement.

The Nature of Fans

"The fan" as a term is rather misleading because opinions differ widely when it comes to defining "a fan." For example, the Collins English Dictionary describes a fan as "an ardent admirer of a sports team." The Cambridge International Dictionary of English, however, notes that a fan is "a person who has a great interest in and admiration for a sports team." For the Sir Norman Chester Centre for Football Research (2003), a fan is simply anybody who follows a club. Lenhard (2002) in his work discusses the most relevant definitions and develops a more sophisticated one:

> A fan or supporter respectively is a human being who identifies with a particular sports club on a cognitive, affective and behaviour-specific level. (p. 38)

Lenhard adds that neither an empirical system of measure nor an identifiable threshold value between "fan" and "not-fan" exits because each and every sports supporter shows different levels of identification.[1] In the context of business and marketing, it is important to note that "typical" football supporters differ in numerous ways from ordinary consumers of ordinary companies. First, they are usually *more passionate* about their favourite football club than consumers are about their preferred brand. Or have you ever seen someone in a supermarket adoring and celebrating a shelf full of Coca-Cola or insulting another one packed with

1 Wiid and Cant (2015) distinguish between "spectators" and "fans" and provide some interesting arguments for such a distinction. In this chapter, though, fans and spectators will be used synonymously.

Pepsi? Second, fans show a *high level of loyalty* to their sports team. Whereas some people might switch from one car brand to another, sports fans stick to their favourite team forever (Nufer and Bühler, 2013). Dempsey and Reilly (1998) explain this loyalty with the fact that supporters find something in sports that they cannot find anywhere else, for example, the escape from the ordinary workaday world, the adrenalin rush and thrill of a match or the feeling of being part of a community. Therefore, fans pledge allegiances to their clubs. Hornby (1996), in his bestseller *Fever Pitch*, illustrates the fan loyalty from a football supporters point of view:

> I had discovered after the Swindon game that loyalty, at least in football terms, was not a moral choice like bravery or kindness; it was more like a wart or a hump, something you were stuck with. Marriages are nowhere near as rigid – you won't catch any Arsenal fans slipping off to Tottenham for a bit of extra-marital slap and tickle, and though divorce is a possibility (you can just stop going if things get too bad) getting hitched again is out of the question. There have been many times over the last twenty-three years when I have pored over the small print of my contract looking for a way out, but there isn't one. (p. 35)

Passion and loyalty leads to the third difference: sports fans are often *irrational in their consumer behaviour.* Purchase decision are seldom taken on commercial grounds, or as Cashmore (2003, p. 23) puts it: "Part of being a fan involves buying all manner of product related to the object of adulation" regardless of price or quality. A related consequence of loyalty is the fact that supporters do not have a real choice when it comes to purchase decisions. While ordinary consumers may have their preferences, they normally have a choice between several products. Sports fans, however, would rarely change to another club only because the ticket price of the competitor is more reasonable.

Apart from that, football supporters are just as important when it comes to the product itself. Morrow (2014) notes the important role of the fans in creating the product, which they actually consume. The atmosphere not only is a crucial part of the attractiveness of the game, but it is created by the supporters. In this respect, the fans can be seen as *co-producers* of an event they pay for in order to attend. Therefore, fans are also called "*co-creators of value*" or "*prosumers*" (a combination of producer and consumer) in the context of sporting events (Nufer and Bühler, 2013, p. 11).

Another approach to describe the personality of sports fans comes from social psychologists. Elements of the social identity theory have been used to analyse the behaviour of dedicated supporters with "*BIRGing*" and "*CORFing.*" "BIRGing" (= basking in reflected glory) means that people are trying to connect with successful others to demonstrate their own success. People who BIRG are trying to portray themselves as successful by publicly displaying a common trait of the entity they relate to. There is clear empirical evidence, that more people wear the club's shirt when their team has won. In the same way, fans like to say "we won" while in the case of a defeat the linguistic phrase is rather "they lost." CORFing therefore reflects the latter. If a team loses, some fans try to CORF (cutting out reflected failure) in order not to be associated with a loser image (Strauss, 2006; Bühler and Nufer, 2014).

The differences mentioned earlier are one of the main reasons why the relationship between sports clubs and their supporters cannot be adequately captured in purely economic terms. Morrow (2014) claims that the customer concept is incomplete because it fails to consider the idea of a *fan's identity* with a club. Support for this interpretation comes from Lenhard (2002, p. 19), who states that "identity and identification are significant themes" in professional sports.

The whole issue of fan loyalty, irrational consumer behaviour, passion, identity and identification lead economic analysts and professional investors to the conclusion that sports fans are "*captive consumers*" within a "captive market" (Banks, 2002; Conn, 2001; Nufer and Bühler, 2013; Pierpoint, 2000). Captive market is defined in the general marketing literature as a group of consumers who have limited choice in terms of the products they can select/purchase or no other alternative but to buy a product from a specific source, respectively.

However, some authors suggest that the relationship between clubs and supporters is changing and that the new generation of fans will not be as passionate and loyal as the traditional supporters (Morrow, 2014). Grünitz and von Arndt (2002) speak about a trend towards the alienation of fans and players. Lenhard (2002) supports this view by discussing the relationship between fans, players and clubs through the ages. He concludes, for example, that the football stars of today are becoming remote from the game's supporters with regard to daily routine and future perspective on life. He identifies an increasing distance between clubs, players and fans, which is leading to a decrease in identification. Dempsey and Reilly (1998) blame the commercial exploitation of supporters by clubs for the fact that more and more traditional fans have been priced out over the years, especially in professional football. Indeed, the social structure of game attending supporters has changed. Middle-income fans are being attracted to the game and low-income fans are being driven away. Malcolm, Jones and Waddington (2000) mention the shift from the "*traditional fan*" to the "*affluent customer*" in this context. Nearly two decades later, empirical research confirms those forecasts made at the beginning of the new millennia. In 2017, the FC PlayFair!, a non-profit organisation aiming for integrity and sustainability in football, carried out the largest scientific survey in German football (FC PlayFair!, 2017). Some of the results, coming from 17.330 dedicated and long-term football fans, should be a ringing bell for any football authorities:

- 72.4% said that the interests of fans fell by the wayside in view of the ongoing developments in professional football,
- 83.3% warn professional football about an increasing alienation of professional football from its fans,

- 83.4% agree that professional football has long since lost touch with real life because of the huge amount of money involved,
- 86.9% think that it is only just about money in football,
- and more than every second respondent made it clear, that they would eventually turn away from the game if football commercialisation increases further.

This, in turn, not only is a German phenomenon, but one that can also be seen amongst football fans in other European leagues. Football, it seems, is at the edge of losing its basis and therefore its most important stakeholders.

Engaging fans is therefore an essential task for professional football organisations in order to remain their customer base. However, it has also to be noted that there are different types of fans with different interests and different needs, which have to be addressed in the context of fan engagement.

Different Fan Types

It is important not to overlook the fact that football fans are not necessarily the loyal, irrational and passionate supporters as mentioned earlier. Greenfield and Osborn (2001) have observed the development of a *new generation of sedentary armchair fans* resulting from the new sports broadcasting coverage. These fans have another relationship to the clubs in comparison to those who attend live games. Hermanns and Riedmüller (2008) also distinguish between television audience and spectators in the stadium in the first place. Lenhard (2002) examines the latter group in detail and identifies the spectators in the stadium as a heterogeneous group. People who attend live games can be divided into three main categories: First, the *consumption-orientated fan* who wants to have a certain level of entertainment value for his/her money. In this case, the emotional bond to the club is not very well-developed and sports games are more or less an exchangeable leisure activity. Second, the exact opposite is the *sports-oriented fan* who shows the same characteristics as the irrational, loyal and passionate traditional supporter mentioned earlier. Third, the *event-orientated fan* who seeks to have fun in and around the stadium regardless of the match itself, that is, Hooligans, Ultras or Groundhoppers. Ultras are specific fan movements who have their origins in Italy. Ultras consider themselves as being responsible for the atmosphere in the stadiums and therefore organise extensive choreographies or flags for example. Groundhoppers, however, are truly football fans who made it their business to visit as many football games and stadiums as possible whether their own club is involved or not. Lenhard (2002) notes that the line cannot be drawn clearly as the example of Ultras and Groundhoppers shows. Both groups are indeed sports-orientated but want to experience more than a pure sporting competition. Lenhard's fan interpretation scheme was one of the first ones and therefore added scientific value to the ongoing question who a fan is and what types of fans there are. However, Lenhard's scheme from 2002 is somehow outdated today. For example, nearly two decades later, the term "event-orientated fan" has a different meaning than in 2002, at a time when the eventisation of sports (i.e., turning sporting competition into an event or spectacle) was only in its beginning and is therefore a misleading term in today's context.

Over the years, different authors (e.g., Crawford, 2004; Stewart, Smith and Nicholson, 2003; Reysen and Branscombe, 2010; Wiid and Cant, 2015) have tried to *conceptualise fans into different categories*, but none gained overall acceptance. There were also some attempts by market research and media agencies, for example, Carat, which differentiated between "maniac," "passionate," "congenial" and "affine" fans (Dentsu, 2019). Their typology, however, is clearly marketing-driven and published to sell their consulting services. Also business-motivated, but far more enhanced, is a *football fan typology* created by the European Club Association (ECA, 2020), which carried out a representative survey across seven football markets. According to the data, they identified the following six fan types:

- *Football Fanatics*: They follow football with a strong emotional engagement. The key to their enjoyment is a sense of community, which football provided. They prefer to go to the stadium to experience the feeling of togetherness. Football Fanatics are attached to their respective club, but are also engaged widely with lower league football.
- *Club Loyalists*: They are long-term football fans, who follow their club closely. They watch football regularly and keep up to date with news. Part of their identity is a strong emotional attachment to their club.
- *Icon Imitators*: They have a moderate to strong interest in football because they play regularly. The Icon Imitators follow specific players and find them relatable. They prefer playing to watching, are not competition focussed, but nonetheless enjoy big games featuring the best footballers.
- *FOMO (fear of missing out) Followers*: They are frequently engaged with football via news, illegal streaming and sharing football stories, but are less emotionally engaged. They prefer to follow the big teams and big competitions as it provides higher quality of entertainment. For them, football is a social currency.
- *Main Eventers*: They show a low engagement frequency, which increases around the big matches and tournaments. As moderate fans they are more interested in the event and are less bothered about the result.
- *Tag Alongs*: In terms of fan engagement, the lightest football fans with low emotional and intellectual engagement. The interest in football is rather prompted by national team performance or by friends/family, interest increases around big tournaments.

All these different fan types are addressed by FIFA through their various competition formats, though some competitions only attract specific fan types as will be shown later on. The next sub-chapter, however, will have a closer look at the different concepts of engaging fans.

Engagement of Fans

Fan engagement has become a buzzword within the past years – both in the sports marketing literature and the business of sports. But what exactly is it? The Connected Fan (2020) defines fan engagement from the football entities' perspective as an "intense and deeply rooted connection with the fan base" and as "the manner in which a club or brand communicates with the fan base." Schnater (2016) in his blog discusses various approaches to defining fan engagement and eventually proposes the following definition:

> *Fan engagement* is the "growth strategy of long-term relationship management between sports institution and fan groups, where institutions facilitate fans in self-expression and in-group acceptance, using both modern online and offline technologies, with the goal of creating social value for fans, which can be transformed into profit optimisation."

This sub-chapter explores the status quo of academic research in the field of fan engagement and also describes some concepts and instruments football entities might use to engage their fans.

Empricial studies and academic papers on fan engagement

There are various empirical studies examining the concept of fan engagement in different contexts. For example, Yoshida et al. (2014) tried to conceptualise and measure fan engagement by proposing a *fan-engagement scale* composing of three dimensions (i.e., management cooperation, prosocial behaviour, performance tolerance). They also showed that team identification and BIRGing plays a particularly important role in increasing the three dimensions of fan engagement.

Stander and De Beer (2016) were exploring the potential of *fan engagement as a predictor of positive consumer behaviours* in the context of South African football. As a result, they established a structural path between fan engagement and match attendance, as well as fan engagement and expenditure on team merchandise.

Huettermann, Uhrich and Koenigstorfer (2019) showed in their study of European professional sports teams that fan engagement can include *positive components* (e.g., fan resource integration, fan learning and fan knowledge sharing) or *negative components* (e.g., fan norm violation and fan resistance to the team). These components, in turn, can have both *benefits* (e.g., fan resource development, fan value co-creation) and *detriments* (e.g., fan value destruction, fan identity conflict development).

Pradhan, Malhotra and Moharana (2020) focused on the *impact of fan engagement on sponsorship*. In the context of professional football, they identified a positive influence of fan personality/sponsor brand personality congruence on sponsor brand attitude and brand purchase intention. In addition, they revealed that *in-role behaviours* (e.g., buying tickets, watching club games and BIRGing) and *extra-role behaviours* (e.g., wearing club apparel and displaying logo of club) are not only relevant but also distinct components of fan engagement.

Some other studies were examining the concept of fan engagement in the context of football club's *social media activities*. Vale and Fernandes (2018), for example, gained a broader understanding of why and how sport fans engage with clubs on social media. It also revealed additional opportunities for sporting organisations to engage their respective fan base online. Parganas and Anagnostopoulos (2015) analysed fan engagement by social media in the context of English professional football. According to their findings, all media channels of the club should be integrated to allow for a more targeted and engaging approach towards its fans. They also concluded that the appropriate balance between purely commercial content and content increasing fan interaction and fan engagement is major challenge for sports marketing managers. In the context of European football, Aichner (2019) found that social media users like, comment and share postings by football clubs independently of the content of the posting. The study also concludes that user engagement and reach of advertisements can be increased significantly by employing football-related content.

In addition, there are studies examining the different levels and concepts of *fan engagement in different cultures*. Sullivan et al. (2021), for example, found out that Chinese football fans tend to support more than one club, often one domestic and one foreign club. They also noted distinct methods of consumption, which eschew traditional forms such as match attendance.

Instruments to engage fans

The relevant sports marketing literature as well as blogs from sports marketing practioniers offer a wide range of instruments in the context of fan engagement. Bühler and Nufer (2010), for example, describe three relationship marketing instruments that professional football organisations can use to engage their fans. First, *member clubs* and *membership schemes* give fans and clubs the opportunity to strengthen their bond. Although most member clubs are directed to adult fans, more and more football clubs realise that they have to engage in relationships with the younger fans as well. Therefore, some football clubs introduced so-called kids clubs, offering discounts and exclusive membership content for the youngest fan base. Second, *fan loyalty programmes* are designed to reward and therefore encourage loyal buying behaviour amongst football fans. Third and in view of the fact that football organisations should also engage with unsatisfied and unhappy fans to remain a healthy relationship, a systematic and professional *complaint management programme* might a good instrument. This is a field, where especially FIFA has significant potential for improvement.

In their *fan engagement model*, Fowler and Wilson (2016) differentiate between fan engagement in four categories: *On matchdays* and *non-matchdays* as well as *onsite* and *offsite*. With fans in the sporting venue on a matchday, the challenge for sporting organisations such as FIFA is to enhance the live experience. Here, the supporting programme before a match and during half-time is essential. Also providing live stats about players during the game might engage fans deeply into the live experience. Social Media and virtual reality technology comes into play on a match-day to engage fans who do not attend in person. This is especially important for FIFA in view of the fact that the majority of people follow the FIFA competitions on television or via livestreams. On a non-matchday, fans can also be engaged onsite by offering exclusive stadium tours. For the offsite version of non-matchday fan engagement, sports entities should try to connect fans with their organisation by virtual reality, club-related content on the clubs' social media accounts and e-sports.

Mons (2021) postulates some requirements to meet the expectations of *fan engagement in the future*. For fans to be engaged on matchdays onsite, stadiums have to be upgraded and exclusive content inside stadiums (sportainment) has to be created. The FIFA World Cup Qatar 2022™ is expected to set new standards when it comes to stadium shows before and during the games. Fans, watching the sporting event from home, should be engaged by facilitating virtual and augmented reality and by offering alternative media to attract fans. Here again, FIFA will introduce the newest technology for covering their forthcoming competitions, especially those designed for a younger generation (i.e., the FIFA Beach Soccer World Cup™ and the FIFA Futsal World Cup™). On non-matchdays, clubs need to engage fans on their site by offering them museums, field trips or virtual experiences. Mons also argues that the "the biggest battlefield for clubs where fan engagement is concerned will actually take place outside the stadium" on non-matchdays. Here, digital transformation, big data, market segmentation, individualised marketing approaches and storytelling is the key to increase fan engagement in the future.

A very important aspect, when it comes to fan engagement in combination with social media is the *concept of second screens*. A study from Carat (Dentsu, 2019) revealed that around 76% of football fans in Germany use a second screen to look for brands or products during a game or simply to chat about the game itself using messenger services or social media like Twitter, Facebook or Instagram. As will be shown later, FIFA has recognised the importance of second screens and therefore not only provides social-media-content before or after a game, but also during a match. According to the Connected Fan (2020), various devices such as smartphone or smartwatches might offer additional options for football clubs to engage with fans.

However, Davey and Richardson (2018) provide an important *word a warning* when it comes to fan engagement. They emphasise that all efforts undertaken to engage fans should be authentic and meaningful to fans. If fans have the impression that engagement is forced on them, fans might do exactly the opposite of what the sporting organisation intended them to do.

Engaging Fans at the FIFA World Cup™

Every four years the world experiences the largest football event: The FIFA World Cup™. It is also the largest migration worldwide with hundreds of thousands football fans travelling to the host nation from different corners of the planet to support their respective national team. In addition, it attracts literally billions of people around the world, who watch the games on television, via livestreams on the internet or at public viewing events. For sports marketing managers, the FIFA World Cup™ is both a dream and a challenge when it comes to fan engagement. This sub-chapter explores how FIFA actively engages fans in their various tournaments.

FIFA has established a sophisticated competition portfolio over the past years. Currently, if offers a total of 15 different competitions to engage different fan types to their world of football. Whereas the FIFA World Cup™ nearly includes all manners of fan types as mentioned earlier (from *Football Fanatics* to the *Main Eventers* and *Tag Alongs*), some other competitions only target very specific types of fans. For example, the FIFA Club World Cup™ mainly relates to *Club Loyalists*, *Icon Imitators* and *FOMO Followers*, who engage themselves on an individual club or player level. The FIFA Beach Soccer World Cup™ and the FIFA Futsal World Cup™ are designed for non-traditional football fans, that is, a younger generation, which is attracted by new forms of football. To engage more women and girls into football, the world governing body extended its portfolio on women's football competitions significantly over the years with the Women's Youth Olympic Futsal Tournament being the latest addition to it.

Whilst those different tournaments will be appreciated in this sub-chapter, the main focus will be on the men's World Cup because it not only is the oldest tournament but also the one which attracts most football fans – men, female, diverse, old and young – across the world. It therefore is a truly global phenomenon and one, which requires a deeper insight. Figure 12.1 offers an overview of how many fans attended the World Cup tournaments in men's and women's football so far.

To compare the amount of fans attending a certain World Cup tournament, the average attendance per game is a good indicator in view of the fact that the various tournaments differ in terms of teams attending and games played. Figure 12.1 clearly shows that the men's World Cup nowadays attracts far more spectators than the women's World Cup. It also shows that there is no linear development of attendance but that it strongly correlates with the respective host nation. The 1994 FIFA World Cup USA™, for example, showed a very high attendance rate due to the large stadiums as well as the attractiveness and easy accessibility of the host nation. The most recent competition, the 2018 World Cup Russia™, on the other side, attracted fewer fans, which might be explained by the fact that visiting fans first needed to obtain a visa to travel to Russia. The rather homophobic and unfriendly nature of the Russian government did not really add to fans' willingness to attend the 2018 FIFA World Cup Russia™ as

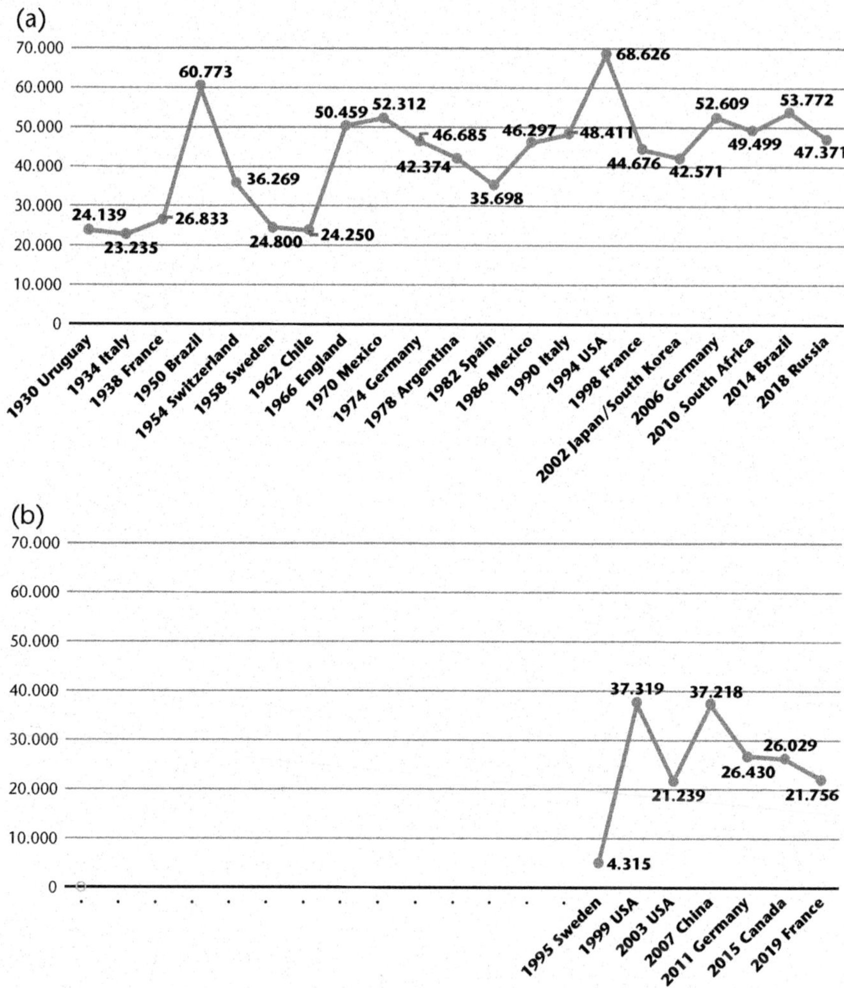

FIGURE 12.1 Average Attendance of football fans at the FIFA World Cups to date

Sources: Statista (2021a, 2021b), own illustration.

they usually did. In addition, the Foreign Affairs Committee of the UK House of Commons published a report warning British citizens planning to visit the FIFA World Cup™ in Russia about alleged threats. Among them the lawmakers named anti-UK sentiment, racism, hooliganism, violence based on ethnic grounds. Nevertheless, despite all this problems, more than 633,000 foreign football fans entered Russia using FAN IDs with China, the United States and Mexico accounting for the largest number of fans who arrived in Russia for the 2018 FIFA World Cup™ (TASS, 2018).

It might be safe to conclude that most football fans attend World Cup tournaments for a *variety of motives*. Of course, they want to support their respective national team. There is also the ever present hope to be part of something big, to be part of history making when the own team really might win the World Cup. Apart from the sports aspects, most fans are travelling to World Cup tournaments, to experience the special atmosphere of the largest football event, to be part of a truly global movement, which takes place in a single nation. Attending a World Cup is more than just the sports involved. Therefore, FIFA and the host nations try to engage fans both onsite and offsite. *In and around the stadium* there are multiple ways to be engaged as a fan before and after the respective matches. For example, the FIFA partners are presenting themselves at stands, providing entertainment and engaging fans in various types of sweepstakes. FIFA itself offers official merchandise in a number of stalls at the venue. Inside the stadiums, there is a well-orchestrated stadium show, which climax when both teams enter the field and stand for the national anthems.

World Cups, however, are not only for those attending games. Every World Cup tournament in the past 30 or so years experienced thousands of football fans following their respective national teams from one host city to another without being able to watch the matches in the stadium. Simply because they could not get hold of a ticket because matches were sold out or the tickets were too expensive. In addition, there are millions of football fans in the host nation, which want to be part of the World Cup experience, but cannot get hold of tickets either. At the 2002 FIFA World Cup South Korea™*public viewing events* became a huge success. FIFA recognised the potential to market such public viewing events and therefore introduced the so-called *FIFA Fan Fests* as an essential part of the official programme of the FIFA World Cup™ since the 2006 edition in Germany. FIFA Fan Fests take place in iconic locations of the host cities and feature broadcasts of the World Cup matches on large screens as well as live concerts, parties, food, beverages and other activities and entertainment. The 2014 FIFA World Cup Brasil™ noted more than 5.2 million visitors at the FIFA Fans Fests, where the top venue Rio de Janeiro had 937,330 visitors in total. The FIFA Fan Fests at the 2018 FIFA World Cup Russia™ saw an even larger outcome. 7.7 million local and international football fans visited the 11 FIFA Fan Fests, watching a total of 917 hours of live football and enjoying a music and cultural entertainment programme with 646 bands playing 323 hours of live music, all free of charge (FIFA, 2018a).

The most recent World Cup tournament in Russia also showed records when it comes to *fan engagement via social media.* FIFA noted over 7.5 billion engagements across all FIFA digital platforms, 1.25 billion video views and over 580 million interactions on FIFA social media platforms during the tournament. According to FIFA it provided fans more opportunities to follow, engage and connect with the 2018 FIFA World Cup Russia™ than ever before. Drivers of *virtual fan engagement* were images from across the 11 host cities, and the proliferation of videos, which contributed to an increase of more than four million new subscribers to FIFA's YouTube channel. FIFA.com was ranked as the number one football website worldwide during the tournament, while the FIFA official app for the 2018 FIFA

World Cup Russia™ became the number one sports app in over 128 countries. To give fans the opportunity to follow their respective team throughout the tournament, FIFA employed 32 team reporters who were delivering exclusive content in 16 languages on multiple platforms before, after and during the 64 matches. Through interactive games, FIFA was able to generate *fan engagement opportunities for their official partners*, as over 25 million fans took part in apps such as Hyundai's FIFA World Cup Match Predictor, McDonald's FIFA World Cup Fantasy or the Panini Digital Sticker Album presented by Coca-Cola. (FIFA, 2018b). FIFA also used various technical options such as timely tweets, phone wallpapers, vibrant GIFs as goal alerts, and exclusive emojis to bringing the 2018 FIFA World Cup 2018 Russia™ to life on Twitter (Stranges, 2018).

Conclusion

Fans are the lifeblood of every sporting organisation. Without supporters the business of football would not be a business because there would be no audience paying for tickets, no spectators watching sports on TV or the internet, no recipients reading the sports news, no fans buying merchandising, and no potential customers for the sports entities' sponsors. Nearly everything in the football business is aimed at fans. However, fans are much more than potential income for the profit-orientated stakeholders of the football business. Fans create atmosphere, they are part of the attraction (and sometimes they are the only attraction). All this leads to the conclusion that fans are essential for football organisations. That is why more and more clubs and associations realise that they have to focus on fan engagement.

However, this also comes with a word of warning. One of the mysteries – or rather paradoxes – of the football business is the notion to transform fans into customers by offering them more and more products and services. It is a paradox because normal companies of nearly all other business sectors are trying to transform their customers into loyal and long-term fans. Engaging fans therefore are two sides of the came coin. Just to turn fans into customers for the pure maximisation of profits is not sustainable. Sporting organisations have to make money, no doubt about that. But, there is a fine line between providing a fan something beneficial and exploiting supporters. Therefore, sporting organisations always have to bear in mind that their customers are extremely loyal, but that their loyalty is not blind loyalty. A healthy relationship should benefit both – the sports entity and the fans. This is also true in the context of the FIFA World Cup™ tournaments.

The FIFA World Cup 2022 Qatar™ will be a completely new experience in the history of football in view of the fact that the 2022 World Cup will be hosted for the first time by a nation with no football tradition whatsoever. Due to the heat during the summer months, the FIFA World Cup 2022 Qatar™ will take place during December, therefore breaking with another tradition in football. However, it could also lead to a completely new experience in terms of fan engagement both at the venues and on the internet. The stadiums of the FIFA World Cup 2022 Qatar™ will be state of the art and therefore be able to set new standards when it comes to fan engagement. For example, the stadium show before the game and in half-time can be expected to be something the sports world never experienced before. In addition, the FIFA World Cup 2022 Qatar™ might also be a benchmark when it comes to engaging fans on social media with millions of people watching the games on television or via livestreams, while simultaneously exchanging views on Twitter, Facebook, Instagram and TikTok. But despite any marketing efforts – and that is the bottom line of this chapter – the "beautiful game" and its fans should remain the core of the football business.

References

Aichner, T. (2019) Football Clubs' Social Media Use and User Engagement, *Marketing Intelligence & Planning*, 37(3), 242–257.

Banks, S. (2002) *Going Down – Football in Crisis*. Edinburgh: Mainstream Publishing Ltd.

Bühler, A. & Nufer, G. (2010) *Relationship Marketing in Sports*. Oxford: Elsevier.

Bühler, A. & Nufer, G. (2014) *International Sports Marketing. Principles and Perspectives*. Berlin: Erich Schmidt Verlag.

Cashmore, E. (2003) The Marketing Midas with a Golden Boot, *The Times Higher*, 26 September 2003, 22–23.

Conn, D. (2001) *The Football Business*. 5th edn. Edinburgh: Mainstream Publishing Ltd.

Crawford, G. (2004) *Consuming Sport: Fans, Sport and Culture*. Milton Park: Routledge.

Davey, T. & Richardson, M. (2018) *Wie erschafft man unvergessliche Fan-Rituale mit Kultstatus?* Available at: https://www.munich-business-school.de/insights/2018/fan-engagement/ [Accessed 30 April 2021].

Dempsey, P. & Reilly, K. (1998) *Big Money, Beautiful Game – Saving Soccer from Itself*. London: Nicholas Brealey Publishing Limited.

Dentsu (2019) *Carat Fantypologie 2019*. Hamburg: Dentsu Aegis Network.

ECA (2020) *Fan of the Future – Defining Modern Football Fandom*. Nyon: European Club Association.

FC PlayFair! (2017) *Situationsanalyse Profifußball 2017*. Berlin: FC PlayFair! Verein für Integrität und Nachhaltigkeit im Fußball e.V.

FIFA (2018a) *7.7 Million Football Fans Visit FIFA Fan Fest during Russia 2018*. Available at: https://www.fifa.com/worldcup/news/7-7-million-football-fans-visit-fifa-fan-fest-during-russia-2018 [Accessed 30 April 2021].

FIFA (2018b) *Russia 2018 most engaging FIFA World Cup ever*. Available at: https://www.fifa.com/worldcup/news/russia-2018-most-engaging-fifa-world-cup-ever [Accessed 30 April 2021].

Fowler, D. & Wilson, G. (2016) Fan Engagement: From Match Day to Every Day. *The Business of Sport*. Available at: https://geoffwnjwilson.com/2016/08/25/254/ [Accessed 30 April 2021].

Greenfield, S. & Osborn, G. (2001) *Regulating Football – Commodification, Consumption and the Law*. London: Pluto Press.

Grünitz, M. & von Arndt, M. (2002) *Der Fußball-Crash*. Stuttgart: RRS.

Hermanns, A. & Riedmüller, F. (2008) *Management-Handbuch Sportmarketing*. 2nd edn. Munich: Verlag Vahlen.

Hornby, N. (1996) *Fever Pitch*. London: Indigo.

Huettermann, M., Uhrich, S. & Koenigstorfer, J. (2019) Components and Outcomes of Fan Engagement in Team Sports: The Perspective of Managers and Fans, *Journal of Global Sport Management*, 1(1), 1–32.

Lenhard, M. (2002) *Vereinsfußball und Identifikation in Deutschland – Phänomen zwischen Tradition und Postmoderne*. Hamburg: Verlag Dr. Kovac.

Malcolm, D, Jones. I. & Waddington, I. (2000) The People's Game? Football Spectatorship and Demographic Change, *Soccer & Society*, 1(1), 129–143.

Mons, J.K. (2021) *14 Awesome Ways How Fan Engagement Will Improve in the Future*. [Blog] *Sport Tomorrow*. Available: https://sporttomorrow.com/how-to-improve-fan-engagement-in-the-future/ [Accessed 30 April 2021].

Morrow, S. (2014) *The New Business of Football – Accountability and Finance in Football*. London: Palgrave MacMillan.

Nufer, G. & Bühler, A. (2013) *Marketing in Sport*. 3rd edn. Berlin: Erich Schmidt Verlag.

Parganas, P. & Anagnostopoulos, C. (2015) Social Media Strategy in Professional Football: The Case of Liverpool FC, *Choregia*, *11*(2), 61–75.

Pierpoint, B. (2000) Heads above Water: Business Strategies for a New Football Economy. In Garland et al. (eds) *The Future of Football – Challenges for the Twenty-First Century*. London: Frank Cass Publishers, pp. 29–38.

Posten, M. (1998) Basking in Glory and Cutting of Failure. [Blog] *Psybersite*. Available at: http://www.units.muohio.edu/psybersite/fans/bc.shtml [Accessed 30 April 2021].

Pradhan, D., Malhotra, R. & Moharana, T.R. (2020) When Fan Engagement with Sports Club Brands Matters in Sponsorship: Influence of Fan–brand Personality Congruence, *Journal of Brand Management*, 27(1), 77–92.

Reysen, S. & Branscombe, N.R. (2010) Fanship and Fandom: Comparisons between Sport and Non-sport Fans, *Journal of Sport Behavior, 33*(2), 176–193.

Schnater, B. (2016) Defining fan engagement. [Blog] *LinkedIn*. Available at: https://www.linkedin.com/pulse/defining-fan-engagement-bas-schnater [Accessed 30 April 2021].

Sir Norman Chester Centre for Football Research (2003) *Fact Sheet 11 – Branding Sponsorship and Commerce in Football*. Leicester: Sir Norman Chester Centre for Football Research.

Stander, F.W. & De Beer, L.T. (2016) Engagement as a Source of Positive Consumer Behaviour: A Study amongst South African Football Fans, *South African Journal for Research in Sport, Physical Education and Recreation*, 38(2), 187–200.

Statista (2021a) *Average and Total Attendance at FIFA Football World Cup Games from 1930 to 2018*. Available at: https://www.statista.com/statistics/264441/number-of-spectators-at-football-world-cups-since-1930/ [Accessed 30 April 2021].

Statista (2021b) *Average Number of Spectators at Games of the FIFA Women's World Championships from 1991 to 2019*. Available at: https://www.statista.com/statistics/272800/average-number-of-spectatators-at-the-fifa-womens-world-cup/ [Accessed 30 April 2021].

Stewart, B., Smith, A. & Nicholson, M. (2003) Sport Consumer Typologies: A Critical Review, *Sport Marketing Quarterly*, 12(1), 206–216.

Stranges, E. (2018) 10 Ways FIFA brought the World Cup to life on Twitter. [Blog] *Media Twitter*. Available at: https://media.twitter.com/en/articles/case-study/2018/10-ways-fifa-brought-the-world-cup-to-life-on-twitter.html [Accessed 30 April 2021].

Strauss, B. (2006) Das Fußballstadion als Pilgerstätte, *Fußball und Politik*, 1, 28–48.

Sullivan, J., Zhao, Y., Chadwick, S., & Gow, M. (2021) Chinese Fans' Engagement with Football: Transnationalism, Authenticity and Identity, *Journal of Global Sport Management*, 1–20.

TASS (2018) *Largest Number of FIFA World Cup Fans in Russia came from China, US, Mexico.* Available at: https://tass.com/sport/1016093 [Accessed 30 April 2021].

The Connected Fan (2020) *What is Fan Engagement?* [Blog]. Available at: https://theconnectedfan.com/fan-engagement/ [Accessed 30 April 2021].

Vale, L. & Fernandes, T. (2018) Social Media and Sports: Driving Fan Engagement with Football Clubs on Facebook, *Journal of Strategic Marketing*, 26(1), 37–55.

Wiid, J.A., & Cant, M.C. (2015) Sport Fan Motivation: Are You Going to the Game?, *International Journal of Academic Research in Business and Social Sciences*, *5*(1), 383.

Yoshida, M., Gordon, B., Nakazawa, M. & Biscaia, R. (2014) Conceptualization and Measurement of Fan Engagement: Empirical Evidence from a Professional Sport Context, *Journal of Sport Management*, 28(4), 399–417.

13

MANAGING RISK AND SECURITY AT FIFA WORLD CUPS

Jan Andre Lee Ludvigsen and Alexander J. Bond

Introduction

The World Cup is one of the largest sporting spectacles globally. Subsequently, the tournament has been employed as a scholarly site of analysis across economic, political, social and cultural fields. Within these fields, "risk" and "security" of previous men's World Cups have been examined from management, tourism, sociology and political science perspectives (Cornelissen, 2011; Jennings and Lodge, 2011; Klauser, 2008; Lee Ludvigsen, 2018; Rookwood, 2019; Toohey et al., 2003; Toohey and Taylor, 2014; Wong and Chadwick, 2017). Against this background, this chapter examines the processes of risk and security management at the World Cup. The chapter explores contemporary concepts, issues and cases related to the World Cup's risk and security management.

While risk management is challenging to define, we refer to the "proactive process" involving "assessing all possible risks to the events and its stakeholders by strategically anticipating, preventing, minimising, and planning responses to eliminate or mitigate those identified risks" (Leopkey and Parent, 2009, p. 199). Therefore, the World Cup is exposed to diversely complex risks (real and perceived) and security issues. In the growing, interdisciplinary literature, the emergence of risk and security complexes at sport mega-events are often pinpointed to the terrorist attacks at the 1972 Olympic Games in Munich and the 11 September (9/11) attack in the United States (Giulianotti and Klauser, 2012; Lee Ludvigsen, 2018; Wong and Chadwick, 2017). While the risk context and risk profile of every separate World Cup is unique, there are typical considerations, as this chapter discusses further.

Our chapter starts with unpacking what types of risks and threats organisers, planners, and stakeholders must account for before World Cup staging. Throughout our discussions, we employ examples from previous World Cups.

DOI: 10.4324/9781003121794-13

Second, we discuss the concept of "security knowledge networks" (Boyle, 2011), applying this to the 2010 World Cup in South Africa. Third, our chapter explores the management of risks and security in stadiums and fan zones as two critical spaces at contemporary World Cups. Fourth, we highlight some more general risks associated with staging a World Cup including resource allocation and infrastructure investment. Finally, our conclusions are provided with some recommendations for future research.

Risk Types and Security Issues

As this chapter argues, the risks and security issues that mega-events like the World Cup are exposed to are complex. They vary according to the risk profile of the relevant tournament. Moreover, the relevant World Cup's risk profile will depend on both *internal* (such as the geographies of the host country, upcoming "rival" fixtures', football-related violence trends) and *external* circumstances and factors (e.g., terrorism trends, a global pandemic or the political climate surrounding the event). Therefore, the key point is that World Cups are never isolated from their broader contexts and surrounding uncertainties. As Wong and Chadwick (2017, p. 595) write, the World Cup – as the most-watched sporting event worldwide – "carries exceptional risks including terrorist incidents, football violence, protests, budget overspends [and] operational failures." In that sense, the forthcoming subsections employ recent World Cup cases as examples to highlight the types of risks and security problems that might exist before and during a World Cup. However, we acknowledge that the discussed categories, risk examples do not represent an exhaustive list. Instead, we discuss significant risks requiring consideration.

Supporter violence

One prominent risk that World Cups are exposed to is supporter violence, or "hooliganism" – the latter being a term lacking a universal definition. This is exemplified by the case of the Germany World Cup in 2006. Although there were no major incidents, there were disturbances recorded at three games (Poland vs. Germany, England vs. Sweden and England vs. Ecuador; Wong and Chadwick, 2017). On the day of Germany vs. Poland, more than 432 arrests in Dortmund were reported, many of which preventative arrests related to the match. These arrests came in addition to several police-fan confrontations and stand-offs (Schreiber and Adang, 2010, p. 483).

Episodes of supporter violence at the World Cup are not necessarily confined to the inside of the stadiums or fan zones. As the evidence suggests, they may occur across the various host cities: in public squares, bars or city centres throughout the event (ibid). Moreover, the media discourses leading up to World Cups usually speculate on the prospects of World Cup-related supporter violence (Lee Ludvigsen, 2018). Ultimately, to counter any issues related to supporter violence, World Cups require large-scale policing and crowd management operations (Stott and Pearson, 2007) including transnational information exchange and collaboration (FIFA, 2010). In a pre-emptive manner, different games and fan groups are also commonly classified according to risk assessments (i.e., "high" or "low" risk games).

Terrorism

As Giulianotti and Klauser (2010, p. 52) discuss, the threat of terrorism and political violence represents both a symbolic and political threat, one that can "endanger the athletes, spectators, and local population" of a sporting event. Whilst no major incidents have taken place at recent World Cups, mass crowds and events *have been* targeted by terrorists in the recent years. In November 2015, a terrorist attack targeted *Stade de France* in Paris, where France played against Germany in a friendly game. This attack had considerable impacts on football events' security and risk management (Cleland and Cashmore, 2018). The threat of terrorism at sporting events is commonly secured against through exceptional security measures. For example, the South Africa World Cup's security measures in 2010 included human-crewed aircraft and bomb-squad tools and expertise (Giulianotti and Klauser, 2010). Whether the terrorist threat remains perceived or real, organisers, planners and authorities cannot ignore it. Doing so can construct a climate of fear and anxiety among event tourists and travelling supporters.

Crime

According to Giulianotti and Klauser (2010), urban crime is one risk that event planners must account for pre-event. One of the primary concerns before the 2010 South Africa World Cup was the "prevalent criminal activity in South Africa" (Wong and Chadwick, 2017, p. 586). Before the 2010 World Cup, it was argued that "crime and safety issues in South Africa are still clouding the destination image of South Africa and thus damping the general enthusiasm among local and international stakeholders for 2010" (Donaldson and Ferreira, 2009, p. 3). As this case shows, the host city's crime rates will often be frequently referred to in the media before tournament commencement (BBC, 2010; The Guardian, 2009).

For the 2010 World Cup, the authorities, therefore, took extra measures against criminal activity. As Cornelissen and Maennig (2010) write:

> A few incidents of crime occurred against Confederation Cup visitors (mainly robberies), which were widely reported in the international media. A well developed and efficiently implemented security plan was a major component of the positive atmosphere that reigned at the 2006 World Cup. To gain the same effects, South Africa had to do much to counter widespread cynicism about the ability of overstretched security and policing infrastructure to deliver an effective World Cup anticrime strategy. For the 2010 World Cup 41 000 security staff were eventually deployed (p. 103).

Subsequently, serious crime declined during this World Cup, whereas the tournament "proceeded with few major incidents" (Cornelissen, 2011, p. 3231). Consequently, a host country's (or city's) crime rates are a distinctive risk that event organisers – in tandem with authorities – must counter to ensure that visitors and fans feel safe and to improve destination image.

Infectious diseases

The coronavirus disease-2019 (COVID-19) pandemic impacted the whole "Football World" and showed that sports events are incredibly vulnerable to infectious diseases (Parnell et al., 2020). However, sporting events were impacted by epidemics or pandemics in a pre-COVID-19 age, too. The 2003 Women's World Cup best exemplifies this risk, originally due to be staged in China between 23 September and 11 October 2003. In light of a SARS epidemic in the region, FIFA – consulting with the World Health Organisation (WHO) (FIFA, 2003) – moved the tournament to the United States, hosted by six cities. Meanwhile, China hosted the 2007 World Cup. Indeed, the organisation of future World Cups may be impacted by infectious diseases, too. It has already been reported that the venue selection of the 2026 Men's World Cup in Mexico, Canada and the United States was delayed because of the COVID-19 pandemic (Reuters, 2020). Collectively, what this demonstrates, is that epidemics and pandemics are inherently unpredictable risks that event organisers and stakeholders have to account for before and throughout tournaments, alongside the other risks and security issues.

A Networked Approach to Risk and Security Management

Any mega-event is the culmination of different networks. These differing and overlapping networks or stakeholder are imperative to event delivery. Therefore, any World Cup is structured through ties, interrelatedness, and interdependence between many individuals and organisations. For example, an event is made of and relies on, multiple government departments, tourism, events, sports, media, and other private sector organisations, creating inter-organisational networks. These organisations most likely involve multiple cities and cross international boundaries, creating inter-city and inter-country networks, respectively. These inter-organisational and transnational networks are vitally important, not only for successful event delivery but also for managing risk and security.

The concept of "knowledge networks" (Boyle, 2011) can be regarded as particularly useful and relevant to understand risk and security management at sport mega-events in the current world. Whilst the tournament-specific regulations and requirements may be relatively fixed for every World Cup; each security delivery remains influenced by the event's local characteristics. However, in sport mega-event risk and security management, host nations and event organisers are increasingly drawing on examples, templates and knowledge that derive from previously staged events (Boyle, 2011; Cornelissen, 2011).

The actors, agencies and organisations involved as security stakeholders cut across private, public and voluntary sectors (Taylor and Toohey, 2015). The linkages between these actors are typically networked. Boyle (2011, p. 170) refers to these shifting linkages as "security knowledge networks" based around knowledge transfer and learning. These networks do not merely "facilitate the movement of event-specific security expertise between geographically and temporally distant locales" (ibid) but also facilitate the movement of security rationales and technologies on a global level. Therefore, through networks of relevant knowledge and expertise, involving; law enforcements, intelligence agencies, sporting federations, security consultants and technology firms (ibid), relevant know-how is transferred onto upcoming football mega-events and applied by the organisers and wider stakeholder groups who are responsible for the risk management and public safety.

We may use the concept of "security knowledge networks" to make sense of the important case of the 2010 World Cup in South Africa. This was the first World Cup to be staged in Africa and took place between the 11 June and 11 July 2010 in ten stadiums spread across nine host cities. As aforementioned, the pre-event discourses were characterised by scepticism concerning the event's organisation, logistics and the country's reputation for being crime-ridden (Wong and Chadwick, 2017). Despite this scepticism, it was stated prior to the World Cup by then-FIFA President Joseph Blatter that:

> Security is a matter for the government, and we have received adequate guarantees in this regard, so there is no reason to have any doubts. The FIFA World Cup is about enjoyment, and I am convinced that we will have a wonderful festival in South Africa (quoted in FIFA, 2010)

Accordingly, this World Cup's security costs came to around 13 billion Rand (Toohey and Taylor, 2014). And moreover, it was reported that South African authorities "drew assistance from the organisers of the 2006 FIFA World Cup, mainly in the form of information and intelligence sharing and contingency training" (Cornelissen, 2011, p. 3227). Furthermore, the police – in collaboration with Interpol and international football authorities kept a database of "known hooligans or criminals" to prevent these individuals from entering the stadiums (ibid, p. 3229). As stated, before the event, Interpol would also provide South African police with key operational support (FIFA, 2010).

First, this yields insight into knowledge transfer processes between a past event (i.e., Germany 2006) and an upcoming event (South Africa 2010). Additionally, the 2009 FIFA Confederations Cup also seemingly served as an important platform for learning and knowledge acquisition (ibid). Second, we can see how information sharing occurred *throughout* the month-long tournament as well. Furthermore, throughout the event's duration, the security delivery was made up of an assemblage of private and public actors. This included private security partners, national and local law enforcement, and volunteers, who operated within the same overarching security field and dealt with various and overlapping security and risk responsibilities (Eisenhauer et al., 2014). However, given the many actors involved in an event's security delivery, this may lead to complications. For example, it was reported that over 100 private security guards went on strike during the South Africa World Cup over payment disputes, which meant that local police had to take over the stewards' responsibilities (CNN, 2010).

Overall, the knowledge network approach (see Boyle, 2011) to the security and risk governance at the World Cup demonstrates wider security and risk management trends. This includes transnational collaboration and the networked structure of private/public security actors as apparent in the contemporary world (see Dupont, 2004). Moreover, the World Cup's specific editions may reveal the overlapping responsibilities of private/public agencies who operate within many of the same spaces and places of the World Cup, two of which we turn to next: the stadium and the fan zone.

Stadiums and Fan Zones

A World Cup's risk management and security delivery are always likely to leave significant footprints on the relevant host city's or country's places and urban life. However, this section zooms in on two of the main event spaces within the vast World Cup "theatre." That is the stadium where matches are played and the fan zone where fans can assemble to watch live-actions on enormous screens. Naturally, these are among the most heavily visited spaces through the life-time of any World Cup. Subsequently, the need to make these spaces safe and secure increases in line with the mass crowds gathered within them.

Typically, the stadiums used in FIFA competitions will conform to strict safety and security regulations (FIFA, n.d.a). Typically, stadium entry is subject to checks and necessary accreditation and identification to access the different stadium zones (VIP rooms, media stands). Stadiums, meanwhile, are typically policed by stewards, private security and other surveillance technologies such as CCTV. Moreover, as Klauser (2008) writes, so-called "outer security rings" are typically set up outside the World Cup stadium. These may extend for up to a kilometre outside the relevant stadium and operate as a pre-defined space and fenced barrier to the stadium for arriving fan groups. Accordingly, these represent "neutralised spaces" in which the official partners and sponsors primarily are facilitated for (ibid, p. 181). Meanwhile, stadium rings are typically populated by different security actors, including volunteers and private and public security services (Eick, 2010).

So-called "fan zones" have emerged as popular spaces at recent World Cups where they are officially named and branded as "FIFA Fan Fests" (FIFA, n.d.b). This is in light of the increased popularity of World Cups as tourist destinations for football enthusiasts. They have increased their popularity following the 2006 World Cup in Germany, where fan zones were popularly erected and visited (Kolyperas and Sparks, 2018; Haferburg et al., 2009). Fan zones are geographically confined areas surrounded by fences. They are accessible to the general public and live-screen World Cup matches and actions on giant screens. Because they are often free to enter, fan zones are primarily visited by fans who have travelled to the World Cup host cities without stadium tickets. Yet, they are sometimes used as a pre-game or post-game destination by fans with match tickets.

Inside these temporary spaces, public viewing events are staged, and supporters may engage in various activities (Lee Ludvigsen, 2021). Fan zones are often characterised by their many consumption opportunities and entertainment activities, including live music and competitions. This again contributes to making fan zones spaces of celebration and festivity. According to FIFA (n.d.a), the highest registered combined attendance in a fan zone on a World Cup match-day was on the 25 June 2018 when Uruguay played against host nation Russia, when 499,000 fans attended the 11 different fan zones that were set up in the various host cities.

Due to fan zones' increased popularity inside the World Cup landscapes and in the world of sport mega-events, so has the need to secure fan zones increased. As Toohey and Taylor (2014, p. 192) argue, World Cup security has, since 2006, extended geographically to include fan zones. In terms of security and surveillance, the public viewing events inside fan zones are in "many ways treated like stadiums" (Klauser, 2008, p. 64). As existing research on fan zone security and surveillance demonstrates, fan zones provide an opportunity for the event organiser to govern fans "by fun" (Lauss and Szigetvari, 2010). While fans are engaged in consumption-related activities, they are simultaneously monitored and regulated by various surveillance features and security actors (ibid).

Simultaneously, the fan zone risk and security management involve numerous precautionary security measures such as, bag checks, control over people admitted/exiting the fan zone, and limited entry at certain times (Haferburg et al., 2009). Moreover, it is heavily restricted which items visitors may bring into the fan zones. Typically, fans will not be allowed to bring their own drinks or snacks (ibid) since official sponsors and partners enjoy exclusive rights to advertise and sell their products (Eisenhauer et al., 2014). Thus, whilst representing separate spaces, the stadium and fan zone share some similarities in security practices and policies and risk management. However, fan zones may be more unpredictable than stadiums in terms of attendee numbers (Toohey and Taylor, 2014). They are more cluttered and free-flowing, as visitors are not assigned to specific seats as they would be inside stadiums.

Economic Risks

While some would argue hosting a World Cup speeds up much-needed infrastructure investment and development, this is often a fallacy. This "opportunity" comes at a substantial cost, on average, 252% higher than budgeted (Flyvbjerg and Stewart, 2012). Here lies another considerable risk, resource allocation. The lack of effective budgeting, rising costs, lack of time, among other factors, mean the overspending takes resources away from other, potentially better returning, infrastructure investment. For example, Brazil, hosting the 2014 World Cup, overspent their stadium budget by approximately $2 billion, meaning their light rail, monorail, airport infrastructure, among other critical infrastructure, were not completed. Brazil's reported total expenditure was roughly $11 billion, for in effect, 12 mostly disused stadiums and unfinished national infrastructure. Consequently, allocating resources for hosting the World Cup meant Brazil did not allocate resources to complete the economically viable infrastructure. Considering Brazil is struggling to manage deepening economic inequality, improving a fragmented education system would have been a better investment (Medeiros, 2016).

The risk of significant infrastructure investment is not just ineffective resource allocation but presents labour force risks. Since the infrastructure projects are condensed into unusually tight (often unrealistic) timescales and coincide, there needs to be a considerable and experienced labour force. Given the rarity of such events, it is unlikely many nations have a labour force to fulfil such projects: the result, the migrant workforce. While there are risks such as leakage from the hosts economy, relying on a large migrant workforce, safety is more apparent. For example, in preparation for hosting the World Cup in 2022, Qatar has probably the most ambitious infrastructure plan, spending $200 billion on stadiums, new airport, new city centre, hotels, new road and rail networks, to name a few. The problem is they have a small labour force; consequently, they rely predominantly on a migrant workforce, which has grown 39% to 2.1 million – 75% of the population. Unfortunately, this heavy reliance on migrant labour (without getting into national policy) has resulted in 6,500 reported migrant worker deaths (Pattisson et al., 2021); which will forever overshadow Qatar's World Cup story.

Conclusion and Future Research

Every World Cup is surrounded by a set of diverse, unpredictable and unique risks that must be mitigated, eliminated or identified. In this vein, this chapter examines World Cup risk and security management processes. This chapter argues that both internal and external trends largely impact the security-related efforts and the risk management processes of a World Cup. Here, the internal trends speak to the popularity of World Cups as tourist destinations, the rise of fan zones, local contexts, regulations and legislation. The external trends relate to global events, the geopolitical context of the tournament, and prospects of terrorism, crime, or epidemics surrounding the event. Collectively, this impacts the exclusive risk profile of each World Cup, and security stakeholders must act pre-emptively whilst drawing upon existing knowledge from past events. This chapter shows the networked structure of security and risk planning, which occurs between editions of the World Cup. In that sense, we argue that the concept of "security knowledge networks" (Boyle, 2011) can be usefully applied to make sense of the global, local and, indeed, "glocal" processes of risk and security management before, during and after World Cups. Although their transient timespan characterises each World Cup tournament, these networks may (re-) activate ahead of forthcoming tournaments, facilitating a continuous learning cycle.

To add to the existing evidence base (see Cornelissen, 2011; Klauser, 2008; Wong and Chadwick, 2017), we end this chapter by suggesting three specific recommendations for future work in risk and security management at the World Cup. These are also relevant to the wider socio-economic study of global sport. As shown, the study of the World Cup and sport mega-event "risk" and "security" is interdisciplinary. It includes contributions from sports management, tourism and event management, sociology and political science. Therefore, we encourage an interdisciplinary approach to the following research questions. First, as Taylor and Toohey (2015, p. 393) argue, different cultures can impact the "expectations and approaches to managing security and safety issues" at sporting events. To this end, researchers should examine the importance of geographical, cultural, social and political contexts on forthcoming World Cups' risk and security management and planning. Particularly, there is a pressing need for future research on the risk management of Women's World Cups and the World Cups below senior level (e.g., FIFA U-20 or U-17 World Cup).

Second, and more event-specific, it will be interesting to explore how "security" and "risk" are framed in the pre-event discourses before the 2026 World Cup to be co-hosted by Canada, Mexico and the United States (Beissel and Kohe, 2020). Especially given the geopolitical questions and power dynamics attached to this World Cup format.

Finally, we underline the importance of understanding the risks associated with infrastructure investment and resource allocation, especially as more developing countries enter the World Cup hosting market, is vital to understanding the broader risks of hosting a World Cup.

References

BBC (2010) *How Dangerous is South Africa?*. Available at: http://news.bbc.co.uk/1/hi/8668615.stm

Beissel, A.S. & Kohe, G.Z. (2020) United as One: The 2026 FIFA Men's World Cup Hosting Vision and the Symbolic Politics of Legacy, *Managing Sport and Leisure*, 1–21.

Boyle, P. (2011) Knowledge networks: megaevents and security expertise, in C. J. Bennett & K. D. Haggerty (eds.), *Security Games: Surveillance and Control at Mega-Events*, pp. 169–184. London: Routledge.

Cleland, J. & Cashmore, E. (2018) Nothing Will Be the Same Again After the Stade de France Attack: Reflections of Association Football Fans on Terrorism, Security and Surveillance, *Journal of Sport and Social Issues*, 42(6), 454–469.

CNN (2010) *Security Guards Strike at World Cup Matches in South Africa*. Available at: https://edition.cnn.com/2010/SPORT/football/06/15/world.cup.strike/index.html.

Cornelissen, S. (2011) Mega Event Securitisation in a Third World Setting: Glocal Processes and Ramifications During the 2010 FIFA World Cup, *Urban Studies*, 48(15), 3221–3240.

Cornelissen, S. & Maennig, W. (2010) On the Political Economy of 'Feel-Good' Effects at Sport Mega-events: Experiences from FIFA Germany 2006 and Prospects for South Africa 2010, *Alternation*, 17(2), 96–120.

Donaldson, R. & Ferreira, S. (2009) (Re-)creating Urban Destination Image: Opinions of Foreign Visitors to South Africa on Safety and Security?, *Urban Forum*, 20(1), 1–18.

Dupont, B. (2004) Security in the Age of Networks, *Policing and Society*, 14(1), 76–91.

Eick, V. (2010) A Neoliberal Sports Event? FIFA from the Estadio Nacional to the Fan Mile, *City*, 14(3), 278–297.

Eisenhauer, S., Adair, D. & Taylor, T. 2014) FIFA-isation: Spatial Security, Sponsor Protection and Media Management at the 2010 World Cup, *Surveillance and Society*, 11(4), 377–391.

FIFA (2003) *When SARS Spelt STOP for Football.* Available at: https://www.fifa.com/who-we-are/news/when-sars-spelt-stop-for-football-87201

FIFA (2010) *Confidence Shown in Security Plans.* Available at: https://www.fifa.com/worldcup/news/confidence-shown-security-plans-1177654

FIFA (n.d.-a) FIFA Stadium Safety and Security Regulations. Available at: https://img.fifa.com/image/upload/xycg4m3h1r1zudk7rnkb.pdf

FIFA (n.d.-b) FIFA Fan Fest™. https://www.fifa.com/what-we-do/marketing/programmes/fan-fest/

Flyvbjerg, B., & Stewart, A. (2012). Olympic Proportions: Cost and Cost Overrun at the Olympics 1960-2012 (1st June, 2012). Saïd Business School Working Papers, Oxford: University of Oxford. 10.2139/ssrn.2238053

Giulianotti, R. & Klauser. F (2010) Security Governance and Sport Mega-events: Toward an Interdisciplinary Research Agenda, *Journal of Sport and Social Issues*, 34(1), 49–61.

Giulianotti, R. & Klauser, F. (2012) Sport Mega-events and "terrorism": A Critical Analysis, *International Review for the Sociology of Sport*, 47(3), 307–323.

Haferburg, C., Golka, T. & Selter, M. (2009) Public Viewing Areas: Urban Interventions in the Context of Mega-events, in U. Pillay, R. Tomlinson & O. Bass (eds.), *Development and Dreams: The Urban Legacy of the 2010 Football World Cup.* Cape Town: HSRC Press.

Jennings, W. & Lodge, M. (2011) Governing Mega-Events: Tools of Security Risk Management for the FIFA 2006 World Cup in Germany and London 2012 Olympic Games, *Government and Opposition*, 46(2), 192–222.

Klauser, F. (2008) Spatial Articulations of Surveillance at the FIFA World Cup 2006, in F. Aas, H. Oppen Gundhus & H.M. Lomell (eds.), *In Technologies of (In)security: The Surveillance of Everyday Life.* London: Routledge, pp. 61–80.

Kolyperas, D. & Sparks, L. (2018) Exploring Value Co-creation in Fan Fests: The Role of Fans, *Journal of Strategic Marketing*, 26(1), 71–84.

Lauss, G. & Szigetvari, A. (2010) Governing by Fun: EURO 2008 and the Appealing Power of Fan Zones, *Soccer & Society*, 11(6), 737–747.

Lee Ludvigsen, J.A. (2018) Sport Mega-events and Security: The 2018 World Cup as an Extraordinarily Securitized Event, *Soccer & Society*, 19(7), 1058–1071.

Lee Ludvigsen, J.A. (2021) Between Security and Festivity: The Case of Fan Zones, *International Review for the Sociology of Sport*, 56(2), 233–251.

Leopkey, B. & Parent, M.M. (2009) Risk Management Issues in Large-Scale Sporting Events: A Stakeholder Perspective, *European Sport Management Quarterly*, 9(2), 187–208.

Manfred, T. (2015). *Brazil's $3 billion World Cup Stadiums Are Becoming White Elephants a Year Later, Business Insider.* Available at: https://www.businessinsider.com/brazil-world-cup-stadiums-one-year-later-2015-5?r=US&IR=T

Medeiros, M. (2016) *World Social Science Report 2016: Income Inequality in Brazil: New Evidence from Combined Tax and Survey Data, United Nations.* Available at: https://en.unesco.org/inclusivepolicylab/sites/default/files/analytics/document/2019/9/chap_21_05.pdf

Parnell, D., Bond, A.J., Widdop, P. & Cockayne, D. (2020) Football Worlds: Business and Networks During COVID-19, *Soccer & Society*, 1–8.

Pattisson, P., McIntyre, N., Mukhtar, I., Eapen, N., Mukhta, I., Bhuya, O., Bhattarai, U. & Piyari, A. (2021) *Revealed: 6,500 Migrant Workers Have Died in Qatar Since World Cup Awarded. The Guardian*. Available at: https://www.theguardian.com/global-development/2021/feb/23/revealed-migrant-worker-deaths-qatar-fifa-world-cup-2022

Reuters (2020) *Venue Selection for 2026 World Cup Delayed by COVID-19 – FIFA*. Available at: https://uk.reuters.com/article/uk-soccer-worldcup/venue-selection-for-2026-world-cup-delayed-by-covid-19-fifa-idUKKBN2472I7

Rookwood, J. (2019) Access, Security and Diplomacy: Perceptions of Soft Power, Nation Branding and the Organisational Challenges Facing Qatar's 2022 FIFA World Cup, *Sport, Business and Management: An International Journal*, 9(1), 26–44.

Schreiber, M. & Adang, O. (2010) *The Poles are coming! Fan behaviour and police tactics around the World Cup match Germany vs. Poland (Dortmund, 14 June 2006), Sport in Society*, 13(3), 470–488.

Stott, C. & Pearson, G. (2007) *Football 'Hooliganism': Policing and the War on the 'English Disease'*. London: Pennant Books.

Taylor, T. & Toohey, K. (2015) The security agencies' perspective, in M. Parent & J. L. Chappelet (eds.), *Routledge Handbook of Sports Event Management* (pp. 373–396). Routledge: Oxon.

The Guardian (2009) *Crime Fears Grow as South Africa Readies for Football World Cup*. Available at: https://www.theguardian.com/world/2009/sep/22/south-africa-worldcup-crime-fears

Toohey, K. & Taylor, T. (2014) Managing Security at the World Cup, in S. Frawley & D. Adair (eds.), *Managing the Football World Cup* (pp. 175–196). London: Palgrave Macmillan.

Toohey, K., Taylor, T. & Lee, C.K. (2003) The FIFA World Cup 2002: The Effects of Terrorism on Sport Tourists, *Journal of Sport Tourism*, 8(3), 186–196.

Wong, D. & Chadwick, S. (2017) Risk and (In)security of FIFA Football World Cups – Outlook for Russia 2018, *Sport in Society*, 20(5-6), 583–598.

14

MARKETING, SPONSORSHIP AND MERCHANDISING AT FIFA WORLD CUPS

Argyro Elisavet Manoli, Michael Anagnostou, and Lingling Liu

Introduction

Marketing the FIFA World Cup is a challenging task and one of great financial importance. Indeed, over the course of the 2015–2018 cycle, FIFA's revenue reached a new high of USD 6,421 million – 83% of it coming from the 2018 FIFA World Cup Russia alone (Deloitte, 2020), signifying the importance of the event to the federation. While it comes as no surprise that football as a sport has a global appeal across all geographic regions, it is the FIFA World Cup that particularly enjoys remarkably high media publicity, fan coverage and interest, making it the biggest mega-sport event globally, together with the Olympic Games (Ennis, 2020). Mega-sport events like the FIFA World Cup are entities with their own distinct brand, and as such they can be included in the main types of marketed entities that Kotler, Keller and Manceau (2016) discuss in their study. As a result, FIFA's marketing team, as the brand manager of such a branded entity needs to explore the best mix of communication, distribution, and service channels for their offerings. However, in the case of the FIFA World Cup where the location of the event changes every time the event takes place, it is not only the event that has to be marketed before, during and after its staging, but also the host country itself. Indeed, it could be argued that possibly the most challenging task for FIFA is to combine the brand management and goals of the event itself (FIFA World Cup) and the ones of the host country of each event as a destination. In order for this challenging task to manage these interconnected elements to be better appreciated, this chapter focuses on the examination of the brand of the event, its links with sponsorship and merchandise, and the wider connection between the event and the destination brand of the host country.

DOI: 10.4324/9781003121794-14

Brand and Brand Elements

The FIFA World Cup is a brand in itself. A *brand* is a product or service offering from a recognised source, a value proposition and a combination of benefits, products, services, information and experiences with the purpose to satisfy the needs and wants of the customers. (Kotler, Keller and Manceau, 2016). The way in which this brand is then managed represents one of the most researched and debated issues in the world of academia (Manoli, 2018; 2020). Brand management aims to differentiate the brand through establishing brand awareness – that is, identifying and recalling the brand name, or in other words imprinting the knowledge of the brand on individuals' memories, and brand image – that is, creating a set of opinions about brands, the personality of the brand which, in turn, forms the attitudes individuals bear towards the brand (Kenyon et al., 2018; Manoli and Kenyon, 2018). Brand image is in fact considered by Keller (1993) the outcome of how positive, bold and unique the associations are and what kinds of brand associations the consumer recalls in terms of a brand's attributes, benefits and attitudes. Brand associations refer to anything linked to an individual's memory concerning a brand and inform the final image that the individual holds of the brand (Aaker, 1991).

Both awareness and image generate brand equity, that is, "*a set of brand assets and liabilities linked to a brand, its name and symbol, that add to or subtract from the value provided by a product or service*" (Aaker, 1991, p. 15). Aaker (1991) through his seminal work, indicates that the elements of brand equity include both brand building aspects, that are memorable, meaningful, and likable, and defensive traits that are transferable, adaptable and protectable. Kotler, Keller and Manceau (2016) further elaborate that there exist three main groups of brand equity drivers: (a) the early selections for the brand elements or identities for the brand such as brand names, official logos, symbols, URLs, characters, spokespersons, slogans, jingles, signage and packages, (b) the marketing activities and supporting programs and (c) other associations secondarily conveyed to the brand (e.g., persons, places or things).

Brand loyalty is the end result of the brand management process and it can be demonstrated through the favourability (attitudinal loyalty) or repeat consumption (behavioural loyalty) of brands over all others in a particular product or service category (Shank and Lyberger, 2014).

Brand Associations in Sports

The extant academic literature on brand management in sport has identified various association models or specific brand associations (attributes, benefits, attitudes) that exist in the world of sport and in particular in sport teams and clubs (Bauer et al., 2008; Ferrand and Pages, 1999; Gladden and Funk, 2002; Ross, James and Vargas, 2006) in international sport events (Ferrand and Pages, 1999; Papadimitriou et al., 2016), in sport leagues (Anagnostou and Tzetzis, 2021;

Kunkel et al., 2014), and in elite football competitions (Anagnostou and Tzetzis, 2021).

The associations commonly found influencing brand loyalty in sports teams or events include both attributes and benefits, as they are detailed later. In terms of the former, attributes such as star/elite player, competition-rivalry/balance, atmosphere, excitement, management, team success, team history, head coaches, product delivery, tradition, logo design and corporate marks have been found to influence brand loyalty as studies suggest (e.g., Anagnostou and Tzetzis, 2021; Daniels, Kunkel and Karg, 2019; Gladden et al., 1998; Gladden and Funk, 2002; Kunkel et al., 2014; Ross, James and Vargas, 2006). In terms of the latter, benefits such as feelings of escape from everyday life, identification, nostalgia, pride in place, escape and peer group acceptance have been identified as factors of influence to brand loyalty (Anagnostou and Tzetzis, 2021; Gladden and Funk, 2002).

In particular, in the case of elite football competitions, certain brand associations found to be connected to the image of the competitions also contributed to the creation of brand equity. These include elite management, entertainment, elite sportsmanship, participants, escape, elite refereeing and corporate identity (Anagnostou and Tzetzis, 2021). While the study by Anagnostou and Tzetzis (2021) uncovered that new brand associations and elements such as fast football and the competition/event anthem would co-exist with the competition's logo, only elite management, entertainment, escape and corporate identity were found to influence the variables of brand loyalty.

At the same time, spill over effects frequently take place between two or more brands found in the same brand portfolio (Cobbs, Groza and Rich, 2015). So, in the case of FIFA and its various competitions that comprise their portfolio, it can be argued that a spill over effect occurs among said competitions, potentially transferring associated elements from one competition such as the Men's World Cup to another competition, such as the Women's World Cup. Indeed, as Kunkel and Biscaia (2020) argue, brands influence each other in the sport brand ecosystem, especially when they are so closely associated. As a result, a positive trait of one competition, such as the FIFA Men's World Cup, for example, the elite sportsmanship that one could associate it with it, could potentially influence how people view a closely associated competition, for example, the FIFA Women's World Cup and the sportsmanship associated with it. Unfortunately, such a spill over effect could also occur with potentially less favourable traits and associations of brands, when belonging in the same brand portfolio, possibly transferring unfavourable associations from one elite competition to the other. This becomes more apparent in the case of FIFA, since the brand of a federation, can affect the brands within its portfolio and as a result activate specific behavioural responses (Kunkel, Doyle and Funk, 2014). This could in turn lead to some unfavourable associations that individuals might have for the organisation, influencing the way in which these individuals view and perceive the organisations' competitions, such as the World Cup, as it is discussed later.

Negative brand associations

It is argued that unethical actions of governing bodies might cause adverse emotions which may deduct value from the brand equity and cause a spill over effect to the sport brand ecosystem of the event (sponsors, host country, officials) the governing body might be organising (Kulczycki and Koenigstorfer, 2016). Intense negative media coverage following such questionable actions occurred in 2015, where FIFA found themselves in the middle of a number of serious corruption accusations regarding bribery, nepotism and unregistered payments (Boudreaux et al., 2016). While examining these accusations goes beyond the scope of this chapter, recognising the negative brand associations they might have created towards the brand of FIFA is imperative in appreciating any spill over effects they might have had towards the brands within FIFA's brand portfolio, such as the World Cup. These were further sharpened by the already existing negative associations the World Cup events have been connected with, concerning the violation of labour rights and health and safety issues raised around the organisation of the 2010 South Africa, 2014 Brazil and 2022 Qatar FIFA World Cups (Carey and Mason, 2016; Heaston, Mitchell and Kappen, 2020). As the studies exploring these events have illustrated, the negative media attention that the issues that arose around those events captured, intensified any negative associations for their brand, which were also paired with potential spill overs from the unfavourable associations with FIFA's brand overall.

It is believed that associations with corrupt organisations create negative reactions in sponsors and other stakeholders (Kulczycki and Koenigstorfer, 2016). In the case of FIFA, corruption allegations towards the organisation had a negative impact on the local population opinions towards the FIFA 2014 World Cup and the event sponsors. The opinions toward the event sponsorship are not only impacted by the local population's assessment of the event itself (e.g., Chien, Cornwell and Pappu, 2011; Gwinner and Eaton, 1999) but also by the assessment of the event governing body because, as it was mentioned earlier, the event brand is highly associated with the brand of the sport-governing body (Kulczycki and Koenigstorfer, 2016).

Sponsorship

It is these brand associations that form the basis of one of the key considerations of organisations that might chose to partner with FIFA in regards to sponsorship. Sponsors are organisations that opt to enter in a commercial agreement with outward facing organisations, such as sport-governing bodies and sport teams, to enhance their brand management among other objectives. In more detail, the objectives of sponsorship include building a non-sporting organisation's brand awareness through their association with a sport brand (Amis, Slack and Berrett, 1999). Through a commercial agreement between a sporting and a non-sporting entity, the latter's name and brand can become known in the minds of a specific target audience that is already attracted to the sport brand. This can be particularly useful at an international level where the non-sporting brand might not be popular in, thus assisting in "spreading" their brand quickly and effectively (Manoli and Kenyon, 2018). Sponsoring a well-broadcasted event like the FIFA World Cup would mean that more focus might be placed on attracting the attention of indirect broadcast media spectators, rather than direct attendees, while it ensures that media exposure is gained for a minimal cost and a rather consistent form when compared to a similar exposure through an advertisement (Manoli, 2014).

An additional objective would be to build a non-sporting company's brand image and associated perceptions, which include the ideas, beliefs and impressions held by the consumers about the company and its products or services (Biscaia et al., 2013). The goal in this case would be to be associated with an entity that is popular and interesting in order for a potential transfer to occur of some of the positive values they bear on the non-sporting company's image. This would suggest that a potential sponsor of the FIFA World Cup could associate themselves with elite sportsmanship in an attempt for some of the event's positive characteristics to spill over to them and their brand. Additional advertising built around a sponsorship agreement could also help reinforce this relationship and activate it for the non-sporting company, in order for any possible benefits to be gained through the association of the two brands.

While partnering with an outward facing organisation such as a sport-governing body and its respective mega-sport events, in this case FIFA and its World Cup which attracts the attention of millions of people around the globe (Deloitte, 2020), can significantly increase a sponsor's brand awareness, it is often argued that sponsor organisations primarily select such a sponsee in order for the latter's favourable attributes to spill over to them through their mutual association (Manoli and Kenyon, 2018). The emphasis placed on the latter, brand associations, can be better illustrated through the examination of FIFA's World Cup sponsorship strategy, which represents a carefully structured strategy differentiating among the various sponsor organisations with which they partner (FIFA, 2018). The way in which the strategy is designed and implemented for the 2018 and the 2022 FIFA World Cup tournaments is discussed later and is based on the on the strategy of FIFA as it is reported on their official website (FIFA, 2018).

As FIFA promote on their official communication, FIFA partners, found at the top of their sponsorship pyramid have the highest level of association with FIFA and all FIFA events. This association is further strengthened through the sponsors' involvement in supporting FIFA in their efforts to develop football around the world in multiple levels, ranging from grassroots to the top level represented in the FIFA World Cup. This in turn allows FIFA and its selected partners to form what FIFA argues is a "true" partnership, which is expected to add great value to the engagement for both sides. Right below this category, the FIFA World Cup sponsors, through their commercial agreements with FIFA, gain rights to what was originally planned to be the FIFA Confederations Cup (and has since been replaced by the FIFA Arab Cup) and the FIFA World Cup on a global basis. Sponsor companies at this level enjoy a strong brand association with these two global tournaments, the use of selected marketing assets and media exposure, as well as other associated benefits. When compared to the partner category discussed earlier, these sponsors are expected to have a weaker association with the federation, but are believed to be tightly connected with the two mega-sport events. Finally, the regional supporter level, the third level on FIFA's sponsorship strategy, represents the lower level of FIFA's sponsorship structure, as it is reported in their official communication. FIFA suggests that companies that belong to this level are expected to promote their association with the FIFA World Cup in the domestic market in which they operate to further build their brand awareness and ultimately their brand image through their association with such a mega-sport event. The structure discussed represents FIFA's re-designed sponsorship strategy for the World Cup events, introducing the regional sponsors as a new category to attract additional organisations more focused on particular regions that might have been overlooked before.

Merchandise

As the earlier analysis illustrates, mega-sport events such as the FIFA World Cup, represent some of the strongest brands in today's sport ecosystem. FIFA and the host countries try to ensure that brand elements depict the best football tournaments in the world in combination with unique characteristics of the host country, as it will be discussed later (Weszka, 2011). In this effort, the creation of a logo, symbol or emblem is the foundation of brand identity can help to construct the brand of a mega-sport event, such as the FIFA World Cup (Buttle and Westoby, 2006). The logos, symbols or emblems have to identify clearly and plainly the entity represented and transmit its personality, character and nature (Hem and Iversen, 2004). They are formed to support a brand by helping to establish its brand identity and any favourable brand associations (Garretson and Niedrich, 2004). Properly managing an identity can become a competitive advantage and a way for an organisation to improve its reputation (Baker and Balmer, 1997; Olins, 1989).

Logos and marks also accelerate the recognition of a brand, further assisting initially in a quicker and wider brand awareness and ultimately acting as tools of brand image (Hem and Iversen, 2004). Since images are believed to be quicker than words, entities can strengthen the image of a brand through the use of their logos (Biehal and Sheinin, 1998), something that FIFA has taken on board, not only through their clearly designed logo, but also through the careful design of individualised logos and signage for each World Cup event. Throughout the organisation of a FIFA World Cup, signage is a particularly significant element. The signs exist not only to direct and inform the fans but also to support and be consistent with all the branding of the event (Weszka, 2011).

Most importantly, logos and visual representations of the brand form the basis for one additional income source of mega-sport events like the FIFA World Cup, the official event merchandise. The official merchandise of an event captures a wide variety of products that are licensed with sport logos, symbols and/or trademarks (Apostolopoulou et al., 2012). A key element in creating event merchandising is the licencing agreement, which refers to the commercial agreement between a sports organisation or a sport individual and a production company that makes the products which are to bear the organisation's, event's, league's or individual's logos and trademarks. The agreement covers the use of the logo or name in exchange for a royalty or fee, and is considered to be a key "branding strategy" in its own right (Shank and Lyberger, 2014). That is because licencing is not always a simple agreement between a provider and a sport brand, but it can be a close and potentially two-way relationship between a sport brand and an equally well-known manufacturer, such as a sport apparel company. In fact, it is argued that a sport brand should recognise its "licencing power" and bear in mind that a strong brand can attract lucrative licencing deals, which if chosen carefully, can lead to a potential increase in its brand equity (Shank and Lyberger, 2014). In their study, Shank and Lyberger (2014) argue that the brand holder, in this case a sport organisation like FIFA, has a number of advantages and disadvantages to consider when becoming a licensor. The former (advantages) would include their possible expansion into new markets through the promotion of new products with their brand and logo, their ability to further penetrate existing markets through additional and more specialised products better targeted at their audience, a heightened awareness of the sport brand, and overall an increased equity if paired with the appropriate licensee. The latter (disadvantages), entails a possibly reduced control over the marketing mix elements of the merchandise products to be produced, the product design due to potential producers' restrictions, the product quality, and its price. An additional disadvantage would also include a possible decrease of the perceived image of the brand if the licencing agreement is not successful and the merchandise products produced do not represent the brand of the sport organisation in terms of quality or price. As a result, through licencing, an organisation's logo and brand symbol can become a symbol of alliance for those who carry it, and ultimately the object of lucrative deals with non-sporting companies (Kwon et al., 2007).

Merchandise, according to Apostolopoulou et al. (2012), attracts avid sport fans who will demonstrate a high identification with the sport brand whose logo is on the licensed products. These fans are also believed to be very involved, attending the events in question and following their favourite team or event also through the media, be it through live broadcast or the promotion of non-live content, such as highlights and interviews with key sport people. The individuals who buy merchandise, according to the same study, are also willing to participate in other functions associated with, but peripheral to, a sport event, and they also tend to wear the merchandise bought not only on the day(s) of the event(s), but also on other days, allowing them in this way to further stress their alliance with the brand.

Moreover, Kwon et al. (2007) argue that individuals who buy merchandise do so because they clearly identify with the brand of the organisation whose logo they bear, however, their identification is not always to be taken for granted. In their study, they argued that sport merchandise consumers are price sensitive and thus even for highly identified fans, prices matter. In fact, it is highlighted that price sensitivity is higher for merchandise than for ticketing, something that brand managers should take into account when entering licensing agreements. Kwon et al. (2007) also suggest that it is the perceived value of the licensed product that drives sales, and as a result sport brands should always aim to partner with quality production companies to ensure that both the quality and the price of the merchandise is appropriate for the intended audience.

Apostolopoulou et al. (2012) add further information on the individuals who purchase merchandise, suggesting that through the purchase, their association (including the brand association) with the team, event or individual whose logo is on the product grows stronger. Most importantly, however, purchasing, using and thus displaying these branded items shows this association to others as a sing of loyalty for the buyers. Apart from being an event attending ritual for some individuals, Apostolopoulou et al. (2012) suggest that buying and displaying merchandise makes people feel that they are part of a team or part of an event, since it can make the buyers feel more connected with other fans and ultimately with the team, the players and the event itself. As a result, merchandise products have a number of meanings for those who purchase them (Apostolopoulou et al., 2012). First, they carry a social symbolic meaning which is based on their expression of fan identity and the social relationships and connectedness that the merchandise products allow them to build, feel and further enhance. Second, they bear a private symbolic meaning which is related to the individuals' values, history, experiences and personal achievements. Finally, they carry an experiential meaning which is pleasured-based. As such, they bring emotions and feelings to the ones wearing and displaying them, while arguably having less if any functional meaning at all.

Destination Brand

Another important aspect to examine regarding the brand of a mega-sport event is how it can influence the brand of the host nation that will be staging it. The connection between FIFA World Cup and its host countries could be defined as a relationship built on co-branding. Co-branding is merging two or more brands into a composite brand or marketing them together (Helmig, Huber and Leeflang, 2008). A co-branding relationship often comprises of a strong parent brand and a secondary brand (Washburn, Till and Priluck, 2000). The parent brand, belonging in the case of mega-sport events to the sport-governing body, is determined by the product category driver. The sport-governing body that is in control of the parent brand tends to have control over most marketing and distribution systems, while embracing a status of a modified brand and in reality possessing the wider consumers base (Uggla, 2004). Thus, in the case of the FIFA World Cup, it could be assumed that the FIFA World Cup is the well-known parent brand and as a result it controls or heavily influences the marketing of each event, and its overall distribution. The brand of each World Cup event is reformed by the destination brand by including the destination theme in the event branding. FIFA, the parent brand, also "owns" the fan base of the event, which they authorise the destination brand to access. The mission of the subordinate brand (destination) is to offer brand equity to the parent brand via strong and unique brand associations (Uggla, 2004). These brand associations should be secondary to those of the parent brand, that is, the FIFA World Cup. Thus, every FIFA World Cup is given a unique set of features originating from the specific destination where each one is held, which are in turn transmitted through the co-branded brand elements (Weszka, 2011).

It is worth noting that at the turn of the century, FIFA decided to rebrand the FIFA World Cup as part of a wider rebranding exercise within the organisation. The new officially trademarked FIFA World Cup did not deviate from the historical brand name but was rather built on its heritage (Chalip and McGuirty, 2004). The host country brands' importance was also further highlighted, and FIFA acknowledged the rising importance and dependability on host countries and event destinations. A bold and focused brand associated with the activities of FIFA, consistent in conveying the right brand elements together with the host destination elements was thus built, which in turn could make it easier to build associations while potentially being more tough to ambush (Chalip and McGuirty, 2004).

Research suggests that strategic and cultural matching of sport event brands and host destinations brands is able to favourably impact tourists' views for both (Weber, et al., 2012), making mega-sport events like the FIFA World Cup attractive for potential host countries. Direct involvement of the event followers can generate a stronger knowledge of the host country, and it can also impact relevant behaviours such as buying products, recommending the event to others, and revisiting the host country (Papadimitriou, Apostolopoulou and Kaplanidou, 2016). South Africa, for instance, organised the 2010 FIFA World Cup to build on such an effect, with recent research suggesting that they have indeed thrived in improving the location's image as a tourist destination (Hemmonsbey and Tichaawa, 2019). Another study by Swart et al. (2019), aiming to assess the brand image legacies that originated from holding the 2010 FIFA World Cup in South Africa in relation to football tourists' perceptions of South Africa, produced similar results. Within it, it is suggested that the core brand image legacy that stemmed from South Africa's 2010 FIFA World Cup remains in the perceptions of international football tourists who visited South Africa, even six years after their visit. Thus, it is argued that the 2010 FIFA World Cup helped in reinforcing positive perceptions of South Africa and to reduce the influence of the negative perceptions regarding safety, security and segregation. Another important brand image legacy that originated from the FIFA World Cup, according to the same study, is destination profiling. The 2010 FIFA World Cup showed South Africa as a nation capable of hosting upcoming mega-sport events. The results seem to suggest that six years after the World Cup, the event has successfully altered and indeed improved the general perceptions of South Africa as a sport tourism destination, thus improving its brand image.

However, it is also worth noting that there is no assurance that hosting a mega-sport event will favour a destination's image (Knott et al., 2017), since a favourable impact on a destination's image does not always occur after a mega-event. This in turn can complicate the decision-making process of bidding for hosting such a mega-sport event, since the brand benefits of doing so cannot be guaranteed. Indeed, it is argued that it is vital that the organisers (sport-governing bodies) and the hosting country itself collaborate closely in order for any brand benefits from hosting the mega-sport event to be achieved. A mega-sport event may interest visitors who are not following the sport as the focal drive for their travel, while visitors who travel only because of the sport mega-event would not otherwise make this trip. If event visitors, who had poor knowledge of the country before the visit, find desirable aspects of the destination, their opinion of the destination will most possibly be positive (Florek et al., 2008). At the same time, the mega-sport event itself was found to be the most important factor for visiting a mega-sport event hosting destination in the case of the 2018 FIFA World Cup (Andersson, Bengtsson and Svensson, 2021).

Destinations with an already widespread positive brand image may face a bigger risk when hosting a mega-sport event, although organising a mega-sport event can indeed be successful. Destination brand image enhancement through mega-sport events can occur if the experiences they have are in line with travellers' prospects. That is, the destination image can be positively enhanced by mega-sport events if the organisers satisfy visitors' expectations. However, more longitudinal studies are required to test whether an improved destination brand image can eventually lead to a change in actual visits to the destination (Andersson, Bengtsson and Svensson, 2021).

Conclusion

This chapter aimed at offering an examination of the brand and the brand elements of a mega-sport event such as the FIFA World Cup, in an attempt to better capture how the brand associations created with it form the basis of important aspects, such as its sponsorship, its merchandise and ultimately the host country's destination brand. Examining the key role that brand associations play in the development and management of the event's brand, in the sponsorship and licensing agreements made with external partners, and in the decision and management of the destination brand of the host country, as they were detailed in this chapter, can allow for a better illustration of the challenging task of co-ordinating and managing these inter-connected issues by a mega-sport event organiser like FIFA, alongside of course the difficult task of managing the organisation's own brand.

References

Aaker, J. L. (1991) The Negative Attraction Effect: A Study of the Attraction Effect Under Judgment and Choice, *Advances in Consumer Research*, 18, 462–469.

Amis, J., Slack, T. & Berrett, T. (1999) Sport Sponsorship as Distinctive Competence, *European Journal of Marketing*, 33(3/4), 250–272.

Amis, J., Trevor, S. & Berrett, T. (1999) Sport Sponsorship as Distinctive Competence, *European Journal of Marketing*, 33(3/4), 250–272.

Anagnostou, M. & Tzetzis, G. (2021) Greek Sport Fans' Evaluation of Football Leagues' Brand Associations and Their Influence on Brand Loyalty. The Case of UEFA Champions League, *Sport, Business and Management: An International Journal*, 11(4), 430–450.

Andersson, S., Bengtsson, L. & Svensson, Å. (2021) Mega-Sport Football Events' Influence on Destination Images: A Study of the of 2016 UEFA European Football Championship in France, the 2018 FIFA World Cup in Russia, and the 2022 FIFA World Cup in Qatar, *Journal of Destination Marketing and Management*, 19, 100536.

Apostolopoulou, A., Papadimitriou, D., Synowka, D. & Clark, J. S. (2012) Consumption and Meanings of Team Licensed Merchandise, *International Journal of Sport Management and Marketing*, 12(1), 93–110.

Baker, M.J. & Balmer, J.M.T. (1997) Visual Identity: Trappings or Substance, *European Journal of Marketing*, 5(3), 366-382.

Bauer, H., Sauer, N. & Exler, S. (2008) Brand Image and Fan Loyalty in Professional Team Sport: A Refined Model and Empirical Assessment, *Journal of Sport Management*, 22, 205–226.

Biehal, G.J. & Sheinin, D.A. (1998) Managing the Brand in a Corporate Advertising Environment: A Decision-Making Framework for Brand Managers, *Journal of Advertising*, 27(2), 99–110.

Biscaia, R., Correia, A., Rosado, A.F., Ross, S.D. & Maroco, J. (2013) Sport Sponsorship: The Relationship Between Team Loyalty, Sponsorship Awareness, Attitude Toward the Sponsor, and Purchase Intentions, *Journal of Sport Management*, 27(4), 288–302.

Boudreaux, C.J., Karahan, G., Coats, M., John, C., Gokhan, B., Morris, K. & Sanchez, A.R. (2016) Managerial Finance Bend it Like FIFA: Corruption on and off the Pitch, *Managerial Finance*, 42, 866–878.

Buttle, H. & Westoby, N. (2006) Brand Logo and Name Association: It's all in the Name, *Applied Cognitive Psychology: The Official Journal of the Society for Applied Research in Memory and Cognition*, 20(9), 1181–1194.

Carey, K.M. & Mason, D.S. (2016) Damage Control: Media Framing of Sport Event Crises and the Response Strategies of Organizers, *Event Management*, 20(2), 119–133.

Chalip, L. & McGuirty, J. (2004) Bundling Sport Events with the Host Destination, *Journal of Sport and Tourism*, 9(3), 267–282.

Chien, P.M., Cornwell, T.B. & Pappu, R. (2011) Sponsorship Portfolio as a Brand-image Creation Strategy, *Journal of Business Research*, 64(2), 142–149.

Cobbs, J., Groza, M.D. & Rich, G. (2015) Brand Spillover Effects within a Sponsor Portfolio: The Interaction of Image Congruence and Portfolio Size, *Marketing Management Journal*, 25, 107–122.

Daniels, J., Kunkel, T. & Karg, A. (2019) New Brands: Contextual Differences and Development of Brand Associations Over Time, *Journal of Sport Management*, 33(2), 133–147.

Deloitte (2020) *Annual Review of Football Finance 2020*. Manchester: Deloitte.

Ennis, S. (2020) Introduction: The Sports Sector in a Global Context. In S. Ennis (ed.), *Sports Marketing* (pp. 1–7). London: Palgrave Macmillan, Cham.

Ferrand, A. & Pages, M. (1999) Image Management in Sport Organisations: The Creation of Value, *European Journal of Marketing*, 33, 387–401.

FIFA (2018) *2018 FIFA World Cup Russia™ - Sponsorship Strategy*. Available at: https://resources.fifa.com/image/upload/2018-fifa-world-cup-russiatm-sponsorship-strategy-2711471.pdf?cloudid=vcvu2vfjhaphrxmmggsv#:~:text=Cup%20Russia%E2%84%A2,%2D%20Sponsorship%20Strategy,and%20value%20for%20interested%20companies.

Garretson, J.A. & Niedrich, R.W. (2004) Spokes-Characters: Creating Character Trust and Positive Brand Attitudes, *Journal of Advertising*, 33(2), 25–36.

Gladden, J.M. & Funk, D.C. (2002) Developing an Understanding of Brand Associations in Team Sport: Empirical Evidence from Consumers of Professional Sport, *Journal of Sport Management*, 16(1), 54–81.

Gladden, J.M., Milne, G.R. & Sutton, W.A. (1998) A Conceptual Framework for Assessing Brand Equity in Division I College Athletics, *Journal of Sport Management*, 12(1), 1–19.

Gwinner, K.P. & Eaton, J. (1999) Building Brand Image Through Event Sponsorship: The Role of Image Transfer, *Journal of Advertising*, 28(4), 47–57.

Heaston, W.R., Mitchell, M.C. & Kappen, J.A. (2020) Institutional Reflections on Organisational Corruption Control: The Case of FIFA. *Global Governance: A Review of Multilateralism and International Organisations*, 26(3), 403–427.

Helmig, B., Huber, J.A. & Leeflang, P.S. (2008) Co-branding: The State of the Art. *Schmalenbach Business Review*, 60(4), 359–377.

Hem, L.E. & Iversen, N.M. (2004) How to Develop a Destination Brand Logo: A Qualitative and Quantitative Approach, *Scandinavian Journal of Hospitality and Tourism*, 4(2), 83–106.

Hemmonsbey, J.D. & Tichaawa, T.M. (2019) Using Non-mega Events for Destination Branding: A Stakeholder Perspective, *GeoJournal of Tourism and Geosites*, 24(1): 252–266.

Keller, K.L. (1993) Conceptualizing, Measuring, and Managing Customer-based Brand Equity, *Journal of Marketing*, 57(1), 1–22.

Kenyon, J.A., Manoli, A.E. & Bodet, G. (2018) Brand Consistency and Coherency at the London 2012 Olympic Games, *Journal of Strategic Marketing*, 26(1), 6–18.

Knott, B., Fyall, A. & Jones, I. (2017) Sport Mega-events and Nation Branding, *International Journal of Contemporary Hospitality Management*, 29(3), 900–923.

Kotler, P., Keller, K.L. & Manceau, D. (2016) *Marketing Management*, 15e édition. New Jersey: Pearson Education.

Kulczycki, W. & Koenigstorfer, J. (2016) Why Sponsors Should Worry About Corruption as a Mega Sport Event Syndrome, *European Sport Management Quarterly*, 16(5), 545–574.

Kunkel, T. & Biscaia, R. (2020) Sport Brands: Brand Relationships and Consumer Behavior, *Sport Marketing Quarterly*, 29(1), 3–17.

Kunkel, T., Doyle, J.P. & Funk, D.C. (2014) Exploring Sport Brand Development Strategies to Strengthen Consumer Involvement with the Product–The Case of the Australian A-League, *Sport Management Review*, 17(4), 470–483.

Kwon, H.H., Trail, G. & James, J.D. (2007) The Mediating Role of Perceived Value: Team Identification and Purchase Intention of Team-licensed Apparel, *Journal of Sport Management*, 21(4), 540–554.

Landa, R. (1996) *Graphic Design Solutions*. U.S.: Delmar Publishing.

Manoli, A.E. (2014) The Football Industry Through Traditional Management Analysis, *Scandinavian Sport Studies Forum*, 5(1), 93–109.

Manoli, A.E. (2018) Sport Marketing's Past, Present and Future; An Introduction to the Special Issue on Contemporary Issues in Sports Marketing, *Journal of Strategic Marketing*, 26(1), 6–18.

Manoli, A.E. (2020) Brand Capabilities in English Premier League Clubs, *European Sport Management Quarterly*, 20(1), 30–46.

Manoli, A.E. & Kenyon, J.A. (2018) Football and Marketing, In S. Chadwick, D. Parnell, P. Widdop, & C. Anagnostopoulos (eds.), *Routledge Handbook of Football Business and Management* (pp. 88–100). Oxon: Routledge

Olins, W. (1989) *Corporate Identity Making Business Strategy Visible Through Design*. London: Thames and Hudson.

Papadimitriou, D., Apostolopoulou, A. & Kaplanidou, K. (2016) Participant-Based Brand Image Perceptions of International Sport Events: The Case of the Universiade, *Journal of Convention and Event Tourism*, 17(1), 1–20.

Ross, S.D., James, J.D. & Vargas, P. (2006) Development of a Scale to Measure Team Brand Associations in Professional Sport, *Journal of Sport Management*, 20(2), 260–279.

Shank, M.D. & Lyberger, M.R. (2014) *Sports Marketing: A Strategic Perspective*, 5th ed., London: Routledge.

Swart, K., Moyo, L.G. & Hattingh, C. (2019) Brand Image Legacies of the 2010 FIFA World Cup^{TM}: A Long-term Assessment, *Sport in Society*, 22(11), 1848–1863.

Uggla, H. (2004) The Brand Association Base: A Conceptual Model for Strategically Leveraging Partner Brand Equity, *Journal of Brand Management*, 12(2), 105–123.

Washburn, J.H., Till, B.D. & Priluck, R. (2000) Co-branding: Brand Equity and Trial Effects, *Journal of Consumer Marketing*, 17(7), 591–604.

Weber, K., Ali-Knight, J., Yu, L., Wang, C. & Seo, J. (2012) Mega Event and Destination Brand: 2010 Shanghai Expo, *International Journal of Event and Festival Management*, 3(1), 46–65.

Weszka, P. (2011) FIFA World Cup Brand Elements and Local Inspirations, *Sport Marketing Quarterly*, 20(3), 174.

15

BROADCASTING AND THE FIFA WORLD CUP: PRIVATISATION AND TECHNOLOGY

Gerard A. Akindes

Introduction

The relationship between sport and media, almost non-existent in the early 1950s, emerged initially when print media began to report sports information. Radio broadcasting (and later, the emergence of television broadcasting of live sports events) quickly modified the essence of the relationship between media and sports. Rowe argues that sport and media supply each other with capital, audience and content (Rowe, 2004). The amplitude of this interconnection is evident in the size and diversity of the audience of international sport events, such as the men's football World Cup and the Olympics. The FIFA World Cup (FWC) is the most significant event of the immense and continuously growing relationship between sport and television broadcasting (see Chapter 9 in this *Handbook*). Globally, football, as the most popular sport in many countries, has gradually built a privileged relationship with television, extending back to television's earliest presence in Europe.

New technologies in the past decade, such as satellite television coupled with the Internet, played a significant role in the transformation of broadcasting rights and their exponential increase in major football nations such as England, Germany, Spain, France and Italy since the 1990s (Clarke, 2002; Jeanrenaud and Kesenne, 2006). The new technologies provided football with a global audience (see Chapter 16 for a more detailed account on these new technologies). The liberalisation of broadcasting policies and new technologies gave new local and international broadcasters license to penetrate targeted local markets and allowed new players to commercially challenge the traditional Public Service Broadcasters (PSB). A noteworthy outcome of new television technologies is an unmatched capacity to reach football audiences across the world. This permitted the FIFA

DOI: 10.4324/9781003121794-15

World Cup, the biggest single global event in sports, to leverage television broadcasting to become a fully global event.

This chapter examines the joint evolution of the FWC global expansion with television broadcasting technologies, and the commercial implications of this historic partnership with a significant milestone during the 1966 FWC. The success in televising the FIFA World Cup in 1966 launched an economically interdependent partnership among football, FIFA, and television broadcasting, which grew over time and continues to evolve with the Internet.

The Early Years of the FIFA World Cup and Television

Television broadcasting without television live games

When the first FWC happened in 1930, the already-existing technology to film football games for television was available, but live football was not yet broadcast in the United States. Without live broadcasting, games were recorded and the films shown later. Boyle and Haynes argue that in 1938, the World Cup finals appeared in cinema documentaries across the world and were covered on short-wave radio across Europe and Brazil.

For several reasons, the FWC was not an active participant in the early years of television. Several factors slowed down the partnership between television and the FWC. Sports organisations were suspicious of live broadcasting. Football was not yet a globalised sport. The FWC involved only a few countries. In fact, only a few nations were members of FIFA and could be part of FWC. The early years of FWC competition were only between Europe and South America. The rest of the globe was either not introduced to the game or still under colonial rule. Only two countries outside Europe and the Americas participated in the FWC before the 1960s. Egypt in 1934 and Indonesia (then the Dutch East Indies) in 1938 were the only African and Asian nations or territories that participated in the FWC until 1970. In parallel, television broadcasting access was still globally marginal and limited to a few nations. Those nations with television broadcasting had a small audience. This combination of factors was not conducive to television broadcasting of the early editions of the FWC.

Live football broadcasting

Post-World War II marked the effective construction of an interdependent, economic relationship between sport and television. The FWC television broadcasting became effective at the 1954 World Cup in Switzerland. This tournament was live on the BBC and in Europe through the newly established European Broadcasting Union (EBU). The EBU broadcast nine FWC matches to five European countries (Union (EBU), 2010). In fact, most countries had only started regular programming one or two years prior to the FWC. In Italy, the inaugural station RAI was launched in January 1954 while Spanish television would not start until 1956 (Tyers, 2014).

The first FWC live TV broadcast had a marginal audience. The limited implementation of television broadcasting capacity confined the FWC to a few European countries that already had a television broadcasting infrastructure and EBU members. The notion of broadcasting rights was initiated. The Swiss football association was paid about $2,500 (£1,500) by the EBU for nine World Cup games (Tyers, 2014). The fee was paid to support the production cost of the games.

The FWC broadcasting in Europe by the EBU and a tradition of access for all the European members of the EBU was established. The rest of the world without television broadcasting capacity remained without live images of the World Cup. The only option available to visually experience the competition was the recorded and film documentary projected several weeks or months later in movie theatres.

The 1958 World Cup in Sweden was broadcast in Europe through the EBU and the Eurovision system. The EBU growth with more members naturally delivered a wider audience for the World Cup. The 1958 World Cup also established the commercial value of television broadcasting. The EBU paid 1.5 million Kronar to Sweden for rights to the finals (Boyle and Haynes, 2017). According to Boyle and Haynes, "a symbiotic relationships between broadcasters and World Cup organisers began to emerge, as stadia were adapted to accommodate commentators …. but it also opened up opportunities for television producers to pursue more interventionist strategies with World Cup hosts, such as ensuring stadia accommodated cameras and commentators" (2017, p. 7).

In 1962, the FWC was in Chile. Satellite broadcasting, still in its infancy, was not fully operational for transatlantic live broadcasting. The limitations of terrestrial broadcasting prevented European countries with already-existing television capacity to receive the games live. Only recorded tapes were shipped to be shown a few days later. The Radio Times cited in a BBC blog described the logistics that had to be in place to allow the games to be on British TV screens. "Each film must be flown from Santiago to Lima, Peru—from Lima to Panama—Panama to Miami and Miami to New York. That takes approximately 14 hours. Then the 90 minutes of film must be processed in New York and rushed to Idlewild Airport to be put on the first available transatlantic jet" (Williams, 2016).

The ability to broadcast the games on television even with a few days' delay remained the privilege of many European countries and the United States. In Europe, the EBU negotiated the rights for delayed broadcasting with FIFA and paid $75,000 for the 1962 World Cup in Chile (Chisari, 2006). Only Europe fulfilled the conditions to become an FWC broadcasting market for FIFA. This included three factors: (1) Television broadcasting had penetrated European nations substantially. (2) Europe was the main football continent with South America, and therefore had an audience. (3) The collective capacity of the EBU could now negotiate and pay for the rights. The rest of the world did not have a strong enough interest in football viewing, the financial resources, or the television broadcasting and penetration to broadcast the FWC. In the rest of the world, the only visual connection to the FWC remained the films projected in movie theatres as documentaries.

Globalising FIFA World CUP and the Beginning of Transatlantic Television Broadcasting

The 1962 FWC was the last World Cup without live transnational broadcasting. In fact, the first communication satellite, Telstar, was launched the same year but three weeks after the World Cup (The Editors of Encyclopaedia Britannica, 1999). Telstar, developed by the American Telephone and Telegraph Company (AT&T), was the world's first active communications satellite and the first communication bridge between the United States and Europe. It opened the era of global television broadcasting and contributed to reinforcing the commercial partnership between FIFA and broadcasters. As stated by Bignell and Fickers, "Telstar satellite inaugurated the age of global television coverage" (2008, p. 50).

The 1966 FWC is acknowledged as a marking moment in the political and commercial history of the FWC. Chisari states that "to some extent, the 1966 World Cup deserves to be regarded as the key moment in the … globalisation of football" (2006, p. 43). As per Chisari's statement, a few factors were important in changing the dynamic between the FWC and television broadcasting. New technologies (the launch of Telstar), many more broadcasters expanding the audience beyond a limited number of countries, and the increased popularity of football were instrumental in this change. In contrast to the 1962 FWC without live broadcasting, 1966 was live in many European countries while recorded games continued to be shown across the world.

The FWC back in Europe allowed the EBU to bid in a Eurovision broadcasting competition. The negotiations for 1966 were initiated along with the 1962 FWC. However, there were substantial differences in the rights paid by the EBU in 1962 and those paid for the 1966 FWC. In fact, the EBU paid $800,000 (Chisari, 2006, p. 44) for the 1966 FWC. The majority of western European countries had an established television broadcasting capability and were members of the EBU. A wider audience and live broadcasting justified the radical increase in the rights paid by the EBU to FIFA to broadcast the 1966 FWC. The EBU in partnership with the main British television broadcasters, the BBC and ITV, provided live broadcasting as well as recordings to be shown on television. The launches of Telstar 1 and 2 created the ability to transmit television signals between Europe and North America and thus initiated the live transatlantic broadcast of the FWC in 1966.

Outside Europe, Mexico and the United States, film recording of the games complemented the live broadcasting to make the 1966 FWC the first globally watched World Cup. Seventy-five countries broadcast the event live or on delay with recorded films. Table 15.1 displays the various countries and broadcasters that aired the games.

TABLE 15.1 Countries and broadcasters that aired the 1966 games

Eurovision				
Europe				
ARD West Germany (Public Television Service)	ORTF France	BRT Belgium (Belgian Flemish)	SSR Switzerland (Swiss French)	RTE Eire
NRK Norway	RTB Belgium (Belgian Walloon)	CLT Luxembourg	TVE Spain	TSI Switzerland (Swiss Italian)
RAI Italy	JRT Yugoslavia	NTS Holland	ZDF West Germany (2nd Television Service)	SRG Switzerland (Swiss German)
SRT Sweden	RTP Portugal	DR Denmark	ORF Austria	YLE Finland
North Africa				Europe
RTM Morocco	RTA Algeria	RTT Tunisia		Greece
Intervision				Cyprus
BT Bulgaria	CST Czechoslovakia	TVR Romania	DFF East Germany	Tunisia
MT Hungary	TVP Poland	TSS U.S.S.R.		
Rest of the World				
South America		Caribbean	Africa	Middle East
Argentina	Mexico	Barbados	Sudan	Kuwait
Brazil	Peru	Bermuda	Rhodesia	Saudi Arabia
Chile	Venezuela	Trinidad	Mauritius	United Arab Republic
Colombia	Uruguay	Jamaica	Ethiopia	Aden
Ecuador	Pacific	Asia		
North America	Philippines	Honk Kong	Japan	Singapore
Canada	New Zealand	Iran	Malaysia	South Korea
NBC New York	ABC Australia	Iraq	North Korea	

In addition to Telstar satellite technology's growing influence, the use of slow-motion clips in football broadcasting is another marker of the nascent importance of technology in broadcasting and viewing of the FWC. By 1966, the BBC had integrated slow motion into their FWC broadcasting. For the first time, slow motion and replays were used in a FWC broadcast (Chisari, 2006).

Beginning with the 1966 World Cup, FIFA took control of broadcasting rights, which became the integral part of the revenues for the governing body. The 1966 FWC was a success, with broadcasting across all the continents for the first time, despite having the competition played by essentially South America and European countries. Only North Korea represented Asia. North Korea earned their qualification without having to play in an Asian–African qualifying tournament. In fact, 1966 was also a political turning point of the FWC with the boycott of African and Asian countries. With a wave of independence in Africa and Asia, 65 associations from these continents were FIFA members. However, only one representative for the Confederation of African Football (CAF) and the Asian Football Confederation (AFC) could qualify for the FWC in 1966. In protest of the fact that the African and Asian teams had no route to direct qualification to the FWC, Kwame Nkrumah, the president of Ghana, instigated the boycott of African teams, which withdrew from the qualifiers (Darby, 2002). It was a significant moment in the history of the FWC and FIFA. The boycott, however, did not affect the global expansion of the FWC. The FWC broadcast in 1966 constituted the globalisation of FIFA representation with the integration of new members for the Global South.

The Global Television Broadcasting of the Global FIFA World Cup

After the 1966 boycott by African nations, Africa and Asia had for the first time their distinct representatives. A final tournament included teams from all the continents. Moreover, for the first time, the FWC was shown outside South America and Europe. On a political and governance background, broadcasting technologies contributed to facilitating the growing global interest from the FWC in 1970.

For the first time, the FWC was broadcast in colour. Already in testing, colour television was not available yet in 1966 but became the norm by the FWC from 1970. Green (cited by Whannel) posits that "by 1970, there were 250 million sets in 130 countries with live broadcasting in colour" (2009, p. 208). For the first time, the FWC outside Europe was broadcast live in Europe.

The 1970 FWC reinforced the importance of television broadcasting influence and the importance of the European audience to the event. In fact, to adjust to the European time zone and fit in primetime TV time slots, games were scheduled to be played at midday (Darby, 2005). The global penetration of television, satellite technology, and the success of Brazil with its player Pele made the 1970 FWC one of the most significant World Cups. A new black-and-white ball supplied by Adidas replaced the brown leather balls used from the inception of the FWC until 1966. As per FIFA, "The name of the original Telstar came from its status as 'the star of television.' The first ball to be decorated with black panels, the pattern was designed to stand out on black-and-white TVs, and changed football design forever". Television broadcasting technology and the ball by Adidas reinforced the collaboration between broadcasting technology transformation and the ability for the FWC to build a global audience and commercial partnerships. Adidas remains the official ball supplier of FWC.

The sum of the commercial tendencies established in 1970 accelerated with the change in leadership of the FIFA in 1974. Joao Havelange became the first non-European FIFA president on 11 June 1974 after winning the election against the British Sir Rous. Havelange campaigned for a full integration and recognition of the Global South and a business transformation of the organisations. Coca-Cola and Adidas accompanied Havelange as main sponsors of FIFA and the subsequent FWC.

The television landscape continued to evolve globally. Already independent African countries and more Asian countries and their national government introduced television broadcasting with the creation of Public Service Broadcasting (PSB). Overall, except for the United States and ITV in Great Britain, television broadcasting was mostly led by governments and was Free-To-Air (FTA).

Globalisation, Accelerated Commercialisation and the Evolution of Broadcasting Technologies

The 1974 World Cup in Germany confirmed the transformation of FIFA and the broadcasting and commercial expansion that was initiated in 1966. It was the first FWC under Havelange's presidency and the sixth one in Europe. Live and recorded broadcasting of the games increased with the growth of television broadcasting. In 1978, more than 100 countries received live broadcasting or recorded films of the World Cup. During the Havelange presidency between 1970 and 1998, a radical transformation in the commercialisation of the FWC and FIFA took place (Milne, 2016). Marketing and broadcasting were the epicentre of the transformation.

Communication satellites

The next major transformations occurred in the late 1980s and early 1990s. Direct-to-home (DTH) broadcasting via satellite transformed the worldwide mediascape. The transformation was accelerated by deregulation, which allowed broadcasters to deploy their activities across political and geographic borders. Private domestic and transnational broadcasters emerged, disrupting the government broadcasting-dominated mediascape and challenging long-lasting monopolies.

The satellite relays permitted cable television to reach all possible areas. This was prevalent in the United States where cable television was already well established. After the early Telstar satellites, geostationary satellite television, such as Intelsat with DTH broadcasting, added another dimension to the global market. Broadcast Satellite Services (BSS) were launched to deliver radio or television entertainment directly to end users through a small receiver terminal. BSS was economical, efficient, and easy to install and operate (Pelton, 2013). In Europe, the launch of the satellite Astra by the Luxembourg-based company SES in 1989 opened new broadcasting possibilities to DTH broadcasting. The launch of many other geostationary Intelsat satellites since the early 1980s, such as the Eutelsat, Arabsat, and Nilesat, provided full coverage of the planet with DTH capacity.

Privatisation of Sports Broadcasting, Public Service Broadcasters and Media Rules

Satellite technology accelerated the entrance of the private television broadcaster into the global mediascape. National and regional media laws had determined the nature, pace and type of impact private broadcasters had in each country. With the exception of the United States and Brazil, where private broadcasters occupied the mediascape very early, Public Service Broadcasters (PSB) were dominant in the rest of the world and often held national monopolies. The privatisation of existing PSB and the entry of transnational broadcasters or new local private players transformed the mediascape.

Despite these transformations, the PSBs retained their control over the FWC for several years. Milne posits that the primary sale of the FWC broadcasting rights to public broadcasters – principally the European Broadcasting Union (EBU) – was unchallenged until 1996. In Europe, the EBU remained a principal rights holder for the multiple FWCs. Despite the increased privatisation of European broadcasters, the EBU did not confront any competition for the FWC's broadcasting rights until 1996 (Milne, 2016). Despite the overall favourable legal environment for private broadcasters, media regulations and law protected selected content in the public domain. The PSBs with FTA broadcasting remained the primary rights holders for the FWC, especially when a local or national team was in competition.

Regulation of sport broadcasting was defined by each country. Political and social intentions varied widely. As argued by Smith et al. (2015), sport broadcasting depended on each country's desire to strongly regulate or not and desire to guarantee FTA coverage of major events. They classified the European countries in three categories: market driven, a balanced approach and strong regulation, depending on how far the country wanted to control what content should be part of the public domain (Smith et al., 2015). The rules therefore established what must be broadcast on FTA TV or could appear on PayTV. According to the country, "strong regulation" or not, PSBs (or commercial free-to-air) broadcasters are granted a dominant role in sports broadcasting. They are supported by a regulatory approach that guarantees free-to-air television coverage for an extensive list of major (and not so major) sporting events.

In France, the media regulatory authority, the Audiovisual Superior Council (Conseil du Supérieur de l'Audiovisuel or CSA) listed sports competitions considered of major importance, which must be accessible on FTA television. These competitions include the matches of the French football team on the calendar of the International Federation of Association Football (FIFA), open games, the semi-finals, and the finals of the FWC (CSA, s.d.). The French regulatory approach is within a broader regulatory rule by the European Union. Without violating the European free-market rules, each country is authorised to have a list of events of major importance to society that must be available via FTA. These rules in Europe played an important role in ensuring PSBs will remain one of the key broadcasters of the FWC. The FTA exception for the FWC ensures that the competition retained a wide audience throughout the years, which goes hand-in-hand with high marketing value and supports the increase commercialisation of FIFA since the 1990s.

The global trend of privatisation and deregulation of media rules from the 1990s brought new players in the sports broadcasting space without fully transforming the commercial dynamic in the early years of that decade. The global penetration of television with satellite technology was the main boost in FIFA's commercialisation. However, national terrestrial television broadcasting and cable television were still prevalent in many countries. Besides selected broadcasters with satellite transnational capacity, such as Sky, Canal+, ESPN and Fox, many private broadcasters remained local with terrestrial coverage. A new era of the commercialisation of FIFA with a stronger impact of television broadcasting would start in the late 1990s and early 2000s.

Transnational Television Broadcasters and PSB

From the 1990s, private television and transnational broadcasters were fully established across borders and media markets. In addition to FTA broadcasters and PSBs, private PayTV was in control of many sports football properties. PayTV penetration started in the 1990s and has drastically increased in most developed markets in Europe, Australia, and part of Asia where watching the most popular sports events and competitions was only possible on PayTV. In Africa and certain parts of Asia, although the penetration was slower mostly for economic reasons, satellite transnational broadcasters were present with sports as their main content to recruit subscribers. Broadcasters such as ESPN, Star Sports, Fox sports, beIN Sports, Canal+ and SuperSport became important actors within the mediascape of Africa and Asia.

Many football properties such as the English Premier League, the French Ligue 1, and the Spanish La Liga, became exclusivity available on PayTV. The FWC had a similar trend, but not everywhere in the world. The diversity and multiplicity of world media systems, media rules and law, and technological capacities influenced how and who broadcast the FWC from the 1990s.

In many instances, PSBs with the backing of governments' resources had exclusive rights for FWC in their specific country. As discussed by Solberg and Gratton (2014), PSBs still hold a strong position in sport broadcasting despite the increased share of the sports broadcasting rights captured by PayTV. In the early 1990s, in many countries mostly in the Global South, the PSBs were often the only ones with national terrestrial coverage and did not have the competition of strong national broadcasters capable of competing with them. Transnational broadcasters with satellite global expansion remained limited. In Africa, only Canal+ entered the

Francophone market in the early 1990s. In 1991, Satellite Television Asian Region (STAR), a subsidiary of News Corps. and the main transnational broadcaster in Asia, was also in its early years of commercial television broadcasting. In China, PSBs under the China Central Television Broadcasting Company maintain a strong dominance over television broadcasting. Technological limitations with the nascent satellite broadcasting DTH capacity and national television, existing national penetration, and media rule constraints contributed to keeping PSBs as key broadcasters of the 1990s FWC in Africa and Asia.

In many countries where PayTV or cable were well-established, PSBs nevertheless remain prevalent. Having the FWC free-to-air for political incentive, media rules and laws and the lowest business cost benefit for private PayTV broadcasters-maintained PSBs' competitiveness in acquiring the FWC broadcasting rights. Nonetheless, the FWC's broadcasting rights are allocated through a bid process. In Europe, for instance, for the first time in 1996 the EBU lost the rights of the FWC to ISK/Kirk (Solberg, 2007). The ISK/Kirk also acquired the rights to part of Asia for the 2002 and 2006 FWC. The move of the FWC to private broadcasters also occurred in a few other geographic areas. The United States sports broadcasting mediascape, which was historically private and controlled by cable networks, acquired the FWC broadcasting rights when they acknowledged the commercial value of the competitions. In fact, the United States effectively started consistently broadcasting the FWC live in 1986 on ESPN and NBC.

In the 1990s, the fast penetration of DTH satellite television broadcasting and cable television opened new opportunity for FIFA to leverage competition between broadcasters for rights acquisition. The diversity of the global mediascape opened new selling opportunities but did not transform the global market into a fully open, competitive buyers' market. PSBs kept their privileged position with large penetration of their television signal and the ability to mobilise resources to acquire the rights. Transnational private PayTV broadcasters (except Europe and the fully privatised United States mediascape) did not engage in acquiring the FWC broadcasting rights. Despite the commercially low interest of PayTV in the early 1990s, the appeal of FWC broadcasting rights grew and took a drastic turn in the early 2000s.

Increased Globalisation and Commercialisation

The 2002 FWC in Japan and South Korea asserted the global identity of the FWC. It was the first co-hosted FWC and the first one outside Europe and the Americas. The FWC was now fully available to the Asian continent. The 2002 FWC in Japan and South Korea also marked the drastic transformation in the commercialisation of the World Cup. Following the bankruptcy of the ISL and ISMM sports marketing organisations, FIFA cancelled the licensing contracts for the marketing and television rights to the 2002 and 2006 tournaments. In fact, ISL and ISMM had acquired the global broadcasting rights (except for Europe and the

United States) for the 2002 and 2006 FWCs (Sportcal, 2001). Following ISL and ISM's bankruptcy, the KirchMedia GmbH group won the right to sell the broadcasting rights of the 2002 and 2006 FWC. The Kirsch Group paid $2.36 billion for 2002 and 2006. In 2001, the group also signed a contract with FIFA to market television and radio broadcasting rights to the United States market (Sportcal, 2001). Following some restructuring, KirchSport AG became Infront in 2002 (SportBusiness, 2002) and became responsible for selling the broadcasting rights of the FWC globally (Sportcal, 2002).

FIFA also signed a contract with Host Broadcast Service (HBS), a subsidiary of KirschSports AG. HBS then became the Host Broadcaster (HB) for all the FWC in 2002. Host broadcasting was initially controlled and managed by the host country of the FWC. After taking charge of the broadcasting rights of the FWC, FIFA took control of all the production components of the competition, with the contract with HBS in 2002. Since 2002 up to the Qatar 2022 FWC, HBS is the broadcasting partner of FIFA World Cup. The 2002 and 2006 FWCs revealed the intention to take advantage of a rapidly globalising market for broadcasting rights (FIFA.com, 2006).

Boyle and Haynes (2017) suggest that 2002 was the start of a new era for television and the FWC. In fact, as satellite television continued to expand globally, the FWC broadcasting rights continued to grow. Furthermore, the global expansion of satellite television increased the emergence of new national and transnational, privately owned FTA or PayTV broadcasters. The global mediascape created new entrants and competitors nationally, regionally and globally. These led to more broadcasters competing for the FWC rights. The FIFA posited that in 2006, FWC had the highest number of broadcasters (more than 500) in the history of the competition, with coverage provided in virtually every country of the world (FIFA, 2007). The diversity of the type of broadcasters is illustrated by the list in three major markets provided by Infront Sport (2006).

- In Germany, the host country, three free-TV (ARD, ZDF and RTL) and one PayTV agreements (Premiere).
- In France, two free-TV (TF1 and M6) and two PayTV (Canal+, Eurosport France).
- In Brazil, PayTV (Bandsports, DirecTV, ESPN do Brazil, Globosat) and one free-TV (TV Globo).

This indicates that the FWC broadcasting rights are not exclusive and are in different packages defined by selected games, types of broadcasting platforms, or simple reattribution of one licensee to another. The packages are also retail offerings that include highlights and magazine programming; the number of games including the opening match, final, and both semi-finals; and selected teams' matches. Geographic coverage, audience size, and so on are also determining factors.

In 2006, each country would present a different scenario, determined by the financial capacity of various bidders and their ability to comply with local media rules about the type of games that have to be FTA and accessible to the large majority of the national population. In England and Germany, government-owned broadcasters retained their rights to the FWC. In fact, the BBC, a public broadcaster, was the only rights holder in the United Kingdom for the 2006 FWC. PSBs acquired the exclusive rights in some countries while privately owned broadcasters acquired exclusivity of rights in other countries.

In the Middle East, Arab Radio Television (ART) acquired the rights for the 2006 FWC for the first time. This shifted the competition from government FTA broadcasters to privately owned PayTV. The ART exclusive rights to the FWC highlighted regional and national dissimilarities and nuances to consider when addressing the penetration of satellite television and PayTV penetration globally. In fact, in the early years, PayTV in the Global South was only accessible to an economic elite that could afford the high fees required for decoders and subscriptions. The very high fees required by ART excluded a large portion of Arab football fans who could not afford PayTV or did not have access to collective viewing in a household, coffee shop or any other space. Malkawi (2007) argued that ART exclusive rights to the 2006 FWC were detrimental to Arab viewers because of the high cost of the equipment and subscription. Malkawi (2007) and Amara (2007) discussed the social and political consequences of the privatisation of the FWC broadcasting rights in the Middle East. This rapid transformation led to the sudden switch of the FWC broadcasting from FTA government-owned broadcasters to PayTV, which indicated the capacity for a privately owned broadcasting entity to outbid the Arab State Broadcasting Union (ASBU). Despite the protest of the ASBU, the FWC broadcasting privatisation in the Middle East became a fait accompli in 2006 (Kuwait News Agency, 2006). Following ART, Al Jazeera Sport, which became beIN Sport, acquired the rights to the 2010, 2014, 2018 and 2022 FWC. With the exceptions of agreements between beIN Sports and government-owned broadcasters, the FWC broadcasting rights did not return to FTA government-owned broadcasters. The rise of beIN Sport and its control of the broadcasting rights of most of major international sports events and competitions to a global sports broadcasting player and right holder of several FWCs is largely discussed by various authors (Akindes, 2017; Amara, 2007, 2012; Samuel-Azran et al., 2014; Ziyati and Akindes, 2014).

The broadcasting of the FWC on PayTV in the Arab world and the fact that the EBU did not have the rights to the 2002 and 2006 FWC illustrate two important facts that increasingly define the FIFA broadcasting rights commercialisation. FWC television broadcasting is a global, commercial property. The higher bidder acquired the broadcasting rights of the FWC regardless of the geographic space.

Higher Privatisation, Higher Revenues for FIFA

The ART acquisition of the 2006 FWC illustrates a global trend of PSBs potentially challenged by private broadcasters and FIFA's desire to go through a bid

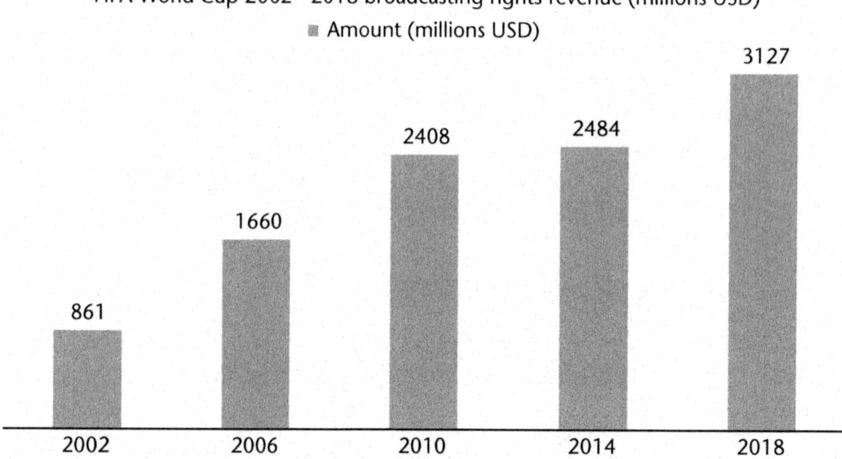

FIGURE 15.1 FIFA World Cup 2002–2018 Broadcasting Rights Revenues (FIFA, 2003, 2007, 2011, 2015, 2019)

process. Regardless, the market may not benefit PSBs and viewers with limited economic capacity to afford PayTV. A more revenue-driven FIFA contributes to creating a new, competitive global market for the FWC broadcasting rights. Since 2006, FWC revenues steadily have drastically increased while broadcasting technologies continue to evolve. Figure 15.1 shows the FIFA World Cup media rights revenue from 2002 to 2018.

The global mediascape transformation is ongoing with new communication technologies such as Digital Terrestrial Television (DTT), which is establishing a global digital television space, allowing new entrants and creating competition for broadcasting rights acquisition.

In Europe, although the EBU regained the broadcasting rights for 40 or more European countries and territories for the 2010, 2014, 2018, and 2022 FWCs, the biggest football European markets (such as France, England, Italy, Spain and Germany) along with the Nordics and Russia are distinct markets out of EBU's collective rights negotiation. The regional broadcasting unions, such as the EBU, ASBU and AUB, collectively had negotiated the broadcasting rights of their predominantly PSBs members. The competitive advantage from national FTA coverage with the ability to reach national audiences is made obsolete by the global coverage of satellite broadcasting and Internet-supplied television content. Despite the ability of broadcasting unions to leverage multiple countries' audiences, the PSBs must compete against privately owned, transnational broadcasters. Transnational broadcasters with sufficient financial capacities compete to acquire regional broadcasting rights with audiences as large as broadcasting unions could offer. Despite the undeniable privatisation of the FWC broadcasting across the globe, FTA broadcast viewing remains prevalent.

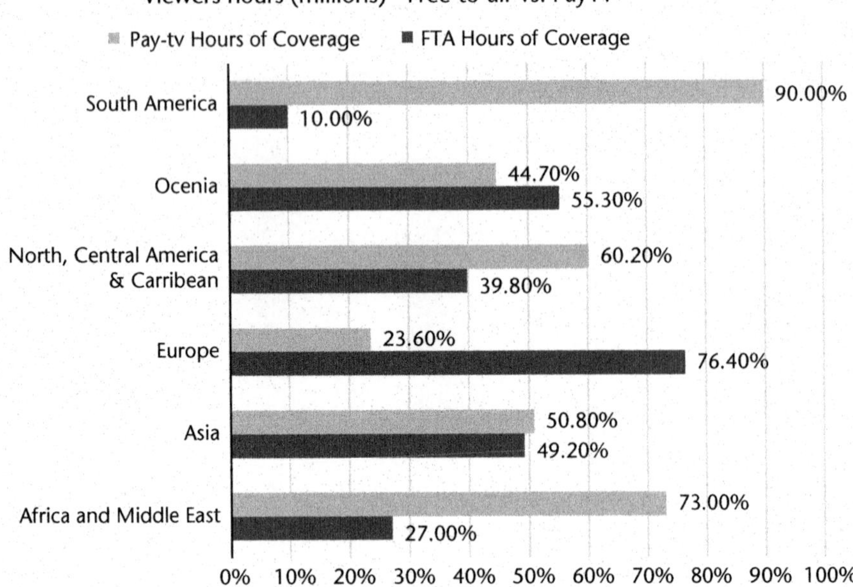

FIGURE 15.2 Hours of coverage, Free-to-air vs. PayTV Hour

Adapted from 2018 FIFA World Cup Russia Global broadcast and audience summary (FIFA.com, 2018, p. 17).

Figures 15.2 and 15.3 show how PayTV shared broadcasting hours with PSBs or FTA broadcasters during the 2018 FWC. Except for Europe, PayTV has more coverage hours than FTA in all regions. In addition to FTA rights acquisition, retroceding all or a portion of the broadcasting rights is a common practice, which could explain a much larger viewership on FTA television. Except for Africa and the Middle East, FTA broadcasting has more viewers all over the world. The analysis of the 2018 FIFA World Cup Russia Media Rights Licensees provides some indications about what could explain the continuous prevalence of FTA viewership (FIFA.com, 2018).

In the Middle East and North Africa, because of beIN Sports' exclusive rights, there was no other broadcaster for the 2018 FWC. In sub-Saharan Africa for the 2018 FWC, four private communication and media corporations (SuperSport, Econet Media Limited, StarTimes and Canal+ International) owned the broadcasting rights. The ABU was outbid by Econet Media Limited. SuperSport acquired the exclusive rights for South Africa and shared rights for the rest of sub-Saharan Africa with StarTimes and Canal+ International. In a few countries, the license was retroceded by Econet Limited to some government-owned and privately owned FTA broadcasters. Although language de facto limited Canal+ International to Francophone Africa and SuperSport to Anglophone Africa, StarTimes crossed the linguistics barriers with programming in French and English. In Africa, transnational broadcasters with aggregated audiences and

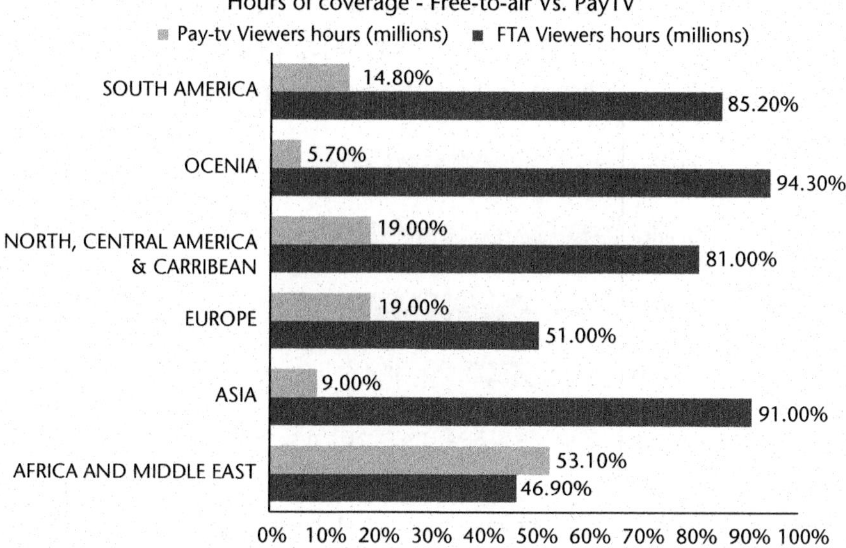

FIGURE 15.3 Viewers hours Free-to-air vs. PayTV

Adapted from 2018 FIFA World Cup Russia Global broadcast and audience summary (FIFA.com, 2018).

stronger financial capacities than the often-underfinanced government broadcasters frequently control the 2018 FWC. This shifted the competition entirely to PayTV. The initial AUB agreement did not sustain FIFA's leadership change in 2016 when Gianni Infantino was elected president of FIFA.

As shown in Figure 15.4, the proportion of Europeans and South Americans who watched the 2018 FWC is the highest in the world. These numbers can be explained by the higher number of European and South American teams in the FWC from the first rounds to the finals, and by the long-lasting culture of football in those two continents. Nevertheless, other factors such as television broadcasting penetration, access to the games on PayTV vs. FTA, and the overall interest of non-participating nations in the competition are important factors. In Asia, one of the most populous nations, India, is primarily a cricket nation with some interest in football.

Despite a lower watching percentage, Asia, with 43.7% (2018, p. 10) of the global total, was the largest viewer of the 2018 FWC (see Figure 15.5). With 18.4% (FIFA, 2018, p. 10) of the global total, China was the largest single country viewer of the 2018 FWC. In comparison to its population size, Africa appears to have the lowest viewership among the continents, with 11% of the global viewership. With the lowest TV and PayTV penetration due to historic and socio-economic challenges, sub-Saharans are less likely to watch many games outside the African teams (Figure 15.6).

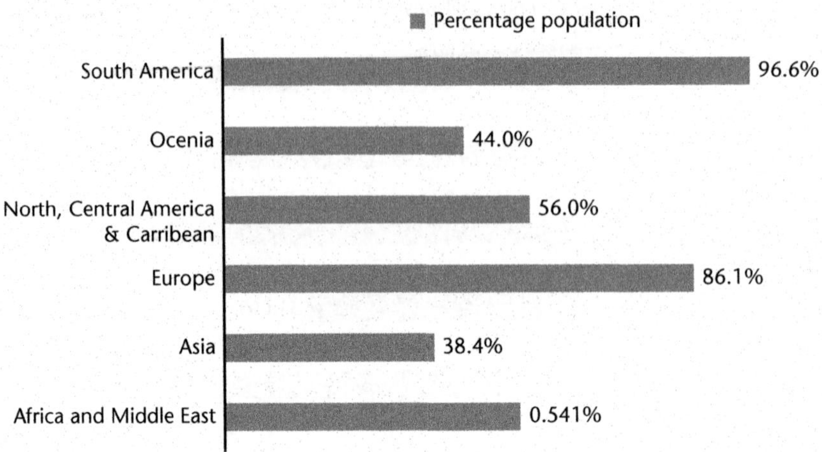

FIGURE 15.4 Proportion of countries that watched the 2018 FWC

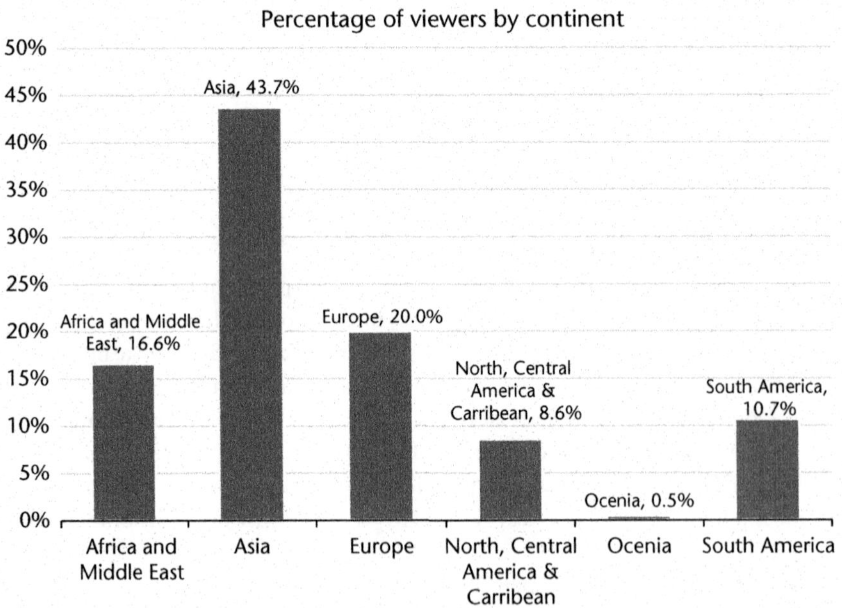

FIGURE 15.5 Viewing of the 2018 FWC by region

Adapted from 2018 FIFA World Cup Russia Global broadcast and audience summary (FIFA.com, 2018, p. 17).

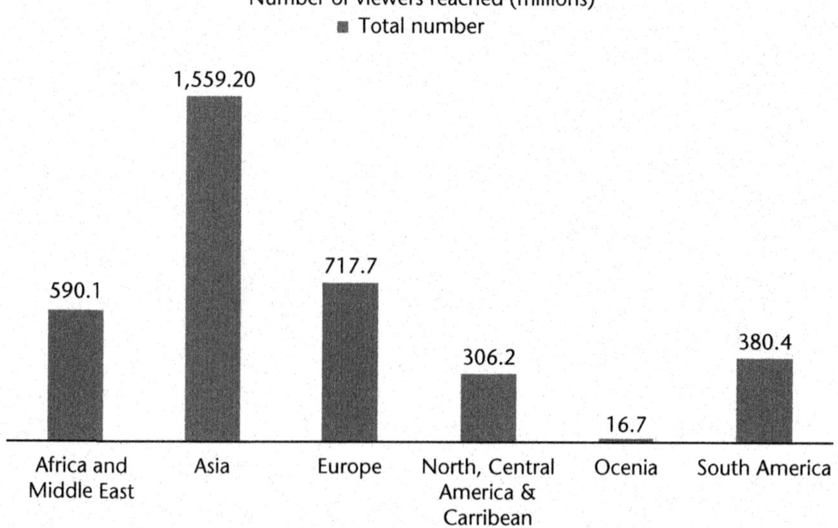

FIGURE 15.6 Viewing of the 2018 FWC by region

Adapted from 2018 FIFA World Cup Russia Global broadcast and audience summary (FIFA.com, 2018, p. 10).

The Internet Transforming Effect

In terms of revenue, Europe remains the first broadcasting rights payer to FIFA (Figure 15.7). Private PayTV broadcasters and the EBU continue to ensure that Europe remains as a single geographical entity and the largest contributor to the FIFA broadcasting rights revenues. The potential audience, which could have been the competitive advantage for PSBs when terrestrial television broadcasting was the norm, is less relevant. Following the rise of satellite television broadcasting with DTH broadcasting, Digital Terrestrial Television (DTT), television distributed over the Internet has transformed sports broadcasting globally for the past decade. Lotz believes that Internet-distributed television (now called *Over-The-Top* or *OTT*) emerged in 2005, but it was uncommon until 2010. FIFA states that "the trend in TV broadcasting towards digital streaming audiences has increased as expected—research also showed that 22% of those viewers watched the 2018 FIFA World Cup in Russia out of home or on computers/mobile devices." The FIFA's statement in the 2018 financial report indicates that 42% of the viewers intended to watch the FWC through OTT (*Infographic*, s.d.).

The data published by Statista based on an Ipsos survey conducted in 27 countries between April 10 and May 4 indicated that television remains the dominant medium for watching the FWC. However, in countries such as India, China, and Saudi Arabia, the survey indicates that 70% to 90% of viewers intended to use the Internet to watch the games. The streaming of the FWC most likely will continue along with more traditional TV viewership. The multiple options

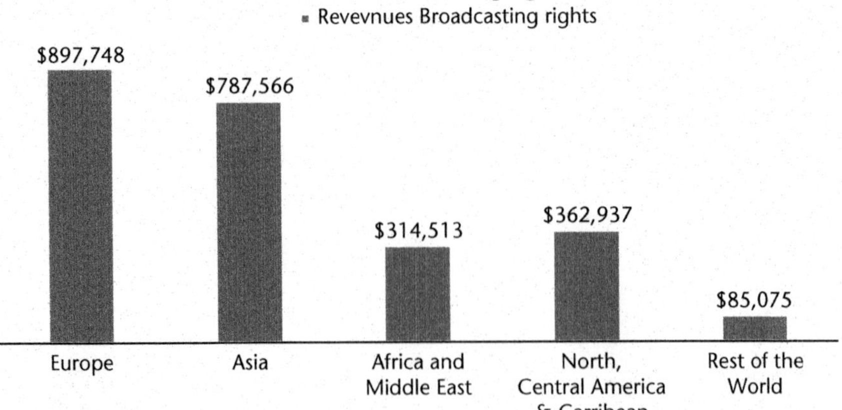

FIGURE 15.7 FIFA television broadcasting rights revenue by region 2018 (in million U.S. dollars). Adapted from FIFA Annual report 2019 (FIFA, 2019, p. 154)

available to watch sports content is transforming viewership habits globally. How these trends are going to affect the upcoming Qatar 2022 FWC in term of revenues for FIFA is one the emerging questions.

The 2022 FWC, the first in the Middle East, is happening during a period of rapid transformations in the world of sports broadcasting. Pushed by the COVID-19 pandemic, sporting events migrated to all-digital formats without stadium spectators. Continuing evolution of broadcasting technology will be impacting the FWC even more. In 2018, broadcasting rights were already broken down into television, portable and Internet. With the global expansion of the OTT, the question is how OTT will influence 2022 FWC broadcasting rights globally. Like satellites in their time, DTH broadcasting streaming over the Internet is transforming the global sport mediascape. Internet-distributed television viewed on a TV, tablet or mobile phone is now a global norm.

Indeed, the television set is in competition with Internet, mobile devices, and tablet viewing globally. The OTT has therefore integrated the consumption of FWC viewing. OTT, which depends on the Internet infrastructure, has worldwide influence that led to distribution of television content over these various platforms. The "platformisation," a term coined by Evens and Donders, (2018, p. 1) although in process globally, does not have the same implication for television and sports broadcasting. As discussed by Lotz, portals (2017) is the crucial intermediary service that collects, curates and distributes television programming via Internet distribution. In this case, the portals platform is used to distribute the FWC games to a specific audience. Netflix and Amazon Prime are often cited as examples of the disruption the OTT is creating in the United States. The phrase "cut the cord" is used to warn that many American cable subscribers will soon abandon the dominant cable networks to subscribe to OTT platforms. The recent acquisition by Amazon Prime of a few games of the English Premier League and the National Football League (NFL) Thursday night game indicate that OTT platforms will transform the sports broadcasting rights market. The question is how OTT service providers will transform FWC broadcasting. FIFA has already adapted its rights packaging to include Internet, and mobile (FIFA.com, 2018). The record of the 2018 media licences published by FIFA show that the main broadcasters acquire the rights for the Internet, mobile, television and tablet and may retrocede parts of those rights locally. Except for the radio license, which is not systematically acquired by television broadcasters, the TV right holder is also the holder for Internet, mobile and tablet content. The existence of a few markets with multiple broadcasters for the same geographic region may be indicative of the possible multiple rights holders for different broadcasting platforms in the same country or region. The United States' National Football League has multiple broadcasters, including Amazon Prime and OTT for the broadcasting of "Thursday Night Football." The coming FWCs will clarify potential changes in how FIFA and its market agency Infront could change the broadcasting packages in regard to each region or country.

Conclusion

Throughout the years, the FIFA World Cup has developed a strong business partnership with television broadcasting. Broadcasting technologies and the liberalisation of national or regional media rules and laws have been the engine of the relationship. Satellite television transformed the relationship between sports and broadcasting. Although PSBs were instrumental in establishing the global broadcasting of the FWC, PayTV contributed to make television broadcasting the most important source of revenue for FIFA. More recently, OTT, television over the Internet, is now part of the sports mediascape. Streaming content is a norm that is diversifying the mediascape with multiple players openly challenging the traditional television broadcasters. Amazon Prime and DAZN are among the largest players with live sports content in the United States and globally. But these players have not yet acquired a FIFA license to broadcast the World Cup. With the increased global shift of the FWC to PayTV where national media rules and law allow, the sports mediascape global transformation is being stimulated by better, faster and more accessible Internet. This offers a diversification in watching the FWC. How FIFA will fully leverage these Internet-driven transformations is at its early stages but already these are boosting revenues for the governing body of global football.

References

Akindes, G. (2017) Sports Media Complex and the Business of Football in Africa. In Dodds, M., Heisey, K., Ahonen, A., Wenner, L.A., Billings, A.C. (eds.), *Routledge Handbook of International Sport Business*. London: Routledge.

Amara, M. (2007) When the Arab World was Mobilised around the FIFA 2006 World Cup, *Journal of North African Studies*, 12(4), 417-438.

Amara, M. (2012) *Sport, Politics and Society in the Arab World.* London: Palgrave Macmillan. http://www.netread.com/jcusers2/bk1388/926/9780230307926/image/lgcover.9780230307926.jpg

Bignell, J., Fickers, A., & others. (2008) *A European television history.* Wiley-Blackwell Oxford.

Boyle, R., & Haynes, R. (2017) The Global Event? The Media, Football and the FIFA World Cup. In *Sport, Media and Mega-Events* (p. 85-99). Routledge.

Chisari, F. (2006) When Football Went Global: Televising the 1966 World Cup, *Historical Social Research*, 31(1), 42-54.

Clarke, R. (2002) *The Future of Sports Broadcasting Rights.* SportBusiness Group.

CSA (s.d.) *Sport et audiovisuel—CSA - Conseil supérieur de l'audiovisuel.* Consulté 22 mai 2021, à l'adresse. Available at: https://www.csa.fr/Proteger/Garantie-des-droits-et-libertes/Sport-et-audiovisuel

Darby, P. (2002) *Africa, Football, and FIFA: Politics, Colonialism, and Resistance.* F. Cass.

Darby, P. (2005) Africa and the 'World' Cup: FIFA Politics, Eurocentrism and Resistance, *International Journal of the History of Sport*, 22(5), 883-905.

Evens, T. & Donders, K. (2018) *Platform Power and Policy in Transforming Television Markets.* Springer.

FIFA (2003) *FIFA Financial Report 2002.* Available at: file:///C:/Users/gakin/Dropbox/FIFA/fifa-financial-report-2002–1599446.pdf

FIFA (2007) *FIFA Big Count 2006: 270 MIllion People Active in Football.* FIFA Big Count 2006: 270 million people active in football…Available at: http://www.fifa.com/mm/document/fifafacts/bcoffsurv/bigcount.statspackage_7024.pdf

FIFA (2007) *2006 FIFA Financial Report* (p. 119). Available at: https://resources.fifa.com/image/upload/fifa-financial-report-2006–515265.pdf?cloudid=zq7qokz0hgq1g7jlosqk

FIFA (2011) *FIFA Financial report 2010.* Available at: https://digitalhub.fifa.com/m/42ecabe5116b0ecd/original/n4hhe0pvhfdhzxbbbp44-pdf.pdf

FIFA (2015) *Financial Report 2014 FIFA* [Financial]. Available at: http://resources.fifa.com/mm/document/affederation/administration/02/56/80/39/fr2014weben_neutral.pdf

FIFA (2018) *2018-FIFA-world-cup-russia-global-broadcast-and-audience-executive-summary.pdf.* Available at: https://resources.fifa.com/image/upload/2018-fifa-world-cup-russia-global-broadcast-and-audience-executive-summary.pdf?cloudid=njqsntrvdvqv8ho1dag5

FIFA (2019) *2018 FIFA Financial Report* (p. 152) [Fianancial Report]. Available at: https://resources.fifa.com/image/upload/xzshsoe2ayttyquuxhq0.pdf

FIFA.com (2006) *2006 FIFA World Cup viewing figures in Germany up 51 percent on average over 2002.* Available at: www.Fifa.Com. https://www.fifa.com/worldcup/news/2006-fifa-world-cup-viewing-figures-germany-percent-average-over-2002–13556

FIFA.com (2018) *Media Rights Licensees 2018 FIFA World Cup Rrussia.* Available at: FIBA.com. https://resources.fifa.com/image/upload/media-rights-licensees-2018-fifa-world-cup-russiatm.pdf?cloudid=ncvjqwzuqeags9uqac4r

FIFA.com (2020) *1970 FIFA World Cup™—News—The adidas Telstar begins ball chain—FIFA.com.* Available at: www.Fifa.Com. https://www.fifa.com/worldcup/news/telstar-story-fifa-world-cup-ball-3073424

Infographic: The FIFA World Cup Is One of TV's Last Strongholds. (s. d.) Statista Infographics. Consulté 29 mai 2021, à l'adresse. Avaialable at: http://www.statista.com/chart/14201/devices-used-to-watch-the-world-cup/

Infront sport (2006) *Record Broadcast Coverage for 2006 FIFA World Cup^{TM}*. Available at: https://www.infront.sport/en/news/2006/6/record-broadcast-coverage-for-2006-fifa-world-cup-tm

Ipsos (2018) *Global Attitudes Towards the FIFA World Cup 2018 in Russia*. Ipsos. Available at: https://www.ipsos.com/en/global-attitudes-towards-fifa-world-cup-2018-russia

Jeanrenaud, C. & Kesenne, S. (2006) *The Economics of Sport and the Media*. Edward Elgar.

Kuwait News Agency (2006) *ASBU calls for ending World Cup broadcasting monopoly*. KUNA. Available at: https://www.kuna.net.kw/ArticlePrintPage.aspx?id=1662772&language=en

Lotz, A.D. (2017) *Portals: A Treatise on Internet-Distributed Television*. Michigan Publishing, University of Michigan Library.

Malkawi, B.H. (2007) Broadcasting the 2006 World Cup: The Right of Arab Fans versus ART Exclusivity, *Fordham In*[TEL] *Lectual Property Media and Entertainment Law Journal*, 17(3), 591-610.

Milne, M. (2016) *The Transformation of Television Sport: New Methods, New Rules*. Palgrave Macmillan.

Pelton, J.N. (2013) History of Satellite Communications. In J.N. Pelton, S. Madry, & S. Camacho-Lara (eds.), *Handbook of Satellite Applications* (pp. 27-66). New York: Springer. 10.1007/978-1-4419-7671-0_35

Rowe, D. (2004) *Critical Readings: Sport, Culture and the Media*. Open University Press.

Samuel-Azran, T., Karniel, Y. & Lavie-Dinur, A. (2014) Globalization and Social Justice in Sports Broadcasting: The Case of Al-Jazeera Sport, *Television & New Media*, 15(8), 725-731. 10.1177/1527476414529166

Smith, P., Evens, T. & Losifidis, P. (2015) The Regulation of Television Sports Broadcasting: A Comparative Analysis, *Media, Culture & Society*, 37(5), 720-736. 10.1177/0163443715577244

Solberg, H.A. (2007) Sport Broadcasting – Is it a Job for Public Service Broadcasters? – A Welfare Economic Perspective, *Journal of Media Economics*, 20(4), 289–309.

Solberg, H.A., & Gratton, C. (2014) Broadcasting the World Cup. In *Managing the Football World Cup* (p. 47-52). Palgrave Macmillan. https://doi-org.turing.library.northwestern.edu/10.1057/9781137373687_4

SportBusiness (2002) *KirchSport becomes Infront*. SportBusiness. Available at: https://www.sportbusiness.com/news/kirchsport-becomes-infront/

Sportcal (2001) *Kirch Takes on ISL's Non-European World Cup TV Rights*. Available at: https://www.sportcal.com/News/PressReleases/50318?&f=s%3A1%2FSoccer%7C%24i%3A2%2FLegal%7C

Sportcal (2002) *FIFA: 2002 World Cup Will not be Hit by KirchMedia's Insolvency*. Available at: https://www.sportcal.com/News/PressReleases/31557

The Editors of Encyclopaedia Britannica (1999, mai 27) *Telstar|communications satellite*. Encyclopedia Britannica. Available at: https://www.britannica.com/technology/Telstar-communications-satellite

Tyers, S. (2014) How World Cup TV coverage has changed since the 1950s. *The Guardian*. Available at: https://www.theguardian.com/football/when-saturday-comes-blog/2014/jul/07/world-cup-tv-television-coverage-changed-1954–1958

Union (EBU) (2010) *EBU and FIFA World Cup^{TM}: Football Needs Television and Television Needs Football*. Available at: https://www.ebu.ch/news/2010/ebu-and-fifa-world-cup--football

Whannel, G. (2009) Television and the Transformation of Sport, *The Annals of the American Academy of Political and Social Science*, 625(1), 205-218.

Williams (2016) *Watching the Beautiful Game*. BBC. Available at: https://www.bbc.co.uk/blogs/genome/entries/6a219df7–746f-45f2-aa31–549fbf924e4e

Ziyati, A. & Akindes, G. (2014) It's All About the Beautiful Game of Football, or Is It? On Television and Football in North Africa. In Onwumechili, C., Akindes, G. (eds.), *Identity and Nation in African Football: Fans, Community and Clubs* (p. 36). London: Palgrave Macmillan.

16

DIGITAL AND SOCIAL MEDIA IN THE BUSINESS OF THE FIFA WORLD CUP

Renan Petersen-Wagner

Introduction

In the past 150 years, societies across the globe have witnessed the emergence of distinct information and communication technologies (hereafter ICTs) such as the telegraph, telephone, radio and television that have altered the way individuals and groups connect to each other (Briggs et al., 2020). Nevertheless, it was not until the end of the 20th century when digital technologies – the transformation of all kinds of content into 0s and 1s – the wider adoption of Internet protocols, and the further miniaturisation of microprocessors that we can evidence that there is nothing untouched by media(tisation) (Tomlinson, 2007; Deuze, 2011; McQuail and Deuze, 2020).

Thus, it is important to ask what are the reverberations of the pervasiveness of digital media on one of the most ubiquitous and serious ordinary elements of a truly global popular culture – association football (hereafter football) (Bromberger, 2004). Football, and in particular the women's and men's World Cup events organised by the *Fédération Internationale de Football Association* (FIFA) that were watched by 1 billion and 3 billion individuals in their last two editions, respectively (FIFA, 2018; 2019), symbolise the pinnacle of this novel digital human condition where everything is mediated; however, what are the transformations, disruptions, continuities and discontinuities to the historical symbiotic relationship between media and sport coming out of the digital revolution?

The chapter follows with a review of the symbiotic relationship between mass media and sport, and the digital disruptions when new media collide with this sedimented relationship; then, data from two distinct social media platforms (YouTube and Twitter) are used to illustrate how the digital revolution is better understood as transformations that contain both patterns of continuities and discontinuities; finally, the chapter ends with a discussion on how digital media

DOI: 10.4324/9781003121794-16

transformed the once sedimented relationship between mass media and sport by extending rather than replacing it.

Understanding the Symbiotic Relationship between Media and Sport

To write about the emergence of professional sport without discussing mass media – and vice-versa – is to portray just one side of a coin, and thus neglecting that what we recognise today as sport is intrinsically connected to what we know as mass media. Both sport and mass media are part of the invented traditions of European modernisation (Hobsbawm, 1983), nevertheless traditionally inhabiting complete opposite worlds (Rowe, 2004). The relationship between the two, became indispensable during the past century to a point where Rowe (2004) conceptualises it as a symbiotic relationship. The lowering of production costs, the shifting to a business model where commercialising advertising spaces trumped the selling of access to content, and consequently realising that selling audiences' attentions to those advertisers were their core business (Wu, 2016), led mass media to constantly battle for content that captivates larger audiences (Rowe, 2013). For instance, the 2014 FIFA Men's World Cup in Brazil was broadcasted to over 200 territories (FIFA, 2015). Thus, by providing a constant influx of real human drama (Bellamy, 2013; Jackson, 2013) sport becomes a key content for media and advertisers (Bellamy, 2013). Above that, the open ended quality of sport such as football exceeds what happens during the 90 minutes and involves aspects of norm violations, scandals, and other ramifications that are important for commercial mass media (see Luhmann, 2000).

The symbiotic relationship rose through ICTs developments moving to the newest available media (Owens, 2006), but only found its *home* with live TV broadcasting (Rowe, 1996). The use of sport as a catalyst for *medium* adoption can be witnessed when football is used to lure users into subscribing to bundled offerings (e.g., BSkyB and the formation of the English Premier League) (David et al., 2017), and especially how new technologies (e.g., HD, 3D, 4K UHD) figure prominently when the FIFA Men's World Cup are held (BARB, 2010; FIFA, 2014). Traditional media such as print, radio and television can be characterised as predominantly linear and uni-directional, by moving standardised content to an undifferentiated mass (one-to-many) (McQuail and Deuze, 2020). Those characteristics alongside its historical roots mean that those spaces are reserved for a few who hold *power* (see Herman and Chomsky, 1988). Even that mass media are credited for fostering public spheres (Habermas, 1991), it is important to interrogate who is to be considered the *public* when *filters* (Herman and Chomsky, 1988) lead to situations of gender (Bruce, 2015; Cooky et al., 2021; Petty and Pope, 2019; Petersen-Wagner, 2020b) and sport imbalances (Coche and Tuggle, 2018; Petersen-Wagner, 2020a). As such, in a situation of broadcasting scarcity (Hutchins and Rowe, 2009), those outlets and individuals working for them become powerful gatekeepers in the mediated flow of information (Herman and Chomsky, 1988).

With the rise of the Internet there were possible transformations to this *closed club*. For instance, in their series of studies, Hutchins and Rowe (2009; 2012; 2013) documented how digital plenitude have disrupted this traditional symbiotic relationship, especially when accessibility is pulverised across multiple platforms (Hutchins and Rowe, 2012). For instance, individuals have now a plethora of options in terms of consuming sport to a point where platform selection is both complementary and competitive (Gantz and Lewis, 2014). The arrival of new media platforms was commonly received with enthusiasm in regards of *democratisation* of content prosumption (McQuail and Deuze, 2020).

New media disrupt traditional media in four interconnected areas, such as power asymmetries, social integration and identity, social change, and space and time (McQuail and Deuze, 2020). Those areas are commonly identified when observing the symbiotic relationship with football as in the case of players, clubs and fans creating and distributing content (Anagnostopoulos et al., 2018; Rookwood and Millward, 2011; Rodriguez, 2017; Sauder and Blaszka, 2018), the networked structure of fan relations that concomitantly brings transnational cohesion and fragmentation (Giulianotti and Robertson, 2007; Hayton et al., 2017; Ludvigsen, 2019; Petersen-Wagner, 2017a, 2017b, 2018), how new media can foster loosely defined social movements and social change (Cleland et al., 2017; Hill et al., 2018;Millward, 2012), and above all how new places for consuming football emerge (Lawrence and Crawford, 2018; Petersen-Wagner, 2018; Woods and Ludvigsen, 2021).

In short, the symbiotic relationship between sport and media has metamorphosed by following new distribution technologies (e.g., print, radio, linear TV, over-the-top, social media platforms), nevertheless it is important to highlight how those technological processes are interconnected with the cultural practices associated with *consuming* content (Jenkins, 2006). Thus, understanding what people can afford with distinct delivery technologies is paramount for comprehending the now disrupted symbiotic relationship.

Methods

The impacts of digital transformations were also experienced in sociological enquiry practices to a point where an *enlarged tradition* of research has emerged. For Marres (2017), a digital turn to sociology implies: (i) the acceptance of new places and contexts for research; (ii) the application of distinct methods of research on those new spaces and contexts; and (iii) new platforms for engaging with the public and wider audience. This chapter takes Marres (2017) points to the fore by investigating new places for consuming football and apply novel methods to comprehend how the symbiotic relationship unfolds on those places. In respect of point one, the focus of this chapter is on two distinct social media platforms – namely Alphabet Inc. owned video sharing platform YouTube and Twitter Inc.

microblogging platform Twitter, whereas for point two this chapter uses YouTube Data Tools (Rieder, 2015) to automatically scrap data from YouTube, and Gephi (Bastian et al., 2009) to scrap tweets and perform social network analyses.

Digital and Social Media – YouTube and Twitter

New digital media distinctiveness in relation to traditional analogue media centres around four features in terms of affordances: (i) capacity for interactivity; (ii) on-demand and real-time access; (iii) all users become consumers and producers; (iv) hybridity of mixing one-to-many, one-to-one and many-to-many forms of communication (McQuail and Deuze, 2020). YouTube, as an agnostic content platform (Burgess and Green, 2018), possesses a business model that relies on the constant active engagement of its over 2 billion monthly logged-in users in producing, sharing, commenting and watching content. Users on YouTube are able to produce, share and even monetise their own content (iii), watch others' content anytime/anywhere (ii) – more than 70% of watch time is done on mobile devices (YouTube, 2021) – comment and engage on conversations (i), and both videos and comments provide spaces for a mix of communication models (iv). Twitter as content agnostic platform[1] (Murthy, 2017) also relies on its over 190 million *Monetizable Daily Active Usage* (mDAU) for its business model that is anchored on advertising revenue. Similarly to YouTube, Twitter allows users to tweet, retweet and reply (i) on all distinct forms of communication (iv), consume on-demand content as focused on Twitter's letter to shareholders (Twitter, 2021, p. 5) and interact on real-time (ii), and ultimately provides multiple spaces for creation and consumption of content as through traditional tweets, fleets, direct messages, and spaces (iii) (Twitter, 2021).

FIFA, CONMEBOL and UEFA YouTube channels

YouTube (launched in 2005) was initially conceived as a platform that removed barriers for *non-professionals* to share videos on the web (Burgess and Green, 2018). The platform has metamorphosed over the years and now operates in multi-sided market by hosting *non-professional* videos, and balancing the interests of other *stakeholders* as pro-amateurs and professional content creators, media partners and advertisers (Burgess and Green, 2018). It is possible to talk about two YouTubes (Burgess and Green, 2018) as in one side there are professionally curated channels

1 Both platforms have drew considerable attention because of their nature as content agnostic when hate speech appears (for their hateful speech policies see Twitter 2021a; YouTube 2021a) to a point where there is at the time of writing this chapter a movement for a football-wide boycott on social media platforms in the United Kingdom (BBC, 2021).

TABLE 16.1 Summary from YouTube Channels

Channel	*Creation*	*Subscribers*	*Videos*	*Views*
FIFATV	September 2006	9,510,000	8,631	3,146,037,975
UEFA	March 2006	286,000	3,259	682,128,415
CONMEBOL	February 2014	24,400	2,517	50,541,464

operating similarly to traditional broadcasting, and on the other there is still an *idealised* open-Internet where you can just "broadcast yourself™" (Jarret, 2008).

In respect of sport, YouTube is considered as a secondary medium by its re-mediation characteristic where content previously considered relevant is made available in shorter format (Stauff, 2009)[2]. Hence, governing bodies and clubs realising that the threat imposed by Alphabet's (the parent company of YouTube and Google) digital disruption meant that the sole option was to join it rather than fight it (Hutchins and Rowe, 2012). As Checchinato et al. (2015) argue, football supporters are prone to engage and consume more professionally curated official channels content rather than user-generated-content (UGC), and thus transforming it as an alternative for TV broadcasting.

To check this, the author collected data from the official YouTube channels of FIFA (FIFATV, 2021), CONMEBOL (CONMEBOL, 2021) and UEFA (UEFA, 2021). A summary of the data can be seen in Table 16.1.

To put the above data into perspective just the final game between Germany and Argentina during the 2014 FIFA Men's World Cup in Brazil had an in-home and out-of-home audience (+60s) of over 1 billion (FIFA, 2015). The average length of videos on those channels were 339 s (FIFA), 232 s (CONMEBOL) and 241 s (UEFA), but ranged 10–3593 s, 7–3553 s, 9–3560 s, respectively,[3] with live streamed events (congresses, draws, eSports, futsal, youth and women games) going up to 10 hours. Those figures are in line with Millennials and Generation-Z preferences for shorter video formats that are less than 60s (61% share) and between 120 and 300 seconds long (50% share) (Statista, 2020; Statista, 2021). What the data from FIFATV shows (see Table 16.2) is that there is a statistically significant positive correlation between duration and dislikes, and only a weak but statistically significant negative correlation between duration and comments suggesting that shorter videos might create more engagement.

2 As an example currently not all content on YouTube is remediation, as the Major League Baseball (MLB) YouTube channel streams live regular season games, and the Union Cycliste Internationale (UCI) YouTube channel streamed some of its events such as the 2021 Cyclocross World Championship, whereas BT has offered free live streams of UEFA Men's Champions League finals for the past five years (Forbes, 2019; BT, 2020).

3 Videos with over 1 hour of content had their duration in seconds considered as short of 3600 s according to the data scraped from YouTube (durationSec on YouTube's API)

TABLE 16.2 FIFATV General Stats Correlation

			Correlations					
			durationSec	*viewCount*	*likeCount*	*dislikeCount*	*commentCount*	*totle engagement*
Spearman's rho	durationSec	Correlation Coefficient	1.000	.017	.003	.080**	−.023*	.002
		Sig. (2-tailed)	.	.104	.765	<.001	.036	.821
		N	8628	8622	8566	8566	8610	8628
	viewCount	Correlation Coefficient	.017	1.000	.921**	.861**	.846**	.919**
		Sig. (2-tailed)	.104	.	.000	.000	.000	.000
		N	8622	8623	8567	8567	8611	8623
	likeCount	Correlation Coefficient	.003	.921**	1.000	.867**	.902**	.996**
		Sig. (2-tailed)	.765	.000	.	.000	.000	.000
		N	8566	8567	8567	8567	8567	8567
	dislikeCount	Correlation Coefficient	.080**	.861**	.867**	1.000	.832**	.891**
		Sig. (2-tailed)	<.001	.000	.000	.	.000	.000
		N	8566	8567	8567	8567	8567	8567
	commentCount	Correlation Coefficient	−.023*	.846**	.902**	.832**	1.000	.916**
		Sig. (2-tailed)	.036	.000	.000	.000	.	.000
		N	8610	8611	8567	8567	8611	8611
	total engagments	Correlation Coefficient	.002	.919**	.996**	.891**	.916**	1.000
		Sig. (2-tailed)	.821	.000	.000	.000	.000	.
		N	8,628	8,623	8,567	8,567	8,611	8634

Notes

** Correlation is significant at the 0.01 level (2-tailed).

* Correlation is significant at the 0.05 level (2-tailed).

Following Khan (2017) in recognising both *passive* (views) and *active* (like, dislike, comments) forms of consumption, it is possible to recognise how patterns of cultural consumption associated with television are still dominant. For instance, videos' average views are 364,940 (FIFA), 20,096 (CONMEBOL) and 209,404 (UEFA), whereas the average for all combined *active* consumption activities are 3,100 (FIFA), 60 (CONMEBOL), and 2,171 (UEFA), equating to a *passive/active* ratio of 0.0135, 0.0034, and 0.0544, respectively. This suggests that while YouTube affords users to enhance their consumption, they are still reproducing similar patterns found on TV. Nevertheless, there is a strong positive correlation in respect of FIFATV (see Table 16.2) between all *active* and *passive* forms of engagement suggesting that while the preference is still oriented to a *passive* consumption the platform affordance is utilised by users. Moreover, in respect of FIFATV there was a negative statistically significant correlation (−.188*) between the age of the post in days and the numbers of views, suggesting that older videos become part of the past meaning that remediation still favours *newness*. Nevertheless, it is important to acknowledge that the line of best fit is *skewed* towards the 1,000 days mark that reflects the period of the FIFA 2018 Men's World Cup in Russia.

In as much the digital revolution was initially embraced with optimism, the reality coming out of FIFATV's data paints a more negative picture in respect of gender equality. By analysing and comparing videos on two paired playlists ("FIFA World Cup | Original Content" and "FIFA Women's World Cup | Original Content"; "2018 FIFA World Cup | Match Highlights" and "FIFA Women's World Cup France 2019 | Match Highlights") it was firstly possible to note the discrepancies in number of videos – 44 to 11 on the original content playlists; and 64 to 52 on match highlights playlists – still putting women's football in a disadvantaged position. Moreover, when analysing the average on views, likes, dislikes, comments, total engagement (sum of all views, likes, dislikes and comments), likes by views, and dislikes by views it is possible to note how women's football videos consistently get less engagement across most metrics.

Nevertheless, when performing an independent sample Mann–Whitney *U* test on views, likes, dislikes, comments, total engagement (sum of all views, likes, dislikes and comments), likes by views and dislikes by views it was possible to note that women's highlights have more likes by views than men's highlights suggesting a disruption to traditional symbiotic relationship where women sport is commonly neglected (see literature review). Further to that, the distribution of likes by views in the original content pair is similar across the two genders evidencing that there is a favourable audience for both competitions, even when women's one is smaller in size (viewcount) (see Tables 16.3 and 16.4).

Moreover, it is interesting to highlight that for the two past FIFA World Cup tournaments' highlight playlists the distribution of dislikes by views is similar across Men's (2018) and Women's (2019) edition indicating that the dislike engagement happens irrespectively of the gender of the competition. This might point that the

TABLE 16.3 Gender comparison on Match Highlights' playlists (Mann–Whitney *U*)

Highlights – Hypothesis Test Summary

	Null Hypothesis	*Test*	*Sig.*[a, b]	*Decision*
1	The distribution of viewCount is the same across categories of Gender.	Independent-Samples Mann–Whitney *U* test	.000	Reject the null hypothesis.
2	The distribution of likeCount is the same across categories of Gender.	Independent-Samples Mann–Whitney *U* test	.000	Reject the null hypothesis.
3	The distribution of dislikeCount is the same across categories of Gender.	Independent-Samples Mann–Whitney *U* test	.000	Reject the null hypothesis.
4	The distribution of commentCount is the same across categories of Gender.	Independent-Samples Mann–Whitney *U* test	<.001	Reject the null hypothesis.
5	The distribution of total engagement is the same across categories of Gender.	Independent-Samples Mann–Whitney *U* test	.000	Reject the null hypothesis.
6	The distribution of total engagement by views is the same across categories of Gender.	Independent-Samples Mann–Whitney *U* test	<.001	Reject the null hypothesis.
7	The distribution of dislikes by views is the same across categories of Gender.	Independent-Samples Mann–Whitney *U* test	.289	Retain the null hypothesis.
8	The distribution of likes by views is the same across categories of Gender.	Independent-Samples Mann–Whitney *U* test	<.001	Reject the null hypothesis.
9	The distribution of comments by views is the same across categories of Gender.	Independent-Samples Mann–Whitney *U* test	0.53	Retain the null hypothesis.

Notes

a The significance level is .050.

b Asymptotic significance is displayed.

dissatisfaction expressed through disliking those videos are addressed to FIFA at large reflecting themes found on Petersen-Wagner and Ludvigsen (forthcoming).

2022 Qatar FIFA Men's World Cup UEFA Qualifiers on Twitter

Twitter Inc.'s microblogging platform (launched in 2006) is considered as a space where users can maintain public asynchronous conversations that facilitates the formation of discrete networks (Murthy, 2017). Because of its low bandwidth requirements and similarity to older forms of communication, it was adopted as a

TABLE 16.4 Gender comparison on original content's playlist (Mann–Whitney *U*)

	Original Content – Hypothesis Test Summary			
	Null Hypothesis	*Test*	*Sig.*[a,b]	*Decision*
1	The distribution of viewCount is the same across categories of Gender.	Independent-Samples Mann–Whitney *U* test	<.001	Reject the null hypothesis.
2	The distribution of likeCount is the same across categories of Gender.	Independent-Samples Mann–Whitney *U* test	<.001	Reject the null hypothesis.
3	The distribution of dislikeCount is the same across categories of Gender.	Independent-Samples Mann–Whitney *U* test	.636	Retain the null hypothesis.
4	The distribution of commentCount is the same across categories of Gender.	Independent-Samples Mann–Whitney *U* test	<.001	Reject the null hypothesis.
5	The distribution of total engagement is the same across categories of Gender.	Independent-Samples Mann–Whitney *U* test	<.001	Reject the null hypothesis.
6	The distribution of total engagement by views is the same across categories of Gender.	Independent-Samples Mann–Whitney *U* test	.599	Retain the null hypothesis.
7	The distribution of Dislikes by views is the same across categories of Gender.	Independent-Samples Mann–Whitney *U* test	<.001	Reject the null hypothesis.
8	The distribution of likes by views is the same across categories of Gender.	Independent-Samples Mann–Whitney *U* test	.768	Retain the null hypothesis.
9	The distribution of comments by views is the same across categories of Gender.	Independent-Samples Mann–Whitney *U* test	.721	Retain the null hypothesis.

Notes

a The significance level is .050.

b Asymptotic significance is displayed.

medium for *keeping informed* and participating in *interactive multicasting* (Murthy, 2017). As such, Twitter can be considered as a place for telepresence where users are constantly in-touch without being physically in-touch (Tomlinson, 2007).

In respect of the relationship between sport and Twitter (see Wenner, 2014), the social media platform is broadly conceptualised as a place where the power of *communication* resides on tweets' reverberations (Billings, 2014) that might bypass – either by appropriation or avoidance – traditional gatekeepers. Moreover, Twitter can be considered a disruptive force to the symbiotic relationship by the way the platform evolved concomitantly towards *informative* and *social* aspects, and how it became part of the cultural fabric of consuming sport (Pegoraro, 2014). This is further evidenced by Twitter's unique position within media ecology in providing networking capabilities (many-to-many) (Hutchins, 2011).

In line with Twitter's networking properties, the author scraped tweets from the 2022 Qatar FIFA Men's World Cup UEFA Qualifiers' games. For the 24th March games, it was used Gephi to collect tweets of all involved teams[4] (mentions, tweets, retweets) employing the user network logic that creates a visual representation of the interactions between users. For the 25th March games, tweets were collected using FIFA and UEFA's[5] official hashtags as words to follow with the same user network logic. In respect of the first group of games, the author run eigenvector centrality analysis (Borgatti et al., 2018) and modularity analysis (Blondel et al., 2008) to create the below visualisation (see Figure 16.1) where nodes (users) are sized by their eigenvector centrality and coloured by their distinct communities.

It is possible to identify communities around bigger nodes who are more popular because of their immediate connections, suggesting that those users can be considered influencers within this network. In a way, it suggests that those bigger nodes operate as gatekeepers by controlling the flow of information across a network that contains 36,841 users connected by 80,391 edges. By delving further on the eigenvector centrality measure of the highest 50 users and distributing them by type, it was interesting to note that the most represented category was national federations or national teams (15), followed by new media outlets (11), players (6), and then competitions or international federations (4). In line with digital disruption discussions (see literature review), both traditional media outlets (1) and journalists (1) did not feature prominently in this network suggesting that their role as gatekeepers and mediators were transformed (McQuail and Deuze, 2020).

For the 25th March games, the visualisation in Figure 16.2 focuses on eigenvector centrality (node size), edges weighted degree (size) and colour (mention – purple; retweet – orange; quote – green) to highlight how the interactive multicasting nature of Twitter brought other relevant participants into conversations (18,243 nodes; 41,002 edges). Slightly distinct to the above analysis, by collecting hashtags we have national federations and national teams (16), players (11), old media (5), and then new media (4) with higher centrality measures

4 Turkey (@TFF_Org) vs. Netherlands (@onsoranje); Serbia (@fssrbije) vs. Ireland (@faireland); Malta (@maltafa1900) vs. Russia (@teamrussia); Belgium (@belgianreddevils) vs. Wales (@cymru); Estonia vs. Czech Rep (@ceskarepre_cz); Cyprus (@cyprusfa) vs. Slovakia (@sfzofficial); Finland (@palloliitto) vs. Bosnia Herzegovina (@nfsbih); Latvia (@kajbumba) vs. Montenegro (@fudbalskisavez); Slovenia (@nzs_si) vs. Croatia (@hns_cff); France (@fff) vs. Ukraine (@uafukraine); and Gibraltar (@gifootball) vs. Norway (@nff_landslag)

5 #wcq (FIFA); Israel vs Denmark (#isrden); Bulgaria vs. Switzerland (#bulsui); Sweden vs. Georgia (#swegeo); Germany vs. Iceland (#gerisl); Moldova vs. Faroe Island (#mdafro); Spain vs. Greece (#espgre); Scotland vs. Austria (#scoaut); Romania vs. North Macedonia (#roumkd); Andorra vs. Albania (#andalb); Hungary vs. Poland (#hunpol); Italy vs Northern Ireland (#itanir); England vs. San Marino (#engsmr)

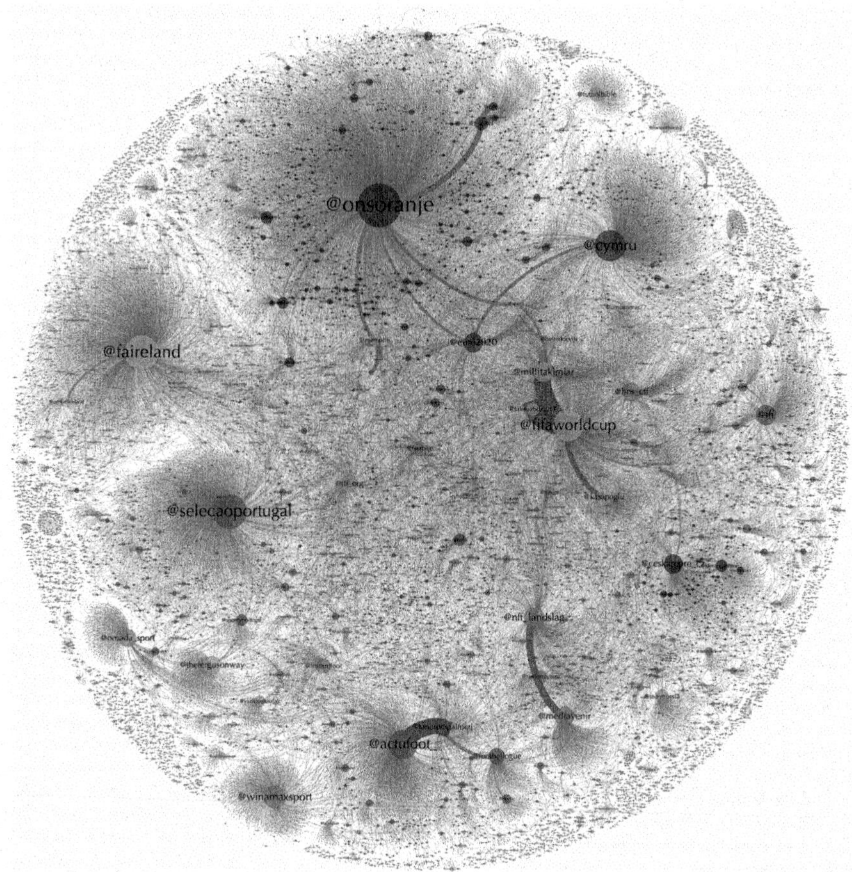

FIGURE 16.1 Twitter communities and influencers

indicating that digital disruption should not be equated to a simple replacement but is better understood as convergence where both old and new co-exist (Jenkins, 2006). Moreover, it is of significance that *ordinary* fans (4) are also influential in shaping discussions, demonstrating how participatory culture and grassroots intermediaries operate in this platform (Jenkins et al., 2013).

What is also important to emphasise is the difference between @england (the Football Association) and @dfb_team (*Deutscher Fussball-bund* – DFB) approaches to social media communication as the latter promotes their star players by mentioning them on different tweets (direction of edges and colour), whereas the former is more often quoted by the players themselves. This can be further evidenced by recognising that out of 11 players with the highest eigenvector centrality measures seven are German and only one is English. Another important point to highlight is the transnational nature of social media platforms as both German and English versions of the DFB, and the Italian and English versions of

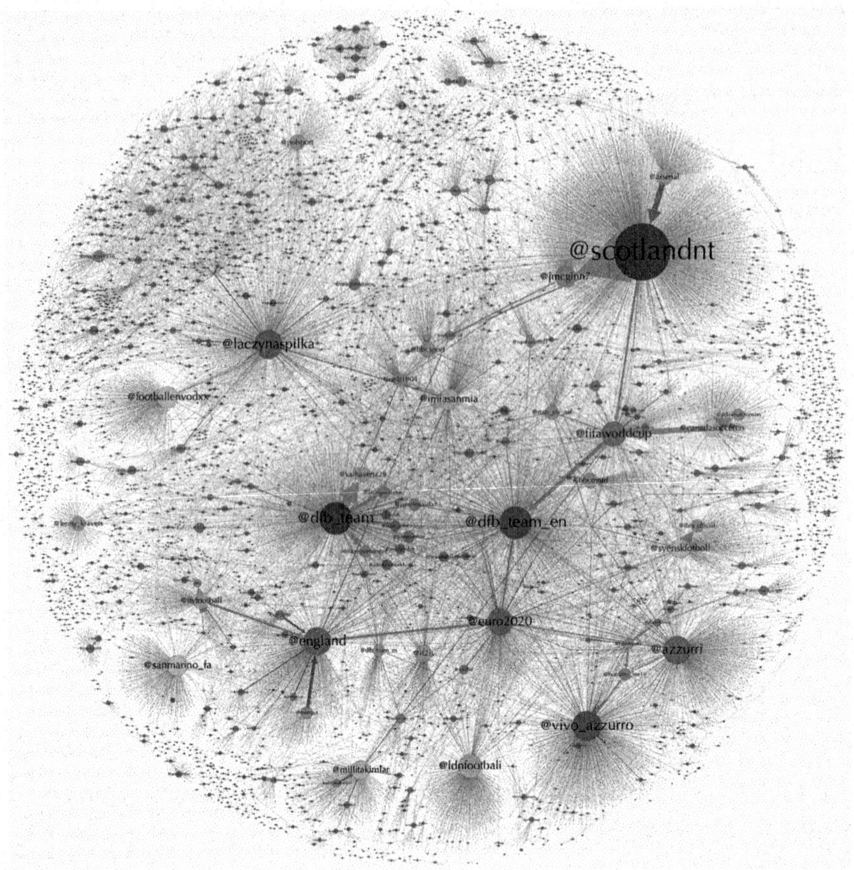

FIGURE 16.2 Hashtag network

the *Federazione Italiana Giuco Calcio* (FIGC) possess higher eigenvector centrality measures (2nd, 3rd, 4th and 6th, respectively).

Discussion

As a proponent of a *total* digital revolution *break*, Negroponte (1995) has predicted that our interaction with media content would evolve towards a total individualisation of consumption experience based on "machines' understanding individuals with the same degree of subtlety (or more than) we can expect from other human beings" (Negroponte, 1995, p. 165), and "our own ability to pull information asynchronously with on-demand content dominating the digital life" (Negroponte, 1995, p. 169). Additionally, the aftermath of digital revolution would see traditional mass media being displaced by new digital media to a point where a *mass* culture would become a thing of the past (see Jenkins, 2006). In as much algorithms dominate our experiences on digital and social media platforms by acting as our digital content butler, and on-demand is pervasive on multiple delivery channels, those transformations have not completely dislodged the shared cultural consumption practices associated with *mass* media. A more subtle analysis of digital revolution is proposed through a convergence paradigm where both old and new cultural practices co-exist (Thorburn and Jenkins, 2004; Jenkins, 2006; Jenkins et al., 2013). Hence, instead of talking about breaks, we should be focusing on both continuities and discontinuities in terms of digital revolution.

The above analyses demonstrate the co-existence of both digital and analogue media *paradigms* where distinct cultural consumption practices happen. While those two platforms similarly possess all new media affordances, the way individuals (e.g., fans, journalists, players) and groups (e.g., clubs, media, national federations) incorporate them into their ecology of media ultimately vary. It can be argued that the variances encountered between the platforms come down to the type of content that is shared through them. On one hand, YouTube as a platform is predominantly used through on-demand remediated shorter format and standardised content; on the other, Twitter's use tends towards immediacy and real-time access. The on-demand or real-time nature of content impact on the other three affordances by encouraging or discouraging interactivity, *prosumption*, and different forms of communication. For instance, YouTube showed low levels of interactivity as cultural consumption practices were predominantly passive emulating the dominant experience of analogue medium of TV. The immediacy of Twitter on the other hand encouraged interactivity from all users as through conversations via official hashtags or mentions/tweets/retweets. The low or high levels of interactivity are then related to the different roles assumed by users as either taking more a *consuming* or *producing* part in the communication flow within that particular medium. For instance, the interactivity nature of Twitter meant that players and ordinary fans became influential in shaping conversations by actively creating and sharing content, while on YouTube this role was primarily taken by the official channels and ordinary users tended to passively engage with the content. Finally, it was possible to perceive how each platform had a predominant form of communication, as on YouTube the content was primarily produced and consumed through the traditional one-to-many model, whereas on Twitter the networking effect of many-to-many was more visible.

Hence, when discussing the disruptions and transformations of digitalisation to the business of football it is important that each platform is considered independently as part of ecology of media instead of assuming that all digital and social media platforms are similar. Whereas both platforms share similar affordances and technologies, the way they weave into the complex fabric of culturally consuming football is distinct. Therefore, the cultural convergence seen on those two distinct social media platforms is part of an accommodation – rather than a disruptive break – between the distinct available media – digital or not – for consuming football. The adjustments materialised by the adoption of a new delivery medium within an already established media ecology is composed by both discontinuities as more evident in the case of Twitter, and continuities as in the case of YouTube.

Conclusion

The pervasiveness of media, digital technologies, and social media platforms mean that we are living in a media life (Deuze, 2011). The cognizance of this condition has bolstered claims of a digital revolution with complete ruptures to our less mediated life and to our analogue relationship with media (Negroponte, 1995). Nevertheless, what has been witnessed since the boom of the Internet and other digital technologies in the 1990s was a period of transformations where older and newer media continue to operate side-to-side (Jenkins, 2006). In a technological perspective, it is possible to argue that digital has predominantly substituted analogue, with older media migrating to digital (e.g., digital TV, news portals, digital radio) and newer media (e.g., social media platforms) emerging at a faster pace. Nevertheless, by observing how individuals and groups incorporate newer media into their lives allows us to avoid a technological deterministic position and to witness patterns of both continuities and discontinuities to our interactions in media. Hence, it is important to understand how distinct digital media technologies are woven on already tie-knitted cultural consumption practices that involve a historical ecology of media. What the aforementioned analyses and discussion demonstrate was that digital revolution in the case of YouTube and Twitter involves more accommodations with patterns of discontinuities and continuities, therefore extending rather than substituting our relationships in and with media. Thus, it is imperative to take a more nuanced and less technological deterministic approach to *digital revolution*, consequently avoiding falling in the trap of fashionable buzzwords.[6]

References

Anagnostopoulos, C., Parganas, P., Chadwick, S., et al. (2018) Branding in Pictures: Using Instagram as a Brand Management Tool in Professional Team Sport Organisations, *European Sport Management Quarterly*, 18(4), 413–438.

BARB (2010) *2010 FIFA World Cup*. Available at: https://www.barb.co.uk/news/2010-fifa-world-cup/ [Accessed 8 April 2021].

Bastian, M., Heymann, S. & Jacomy, M. (2009) Gephi: An Open Source Software for Exploring and Manipulating Networks. *International AAAI Conference on Weblogs and Social Media*, San Jose, CA, pp. 361–362.

BBC (2021) *Social Media Abuse: Premier League Managers Call for Football-wide Boycott*. Available at: https://www.bbc.co.uk/sport/football/56686068 [Accessed 26 April 2021].

Bellamy, R. (2013) Reflections on Communication and Sport: On Institutions and Strategies, *Communication & Sport*, 1(1-2), 43–54.

6 Google Books's Ngram viewer shows a reinvigorated interest on digital revolution a decade after the dot-com bubble (Google, 2021).

Billings, A. (2014) Power in the Reverberation: Why Twitter Matters, but not the Way Most Believe, *Communication & Sport*, 2(2), 107–112.

Blondel, V., Guillaume, J.-L., Lambiotte, R., et al. (2008) Fast Unfolding of Communities in Large Networks, *Journal of Statistical Mechanics: Theory and Experiment*, 2008, 1–12.

Borgatti, S., Everett, M. & Johnson, J. (2018) *Analyzing Social Networks*. London: Sage.

Briggs, A., Burke, P. & Ytreberg, E. (2020) *A Social History of the Media: From Gutenberg to Facebook*. Cambridge: Polity Press.

Bromberger, C. (2004) *Football: La bagatelle la plus sérieuse del monde*. Paris: Pocket.

Bruce, T. (2015) Assessing the Sociology of Sport: On Media and Representations of Sportswomen, *International Review for the Sociology of Sport*, 50(4-5), 380–384.

BT (2020) *BT to show 2020 UEFA Champions League and Europa League finals free-to-air*. Available at: https://www.bt.com/sport/football/champions-league/bt-sport-to-show-free-to-air-uefa-champions-league-europa-league-final [Accessed 27 April 2021].

Burgess, J. & Green, J. (2018) *YouTube: Online Video and Participatory Culture*. Cambridge: Polity.

Checchinato, F., Disegna, M. & Gazzola, P. (2015) *Content and Feedback Analyis of YouTube Videos: Football Clubs and Fans as Brand Communities, Journal of Creative Communications*, 10(1), 71–88.

Cleland, J., Doidge, M., Millward, P., et al. (2017) *Collective Action and Football Fandom: A Relational Sociological Approach*. London: Palgrave.

Coche, R. & Tuggle, C.A. (2018) *Men or Women, Only Five Olympic Sports Matter: A Quantitative Analysis of NBC's Prime-Time Coverage of the Rio Olympics, Electronic News*, 12(4), 199–217.

CONMEBOL (2021) *CONMEBOL*. Available at: https://www.youtube.com/user/laconmebol [Accessed 27 April 2021].

Cooky, C., Council, L., Mears, M., et al. (2021) *One and One: The Long Eclipse of Women's Televised Sports, 1989-2019, Communication & Sport* [OnlineFirst].

David, M., Kirton, A. & Millward, P. (2017) Castells, 'Murdochization', Economic Counterpower and Livestreaming, *Convergence: The International Journal of Research into New Media Technologies*, 23(5): 497–511.

Deuze, M. (2011) Media Life, *Media, Culture & Society*, 33(1): 137–148.

FIFA (2014) *Sony's Ultra High Def 4K at the World Cup*. Available at: https://www.fifa.com/worldcup/videos/sony-s-ultra-high-def-4k-at-the-world-cup-2487018 [Accessed 8 April 2021].

FIFA (2015) *2014 FIFA World Cup Brazil™ Television Audience Report*. Available at: https://img.fifa.com/image/upload/n3z25ncdjj9qdwja1tet.pdf [Accessed 5 May 2021].

FIFA (2018) *Russia 2018 Most Engaging FIFA World Cup Ever*. Available at: https://www.fifa.com/worldcup/news/russia-2018-most-engaging-fifa-world-cup-ever?_branch_match_id=451382109478770048 [Accessed 23 July 2018].

FIFA (2019) *FIFA Women's World Cup 2019™ Watched by More than 1 Billion*. Available at: https://www.fifa.com/womensworldcup/news/fifa-women-s-world-cup-2019tm-watched-by-more-than-1-billion [Accessed 21 February 2020].

FIFATV (2021) *FIFA TV*. Available at: https://www.youtube.com/channel/UCpcTrCXblq78GZrTUTLWeBw [Accessed 27 April 2021].

Forbes (2019) *BT Sport To Show UEFA Champions League Final For Free On YouTube*. Available at: https://www.forbes.com/sites/stevemccaskill/2019/05/21/bt-sport-to-show-uefa-champions-league-final-for-free-on-youtube/ [Accessed 27 April 2021].

Gantz, W. & Lewis, N. (2014) Sports on Traditional and Newer Digital Media, *Television & New Media*, 15(8), 760–768.

Giulianotti, R. & Robertson, R. (2007) Forms of Glocalization: Globalization and the Migration Strategies of Scottish Football Fans in North America. *Sociology*, 41(1), 133–152.

Google (2021) *Google Books Ngram Viewer - Digital Revolution.* Available at: https://books.google.com/ngrams/graph?content=digital+revolution&year_start=1800&year_end=2019&corpus=26&smoothing=3&direct_url=t1%3B%2Cdigital%20revolution%3B%2Cc0#t1%3B%2Cdigital%20revolution%3B%2Cc0 [Accessed 25 May 2021].

Habermas, J. (1991) *The Structural Transformation of the Public Sphere: An Inquiry into a Category of Bourgeois Society.* Cambridge, MA: MIT Press.

Hayton, J.W., Millward, P. & Petersen-Wagner, R. (2017) Chasing a Tiger in a Network Society? Hull City's Proposed Name Change in the Pursuit of China and East Asia's New Middle Class Consumers, *International Review for the Sociology of Sport,* 52(3), 279–298.

Herman, E. & Chomsky, N. (1988) *Manufacturing Consent: The Political Economy of Mass Media.* London: Vintage.

Hill, T., Canniford, R. & Millward, P. (2018) Against Modern Football: Mobilising Protest Movements in Social Media, *Sociology*, 52(4), 688–708.

Hobsbawm, E. (1983) Mass-Producing Traditions: Europe, 1870-1914. In Hobsbawm, E. & Ranger, T. (eds.) *The Invention of Tradition.* Cambridge: Cambridge University Press, pp. 263–307.

Hutchins, B. (2011) The Acceleration of Media Sport Culture: Twitter, Telepresence and Online Messaging, *Information, Communication & Society*, 14(2), 237–257.

Hutchins, B. & Rowe, D. (2009) From Broadcast Scarcity to Digital Plenitude, *Television & New Media,* 10(4), 354–370.

Hutchins, B. & Rowe, D. (2012) *Sport Beyond Television: The Internet, Digital Media and the Rise of Networked Media Sport.* London: Routledge.

Hutchins, B. & Rowe, D. (2013) Digital Media Sport: Technology, Power and Culture in the Network Society. *Routledge Research in Cultural and Media Studies.* London: Routledge.

Jackson, S. (2013) Reflections on Communication and Sport: On Advertising and Promotional Culture, *Communication & Sport,* 1(1-2), 100–112.

Jarret, K. (2008) Beyond Broadcast Yourself™: The Future of Youtube, *Media International Australia,* 126(1), 132–144.

Jenkins, H. (2006) *Convergence Culture: Where Old and New Media Collide.* New York: New York University Press.

Jenkins, H., Ford, S. & Green, J. (2013) *Spreadable Media: Creating Value and Meaning in a Networked Culture.* New York: New York University Press.

Khan, M.L. (2017) Social Media Engagement: What Motivates User Participation and Consumption on YouTube?, *Computers in Human Behavior,* 66, 236–247.

Lawrence, S. & Crawford, G. (2018) Digital Football Cultures: Fandom, Identities and Resistance. In Caudwell, J. & Gilchrist, P. (eds.) *Advances in Leisure Studies.* London: Routledge.

Ludvigsen, J. (2019) Transnational Fan Reactions to Transnational Trends: Norwegian Liverpool Supporters, 'Authenticity' and 'Filthy Rich' Club Owners, *Soccer & Society,* 20(6), 872–890.

Luhmann, N. (2000) *The Reality of the Mass Media.* Cambridge: Polity Press.

Marres, N. (2017) *Digital Sociology: The Reinvention of Social Research.* Cambridge: Polity.

McQuail, D. & Deuze, M. (2020) *McQuail's Media and Mass Communication Theory*. London: SAGE.

Millward, P. (2012) Reclaiming the Kop? Analysing Liverpool Supporters' 21st Century Mobilizations, *Sociology*, 46(4), 633–648.

Murthy, D. (2017) *Twitter: Social Communication in the Twitter Age*. Cambridge: Polity.

Negroponte, N. (1995) *Being Digital*. London: Hodder & Stoughton.

Owens, J. (2006) The Coverage of Sports on Radio. In Raney, A. & Bryant, J. (eds) *Handbook of Sports and Media*. Abingdon: Routledge, pp.124–138.

Pegoraro, A. (2014) Twitter as Disruptive Innovation in Sport Communication, *Communication & Sport*, 2(2), 132–137.

Petersen-Wagner, R. (2017a) Cultural Consumption through the Epistemologies of the South: 'Humanization' in Transnational Football Fan Solidarities, *Current Sociology*, 65(7), 953–970.

Petersen-Wagner, R. (2017b) The Football Supporter in a Cosmopolitan Epoch, *Journal of Sport & Social Issues*, 41(2), 133–150.

Petersen-Wagner, R. (2018) Between Old and New Traditions: Transnational Solidarities and the Love for Liverpool FC. In Lawrence, S. & Crawford, G. (eds.) *Digital Football Cultures: Fandom, Identities and Resistence*. London: Routledge.

Petersen-Wagner, R. (2020a) Sports Media Patterns in the UK. In: Society + Media + Sports. Available at: https://petersen-wagner.biz/2020/03/29/sports-media-patterns-in-the-uk/ [Accessed 19 April 2021].

Petersen-Wagner, R. (2020b) Women's Sport and the Media. In: Society + Media + Sports. Available at: https://petersen-wagner.biz/2020/03/29/womens-sport-and-the-media/ [Accessed 19 April 2021].

Petersen-Wagner, R. & Ludvigsen, J. (Forthcoming) Fan Reactions to VAR on FIFATV YouTube Channel during the 2018 FIFA Men's World Cup.

Petty, K. & Pope, S. (2019) A New Age for Media Coverage of Women's Sport? An Analysis of English Media Coverage of the 2015 FIFA Women's World Cup, *Sociology*, 53(3), 486–502.

Rieder, B. (2015) YouTube Data Tools. 1.22 ed.

Rodriguez, N. (2017) #FIFAputos: A Twitter Textual Analysis Over 'puto' at the 2014 World Cup, *Communication & Sport*, 5(6), 712–731.

Rookwood, J. & Millward, P. (2011) 'We All Dream of a Team of Carraghers': Comparing 'Local' and Texan Liverpool Fans' Talk, *Sport in Society*, 14(1), 37–52.

Rowe, D. (1996) The Global Love-match: Sport and Television, *Media, Culture & Society*, 18(4), 565–582.

Rowe, D. (2004) *Sport, Culture and the Media: The Unruly Trinity*. Maidenhead: Open University Press.

Rowe, D. (2013) Reflections on Communication and Sport: On Nation and Globalization, *Communication & Sport*, 1(1-2), 18–29.

Sauder, M. & Blaszka, M. (2018) 23 players, 23 voices: An examination of the U.S. Women's National Soccer Team on Twitter during the 2015 World Cup, *Communication & Sport*, 6(2), 175–202.

Statista (2020) *Share of Individuals Who Ever Watched Short Entertainment Videos Online in the United Kingdom (UK) in 2019, by Age Group*, Available at: https://www.statista.com/statistics/707978/watching-short-entertainment-online-videos-uk-by-age-group/ [Accessed 3 May 2021].

Statista (2021) *Share of Generation Z and Millennials Watching Mobile Videos Daily Worldwide as of October 2020, by Video Length*. Available at: https://www.statista.com/statistics/12151

92/share-of-gen-z-and-millennials-watching-mobile-videos-daily-by-length/ [Accessed 3 May 2021].

Stauff, M. (2009) Sports on YouTube. In: Snickars, P. & Vonderau, P. (eds.) *The YouTube Reader.* Stockholm: National Library of Sweden, pp. 236–251.

Thorburn, D. & Jenkins, H. (2004) *Rethinking Media Change: The Aesthetics of Transition.* Cambridge, MA: MIT Press.

Tomlinson, J. (2007) *The Culture of Speed: The coming of Immediacy.* London: Sage.

Twitter (2021a) *Hateful Conduct Policy.* Available at: https://help.twitter.com/en/rules-and-policies/hateful-conduct-policy [Accessed 26 April 2021].

Twitter (2021b) *Q4 and Fiscal Year 2020: Letter to Shareholders.* Available at: https://s22.q4cdn.com/826641620/files/doc_financials/2020/q4/FINAL-Q4'20-TWTR-Shareholder-Letter.pdf [Accessed 5 March 2021].

UEFA (2021) *UEFA.* Available at: https://www.youtube.com/user/UEFA [Accessed 27 April 2021].

Wenner, L. (2014) Much Ado (or Not) about Twitter? Assessing an Emergent Communication and Sport Research Agenda. *Communication & Sport,* 2(2), 103–106.

Woods, J. & Ludvigsen, J. (2021) The Changing Faces of Fandom? Exploring Emerging 'Online' and 'Offline' Fandom Spaces in the English Premier League, *Sport in Society,* OnlineFirst.

Wu, T. (2016) *The Attention Merchants: The Epic Scramble to Get Inside Our Heads.* New York: Alfred A. Knopf.

YouTube (2021a) *Hate Speech Policy.* Available at: https://support.google.com/youtube/answer/2801939?hl=en-GB [Accessed 26 April 2021].

YouTube (2021b) *YouTube for Press.* Available at: https://www.youtube.com/intl/en-GB/about/press/ [Accessed 5 March 2021].

17

CULTURE AND THE WORLD CUP: THE CASE OF QATAR

Mahfoud Amara and Youcef Bouandel

Introduction

On 2 December 2010, Qatar was awarded the right to host the 22nd edition of the men's FIFA World Cup. This decision marked a turning point in the history of the World Cup. To date, apart from the 2002 and 2010 tournaments, which were held in Asia (Japan and South Korea) and Africa (South Africa), respectively, all other tournaments have alternated between Europe and North/South America. All previous tournaments have been held either in dominantly Christian countries or where Christianity is widespread. However, the 2022 edition will be different for three main reasons. First, it will be the first time where the World Cup will be held in a completely different geographical and cultural environment: an Arab, Muslim and Middle Eastern country. Second, given the country's size, football fans can practically attend three live games in one day. The farthest distance between stadiums that will host the matches is about 55 kilometres (equivalent to 35 miles), which is the same distance between Old Trafford, home of Manchester United and Anfield, home of Liverpool Football Club. Third, unlike previous tournaments, which were held in June/July, because of the summer heat in Qatar, the tournament was moved to November/December. Consequently, the final of the World Cup in Qatar will be played on December 18, Qatar's National day.[1]

The hosting of the World Cup is certainly a monumental achievement by the state of Qatar. Not only it brings the country to more international exposure, and helps it rip the potential economic benefits, but also it offers the world a window

1 Since 2007, Qataris celebrated 18 December as their National Day instead of 3 September. It was on 18 December 1878 that Sheikh Jassim bin Mohammed Al-Thani succeeded his father, Mohammed bin Thani, as ruler of the Qatari peninsula. He succeeded in uniting the local tribes, combatted external forces and earned a significant degree of autonomy for the tribes. He is known as the "founder" of the country.

DOI: 10.4324/9781003121794-17

onto Qatar's identity, culture and heritage. Similarly, being a Muslim and a conservative country represents a challenge to organisers and population alike. In this chapter, we look at the available cultural opportunities and challenges that Qatar faces as result of hosting the 2022 FIFA World Cup, and how Qatar is responding to these different challenges, communicating to both national and international audiences.

Qatar and National Identity Narrative

Qatar, a former British protectorate, is a relatively new country. It achieved its independence on 3 September 1971. The country was an unknown until 1995, when Sheikh Hamad Ben Khalifa Al-Thani became the Emir. Under his leadership, Qatar has made significant steps forward on the economic, social and political levels. Blessed with the third largest reserves of natural gas, the Qatari establishment has been able to invest in ambitious development programmes under "Qatar National Vision 2030". The Vision sets out a number of challenges such as "modernisation with the preservation of traditions" and among the guiding principles embodied in it, is the protection of "moral and religious values and traditions" (Amiri Diwan, n.p).

Since the turn of this century, Qatar's landscape has changed beyond recognition, and become an important player in mediation (conflict resolution); home of one the most important mass media hub in the Arab world, represented by Al Jazeera news network. The country has been hosting international and regional events, including sport, which – since 2006 and the hosting of the Asian Games – becomes among the important pillars of Qatar's development strategy. The most important of these sport tournaments is, undoubtedly, men's World Cup 2022. This event offers both opportunities and challenges to the country's future developments. On the one hand, it would lead to further developments and investment. On the other hand, it would provoke the contradiction of the conservative elements of society who see that change unfolding too fast, thereby posing a threat to traditional Islamic nature of Qatar's society.

Qatar as other countries in the Gulf Cooperation Council (GCC, henceforth) is undergoing a rapid change, characterised by its urban development, demographic change, level of education, and general effect of globalisation on local culture. Qatari state as other Arab and Muslim countries is working toward striking the right balance between integrating the conditions of modernisation while preserving local authentic culture. On the one hand, opening up to liberalisation and global means of consumption and communication, while maintaining social cohesion and traditional values, on the other. Urban change and planning is a witness of what could be perceived as contrasting process between tradition and modernity. Fadli and Al Saeed (2019, p. 1) argue that:

> Architectural richness of the urban conurbations in the Gulf is displayed through its massive defensive towers, mosques, residences, palaces and

> souks. Through the past few decades, urban heritage within these States, such as in the State of Qatar has been adversely affected due to the rapid urbanisation. In fact, following the discovery/exploitation of oil between 1960s and 1970s, Doha has witnessed a dramatic change affecting the physical, economic, cultural and aesthetics of the traditional historic buildings.

While shared *Khaliji* identity, common dominator to designate shared heritage, culture and religion for population living in the Arabia Peninsula *(Khalij Al-Arabi)*, was stronger before 2017, the blockade has pushed toward the reimagining of a national identity narrative. In Qatar, the emphasis on constructing single-identity cultural policy that reflects equal recognition of nomadic and coastal pasts. At the same time, announcing its respect and appreciation of the diversity that comprises the nation's population (Mitchell and Al Hammadi, 2020). This dualistic identity narrative is yet to be reconciled and accepted as it may conflict with perceived social and economic benefits of citizenship, as well as "the salience of societal divisions, even though they [Qataris] may personally disagree with these divisions and feel they are lessening over time." (Mitchell and Al Hammadi, 2020, p. 258). One could argue that sporting context offers more opportunities to reconciling between unity and diversity, as symbolised by the national football team made of Qataris and naturalised players, who are the product and legacy of Qatari national strategy for sport development and represented by Aspire Academy. The success of the multi-ethic and multi-racial national team in the Asian Football Cup of Nations, in time of adversity (and external threat), came in the right moment to strengthen the importance of cultural diversity and the contribution of both citizens and residents in the developmental project of Qatar and its resilience as a nation.

Displaying Qatari Culture and Identity: The FIFA World Cup Logo and Stadiums

Culture has been one of the pillars of Qatar positioning strategy and visibility in the international map. As stated by Eggling, "the Qatari government strategically uses cultural diplomacy to first produce and then disseminate an elite identity narrative of Qatar being a cohesive, future-oriented and rightfully engaged player in international affairs both inside and outside the state."(2017:720) The author uses the term culture diplomacy as "virtual enlargement" that is, the potential for small states to enlarge their "importance to" and "presence in" the international community by drawing on alternative power resources, such as the promotion of their culture. Hence, in a more (inter) connected world, the traditional and conventional relationship between size, power and influence is being challenged. To this goal, the country has embarked in ambitious tasks to revolutionise the cultural scene in Qatar, with projects such as *Katara* cultural village, Islamic museum, the opening of Qatar National Museum, the rehabilitations of old archaeological sites (e.g., Al-Zubara Fort), and renovations of *souqs* (Souq Waqif in Doha and Al-Wakrah Souq). The goal is to challenge the "orientalist" misperception and statement made "primarily by highly educated westerners, based, it seems on a pre-existing idea of 'cultural heritage' and an expectation of 'Qatari heritage' should look like" (Exell and Rico, 2013, p. 670).

Sport as a form of cultural and artistic expression is at the core of Qatar's cultural project and diplomacy. This was illustrated in the photo exhibition "Hey'Ya: Arab women in sport" organised by Qatar Olympic and Sport Museum (member of Qatar Museum Authority), which was launched in Doha before moving to the centre of London during the London 2012 Olympic Games. The exhibition then travelled to National Football Museum in Manchester as part of Qatar-UK 2013 partnership programme for cultural exchange. It featured large-scale photos by Brigitte Lacombe and documentary films by Marian Lacombe "celebrated the strength and pride of female athletes from the Arab world" and coincided with the participation of Qatari female athletes for the first time in the summer Olympics alongside Saudi Arabia and Brunei. A participation that was facilitated following International Federations decision to lifting the ban on Hijab/the veil in sport. For Qatar, it was important to engage with the debate on Female sport while preparing to take its strategy for biding and hosting sport events to another level. In the same spirit of reconciling traditional and modern sports, as well universality of sport values with local cultures and specifications, the Qatar Olympic and Sport Museum will open its door before the 2022 FIFA World Cup. Located in Khalifa Stadium, which was modernised to host the FIFA World Cup matches, the museum will take visitors through its physical and interactive/virtual gallery exhibits and collections throughout ancient and contemporary sport, including local history and narratives about sport in Qatar. This is evidenced in Abdulla Yousuf Al Mulla, Director of Qatar Olympic and Sports Museum statement "We envision to establish the museum as a testament to Qatar's enormous appetite and enthusiasm for sport and its national ambition for the nation to become more physically active" (Doha News, 2021).

The other important spaces to display Qatari culture is that of stadium architecture and the official logo, which is the focus of subsequent section. Logos, whether for corporate organisations, institutions, sporting clubs or sports events, are not developed in a vacuum. They usually give an identity to the logo holders by symbolising their mission and values. When logos are developed, great care is taken to ensure they reflect the culture, tradition and values associated with the sports tournament. In this sense, logos are brands that become easily recognisable and reflect the identity of those associated with it. In this sense, logos, like national flags, become a vehicle of "inclusion" reflecting the emotional attachment to a particular notion of togetherness and belonging. The logo for Qatar's FIFA World Cup 2022 is no different. It was cautiously designed and crafted, to make sure it reflected the Qatari culture and its launch was carefully choreographed to mark its symbolism.

Indeed, on 3 September 2019, the long awaited logo of the 2022 FIFA World Cup was finally launched. At 20:22 or 08:22 PM local time, (17:22 GMT), the most iconic and historical buildings in Qatar were covered with this logo, which includes *Burj* Doha, Souk Waqif, *Katara* Cultural Village Amphitheatre and the UNESCO World Heritage Site, Al-Zubara Fort. At the same time, the logo was unveiled in at least 24 cities around the world, such as London, Seoul, Mexico City and Johannesburg, to name just a few. The date, September 3, represents the day Qatar formally achieved its independence from Britain. This was yet another opportunity for Qatar to show the world that, less than five decades after becoming an independent state, it has become the focus of the world's attention. The timing of the launch, 20:22 represents the year that Qatar to host the World Cup tournaments. Looking at it from a different angle (08:22), 22 represents the year of the tournament and 8 refers to the number of stadiums that will host the matches.

The logo itself, whilst clearly featuring elements of local Arab culture, with references to football, it has also an international dimension, connecting the whole world. It preserves the iconic shape of the FIFA World Cup trophy. Second, its design looks like the number 8: the number of stadiums that will host the World Cup in Qatar. The logo's swooping curves represent the waves of the desert dunes, which is one of the first things, associated with the Arab peninsula. The form that emblem takes is inspired from the woollen shawl that locals wear during the winter months. The reference to winter in the emblem was inspired by the fact that the tournament would be played in winter – November and December 2022. The typography shows Arabic inscription coalescing tradition and modernity (FIFA, 2019).

The logo is not the only medium whereby Qataris display their cultural heritage. Stadiums are another tool. These are the Al *Bayt* stadium, *Al Janoub* stadium, *Al Rayyan* stadium, *Al Thumama* stadium, Education City stadium, *Khalifa* International stadium, *Lusail* stadium and *Ras Abu Aboud* stadium. These stadiums were either built specifically for the event in question, or have undergone extensive refurbishment (e.g., Khalifa stadium). Designed by some of the best architects in the world, such as the celebrated late Iraqi architect, Zaha Hadid, these venues are destined to leave a long lasting impression. Beyond the design and the incorporated technology, these stadiums have been made to reflect the local identity and culture as well as Qatar's ambition as a nation.

Four exemplary cases are worth mentioning. The architecture of the first stadium, *Al Thumama*, located about 6 km from Doha, is another representation of the region's history, culture and identity. The stadium is built in the shape of Al *Gahfiya*: a traditional knitted white cap worn by males across, not only the Arab Peninsula but also throughout the Muslim world. The *Gahfiya's* symbolism for Muslims is equivalent to what the *Kippah* represents for Jews. In addition to being a religious symbol, usually worn by men for Friday prayers throughout the Muslim world, it is also a vital part of the daily traditional clothing in the Arab Peninsula. The *Ghutra*, a smooth cotton fabric covers the *Gahfiya* and everything is held by the *Agal*: the ornamental black cord that can clearly be seen on men's head in the region.

The second venue is the Al *Janoub* (south) Stadium, situated in the city of Al-Wakrah, about 20 km, south of Doha, is another monument that bridge Qatar's history and its future aspirations. Designed by the renowned Iraqi architect Zaha Hadid, its shape is like traditional dhow boats, which have been, until very recently, the corner stone of the region's economy: fishing and pearl diving. Not only, the dhow boat represents the past, but it also represents Qatar's motivation and ambition to reach beyond its shores. The Third of the stadiums is located in northern city of Al Khor, about 45 km from the country's capital city, Doha. It will host games throughout the tournament until the semifinals. It is known as Al *Bayet* (literarily house), short for *Bayt al Sha'ar* (house of hair or lint), which reflects Qatari hospitality. The structure of the stadium is like a giant tent, made of camel's hair and used by nomadic Bedouin people in the desert. Keeping with the spirit of the Bedouin traditions, the arena will, like a nomad's tent, "move" after the tournament. The fourth case that deserves our attention is the purpose built *Ras Abu Aboud* stadium. Built on the shore of the Gulf, in the Cornish area, about 5 km from the centre of Doha, from modular building blocks including shipping containers. The 40,000-capacity venue will go down in FIFA World Cup™ history as the first fully dismountable and reusable tournament venue.

Reconciling between "Tradition" and Modernity: "East" and "West"

Qatar, since winning the bid to host the FIFA 2022 World Cup, has been at the receiving end of much criticism about its culture, tradition, laws, and even geography, which were depicted as non-compatible with western and football cultures. Qatar has been seen as ultra-conservative hence not tolerant to some subcultures associated with football festivity such as alcohol drinking, gender mixing and spectacle. The authorities in Doha, represented by the Supreme Committee for Delivery and Legacy (SC henceforth), addressed this criticism in a moderate manner. They did in a way to avoid consolidating orientalist clichés and discourse of clash of civilisation, while, at the same time, making sure its response did not offend Qatari society. One strategy was to opt for responding in international press to different "fears," in developing a crafted content in official webpages, and initiating cultural projects to change stereotypes. Among these projects is the annual festivals delivered by the SC's 2022 FIFA World Cup™ cultural stakeholders, the Qatar Tourism Authority, Qatar Museums and Qatar Foundation, in association with the Ministry of Culture and Sport. The organising Committee promised that the 2022 FIFA World Cup will offer many cultural platforms, designed to narrate Qatar's story to local, regional and international audiences.

The SC through its webpage prepared a guide and "things-to-do" in Qatar during the World Cup including a set of questions and answers. The webpage can be considered a space for "argumentative discourse" with the goal of "maintaining certain standards of *reasonableness* and expecting others to comply with the same critical standards … an interest in the use of effective persuasion techniques" (Kock, 2013, p. 437). One of these questions is "will I be able to drink alcohol in Qatar?" The answer to this question illustrates the endeavour of the host nation to finding an in-between zone that is acceptable to all. Emphasising the prospect of openness to different wants of diverse communities of fans [and clients], which is already in place, while explaining rules of order which are not specific to Qatar as Muslim majority country.

Qatar is not a dry state, and alcohol is available at licensed bars, clubs and hotels. Fans should note that not all hotels are licensed to serve alcohol. During the FIFA Club World Cup, alcohol will also be made available at the fan zone hosted at Doha Golf Club. At this tournament, alcohol will not be served inside stadiums during the matches. Fans should note that public drunkenness *(similar to a "drunk and disorderly" offence in many countries)* and drinking in public is not allowed in Qatar (emphasis added) (SC, 2019)

The other issue that received much attestation in the media is the welcoming of LGBTQ fans. To the question "are LGBTQ fans welcome?" the answer put forward is as follow:

> Everyone, regardless of gender, sexual orientation, religion, race or nationality will be welcome. All fans should rest assured that the tournament organisers are taking every *reasonable* effort to ensure their safety and wellbeing during their visit in Qatar. Generally speaking, public display of affection is not part of Qatari culture and therefore locals expect visitors from all backgrounds *to respect the local culture and customs* (SC, 2019).

The answer emphasises that no distinction is to be made, and sexual orientation was included with other forms of ethnic and gender distinctions. In other words, sexual orientation is not be treated as a distinctive variable, which is a manner to deescalate the exaggeration on it, and the tension around it. The term "reasonable" is used to explain tolerance within the possible and the acceptable in relation to, interestingly, aspects of "safety and well-being" of both fans and general population. Finishing with the term "generally speaking" which is not addressed specifically to LGBTQ community but to all visitors, residents and locals alike that displaying of affection [in public] is not part of Qatari culture. It is not the legal discourse being used here, but that of tolerance and respect to local cultures, which you would expect from tourists visiting any country.

Conclusion

Hosting the FIFA 2022 world Cup in Qatar has expectedly raised a number of controversies. When Qatar was awarded the right to host the tournament, the decision surprised many observers, given that Qatar is (at least at that time) not being at the centre of international football culture. Since then, however, Qatar has become a key player at many levels in the world of football, through direct investment (i.e., PSG), sponsorship of football clubs and tournaments, and, of course, thanks to its TV Sport Network, BeINSport. Qatar, both for the Middle East and North Africa region, being the host of the FIFA World Cup for the first time will, no doubt, strengthen the popularity of football in the entire region. The victory of the Qatari national team in the 2019 Asian Cup and the growing local enthusiasm around the national team are strong indicators of the impact that hosting the FIFA World Cup is already having in boosting football culture. Furthermore, for the first time in its history, the World Cup would be held in a completely different environment: in an Arabo-Muslim country. This will inevitable bring different challenges to the organisers (FIFA and the Qatari authorities), visiting fans and the local population alike. Football fans from all around the world, with different cultures and backgrounds, will be coming to Qatar bringing their own football subcultures. Consider for example, alcohol drinking; it is becoming the norm in football, thanks to the huge investment and aggressive marketing of alcoholic beverage companies in football industry. It is perhaps the most significant issue that fans and locals alike will be asked to accommodate. The dress code, too, as well as public display of affection between couples of opposite genders, let alone of the same sex. These matters have been raised in several occasions in the recent past. They seem to be strengthening the "orientalist" perception of the other "the East," the other as the "unknown" (outside the norm), and "intolerant." Qatar is not unique in this respect. Similar issues were raised for other hosting countries including more recently (majority Christian Orthodox) Russia, which had to put in place some specific measures and restrictions during the World Cup, including for the sale of alcohol and crackdown on protests.

Qatar hosting the 2022 FIFA World Cup will provide the country with the perfect opportunity to showcase its culture and heritage. Visitors, as well as those who will follow the tournaments from afar, will be introduced to Qatari culture since the authorities have been engaged in what we can be termed as "a balancing act" of tradition meeting modernity. This has been clearly visible in the World Cup's logo and the architecture of different stadiums hosting the tournament. They are aware of the potential clash between their commitments to FIFA and its corporate partners on the one hand, and their accountability to local population and homeland security on the other. Hence, every effort will be made to cater for visitors needs, which is also an obligation from the stand point of Arab hospitality, but at the same time making sure that local culture and customs are respected and preserved.

References

Amiri Diwan. Qatar national Vision 2030. Available at: https://www.diwan.gov.qa/about-qatar/qatar-national-vision-2030?sc_lang=en

Doha News (2021) *Sports hungry' Qatar to Open New Sports Museum*. Available at: https://www.dohanews.co/sports-hungry-qatar-to-open-new-sports-museum/ (Accessed 3 June 2021).

Exell, K. & Rico T. (2013) 'There is No Heritage in Qatar': Orientalism, Colonialism and other Problematic Histories, *World Archaeology*, 45(4), 670–685.

Eggling, K.A. (2017) Cultural Diplomacy in Qatar: Between 'Virtual Enlargements', National Identity Construction and Elite Legitimation, *International Journal of Cultural Policy*, 23(6), 717. 10.1080/10286632.2017.1308505

FIFA, FIFA World Cup Qatar 2022™ Official Emblem revealed, 03 Sep 2019. Available at: https://www.fifa.com/worldcup/news/fifa-world-cup-qatar-2022tm-official-emblem-revealed

Fadli, F. & Al Saeed, M. (2019) A Holistic Overview of Qatar's (Built) Cultural Heritage; Towards an Integrated Sustainable Conservation Strategy, *Sustainability*, 11, 2277, 10.3390/su11082277

Kock, C. (2013) Defining Rhetorical Argumentation, *Philosophy & Rhetoric*, 46(4), 437–464

Mitchell, J.S. & Al-Hammadi, M.I. (2020) Nationalism and Identity in Qatar after 2017: The Narrative of the New National Museum, *Journal of Arabian Studies*, 10(2): 271. 10.1080/21534764.2020.1854273

Qatar National Vision (2030) Available at: https://diwan.gov.qa/about-qatar/qatar-national-vision-2030?sc_lang=en (Accessed 5 June 2021).

Supreme Committee for Delivery and Legacy(2019) *The Football Fan's Guide to Qatar*. Available at: https://www.qatar2022.qa/en/news/the-football-fans-guide-to-qatar

18

AFTERWORD

Paul Widdop, Simon Chadwick, Christos Anagnostopoulos, and Daniel Parnell

As we sit around the table and talk through the journey of the book and sign off the last chapters, the sports news flashes through social media and we are reminded that today is a relatively important one. We check the time, it is 9:30 a.m. on a chilly Autumn morning in Birmingham, UK. It is 30 September 2021, quite an uneventful day, but in the football world, today is no ordinary day. Indeed, bubbling under the surface, this ordinary day has the power to change the course of football history. Today has global significance, as Arsene Wenger an astute mind and esteemed servant of the game, puts forward an FIFA constitutional plan to layout a roadmap for a bi-annual World Cup, which would end an unbreakable convention of a World Cup tournament that has always been on a four-yearly cycle. As with breaking with any habitual norm, there is tension or what psychologist Leon Festinger terms cognitive dissonance. There is vehement opposition to the plans. But there is more at stake here than Festinger's idea of uneasiness of inconsistent beliefs, there is a global political power game that is threatening to split football down the centre.

Before we explore some of the arguments surrounding what a change in a World Cup structure would bring to the global society, it is important to take one step back and explore how the four-year structure came into existence in the first place. As Tennent and Gillett describe in Chapter 2, this history perhaps demonstrates why there is a need to change, and a desire for FIFA to change a rather outdated model.

In 1929, it was decided that the first ever World Cup would take place in Uruguay from 13 July to 30 July 1930 and from that point on (except for suspension during wartime) the tournament has globe hopped from city to city (predominately the Americas and Europe) on a four-yearly spinning cycle. But why? Initially, the concept for this timeframe was taken from the Olympics, which was based on the Octaeteris calendar and the Greek use of 50 months of one Olympiad, four-year cycle and 49 lunar months for the next Olympiad.

Thus far, the Octaeteris calendar has become normalised and a system of infrastructure has been built around it. It is what football fans have been conditioned and socialised into, and what they come to see as traditional and a normal situation. In fact, the idea has become that entrenched that it reflects a state of nature, one that naturally fits with the environment, and survived as it has because it is the institution that best fits the world of commerce and society. But this is an artificial view, we lose sight of the fact that the World Cup and its timeframe has been socially constructed, created by people on the basis of what appears to be a rather odd ancient calendar. If say, the rules of the game were altered back in 1929 to a two-year model, we would dare say have become that accustomed and socialised to its existence that to consider changing it would be a crime against the very essence of the game. But football is a game of tradition, and changes to its fabric are met with opposition, especially when those appearing to be the guardians of the traditional form of the game have political strength.

For a global game, or one that claims to be for the people for the world in all its continents, the critical voices of the proposal are loudest in Europe. It is Europe where the old seat of power lies, with its impressive football infrastructure, vast colosseums, its global competitions, and famed domestic leagues. Indeed, in the vacuum left by a four-year cycle of the World Cup, UEFA and its European member federations have built their footballing models. The UEFA Champions League, UEFA Euro Tournaments, Premier League, La Liga, Bundesliga, and Serie A, are lucrative and encroachment on their market share will not go unchallenged. Furthermore, whole industries have been forged around this European model, with foreign direct investment from Nation States to State owned investment vehicles and energy companies, all claiming a slice of this lucrative and politically powerful market. There is too much at stake to risk damaging the European product, but tradition is where the battle lines will be drawn.

Whilst the benefits and limitations of the proposal are debated and politized, a structural change in the football calendar reflects wider concerns for humanity, one that goes beyond a feud between Europe and the new world. Indeed, football is often said to mirror the society in which it is played, and humanity is facing an uncertain future, as is football. The structural change to the World Cup tells us something about globalisation and sustainability. These two issues for us, are the two key themes in the future for sport, and for life on the planet.

Globalisation has become a process that unites us all. There is no doubt that the World Cup is a product of globalisation processes, processes which are heavily reliant on fossil fuel-led development and connectivity. Indeed, the forces that shaped global connectivity and propelled us technologically and economically forward has changed football. We are now as a species not restricted by geographic boundaries, and technology has rapidly changed consumption processes. However, these rapid changes have had a long-term impact on the planet we inhabit.

In a globalised world consumer experiences taken on certain expectations. Indeed, technology and the digital revolution has reinvented the way people consume, but this has come at such a pace that we can now differentiate between consumers, with terms of baby boomer, Generation X and Generation Z. Whilst these classifications are based on year of birth, they really reflect the way these groups use technology and wired into the digital matrix. Indeed, Petersen-Wagner cats a wide lens on this subject in the previous pages (see Chapter 16 in this Handbook). Yet, whilst looking innocent enough these classifications have huge implications for the way people consume products, services and experiences, and this has several implications for football. There is no doubt there is conflict throughout European football between the so-called legacy fans and the new GenZ consumers. In reality, the way these groups consume football is very different and a product of globalisation processes. Younger age cohorts have grown into a world of instant gratification, not bound by tradition, setting new conventions. The idea to them of having to wait four years to watch the world's finest sporting competition seems implausible and counterintuitive, embedded in the old world, where tradition is key and the door is locked. FIFA know this of course, and they know the demand for a two-year World Cup, no matter about the procrastinations of the Europeans, is very high.

Yet, these globalisation processes bring about geopolitical tensions. This is the essence of the arguments laid out by Brun and Gomez (see Chapter 4 in this Handbook). As such, 21st-century football has thus far largely been characterised by rights negotiations, sponsorship deals and revenue generation strategies. The origins of this prevailing ideology have been in neoclassical economics and free markets. With patterns of global economic and political power now shifting, countries such as China and those in the Gulf region have become important and influential members of both of the global community and the world of football. However, these countries are characterised by large state sectors and by governments that actively intervene in the activities of industries such as Football. This necessitates a new view of world sport, that is "the geopolitical economy of sport," where connections between geography, politics and economic activity prevail, especially as they pertain to production, trade, government and international relations. There is a shifting power struggle currently gripping Europe and the rest of the world. The football power base is slowly moving East, how far East it goes, we are not yet sure. But let us make no concessions, a two-year World Cup will be a hammer blow to Europe, UEFA and the future of its flagship competitions. Conversely, FIFA cannot fiddle while Rome burns, their secret fear is that without a shift to two-year World Cup, the processes of capitalism and globalisation will eventually propel UEFA's competitions (domestic and international) to consume the World Cup, and reduce it to an historic competition of a bygone era, stripping it of its lustre and significance.

Closely connected to globalising processes is climate change and issues of sustainability. Orr and her colleagues' closing remark is an illustrative one: "the impact of FIFA on the environment and the impact of the environment on FIFA must be a focus in the next century" (see Chapter 8 in this *Handbook*). Indeed, the very processes that brought globalisation to the world have brought the world to the brink of collapse. Indeed, we are seeing unprecedented natural disasters, erosion of the polar ice caps at an unprecedented rate, rising seas and an unprecedented shift in the migration of the world's population. Energy is the dynamic unifying everything, and the use of energy for the global economy and for everyday life is putting severe pressure on the planets eco-system. Therefore, can the world afford a two-year World Cup. Indeed, mega events by their very nature are mass consumers of energy and contributors to detrimental levels of CO_2 and harmful gases, so the very thought of doubling one of the biggest events in human history, seems implausible at best and feckless at worst. For a sustainable future don't we have to limit our consumption to preserve not just the game but life as we know it.

In a world of dense connectedness football allows us to grasp the complexities of the world we inhabit. There are enormous tensions, but football simplifies life, just a game of 11 versus 11. Football does much more to bring us together than it does to separate us. Footballers and managers are becoming the role models we always wanted them to be and standing up to injustices. Football can help us to understand globalisation and it can also help us address the big challenges we face. Whether there is a two-year of four-year World Cup remains undecided. But football is the gift to the world and a resource for hope.

Football will win.

Paul, Simon, Christos, Dan.

INDEX

Page numbers in *italics* indicate figures and **bold** indicate tables.